AS Level
Law

Cavendish
Publishing
Limited

London • Sydney

AS Level Law

Mary Collins, LLB, LLM, PGCE
Solicitor and Senior Lecturer in Law
University of Plymouth

Cavendish
Publishing
Limited

London • Sydney

Third edition first published in Great Britain 2000 by Cavendish Publishing Limited, The Glass House, Wharton Street, London WC1X 9PX, United Kingdom.

Telephone: +44 (0) 20 7278 8000   Facsimile: +44 (0) 20 7278 8080

E-mail: info@cavendishpublishing.com

Visit our Home Page on http://www.cavendishpublishing.com

This title was previously published as *Lecture Notes on A Level Law: Paper I*

340
coc
0019972

British Library Cataloguing in Publication Data

Collins, Mary
AS Level Law – 3rd ed
1 Law – England 2 Law – Wales
I Title
349.4'2

ISBN 1 85941 596 2

Printed and bound in Great Britain

PREFACE

This text aims to cover the new Law Advanced Subsidiary syllabuses of the Assessment and Quality Agency (AQA) and the Oxford, Cambridge and Royal Society of Arts Combined Examination Boards (OCR). Each syllabus is in three parts: the AQA has three modules (Law Making, Dispute Solving and The Concept of Liability in Crime and Tort); and the OCR has three units (Machinery of Justice, Legal Personnel and Sources of Law). The AQA syllabus is wider than the OCR, as it includes the concept of liability. Each of these main areas is dealt with in this book in what is hoped to be both an interesting and stimulating way, so as to encourage students to progress from this level and further develop their knowledge and understanding of law and how it operates in society.

This is a very exciting time to be embarking on a study of the law. Not only will students be given a broader introduction to the study of law via the AS level course, but the legal system is in a state of major change and reform. Several changes in legislation and judicial precedent have already occurred, but more are planned and students are encouraged to follow these developments, not only in their reading, but also through the media and, in particular, the internet. Many of these changes are dealt with in this text, including the impact of the Human Rights Act 1998 (in force from October 2000).

One of the main attractions of studying law is that it develops one's awareness of its place in society. Keeping up to date may be frustrating at times, but everyone can usefully contribute to the debate as to the future development of the law, both in general and in particular areas. Not only is the content of the law important; also of importance is an appreciation of the relationship of law with other subjects, such as sociology, politics and economics.

The techniques by which knowledge is gained will be assessed by the examiners. These include the analysis of information, the organisation of material and an appreciation of the relationships between legal concepts. Clear expression of ideas is essential, as this will demonstrate understanding.

I wish you success in your exploration of this subject, which, although undergoing rapid change, retains much from the past, which adds to its fascination and mystique.

Mary Collins
June 2000

CONTENTS

4 THE PROVISION OF LEGAL SERVICES

Contents

TABLE OF CASES

TABLE OF STATUTORY INSTRUMENTS

TABLE OF EC LEGISLATION

CHAPTER 1

THE NATURE OF LAW

Introduction

In this chapter, we will consider the purposes that law serves in society. We need, first of all, to classify the different types of law. The principal division is between civil and criminal law, but other classifications exist. We then move on to consider the types of rule that exist, such as moral, religious and legal, and consider why people obey rules, how rules change and how we can distinguish rules from other social phenomena, such as habits, customs, conventions and practices. This will then bring us to a discussion of the types of legal rules and their relationship with morality and justice. Finally, we will consider the constitutional context and how the law regulates the relationship between the citizen and the State.

Classification of law

It is useful to be able to classify law for a variety of reasons, including understanding the purposes served by law and its functions in society. Procedure and penalties may also differ according to whether one is considering criminal or civil law. Criminal law has, as one of its aims, the punishment of offenders who commit a crime against society. A person will be prosecuted for a criminal offence, such as murder, theft or robbery. Prosecution is in the name of the Crown and is usually undertaken by the Crown Prosecution Service, which was set up by the Prosecution of Offences Act 1985, although other public bodies may be able to bring a prosecution, such as Customs and Excise and Trading Standards Officers. In some instances, a private individual may be able to initiate a prosecution, as was shown in the Stephen Lawrence case, when the parents of the deceased attempted to prosecute some of the youths alleged to have killed their son. On the other hand, civil law, for example, the law regulating the making of contracts, aims to compensate a party who has been wronged (called a claimant), by making an award of money damages against the wrongdoer (called a defendant). This may be proved to have arisen where the defendant has broken his or her side of the bargain. This is but one type of civil wrong; others are torts, such as negligence, defamation and nuisance. The civil law also regulates the ownership and disposal of property, family relationships, employment and consumer transactions.

Methods of classifying the law

Traditionally, classification of law has taken two forms. We have already mentioned the distinction between criminal law and civil law. Offences such as theft, robbery, burglary and murder are classified as criminal, as these actions are sufficiently anti-social to warrant punishment by the State in the form of imprisonment of the offender or by the imposition of a fine. Civil law, on the other hand, provides for the making of contracts, wills, ownership and transfer of property, and regulates employment, consumer transactions and family matters. Apart from contracts where two or more parties have entered into a binding agreement which can then be enforced, the other main type of civil liability arises in tort. This covers acts or omissions where a person's interests have been adversely affected by the defendant, such as physical injury, damage to property or the publication of defamatory statements.

Another way in which law can be classified is by distinguishing between public international law, which regulates the actions of States and the entering into of treaties between States on the one hand; and municipal law on the other. Municipal law can then be subdivided into private law, such as contract, and tort, which is simply an alternative term for civil law. Public law covers not only criminal law, but also constitutional and administrative law. Private international law regulates conflict between the laws of different States in areas such as contract, tort and family matters.

Before leaving the classification of law, it is worth mentioning one other type of classification, namely, that between substantive and procedural law. Substantive law is the body of rules regulating the making of contracts or the commission of torts or crimes. This crosses the boundaries between civil and criminal, and between public and private law, and is concerned with defining an offence or a tort or the conditions which must be met for a contract to be legally binding. The substantive rules impose liability on a party proved to be in breach of one of the rules, and, if this is a rule of criminal law, a penalty may result, or, if this is a rule of civil law, a remedy may be provided for the claimant.

Procedural rules regulate the conduct of court proceedings and aim to ensure fair play between the parties. Some examples include: the disclosure of evidence to one's opponent; the meeting of deadlines for the service of documents; and the need to prove the facts relied on by evidence such as documents or witnesses. The rules of evidence ensure that the court takes cognisance only of facts which are satisfactorily proved. In criminal trials, there is a general rule against the admission of hearsay evidence (that is, evidence which is outside the direct experience of the witness) as proof of alleged facts. However, in civil trials, the Civil Evidence Act 1995 repeals Pt 1 of the Civil Evidence Act 1968, with the effect that all hearsay evidence is admissible and it will be for the court to assess its worth.

One of the underlying principles of criminal procedure is that the defendant is presumed innocent until proved guilty. The prosecution bears the burden of proving guilt beyond all reasonable doubt.

In the past, the so called right to silence has been linked with this principle, but ss 34–37 of the Criminal Justice and Public Order Act 1994 allow adverse inferences to be drawn where a defendant fails to mention relevant facts when questioned or charged or fails or refuses to account for suspicious marks, objects or substances or his or her presence at the scene of a crime. Failure to give evidence at trial may also give rise to adverse inferences. In the case of *R v Condron and Another* (1997), the defendants refused to answer questions during police questioning on the advice of their solicitor. The solicitor considered that his clients were unfit to answer questions, as they was suffering withdrawal symptoms from heroin. The defendants relied on the advice to remain silent as part of their defence, but did not make known the reason for the advice at the time of interview. The court held that adverse inferences could be drawn from the defendants' silence. A challenge to the Crown Court conviction, which was affirmed by the Court of Appeal, was heard by the European Court of Human Rights (ECHR) (as *Condron v UK*), which ruled in May 2000 that the trial judge had not properly directed the jury as to the issue of the applicants' silence during police interview. This effectively prevented the applicants from receiving a fair trial, which amounted to a breach of Art 6(1) of the European Convention on Human Rights.

What is a rule?

Defining a rule is not an easy task, but it is useful to attempt a definition, since this concept forms the basis of social behaviour. Rules govern a person's relationships with others, and this concept is fundamental to the study of law and the legal system.

The lawyer who is asked to advise a client will be expected to offer advice as to the client's legal position, taking into account the appropriate legal rules. The judge, in reaching a decision in a case, will apply the law to the facts to arrive at a reasoned decision and not one based on whim or bias.

Rules are a phenomenon of society regulating the conduct and relationships of people, so that, whenever one person comes into contact with another, their dealings, whether of a social or business nature, may well be governed by a rule or, more likely, a set of rules. It is useful, therefore, to be able to distinguish rules from other social phenomena, such as habits, and to consider the sources from which a rule may derive, for example, religion or morality.

An essential feature of most, if not all, societies is that of institutions – the family, schools and colleges, the workplace and financial bodies, to name but a few. Such institutions and the groups and individuals which exist within them operate by way of rules. Similarly, clubs and societies operate by rules, and the State itself is regulated through a constitution, both in its parts and its relationship with the citizen, by way of rules. Rules will usually be written, but this is not essential to the definition of a rule. Some rules, as with custom, will invariably be unwritten.

Another useful illustration is that of sports and games, where not only do the players need to be aware of the rules, but also spectators and those vested with authority to enforce the rules. The interpretation and use of the rules will determine whether the game or sport is being played properly, and the consequences that will or could follow from breach of a rule. This may range from a reprimand to the imposition of a penalty such as a fine or disqualification. Usually, the rules will be contained in a 'rule book', and this may also contain provisions for their enforcement and amendment. Alternatively, the rules may change over time by accepted practice, or, in particular instances, players may agree on a particular set of rules or an interpretation of the rules.

This brings us to a broad definition of rule as a norm or guide regulating social conduct. It is a measure or standard by which conduct is gauged, and which may give rise to a consequence such as a penalty when not complied with. We can say that rules are imperative, in that a person who is the subject of a rule does not usually have any choice as to whether or not he or she complies. This is not to say that there may not be exceptions to a rule, or that a person cannot be exempted from a rule, but both of these should be provided for in the rule itself or by the rule making body.

As already noted, rules may be written or unwritten. Legal rules, with only the exception of customary law, are written and derive from a formal source vested with authority within the State. On the other hand, other types of rule, such as moral rules, will tend to be unwritten and there may be no consensus as to their scope and effect and no formal mechanism for their enforcement.

Some rules are expressed in negative and others in positive terms. An example of the former is 'do not walk on the grass' and an example of the latter, 'pedestrians must use the pavement'.

An example illustrates the points made so far. Operators of a car park are authorised by law to levy charges and to regulate the parking of vehicles on their premises. A rule requiring a valid ticket to be displayed is expressed in positive terms and, on breach, a fine may be charged. The above rule could just as easily be expressed in the negative, that is, a car parked without displaying a valid ticket will be subject to a fine. It is usual to associate the notion of 'penalty' with the concept of a rule, in that the rule is attempting to ensure compliance. Thus, if a rule is not complied with, some consequence should follow to 'punish' the rule breaker and to deter him or her and others from future breaches. Thus, those who park without a valid ticket may be liable to a fine. The consequence may be stated as part of the rule itself, or in a subsidiary rule. Some rules are categorical commands, for example, vehicles must stop at a red light, the speed limit is 30 mph or vehicles should not stop on the hard shoulder of the motorway except in an emergency. Most rules will have exceptions, where the otherwise regulated conduct will be permitted or prohibited in special defined circumstances. Using the above scenario of a car park, an example might be that vehicles parked in the car park on a Sunday are not required to display a ticket. Some conduct may be entirely exempt from the application of a rule, for example, invalid carriages are not subject to any charge for parking on any day of the week.

Rules distinguished from other social phenomena

Let us now consider more fully how a rule can be identified and distinguished from other social phenomena. Twining and Miers, in *How to Do Things With Rules* (4th edn, 1999), define a rule as 'a general norm mandating or guiding conduct or action in a given type of situation'. According to Twining and Miers, rules have four aspects:

- rules guide or lay down standards of behaviour;

- rules are normative, in that they prescribe (or proscribe) desirable (or undesirable) conduct, that which is valid, good or lawful;

- rules are not optional but imperative, requiring compliance, expressed in terms that a person must/must not, shall/shall not, ought/ought not conduct him or herself in a certain way;

- rules provide justification for a decision or course of action and its source can persuade a person to obey.

Some would argue that the law is the most authoritative of rules, ultimately deriving its authority from the State and where the most far reaching of penalties can be imposed. Rules have general effect and govern a situation which has arisen in the past and which is likely to arise again. A novel situation cannot be said to be governed by a rule, but, following recurrence, a rule may develop which guides or regulates future conduct.

The concept of a norm is a wide term and, as a result, Twining and Miers are able to include within their definition of rule 'precepts, regulations, conventions, principles and guiding standards'. Other writers, notably Hart (*The Concept of Law*, 2nd edn, 1997), have also analysed the concept of rule and distinguished it from 'habit, prediction, practice, command and value'. A broad definition is useful, in that it can cover the various social phenomena referred to by Twining and Miers which often overlap and which may change over time. Writers and jurists may not always be exact in the use of language, and it is common for judges to use the term 'principle' interchangeably with 'rule'.

At one extreme, a rule may be formal, having derived from an authoritative source, and may set out clearly what is to be done or not to be done. In addition, it may specify, as part of the rule, or separately in another rule, the consequences for non-compliance. Legal rules will often fit into this category.

At the other extreme, conventions, for example, suggest that a course of action is to be preferred (or not) but may have no clear statement as to the consequences of breach or authoritative or written source. These will have developed over time and be passed down from one generation to another. Social conventions regulate etiquette and good manners, for example, replying to a letter or acknowledging a friend or acquaintance in a public place.

Returning to Twining and Miers' definition of rules as including 'precepts, regulations, conventions, principles and guiding standards', we will take each in turn and then consider more fully Hart's distinction between rules and 'habit, prediction, practice, command and value'.

Precepts are maxims or principles related to issues of justice, fairness or morality. Often, such terms as rules, principles and standards are interchangeable, and this is so with the terms precepts and principles. We may say that the fundamental principles of a criminal justice system should be a presumption of innocence, a right to remain silent during police questioning and during trial (possibly subject to the ability of the court to draw adverse inferences from a person's silence), that the burden of proof should rest with the prosecution and that the standard of proof should be beyond all reasonable doubt, and that defendants should have, in serious criminal cases, a right to jury trial. These principles are basic or fundamental to the system, and equally may be described as precepts. In the case of *Airedale NHS Trust v Bland* (1993), Lord Browne-Wilkinson analysed what he described as the moral precept which requires 'respect for the sanctity of human life'. He concluded that the role of the judge in developing the law was a limited one and that it was for Parliament to address itself to the 'moral, social and legal issues raised ...'. However, in the exceptional circumstances of this case, the declaration to cease treatment was to be granted, as this was, on both medical and ethical grounds, in the best interests of the patient.

'Regulation' is a term often used interchangeably with, or in addition to, the term 'rule'. It implies an official body empowered to lay down a code or set of rules. In law, it may have a technical meaning referring to law made by those to whom power is delegated by Parliament. Thus, government ministers may be able to make rules, regulations or orders under an enabling Act of Parliament. The collective term for such provisions is delegated or subordinate legislation.

'Convention' or, as it is sometimes called, 'usage' refers to proper modes or standards of conduct by which an individual will feel bound. The degree to which conventions may be enforced, resulting in some penalty, may be limited and non-compliance tolerated.

It is often difficult to distinguish conventions and custom, although customs (not to be confused with customary law, as described in Chapter 2) are rules which are considered (by those to whom they apply) to be generally obligatory. Social customs may regulate etiquette and good manners, but more generally are concerned with folklore and the traditions which have been passed down from one generation to another. In Derbyshire, for example, annual well dressing festivals take place, and the customary May celebrations held to welcome the coming of spring at Helston and Padstow in Cornwall are well known. Other customs that come to mind include the carrying of the bride over the threshold, eating pancakes on Shrove Tuesday, never opening an umbrella indoors and avoiding walking under ladders. Over time, a course of action which has been customary may become more fluid and be considered to be no more than a convention. Traditionally, it was customary for a man to doff his hat to a lady. This has become outdated for the majority of people, partly because few men wear hats and partly because women generally do not wish to be treated in this way.

The term 'convention' may be used generically to refer to morality, custom, ethics, religion and rules of etiquette. Constitutional conventions are those practices which develop and which are considered binding by those who are the subject of the rule. They often supplement the official rules, making the latter more workable.

In the constitution of the UK, by convention, the monarch does not refuse her assent to Bills which have passed all stages in the House of Commons and House of Lords. In law, the Queen might refuse her assent, but, since the 18th century, the practice has developed whereby it is understood that no such refusal will occur.

In non-developed societies, social regulation may be by way of custom and this may take the form of law, in that it is officially recognised and enforced by those with power and authority who can impose sanctions or penalties for breach. In studying the history and development of the common law, the importance of custom will be seen. The origins of the common law are said to be those local customs collected and moulded by itinerant justices into a common, uniform body of precedent.

Principles are not always easily distinguishable from rules, and certainly judicial statements suggest that these terms are synonymous. We might talk of the rules of natural justice, but equally they may be referred to as principles. We have already referred to fundamental precepts such as the presumption of innocence, but this can just as correctly be referred to as a principle.

A principle may be open-ended and take the form of a maxim or wise saying. Thus, the principle that 'no man should profit from his own wrong', the 'polluter pays' principle and the principle that 'he who comes to equity should come with clean hands' suggest an essential truth or grain of wisdom, but do not suggest the type of conduct which is prohibited or the consequence which will follow non-compliance. This is not to suggest that a rule will always provide for a consequence for non-compliance, but rules will often be more precise as to the situations in which they are to apply.

Principles may conflict, as was shown in the *Airedale* case already referred to, where the House of Lords had to decide whether to grant a declaration permitting the medical treatment of Tony Bland to cease. The court was faced with the dilemma that the principle of the sanctity of human life was said to conflict with the principle of having regard to the quality of life. The court held that these principles did not so much conflict; rather they complemented one another, and it was for the court to arrive at a balance.

As we shall see later, Dworkin disagreed with Hart's narrow definition of law to include only rules and suggested that law is a 'rich fabric' which includes rules and non-rule standards, that is, principles and policies. In Dworkin's view, rules apply in an all-or-nothing fashion, whereas principles may conflict and will have to weighed by the judge in reaching a decision.

This is borne out when considering the development of the common law, in that a judge may be bound by a decision of a higher court. In other words, he or she will have to comply with the rules unless there are means of avoiding the rule, for example, by way of distinguishing. If, on the other hand, the court is not bound by previous decisions, it may reach its decision by calling on principle, as noted by Lord Slynn (dissenting) in *R v Brown* (1993). The court may also seek assistance in reaching a decision by referring to the public interest or public policy, as illustrated by the majority in *Brown*.

Guiding standards may be even more fluid than conventions, and their source will determine the extent to which they may be binding. A useful example is the Highway Code, and others can be found in the various charters established, including the Citizens' Charter, Rail Passengers' Charter, Students' Charter and Taxpayers' Charter.

It is not only in the area of public administration that charters are being adopted. Commercial and educational organisations are also preparing charters setting out the minimum standards to be expected by those who are customers or members of such organisations. Some provide for compensation for breaches in the guidelines, for example, the Passengers' Charter, whereas others do not.

It has become fashionable for government departments and other bodies to issue guidelines, circulars and policy notes so as to assist in the interpretation of legal rules. These will not form part of the law, but may assist in determining its scope and effect.

The Highway Code is an example of a Code of Practice, breach of which does not automatically result in breach of a legal rule. However, breach of the Code may be used in evidence in a court of law to prove breach of a legal rule. For example, a failure to comply with a traffic signal may be used to prove that a driver was negligent in a civil claim for damages and/or in a criminal prosecution for careless or dangerous driving.

We will now move on to consider some of the distinguishing features of habits, predictions, practices, commands and values.

Rules can be clearly distinguished from habits, in that a person who acts out of habit does so without any sense of obligation. An habitual course of conduct may be undertaken regularly, but may at the same time be one which arises by way of either accident or convenience. If I always take a particular route on my way to work, or I always wear a red hat on Fridays, or I eat an apple each day for lunch, these actions can be described as habits. One is neither compelled to do them nor obliged to do them in compliance with a rule. As Hart noted, habits, practices and predictions are capable of verification and are concerned with types of behaviour. The individual who behaves in these ways may not do so out of any sense of duty or from any wish to act correctly. Rules, commands and values, however, involve some internalisation and each attempts to regulate and control behaviour. Some rules may develop from habits and practices, but they take on a normative form, for example, an 'ought', and the original reasons for their existence may be lost.

Rules differ from predictions, in that a prediction is nothing more than a forecast of behaviour and, factually, the prediction may be shown to be true or false. I may attempt to predict the weather for the coming week. I may be shown to be correct or incorrect in my prediction. Rules do not attempt to predict how people will behave, but rather provide guidelines or standards to regulate their behaviour. This is not to say that those involved in advising others about the application of a rule (and most often this arises where a lawyer offers advice to a client as to how the legal rules which govern the client's situation will affect him or her) will not attempt to predict how a particular rule will apply to an individual. The lawyer who is asked to advise a client will base his or her prediction of the extent of the client's liability or the likely success of the client's claim on his or her estimation of how the court will interpret relevant legislation or apply case law to the problem. The prediction will be based on an estimation of how the courts have decided past cases in accordance with the rules of precedent or how a statutory provision will be interpreted by the court.

Commands may overlap with rules, but there are important differences. A command may apply to a purely novel situation, whereas rules will apply in general. Some rules command the doing of something (or refraining from doing something), but others attempt to encourage or facilitate a course of action.

The notion of a command implies a person or body able to command. As we will see later, Austin devised a command theory, where he suggested that legal rules were commands emanating from a sovereign power. He subscribed to the positivist school of legal philosophy, whereby the validity of the law was to be measured not in terms of its moral content, but by the process required for a rule to become law. The process by which law came about was a formal one, recognised as having authority to compel the citizen to comply with the commands of the sovereign body.

Perhaps the most difficult distinction to draw is between rules and values. It is clear that values underlie most rules, and it can be argued that rules are the means by which social values are achieved. Thus, values are ends in themselves and are concerned with right and wrong. Values are closely linked with ideals, and these may often be unattainable but provide standards towards which people strive. The embodiment of values into rules may necessitate the rule having more limited effect than the value which underlies it, and limitations may have to be placed on the rule.

Values are most often associated with morality and what is considered to be right or wrong conduct. The natural law school of thought suggests that legal rules should be judged by standards of fairness, equality or justice and that a rule which fails to meet such a standard at best need not be obeyed and at worst is not to be classed as law. The utilitarian view measures rules according to their consequences. If a rule maximises happiness or well being or some other effect which is deemed good, it will be justifiable. Some suggest that the correct approach is to combine both these theories, with the effect that, if a rule achieves a moral principle or value and has utility, it is justifiable.

Classification of rules

Having considered the definition of rules and compared rules and other social phenomena, it is time to classify types of social rule. Traditionally, rules have been classified into legal rules, religious rules, ethical rules, moral rules, rules of etiquette and customary rules. However, these are not hard and fast categories, and there may be considerable overlaps between one or more. In addition, it is worth reminding ourselves that the concept of a rule may be defined narrowly or widely, depending on context, with the effect that conduct governed by what one person considers to be a rule may be thought of by another as no more than convention or values.

Attempting to classify rules serves to illustrate their origins and other distinguishing features such as the effects of breach, the form that a rule takes and whether a mechanism exists for their enforcement. It must be stressed, however, that, at different times in history in one society, or between different societies, particular conduct may be regulated by one or more types of rule and that legal rules may well have a special relationship with one or more types of rule.

Legal rules

Legal rules are the most formal and, in developed societies, are invariably written. In the UK, the main sources of law are statute and case law, together with law emanating from the European Union (EU). Other sources of law include custom and what are known as subsidiary sources of law, including ecclesiastical law, Roman law and learned works. Only customary law is unwritten, but, once it has been relied on in a dispute decided by the higher courts, it will be recorded in the law reports. It does not, however, depend on being so recorded for its validity.

Legal rules exist as part of a system with machinery for enforcement and amendment of the rules. Agencies such as the police and courts will be vested with legitimate authority to enforce the law in the case of criminal law and prosecutions will be brought in the name of the Crown or State or, in some jurisdictions, the people. The civil law provides a means by which individuals may enforce their rights against others, whether it be in contract, in tort or in relation to a family dispute or a dispute over property rights. An important constitutional principle is the rule of law that the citizen cannot 'pick and choose' which laws to obey, but is obliged to obey all rules which have been made by a properly constituted authority.

Where no moral consensus exists as to the worth of a particular law, how that law is viewed by both the enforcer and those who are subject to the law is of crucial importance. If law is to be obeyed, it will need moral authority and must be seen to be fair in the light of the principles of justice, not only in respect of how it is applied, but also in its content. The imposition of heavy criminal penalties may simply have the effect of 'increasing the stakes', whereby the offender will feel justified in risking a more serious offence, or, in the words of the adage, the offender might as well 'be hanged for a sheep as for a lamb'.

We will look more closely at the definition of law and the different approaches of the positivist and natural law schools to this question when we consider the relationship between law and morality.

Religious, ethical and moral rules

Religious, ethical and moral rules are often difficult to differentiate, and may well have a common root. Those who adhere to a religion will often derive from it their moral code. Christians will look to the Bible for guidance on what is right and what is wrong. Muslims look to the Koran, and Jews to the Torah. Religion will often involve much more than just a moral code, for, to take Christianity as an example, it is concerned with spiritual matters, the afterlife and the relationship of humans with God.

Ethical rules are a branch of morality and usually regulate the conduct of professional people such as doctors, lawyers and teachers, and their dealings with patients, clients and students. Ethical codes will be administered by a governing body, for example, The Law Society, the General Council of the Bar or the General Medical Council, with the aim of ensuring high standards of conduct in relationships where the recipient of the service may be vulnerable, and where the provider of the service exercises authority and power and is in a position of trust. Terminology can sometimes be confusing, and the term 'ethics' may be used simply to refer to an individual's or group's moral code.

Professional ethics may be referred to as professional etiquette. In considering the relationship of solicitors and barristers and their dealings with clients, it is usual to refer to the respective rules of etiquette enforced by The Law Society or the Bar Council.

Morality, as we have noted, may be founded in religious belief, but, for some people, a moral code is based on humanist principles or the fundamental principle, 'do to others as you would be done by'. The political debate initiated by John Major in 1993, under the slogan 'back to basics,' raised the question of what is meant by 'moral code'. This backfired somewhat on the Conservative Government, when it later had to meet allegations of 'sleaze' in relation to both personal and political wrongdoing.

Some suggest that morality is purely a private matter for the individual, and what he or she does in private is the sole concern of that person. This so called 'private morality' is to be distinguished from public morality, where those who hold public positions may be accountable for their actions in so far as they affect the carrying out of public duties. Others suggest that there is no such distinction and that morality affects all aspects of one's life, that is, both private and public, and that, for example, when a public figure breaks a promise made to a member of his or her family, or commits adultery, or engages in sharp financial practice, or has a child outside wedlock, this is of relevance in judging his or her suitability to carry out public or commercial activities.

It is, of course, convenient for public figures or those in positions of authority or trust to distinguish what they do in their private lives from their public position, but such a distinction sits uncomfortably with the notion that morality is all-encompassing in regulating a person's dealings with others. It has been argued that morality has a narrow scope, regulating only sexual conduct and controlling violence to humans and animals. Certainly, any reference to morality brings these two areas to mind. Thus, the acceptability or otherwise of homosexuality, abortion, pornography, incest, extra-marital relationships, bigamy, euthanasia, divorce, cohabitation, vivisection, sado-masochistic practices or human embryo experimentation involve moral issues, and some have been legalised and others not. This last point suggests that, even where a moral consensus on a particular issue exists (in many cases, this may not be so), law does not always follow by reflecting those moral values.

Abortion is one such case: the Abortion Act 1967 permits abortion where specified conditions are met, but extremes of opinion exist as to whether abortion is right or not. At one extreme is the view that life starts at conception and the human being who results should have the full protection of the law; at the other extreme is the view that it is the pregnant woman who should be able to decide whether to abort or continue with the pregnancy.

It is to be noted that this debate has taken a new turn in the light of the scientific developments which suggest that aborted foetuses will, in two or three years' time, be able to be used in fertility treatments. The Human Fertilisation and Embryology Authority, established under the Human Fertilisation and Embryology Act 1990, has called for public discussion of the moral, ethical, social and legal issues involved before proposals are made on changes in the law.

Later, we shall consider the questions whether, on the one hand, legal rules should reflect moral rules and, on the other, whether legal rules should shape and influence moral values. Law and morality may overlap, and this is mostly true of the criminal law, based as it is on moral and religious principles of wrongdoing, fault, punishment and retribution, guilt and the attainment of justice. In other instances, law and morality diverge, and, in some cases, the law regulates 'neutral' conduct, that is, conduct which has no moral element. We shall also consider the extent to which law which fails to comply with moral principles and which is considered to be 'bad' law can be said to be law at all.

Natural and positivist schools

The natural law school of thought suggests that 'bad' law either need not be obeyed or is not law at all, whereas the positivist school holds that, no matter how bad a law is, or the system by which it is made, if the recognised procedures for law making have been complied with, 'the law is the law' and, in legal terms, should be obeyed.

It will be a separate issue, and one with which the jurist is not concerned, as to whether, as a matter of conscience, a citizen will be morally justified in not obeying such a law. It will be for the citizen to decide the extent of his or her moral responsibility, not only to obey, but also to bear any penalty exacted for breach of the legal rule.

Before concluding our remarks on classification of rules, we must briefly mention rules of etiquette and custom. We have already noted that the term 'etiquette' may be used to refer to professional codes of conduct, but, in a general sense, the word denotes good manners and common courtesy. However, in a narrow sense, etiquette has overtones of class division, whereby social inferiors are required to 'keep their place' and show deference to those who consider themselves to be, or who are considered by others to be, socially superior. The old ways die hard, and a person may be judged according to his or her table manners and dress, accent and social connections, and may still be required to do 'the right thing' on social occasions, such as bowing or curtseying to members of the royal family or complying with a dress code in order to gain entrance to the royal enclosure at Ascot. In its widest sense, etiquette remains essential in an increasingly crowded world. Good manners and politeness towards others help to give meaning to the notion of a civilised society as one where its members show care and concern for others and, at the same time, enhance social conditions for all.

When discussing conventions above, we compared these with the notion of custom and noted that it is not always easy to distinguish between the two. Customs tend to be more fixed than conventions and are generally obligatory. Both regulate social conduct and breach may result in disapproval, gossip, ridicule or ostracism. This distinguishes custom and law, in that breach of the latter results in a penalty imposed by or with the authority of the State.

It is not possible to distinguish law and custom by means of the type of action involved, since an action in one society may be a breach of custom and in another a breach of law. In less developed societies, there may be a dependence on custom, in that this passes from one generation to another and the rate of change may be relatively slow. In complex societies, however, custom gives way to more formal rules and mechanisms for change. Vestiges remain, for example, social customs, local customary law and the customs and practices of the constitution.

Why have rules?

In concluding, we may well ask what purposes are served by rules. Given the social nature of humans and that people operate in groups and institutions and enter into relationships with others for the fulfilment of needs and wants, we need standards and guides to behaviour. We need to know what is socially acceptable and the consequences of participating in socially unacceptable behaviour.

Although most rules may be in written form, mechanisms for change are provided and rules may well form part of a network or system. We may well ask why people obey rules, and some answers might be fear of a penalty, internalisation of the 'rightness' of rules, acceptance with or without questioning and a sense of obligation. Later, we will consider some of the theories as to why law is obeyed, including those of Hart, Summers, Farrer and Llewellyn.

Law as a system of rules

We have already defined law as a system of rules imposed by the State or by those having authority which give rise to sanctions or penalties when the rules are not complied with. We have to bear in mind that the concept of a rule may be defined widely, so as to include principles, guiding standards and regulations. Several questions arise when analysing the nature and characteristics of law: first, its role in society and the purposes law serves; secondly, the reasons why people obey law; thirdly, its relationship with morality; and, finally, its relationship with justice.

Some of the roles attributed to law are to maintain order (and this may well involve, in some societies or at some times, the repression of groups or interests within society), to regulate conduct, by means of both criminal and civil law, and to provide a means of settling disputes which arise or ensuring that people can order their affairs so as to avoid disputes. Atiyah suggests that this has its drawbacks, in that it suggests that law is an end in itself and that it has a mind, whereas, in Atiyah's opinion, law, like other concepts, is an abstract social construct made up of 'rules, principles and ideas'. Its purposes or functions are those of the people who make and enforce the law, and it is necessary to analyse the principles and policies underlying legal rules if one is to appreciate their effect. Principles and purposes may conflict, and a law may not have been clearly thought through or its possible effects considered. In any event, circumstances may change and a law may be adapted to meet new needs which are outside its original purposes. This is most often associated with the extent to which the judge has an active role in law making, so as to develop the law by taking into account the purposes that he or she considers the law ought to serve.

The accepted approach

The accepted approach is that the judge must give way to Parliament, which, as the elected representative of the people, is the arbiter of policy issues. The role of the judge is a limited one, concerned with interpreting statutory provisions and developing the common law within the confines of binding precedent. Where the judge is confronted with a hard case and no binding precedent exists, he or she should look to principle to assist him or her in reaching a decision. If, in so doing, the judge extends the boundaries of the law beyond that which is acceptable, it is for Parliament to pass legislation to achieve acceptable policy objectives.

In discussing the functions of law, what law is supposed to do and how effective it is in achieving those purposes must be distinguished. The former concerns the theories that have been devised about the functions of law, and the latter with how law works in practice. Both are useful, in that the former may be used as a measure of the effectiveness of law in society.

As we have noted, one of the main functions of law is said to be to resolve (or provide mechanisms for the avoidance of) disputes. The UK has an adversarial system, as opposed to an inquisitorial one. The parties to a dispute 'do battle', and it is for the claimant to prove his or her case. It must be noted, however, that, following the Woolf reforms of the civil justice system, this ethos will have to change, in that control of civil litigation moves to the court by way of case management provisions in the Civil Procedure Act 1997.

Resolution of disputes

The phrase 'resolution of disputes' properly refers to civil claims where the standard of proof on the claimant is on the balance of probabilities. In criminal cases, the prosecution must prove the defendant's guilt beyond all reasonable doubt. Only in a very wide sense is there a dispute; rather, it is the State imposing a penalty on a defendant found guilty of an act or omission which is considered to be sufficiently serious to warrant a fine, imprisonment or other penalty.

So far as effectiveness is concerned, several questions arise: first, whether the adversarial system is more effective than an inquisitorial one; and, secondly, given the pressures on the civil law system regarding unmet need for legal services and reductions in legal aid and advice provision, whether alternatives to traditional court settlement of disputes should be promoted (for example, arbitration, mediation and conciliation). Lord Woolf and others, including the Lord Chancellor, have promoted the idea of alternative dispute resolution, on the basis that litigation should be a last resort.

Regulation of conduct

Another function of law is the regulation of conduct and the entering into of relationships. Thus, the law might be a means of defining and regulating marriage and divorce, the relationship of parent and child, the ownership and use of property and its disposition by will or on intestacy, the making of contracts, the entering into of business and commercial relationships and the relationship between employer and employee, to mention but a few.

Some or all of these may give rise to sensitive issues and bring into question the extent to which law should be used to regulate such relationships. Other means of social control, such as morality or religion, might be argued to be more effective. A balance between the interests of the individual to own and use property, to marry and have children or decide not to do so, to be free to enter into contracts and so on and the interests of others and society in general has to be struck.

Some would argue that the law should protect individuals in their relationships with others, particularly those who are young, weak or vulnerable. Others suggest that the role of law is a limited one, particularly in matters which are more properly the concern of private morality such as sexual relations, the age of consent and abortion. Again, the distinction between judge-made law and that passed by Parliament has to be borne in mind, in that some take the view that, if law is to regulate matters, it must take the form of legislation and not the decisions of judges made piecemeal as and when a dispute arises.

In some societies the law has not been an instrument to protect or facilitate social arrangements but rather as a means of giving recognition to the actions of a ruling class with power and authority. The legal system and the laws made by it are a means of repression not only of those who present a threat to the existing order, but also of the majority of people. This then ensures continuance of the existing order. Recent history has shown that the use of law as a means of repression is possible despite more enlightened views as to its purposes. The Nazi regime is an oft-cited example of a system of law which was enforced by judges in courts of law and where rules were duly passed in accordance with recognised procedures but which, in its content and effect, was cruel and barbaric. Hart described such laws as too evil to be obeyed.

We will now turn our attention to some theories which explain what law is and the purposes it serves. The main distinction as to what law is is between the positivist and natural law schools of thought. The latter went into decline in the 19th century but saw something of a revival in the 20th century. The proponents of modern positivism are Hart and Kelsen, but, in the 19th century, Austin and Bentham put forward positivist theories of law. We will briefly consider the main principles put forward by Austin and Bentham and then those of Hart and Kelsen.

John Austin, in *The Province of Jurisprudence Determined*, published in 1832, stated that law was the command of a sovereign power within the State enforced by coercion. Thus, in the UK, law was made by the monarch in Parliament and the breach of law gave rise to the imposition of a sanction. The study of law was to be distinct from historical or sociological inquiry, and there was no necessary connection between law and morality. The jurist was to confine his study to what law is and not what it ought to be as measured against some value judgment which, unlike fact, could not be substantiated by proof. He recognised that law is normative, that is, it requires obedience and there may well be both a legal and a moral obligation to obey. Austin was concerned with an analytical study of law and the legal system, including what law is, how it is made and by whom.

Jeremy Bentham's writings lay undiscovered for more than a century after his death in 1832, but were published by Hart in 1970. These revealed Bentham's criticism of the common law. He described precedent as 'dog's law', and proposed urgent reforms so as to demystify the legal system. His theory of law was founded on the principle of utility and he said that the legal system should be rational and accessible and that law should be contained in a code permitting the judge to adjudicate in disputes rather than having power to interpret the law.

Austin had been Bentham's disciple and both defined law as the commands of a sovereign power. Bentham wished to move away from the 19th century natural law doctrine, which measured man-made law against divine law or the law of nature, and concluded that law which conflicted with a higher law was either not law at all or need not be obeyed.

Hart's theory

Hart, in *The Concept of Law*, continues his debate with Dworkin and recognises four main components of positivism, namely:

- law as a command enforced by coercion;

- law and morality are essentially separate;

- a legal system is based on logic so that correct decisions can be deduced from legal rules;

- analysis of legal concepts is distinct from historical and sociological studies and moral judgments cannot be proved by rational argument.

Hart stated that law is concerned with what is, whereas morality is concerned with what ought to be, but he recognised a core of indisputable truth in natural law doctrine. Unlike Bentham and Austin, Hart stated that law is a social phenomenon and not a command of a sovereign backed by coercion. Law is a system of rules which he analysed into primary and secondary rules. Primary rules proscribe basic anti-social behaviour such as theft, the use of violence and fraud. Secondary rules are of three types: rules of change; rules of adjudication; and rules of recognition.

Rules of change apply to both primary and secondary rules and permit changes to be made by Parliament and the courts to the law or legal system. Rules of adjudication confer power on the courts to decide when breaches have occurred in criminal and civil matters. Rules of recognition form the bedrock of a legal system and provide criteria for determining the validity of the system and rules made within it. Officials concerned with the administration and adjudication of the law have to adopt an 'internal point of view', that is, accept secondary rules. Citizens need to obey primary rules and should do so from a sense of obligation.

Kelsen's theory

Hans Kelsen, in *The Pure Theory of Law* (1978), took a scientific approach to the study of law and stated that law is a system of 'oughts' or norms which describe human conduct. The function of law is the use of force to ensure compliance with a rule. A rule would be expressed in terms of 'if X, then Y'. The consequence of breach is the imposition of a sanction. Law is distinct from morality and is to be analysed in terms of a pyramid, at the apex of which was the *Grundnorm* (basic norm), whose validity is presupposed and based on efficacy. The basic norm provides the reason why law is obeyed but is neutral and is not founded in morality.

Criticism of the positivist approach

Extensive criticism has been made of the positivist approach, including that it was an overreaction to the natural law doctrine, drawing on 19th century distinctions between 'is' and 'ought'. It has been said that it takes no account of values and fails to contemplate a connection between law and morality, the emphasis on sanction is not a true representation of law, as some laws impose no sanction and others impose a sanction in the absence of a legal duty. Other laws are power-conferring and it is far fetched to define sanction as including, for example, nullity following a failure to make a will in accordance with the proper rules.

We need to turn our attention now to the natural law doctrine. This analyses the point at which law and morality coincide. It is concerned with what should or ought to exist and measures man-made law against a divine or higher natural law. If the former offends the latter, St Thomas Aquinas was of the opinion that the law lost its moral binding power and that the citizen might be justified, in some cases, in not obeying the law. On the other hand, St Augustine, Plato, Cicero and Aristotle considered that such was not law at all and was not binding. Depending on one's stance, this may well affect not only one's perception of law, but also whether it is to be obeyed or not.

The positivist would argue that, in legal terms, all law, no matter how bad, must be obeyed, but morally it will be for the individual to decide whether or not to do so. The natural lawyer argues that 'bad' law is either not law at all and need not be obeyed, or that although law, morally it need not be obeyed, but that the citizen must expect imposition of a penalty for non-compliance.

Sir William Blackstone, in his *Commentaries on the Laws of England* (1765), stated that a conflict between positive law and God-given principles would nullify the positive law.

The functions of law

Having considered some of the theories defining law, we will now move on to consider some theories which attempt to analyse the purposes of law.

Techniques of law

Summers devised a techniques of law theory in which he set out five techniques or aims of law. Farrer subsequently added another two techniques, namely, constitutive and fiscal functions. Those noted by Summers were as follows:

- grievance-remedial;
- penal;

- administrative/regulatory;

- conferral of social benefits;

- private arrangements.

This theory emphasised the role of the law maker and the techniques available to give effect to social policies. Those who interpret the law will either have to apply the literal meaning of the words used or have to look behind the rules to find their meaning, so as to apply the law to given facts to arrive at a solution.

Law jobs theory

Llewellyn constructed a law jobs theory. In any group, certain needs will have to be met, or, as he referred to them, certain jobs will have to be done. Rules are one of the main ways in which such needs are met, although it is to be noted that law is not the only means of achieving social ends.

Llewellyn was a member of the American realist school of thought, which, like the positivists, was concerned with law as it is rather than with law as it ought to be. Law as an institution performs various jobs including allocation of authority, determination of disputes, the adjustment to change and, by far the most important, the disposition of 'trouble cases' or how officials deal with disputes.

Sociological theory

Brief mention must be made here of the sociological school of thought, which treats law as a social phenomenon and only one way of social control. Writers such as Pound, Durkheim, Weber and Marx put forward sociological views of law and the functions it performs. Pound said that law makers and lawyers were engaged in social engineering and that the law identified and protected various interests by way of rights and duties. He identified three types of interest:

- those of the individual, including personal, domestic and property interests;

- social interests, including general morals, social institutions, security and order;

- the public interest of the State as the guardian of the second type.

Law provides the means by which such interests are secured. Should interests on the same level conflict, they must be weighed against one another with the aim of ensuring that as many as possible are satisfied. Interests on different levels cannot be weighed against one another, so, for example, individual interests should not be weighed against public or social interests.

Durkheim's theory

Durkheim put forward the proposition that society was held together by social solidarity. Law had a central role to play in the transition from a simple system in which law was repressive (mechanical solidarity) to a more complex system based on the division of labour and secularism, where law is restitutive (organic solidarity).

Weber's theory

Weber took a traditional positivist approach to law and defined law in terms of an order imposed by those with recognised authority and one in which coercion would be applied where law was broken. He analysed different systems of law and the ways in which law is made and considered how justice could be achieved.

Marx's theory

Marx saw law as a means simply of class domination and oppression. Law was a necessary evil in capitalist society, whereas in a classless society there would be no need for law, for the means of production would be equally shared amongst all members of society.

Law and morality

Before considering the relationship of law and morality, whether one is shaped by the other and the extent to which one should shape the other, we need to consider what is meant by 'morality'. Earlier, we attempted to distinguish between rules and other social phenomena, and between legal rules and other types of rule, including moral rules. We noted that morality may be described as a body of rules, but equally it may be described as a set of values, beliefs or tenets which govern a person's or group's behaviour. Religion, ethics and morality are intertwined and may be relative according to time and place. However, they are concerned with what is right and wrong and operate on a different level from custom.

To tell lies or act dishonestly is generally considered to be wrong and may offend against not only morality, but also religion and, in some cases, the law, as with fraud or when taking an oath. Customs concern practices which have grown up over time and which are passed down from one generation to another. Failure to comply will rarely give rise to an allegation of guilt or fault or a sense of wrongdoing which is associated with moral rules.

Other types of conduct which are generally considered to be immoral include killing or injuring another person; stealing or damaging another's property; committing adultery; committing incest; taking advantage of another person, particularly one who is vulnerable or weak; and mistreating animals.

The essence of saying that some action or omission is immoral is to attribute blameworthiness, opprobrium and that it ought not to be done. There is a transgression, and invariably it involves a curb on behaviour rather than a positive duty to act. It follows that those who believe in freedom of choice and the ability of freely consenting individuals to do as they please in private resent any attempt to enforce moral ideals subscribed to by the wider society or so called 'do-gooding' individuals such as Mary Whitehouse or Lord Longford.

On the other hand, it might be argued that the law must take a lead either from the wider society and what public opinion suggests is wrong, or in some cases from the enlightened few in that it commands authority and respect sufficient to warrant obedience. In the minds of some, only when a law is passed prohibiting certain conduct will this warrant compliance. It necessitates the authority of the law to ensure that such conduct is not permitted.

Furthermore, implicit in the notion of freedom are knowledge and understanding. For one thing, not everyone is of the same level of intelligence and some, by reason of age, disability or education may be vulnerable and easily led by those more able, persuasive and without scruples or who are driven by money. Thus, the law may seek to protect people from others or from themselves. Caution is needed, however, concerning the question of whether the law should reflect morality. There may be no one moral standard to be applied by the law. It appears that this is certainly true of modern day Britain and there may be no agreement as to whose 'job' it is to enforce moral principles. This ranges from organised religion, the home and the school to the government of the day.

Simply to follow the majority view holds dangers, in that there is no guarantee that the majority reflect any standard other than one which promotes their interests best. If law is to reflect morality and the legislators are not the best equipped, this leaves the judges. Arguments for and against leaving moral issues in the hands of the judges can be put forward. On the one hand, they are appointed and not accountable to the people and therefore should not attempt to impose their views on others whereas, on the other, it can be said that, as they are independent, they can develop the law in an objective way without giving way to popular fashion or whim. Development of the law may well involve the judges in questions of public policy and this, it can be argued, is the province of Parliament, where all relevant issues can be debated before law is enacted.

The relationship of law and morality

We will now move on to consider more fully the relationship of law and morality. Law and morality in some places and at some times overlap, and sometimes diverge. This can be represented by two partly intersecting circles. At the point of intersection, law and morality regulate social conduct, and at the points where they do not intersect, conduct may be regulated by one and not the other. It should be noted, however, that even when they intersect they may not be identical, and that the law may be more specific and allow exceptions, whereas the moral rule may be all-embracing as, for example, with abortion, where a person's moral code may permit either abortion on demand or not in any circumstances. The Abortion Act 1967, as amended by the Human Fertilisation and Embryology Act 1990, permits abortion in specified circumstances.

Another area of overlap is the criminal law, where the State imposes sanctions for the commission of offences considered sufficiently serious as to warrant loss of freedom or fine or other punishment. The offender must 'pay his or her debt to society', and the law attempts to deter the offender and other members of society from such a course of action. The criminal law may also attempt not only to punish, but rehabilitate the offender, so as to re-enter society better able to contribute to it.

The criminal law adopts terminology suggesting wrongdoing and censure, such as guilt, offence, prosecution, sentence, and it regulates conduct which by any standards should be considered to be wrong or anti-social. Serious offences come readily to mind including murder, rape, burglary, theft and robbery, but these are not absolutes. Although founded in a society's values and ideology and the need to protect fundamental principles and standards of conduct, the law develops the meaning and effect of such offences.

Take murder, for example. This is not defined in the same way as killing another person. In some cases, killing a person can be lawful, as was the case before the Murder (Abolition of the Death Penalty) Act 1965, where a person convicted of murder was sentenced to death and this was carried out in the name of the Crown. The moral rule, however, may prohibit all killings, and this may be widely interpreted to include the foetus (from the moment of conception), to the person being kept alive artificially, to the person who is in great agony and wishes to take his or her own life or have another dispense a lethal drug to end life. Some would argue today that the death penalty for murder of police officers and others should be reinstated, so as to give effect to the moral opinion that taking the life of another is not acceptable and deserves the ultimate of penalties. However, Parliament has resisted various attempts to change the law so as to give effect to this suggestion.

The question has to be asked whether Parliament is correct in not passing a law to reinstate the death penalty if the majority of the population hold views whereby it is considered the best course of action. One counter-argument to such a change is that, given the numbers of miscarriages of justice which have been proved to have occurred in recent years through abuses of the criminal justice system, no convicted person should be sentenced to death. One other argument might be that Parliament, as the elected representative of the people, need not, or should not, give way to a majority view of the moment, but should attempt to set standards reflecting fundamental principles which apply long term and transcend mere fad or fashion.

The former appears on the surface to be an argument based on expediency or practicality, whereas the latter is based on morality or what ought, or ought not, to be done. However, it can be said that to discover at a later date that a person who had been hanged for an offence he or she did not commit is in itself repugnant to moral principles.

As we have already mentioned, the law in certain circumstances permits abortion and it is no longer a criminal offence to commit suicide (although it is to aid or abet another in an attempt to commit suicide), euthanasia is not permitted by the law, as was shown in the unreported case involving Dr Cox in 1992, who was convicted of the attempted murder of a patient to whom he had administered a lethal dose of saline solution to end her life. This was commented on by the House of Lords and Court of Appeal in *Airedale NHS Trust v Bland* (1993), where it was decided that a patient in a persistent vegetative state, for whom there was no medical hope of recovery, could have his life-support treatment stopped, resulting in his death. The House of Lords stated *per curiam* that positive steps to end life were unlawful, and that doctors should seek the guidance of the courts before ending life-support treatment, because every case would be different. Lords Browne-Wilkinson and Mustill stated that 'the moral, social and legal issues' should be considered by Parliament. Thus, the law draws the line between taking steps to end life and discontinuing treatment which prolongs breathing artificially when the medical evidence shows that brain death has occurred. To kill another person may be morally wrong, but, translated into law, may be permitted in defined cases.

In other societies, or at other times, taking the life of another may be more widely permitted by the law so as to reflect the moral attitude to human life. In the *Bland* case, both the Court of Appeal and House of Lords discussed the moral dilemma between the sanctity of human life and the quality of life. Both recognised that these were complementary and that, in the absence of legislation, the court's function was to balance the two. The House of Lords concluded that it was right to allow someone in the position of Anthony Bland, who was adult, had not expressed any wish as to what should be done if such circumstances befell him, and for whom there was no medical hope of recovery, to die naturally following removal of life-sustaining treatment.

When considering the issue as to how far the law should attempt to reflect morality on the question of life and death, it is instructive to bear in mind the debate about the imposition of life sentences for murder. In the House of Lords case of *R v Secretary of State for the Home Department ex p Doody* (1993), mandatory life prisoners claimed judicial review of the Home Secretary's decisions as to the length of imprisonment they were to serve. Amongst other things, the case illustrates that although the only sentence for murder is life imprisonment, in practice it is rare for a prisoner to remain in prison for his natural life. How long is served is at the discretion of the Home Secretary. The court ruled that, in the exercise of this power, the Home Secretary is obliged to give such prisoners reasons, but that there is to be no automatic right of challenge simply because a prisoner disagrees with the conclusions reached.

The Independent Committee of Inquiry, chaired by the former Lord Chief Justice, Lord Lane, reported in December 1993, recommending abolition of the mandatory life sentence for murder. In its place, a life sentence would be the maximum sentence reserved for the most wicked and for those who posed a continuing danger. In other cases of murder, the judge should be free to decide the appropriate remedy on the merits of each case and a decision made in open court.

Under the present system, all categories of murderer, in the words of the report, 'from the "mercy killer" and the battered wife to the terrorist and armed robber', are sentenced to life imprisonment and it is then for a member of the executive, the Home Secretary, behind closed doors, to decide on the length of sentence. A notable instance where the Home Secretary's exercise of his powers to determine a life prisoner's eligibility for release has been subject to judicial scrutiny is *R v Secretary of State for the Home Department ex p Hindley* (2000), where the court held that the Home Secretary should not fetter his discretion by deciding beforehand never to release a life prisoner. The result might be that release is not forthcoming, but each case should be kept under review so as to take into account the particular circumstances. This brings into question not only moral issues, but those of justice, which will be considered in the next section.

Given that law and morality may overlap on a particular issue but that the scope and effect will not always be identical, it must be noted that often they diverge. This may be because law is used to regulate types of conduct which have no moral element, for example, minor traffic offences, or simply because no moral consensus exists, so that the law is either not used at all or it reflects only one view current within society.

It might be that law is used in an attempt to change the general moral view and represents what those in authority consider to be appropriate or representative of an enlightened view. Morality may be unable to keep up with rapid medical, scientific or technological change and it will be for the law to give effect to such changes. In any event, over-regulation of every aspect of a person's life by law cannot be desirable and, for good or bad, people must be left to make choices as to personal behaviour even though this is not for their good or that of society generally.

Should law influence or merely reflect morality?

Whether or not law should reflect and reinforce morality depends on one's view of law and the purposes it serves in society. Whether law should go even further and attempt to change attitudes and give a moral lead is more problematic, and may result in the law and legal system losing some of its authority and respect.

In discussing these questions, we need to take account of the natural law school of thought, which we have already briefly described. This emphasises the close relationship of law and morality and a logical conclusion of the theory is that, where law fails to accord with moral principles, either such rules are not properly classed as law or the citizen is not morally bound to obey such law.

Even proponents of the positivist school, such as Hart, recognised a core of moral principle in law and concluded that the Nazi regime was so morally indefensible that the citizen was not morally bound to obey. Dworkin, on the other hand, considers that law is not only made up of rules, but also non-rule standards, and in deciding a hard case the judge calls on moral and political standards (principles and policies). Rules and principles form part of the law and dictate, guide or influence a result. These are properly the province of the judge, whereas policies are the province of Parliament, since they set out a goal to be achieved in social, political or economic matters or which are deemed to be desirable but not necessarily on grounds of morality. The role of the judge is to find the one right answer, not to make law. A judge formulates principle and, if it exceeds the limits, it is for Parliament to state the policy to which the law should give effect.

The Hart-Fuller debate

Present day exponents of natural law doctrine include Fuller, who, in *The Morality of Law*, spoke of the law's 'inner morality' which he formulated in terms of eight procedural requirements, including generality, promulgation, non-contradiction, clarity, non-retroactivity, constancy, the possibility of compliance and congruence between a declared rule and official action. He considered that Nazi law could not be considered to be law. Hart and Fuller entered into what has become known as the Hart-Fuller debate on the morality of law, whereby the former put forward positivist views and the latter the natural law view, that law and morality are inextricably mixed.

Similarly, Lord Devlin stated that law, in particular the criminal law, is based on moral and religious principles. Ultimate standards of right and wrong exist. In other words, society is held together by a binding moral code and the role of the judge is to ensure continuance of this code as a guardian of morality. The judge has to put himself in the position of the reasonable man so as to gauge what is in the public interest. The suppression of vice was 'the business of the law', and consent and prevention of public immorality was insufficient.

This attitude is clearly shown in the cases of *Shaw v DPP* (1961), *DPP v Withers* (1974) and *Knuller v DPP* (1972). *Shaw* has become known as the *Ladies Directory* case, where prostitutes advertised in magazines and where the publishers were convicted of the offence of 'conspiring to corrupt public morals'. In *Knuller*, the publication of advertisements inviting homosexual contacts were said to be undesirable on grounds of public policy and were prohibited, as in *Shaw*. In *R v Gibson* (1991), where a model's head was displayed at a public gallery, and attached to the head were earrings made from freeze-dried human foetuses of three to four months' gestation, it was held that the common law offence of 'outraging public decency' had been committed.

It may be argued that these cases are outdated in their approach and that judges are not suitable to decide such sensitive issues. If they are not to be left to individual discretion and choice, it is for Parliament alone to lay down the ground rules. Hart took a libertarian stance, following JS Mill, that the 'individual is sovereign'.

An issue before Parliament during the debates on the Criminal Justice and Public Order Act 1994 was the age of consent for homosexuals. The Sexual Offences Act 1967 provided that two consenting males aged 21 or over who participated in homosexual acts in private committed no criminal offence. Edwina Currie MP proposed that the age of consent be reduced to 18 and this has now been enacted. Reduction to 16 was rejected. Critics of this proposal suggested that the law should protect young men from unscrupulous members of society and themselves at a time when they may be impressionable and vulnerable. Proponents of this measure suggested that this should be a matter for the individual, and it is not the place of the law to intervene in private matters or seek to enforce a particular pattern of behaviour.

The debate over reducing the age of consent to 16 continues, following the Government's dropping of a provision in what became the Crime and Disorder Act 1998 when faced with opposition in the House of Lords. The Sexual Offences (Amendment) Bill contains a similar provision, and the Government has threatened to invoke the Parliament Acts if the House of Lords continue to oppose this change in the law.

At one extreme, there are those who promote complete freedom of the individual, and, at the other, those who wish to see the law impose limits. This raises the question as to where the line is to be drawn: no restrictions or, if so, how much, and by what means? The Wolfenden Committee Report in 1957 on *Homosexual Offences and Prostitution* made the following statement on the function of the criminal law:

> ... to preserve public order and decency, to protect the citizen from what is offensive and injurious, and to provide sufficient safeguards against exploitation and corruption of others, especially the vulnerable, that is, the young, weak in body or mind, inexperienced or those in a state of physical, official or economic dependence. The law should not intervene in the private

lives of citizens or seek to enforce any particular pattern of behaviour further than necessary to carry out the above purposes.

This statement was considered in the case of *R v Brown* (1993), where the House of Lords by a 3:2 majority held that, where the defendants had committed sado-masochistic acts in private and their victims had consented, public policy demanded that such acts be treated as unlawful under ss 20 and 47 of the Offences Against the Person Act 1861. Lord Mustill, dissenting, took the view that this Act did not cover the defendants' actions and thereby make them unlawful, although clearly such actions were immoral. Where the parties had consented to sado-masochistic practices, these did not fall within the provisions of ss 20 and 47 of the Offences Against the Person Act 1861. These provisions made duelling and prize fighting unlawful, but were not appropriate to the facts of this case. He did not endorse a libertarian view, and considered that right and wrong could be distinguished. However, this was a matter of private morality and it was not the function of the criminal law to impose standards on the individual. The individual should be governed by his or her own moral standards or be subject to the pressures of religion or other community to whose ethical ideals he or she responds. State intervention in the lives of individuals should not be more than is necessary to ensure a proper balance between the interests of the individual and those of the community in which he or she lives. It was for Parliament to decide where the public interest lay.

Lord Templeman, in the majority, asked whether the defence of consent should extend to sado-masochistic practices. This was to be decided on the basis of 'policy and public interest'. A line had to be drawn by the courts and, rightly or wrongly, it had become established that boxing was a lawful activity, as is surgery, ritual circumcision, tattooing and ear piercing. Such activities are lawful and, where practised with consent, actual bodily harm, wounding or serious bodily harm do not give rise to criminal liability. Unlawful activities include duelling and prize fighting, and consent cannot legitimate such activities.

Lord Jauncey, also in the majority, drew the line between common assault, where consent provides a defence, and offences under ss 20 and 47 of the Offences Against the Person Act 1861, where consent is not available as a defence unless the circumstances fall within accepted exceptions, such as sporting contests, chastisement or surgery. The creation of new exceptions was a matter for Parliament, following a full review of the moral, social, medical and other issues. Thus, the majority of their Lordships took the view that all acts above common assault are unlawful, and consent is no defence, unless statute permits such actions. It was not for the courts to allow a defence of consent and make such actions lawful. Lords Mustill and Slynn, dissenting, considered that the Offences Against the Person Act 1861 did not apply to these actions, although clearly they were morally wrong, and so it was for Parliament to prohibit such actions if this was desired.

Following this judgment, protests were raised by civil rights campaigners who demanded a right of privacy to be enshrined in law so as to comply with Art 8 of the European Convention on Human Rights. It was also alleged that the sentences of imprisonment were excessive, that questions of morality were for Parliament and not the courts, which are unrepresentative of the population at large and are only able to make decisions after a dispute or question arises. As the case involved the consent of the parties involved, who were adults conducting themselves in private, the court had imposed an unacceptable limit on personal freedom. A line had to be drawn between the acceptable and the unacceptable. To torture a person and thereby cause his or her death and then plead consent would be unacceptable, but Parliament should determine the proper place of consent, not the courts. The decision was reached by a 3:2 majority, which suggests that, in reality, little consensus exists on such issues, and for the majority to suggest that it is for Parliament to legitimise such activity if thought necessary and for the minority to suggest that such actions are lawful until Parliament prohibits them is equally unsatisfactory. On 20 February 1997, the ECHR ruled in favour of upholding the decision of the House of Lords that consent is no defence and that there had been no infringement of Art 8 of the Convention.

In 1991, the House of Lords made a landmark decision in respect of rape within marriage. In *R v R (A Husband)* (1991), the principle established by Sir Matthew Hale in *History of the Pleas of the Crown* (1736), whereby a husband could not be guilty of rape committed on his wife, 'for by their mutual matrimonial consent and contract the wife hath given up herself in this kind unto her husband which she cannot retract', was rejected.

On the facts of the case, the parties had been separated some 22 days before the alleged rape, but there had been no legal separation or court order prohibiting the husband from molesting his wife. The court held that the time had come to remove Hale's proposition altogether, rather than create further exceptions to the rule. Its terms no longer accorded with what was considered acceptable behaviour. It was never any more than a legal fiction and had been overtaken by events. In the words of Lord Lane, the Lord Chief Justice at the time, 'a rapist remained a rapist subject to the criminal law, irrespective of his relationship with his victim', the common law fiction had become anachronistic and offensive, and it was the duty of the court to remove the immunity created by it.

Lord Keith said that the common law could change and evolve in the light of social, economic and cultural developments. The status of women today is radically different from that in Hale's time, and the institution of marriage is seen as a partnership of equals where a wife is no longer the subservient chattel of her husband. The Law Commission has recommended that rape in marriage be a criminal offence and that a wife who alleges rape against her husband be a compellable witness for the prosecution against her husband. Prosecutions should be brought with the consent of the Director of Public Prosecutions.

We have already referred to the *Bland* case and the issues it raised. It is useful to note here the role of the Attorney General as *amicus curiae* (friend of the court). Given the public importance of the case and the serious medical, moral and ethical questions raised, it was essential that those interests be put before the court. The case was novel, in that it was the first time that the English courts had had to deal with such a question concerning life and death. Furthermore, Tony Bland was not a child or ward of court, he was immune from pain and had given no instructions concerning treatment in the event of his becoming such a patient. In the Court of Appeal, Hoffman LJ stated that, in such an area as this, there should be no difference between the law and what is morally right. The court's decision should be based on accepted ethical values. Both the Court of Appeal and the House of Lords made much use of persuasive authorities from Commonwealth and other jurisdictions in assisting them in reaching the decision that treatment should cease.

The case of *Re J (A Minor) (Medical Treatment)* (1992) was referred to in the *Bland* case. This concerned a severely handicapped baby whose doctor considered that mechanical ventilation procedures would not be appropriate. An injunction was sought to order the carrying out of such treatment, but the court held that in the best interests of the child this was not to be granted. The court adopts the role of *parens patriae* in respect of minors, as illustrated in the case of *Re J (A Minor) (Inherent Jurisdiction: Consent to Treatment)* (1992), where the court held that a 16 year old does not have complete autonomy to refuse medical treatment. The court was also of the opinion that the '*Gillick* competent', that is, a child of sufficient intelligence and understanding, could not refuse treatment. In *Gillick v West Norfolk and Wisbech AHA* (1985), it was held that, at common law, the '*Gillick* competent' could consent to treatment without the need for parental consent or even in the face of the parents' express prohibition. The court can, therefore, override parental refusal of treatment and a child's refusal of treatment.

The conclusion may be drawn, therefore, that the court can protect children and others who are vulnerable or weak from themselves or others, although the jurisdiction of the court in respect of minors has always been considered special. It might be argued that, where Parliament has failed to legislate, it is for the courts to adopt what some might describe as a paternalistic approach in the meantime and then, if the decisions of the courts are unacceptable, for Parliament to set the limits of the law. Recent cases endorse this view, for example, the 13 year old girl ordered by the court to undergo a heart transplant; whereas where both parents agree on the circumcision of their male child on religious grounds, the court will not intervene.

Other issues, which we can but mention and which have a moral dimension, include that of women over the child-bearing age giving birth to test-tube babies; sterilisation of the mentally and physically handicapped; surrogate motherhood; and the use of foetal tissue in embryo experimentation. In 1996, the situation of Mandy Allwood came to public attention when she had to decide whether to proceed with a multiple pregnancy or to selectively abort some of the foetuses. In the result, she decided to proceed, but nature took its course and all the foetuses died. Some time before this, it was made public that another woman pregnant with twins had decided to selectively abort one of the foetuses and later delivered a healthy child. Increasingly, fathers of such foetuses are claiming a voice in deciding their fate. A case in the Scottish Court of Session, brought by the father of a 12 week old foetus, seeking an injunction to prevent his estranged wife from having an abortion, illustrates the dilemma. An appeal was to be made to the House of Lords, but the father decided to drop the case. He had alleged that his wife wanted an abortion because he had been violent to her and that this was not a good reason within the terms of the Abortion Act 1967.

Another issue which has come to prominence recently is the defence of provocation for women with violent partners. The present law on provocation as a defence to murder is said to be to the advantage of men who react in a moment of passion or anger, whereas women who are driven to retaliate against partners, often following many years of violence, do so only after a time in which they plan their actions. Consequently, the defence of provocation is rarely available to such women and this needs to be changed.

The question of the extent to which morality plays a part in the decisions of local authorities to ban hunting over their land came before the High Court in the case of *R v Somerset CC ex p Fewings* (1995) on an application for judicial review. It was held that the moral issues involved in hunting should play no part in a decision whether to impose a ban on hunting over council land and that the ban was *ultra vires* in this case.

An extremely difficult case to come before the courts was that of Diane Blood, whose husband contracted meningitis and who then lapsed into a coma and died. Sperm samples were taken from him after he went into a coma. His widow wished to use them in an effort to become pregnant. It was held that the Human Fertilisation and Embryology Act 1990 required written consent by the sperm donor for its use and as this was not given, Mrs Blood was unable to make use of the sperm in this country. However, the regulating authority had overlooked that Mrs Blood was entitled to such treatment in Belgium, and that Parliament had placed no restriction on the Authority's discretion to permit this. Her appeal was allowed, and the Authority later confirmed that it would permit Mrs Blood to take the sperm to Belgium for treatment.

Two other issues, and their regulation by law, have yet to be decided, namely, whether the law should prohibit childminders from smacking children in their charge, and whether the law should ban tobacco advertising. A proposed ban on tobacco advertising has caused sports organisations to protest that it is only through such advertising income that they are able to offer their sports services. A recent ruling by the ECHR against the use of corporal punishment has resulted in a government announcement that smacking is acceptable, but that the use of canes, slippers and belts are not, nor is hitting a child around the head.

The arguments for and against the involvement of the law in such areas revolve around the freedom of the individual, on the one, hand and of protection of the weak and vulnerable, on the other. If the law is seen as too restrictive of the freedom of the individual, it will lose respect and the result may be criminalisation of conduct considered morally acceptable, whereas, if it is seen to be too liberal, it may lose its moral authority in failing to protect those in need.

Law and justice

What is justice?

The concept of justice is most often linked with that of law, in that the former is an ideal which, in the minds of most people throughout time, should be the aim to be achieved by law. However, justice in the sense of fairness should, as a moral value, permeate all areas of social activity, and it is ultimately for the law and legal system to enforce principles of fairness. It must be noted, however, that in some societies and at different times law does not promote the principle of justice or fairness and may be used as an instrument of repression of a section or sections of society or as an instrument of terror against the general population. Moreover, particular laws may be seen by members of a society as unjust, and the question may arise as to the moral imperative to obey such law.

In considering the English legal system, the words 'law' and 'justice' may often be used interchangeably, for example, with reference to the 'courts of justice', 'justice of the peace', the 'criminal and civil justice systems'; but this is not to say that law or the legal system and justice are identical or that justice is achieved. In relation to the criminal justice system, this appears to be particularly true in the light of a considerable number of appeals to the Court of Appeal alleging miscarriages of justice and radio and television programmes which have publicised failings in the system whereby the guilty go free, either through non-detection or technicalities in the trial process, or the innocent are wrongly convicted.

It might be argued that any criminal justice system must accept the former as the price to be paid for preventing the latter, which by any standard of morality, ethics or fairness is never acceptable. The epitome of the aim of achieving justice in the criminal justice system is the statue of justice on the Old Bailey in London holding outright the evenly balanced scales of justice.

It is to be noted that there are four components to be measured.

The pre-trial process

This is the process by which evidence is collected and a charge is made against an accused. This has been found seriously wanting and, given our accusatorial system, the trial process cannot be any better than the evidence which is brought before the court. If this has been fabricated or obtained as a result of duress, whether physical or psychological, a conviction secured on the basis of such evidence may, many years after the trial, be found to be wrong.

The trial of the Guildford Four, in which Donaldson LJ presided, was at the time described as scrupulously fair, but it was only much later, as a result of press and other pressure, that fabricated evidence was shown to have caused great injustice.

The trial process

This should be fair in its form by which a person is tried and guilt determined. We will consider later some of the fundamental principles which contribute to a fair trial, such as the presumption of innocence, the right to jury trial and the right to silence, which has been amended by ss 34–37 of the Criminal Justice and Public Order Act 1994. It is interesting to note the decision of the ECHR in *Findlay v UK* (1997) that a trial by court martial under the provisions of the Army Act 1995 did not constitute a fair hearing by an independent and impartial tribunal as provided for in Art 6(1) of the Convention.

The adequacy of mechanisms for discovering and rectifying miscarriages of justice

The Runciman Royal Commission on Criminal Justice, which reported in July 1993, recommended the establishment of a criminal cases review body, and the Criminal Cases Review Commission has been set up by s 8 of the Criminal Appeal Act 1995.

Substantive legal rules

The fourth component to be measured is substantive legal rules, whether criminal or civil, and the penalties which can be imposed for breach, governing a person's conduct. If such rules are considered by sufficient numbers of the population to be unjust, this can only result in loss of respect for the law and those who enforce it. The following are good examples: the suggested increase in penalties for drug abuse; the Dangerous Dogs Act 1991; and the recent bans on knives and guns, now to be extended to all handguns, despite the protests from members of gun clubs who assert that they are being penalised for the actions of Thomas Hamilton at Dunblane in 1996.

Theories of justice

As we have already mentioned, law and justice are closely associated, but by no means identical. We need now to consider some of the theories which have been constructed to explain this concept and its relationship with law and other social phenomena. We have already stated that justice can be used as a measure of the quality or fairness of the processes of the legal system and of substantive legal rules. Another way of making this distinction is between formal or procedural justice on the one hand and substantial justice on the other. We will consider each in turn.

Formal justice

Formal or procedural justice requires a legal system to provide rules, principles and machinery for due application of the law to all persons without fear or favour. It is a fundamental principle, founded in morality, that no one should be above the law and those who administer the law should do so without prejudice, bias or fear of recrimination from those with power. The independence and impartiality of the judiciary are essential, and are the main ways in which the citizen is protected from dictatorial government. However, this says nothing of the substance of the rules which are to be administered and applied. They may be considered to be unjust, wrong or immoral.

The positivist looks to the process by which law is made. If this has been complied with, no matter what the content of the rules, they are to be obeyed and applied. The natural lawyer, on the other hand, will question the content or substance of the law and, in very extreme situations, may be willing to question the authority of the legal system itself, and if this is found wanting will either conclude that it is not law at all or that the citizen is not morally obliged to abide by it.

Formal justice depends on the notion of equality. Hart, in *The Concept of Law*, says that 'like should be treated as like'. This necessitates that those who administer the law do so impartially without preference for the rich, the powerful, or members of an elite. As Fuller noted, law should manifest certain characteristics. It should be of general effect, so that everyone falling within the remit of a rule should be treated in the same way. Thus, a person convicted of murder should be subject to the required penalty regardless of whether he or she is black or white, male or female, old or young, or of high or low rank. The rule may well define exceptions so that those, for example, who are insane or of tender years will not be not be subject to penalty. Generality allows people to plan their activities so as to comply with the law. It follows that the law should have prospective effect and only in cases where a statute expressly provides will English law allow it to have retrospective effect. The law should be clear in its effect, provide for the possibility of compliance, and there should be some congruence between the official rule and its application in practice.

Judges, when making decisions, should do so in accordance with recognised principles in the absence of binding precedent so as to ensure that their decisions are reasoned and impartial. Improper considerations and motives should play no part in the decision making process. This comes from training and experience, as well as knowledge and understanding of how the law has developed and appreciation of the purposes it serves.

When considering formal justice, two important doctrines are the rule of law and natural justice.

The rule of law

This forms one of the cornerstones of democratic States and in those with written constitutions it is often guaranteed. Government excess can be found by the courts not only to be illegal, but also unconstitutional, since the constitution is treated as a form of higher law by which the actions of government and others are measured. No person is above the law, and even government itself is subject to law and is required to conduct its activities in accordance with duly established legal rules rather than by way of arbitrary or discretionary means.

It is, however, a broad and rather elusive concept and one which does not sit easily in the UK with the doctrine of sovereignty of Parliament. The role of the courts is also much more limited in respect of government activities. The Government may act by way of statutory or prerogative power and this affords the courts little, if any, means of permitting any challenge by an aggrieved citizen.

However, if delegated powers are used, the delegate, whether a government minister, local authority or public body, can be found to have abused or exceeded the powers granted and the court may declare such actions *ultra vires* and void. A useful illustration is that of the case of *M v Home Office and Another* (1993), where the House of Lords affirmed the decision of the Court of Appeal in holding the Home Secretary in contempt of court for failing to comply with a court order for the immediate return to this country of an asylum seeker unlawfully deported to Zaire pending his application to the court for judicial review of the decision to deport.

The doctrine of natural justice

The doctrine of natural justice is rather a misnomer, in that there is no appeal to natural law or to divine law, but rather to the fundamental need for fairness in the judicial process. The doctrine has been extended to decision makers acting not only in a judicial capacity, but also to those acting quasi-judicially. Such distinctions are not easy to define but the courts have classified, on the one hand, judicial and quasi-judicial decisions and, on the other, administrative decisions where the rules of natural justice have not been strictly applied.

However, this distinction has lost much of its importance following the case of *Re HK (An Infant)* (1967), where it was stated that decision makers, no matter what their capacity, must act fairly.

In *Bushell v Secretary of State for the Environment* (1981), Lord Diplock stated that: '... the only requirement ... as to the procedure to be followed at a local inquiry ... is that it must be fair to all those who have an interest in the decision that will follow it.' In *Council of Civil Service Unions v Minister for the Civil Service* (1985) (the *GCHQ* case), Lord Roskill said that natural justice might now be laid to rest and be 'replaced ... by a duty to act fairly'. Lord Scarman spoke of 'the requirement of natural justice, namely, the duty to act fairly', and observed that this applies to purely administrative acts.

Some cases still speak of the 'rules of natural justice' as opposed to a general duty to act fairly, and so it is not settled whether these are still separate. However, what is clear is that the courts are not concerned with the merits of a claim under the judicial review process (unlike an appeal) and will not substitute its decision for that of the decision maker. Usually, cases are sent back to the decision maker who will be required to make a new decision in accordance with the recommendations of the court as to the extent of its legal powers. Thus, the reference to a duty to act fairly relates to process and not to the merits of a decision.

There are two limbs to the rules of natural justice:

* *nemo judex in res sua* (no man should be a judge in his own cause);

* *audi alteram partem* (both sides have a right to be heard).

We have an adversarial legal system, in which it is for the prosecution in criminal cases, and for the claimant in civil cases, to prove its case. The judge is an independent and impartial 'arbiter' of law and fact (or of law in Crown Court trials where the jury is the arbiter of fact), who decides cases coming before the court on the basis of the evidence produced and his knowledge and understanding of the law as applied to the facts. It follows that, in judicial proceedings, both sides should have a right to make representations to the court, but it is recognised that a defendant, particularly in criminal trials, need not say anything in his or her own defence subject to the power of the court to draw adverse inferences from his or her silence and that the burden of proof rests with the prosecution or claimant.

The rules of natural justice ensure that fair play operates, so that a party knows the case he or she has to answer and the judge has no interest in the outcome. The rules of natural justice have been developed by the judges as part of the common law and, where one or both have not been complied with, the aggrieved person may seek judicial review. The relief granted will be an order of mandamus, certiorari or prohibition as appropriate in the circumstances.

It must be noted that neither rule has been defined with great precision, with the effect that many limitations exist on their scope. This is particularly true of the right to be heard, where there is no absolute right to legal representation. A person should be given adequate prior notice of charges or allegations and a reasonable opportunity to put his or her case. The rules provide for minimum standards so as to ensure safeguards to protect the interests of those in respect of whom decisions are made.

The rule against bias ensures that the judge or decision maker leaves aside his or her personal preferences or prejudices due to age, background, education or sex. It also militates against the espousal of fixed views, as in *R v Bingham Justices ex p Jowitt* (1974), where a magistrate said that he always believed police witnesses in preference to members of the public.

Pecuniary and proprietary interests, personal knowledge and relationships with a party or witness are also included. In short, the decision maker should consider whether his or her position is compromised to the extent that he or she should stand down.

The question of judicial bias arose in the most surprising way in *R v Bow Street Metropolitan Magistrates ex p Pinochet Ugarte* (1998), when it was alleged that Lord Hoffman had failed to disclose his connection with Amnesty International, after this organisation had been asked to address the court, in the case concerning Spain's application for the Colonel's extradition to stand trial for genocide and torture. In a novel move, the decision was found to be void on the basis that apparent bias could arise from a direct interest in the case, apart from the long recognised financial interest. It was stressed that there was no suggestion of actual bias. More will be said on this in Chapter 3.

Over the years, the courts have extended the scope of the rules of natural justice and now apply a wide duty to act fairly. Decision makers are obliged to observe all or some of the aspects of both rules according to the circumstances. However, there are situations where the rules do not apply, including where a statute excludes their operation, where matters are dealt with at a preliminary stage or where a presumption excludes the doctrine. In professional relationships, the rules only apply where a person's rights are affected.

Legitimate expectation

We have already referred to the *GCHQ* case, which involved a union ban issued by the head of the civil service by way of an Order in Council. The House of Lords held that the employees had a legitimate expectation to be consulted before such action was taken. It had become a well established practice for the Government to consult civil servants before making significant changes to their terms and conditions. This regular practice gave rise to a legitimate expectation that it would continue unless notice was given of revocation. Legitimate expectation may arise out of a promise or a regular practice. It may be an expectation of being consulted, or a right to a hearing, or to make representations.

In *AG of Hong Kong v Ng Yuen Shiu* (1983), Ng, an illegal immigrant to Hong Kong, became aware, after registering as an illegal immigrant, of an undertaking from the British Government that repatriation would only be made following an interview and consideration of the merits of each case. Ng was deported without any opportunity of giving his reasons for remaining in Hong Kong. It was held that the undertaking gave rise to a legitimate expectation in Ng that his case would be considered on its merits. In *R v Secretary of State for the Home Department ex p Khan* (1985), K and his wife wished to adopt a child from Pakistan. K obtained from a Citizens' Advice Bureau a standard letter from the Secretary of State stating that he 'may exercise his discretion' and exceptionally allow a child to be brought here for adoption when satisfied on four specified matters. K's application was refused, and it was shown that the Secretary of State took into account a matter not mentioned in his letter. The court held that any change in policy should have resulted in a hearing at which K could have made representations. The Secretary of State was under a duty to act fairly and was obliged to reconsider the matter on the basis of his letter, or if the new policy was to apply, K should have an opportunity of being heard.

R v Secretary of State for the Home Department ex p Ruddock (1987) contains *obiter* statements that a legitimate expectation arose from the publication of the Government's policy on telephone tapping that it would remain unchanged. Any change in policy was to be published. This, as with the other cases, illustrates that legitimate expectation only concerns procedural requirements and not substantive ones. The Government could change its policy for the future, but if it did so it would need to publicise the change so as to ensure those affected by it had due warning. In *O'Reilly v Mackman* (1982), a prisoner had a legitimate expectation of remission and he had *locus standi* under RSC Ord 53 to challenge a decision depriving him of it. In *R v Lord Chancellor ex p The Law Society* (1993), The Law Society challenged regulations made by the Lord Chancellor under the Legal Aid Act 1988, and it was held that The Law Society had *locus standi* and a legitimate expectation of being consulted before changes were made in legal aid provision. In the result, the regulations were found to be *intra vires*.

Two other cases illustrate the continuing use of the concept of legitimate expectation. In *R v Secretary of State for the Home Department ex p Hargreaves and Others* (1997), it was held that prisoners at Risley, who had signed a compact offering them the opportunity to apply for home leave, did not have a legitimate expectation that their entitlement was on the basis of having served one-third of their sentence, the standard which applied on their entry. Rather, their entitlement was that which applied at the date of application for home leave. A change in rules increasing the time served to one-half of a sentence was within the powers of the Home Secretary. Hirst LJ referred to Lord Scarman's statement of principle in *Re Findlay* (1985) to the effect that 'the most that a convicted prisoner could legitimately expect was that his case would be examined individually in the light of whatever policy the Secretary of State saw fit lawfully to adopt'.

The Home Secretary could change his policy, but it is to be noted that the court suggested that, in future, all documents issued to prisoners should be clear and unambiguous so that eligibility for such privileges as home leave would be subject to the rules applicable at the time of application, not on entry to prison.

The case of *R v IRC ex p Unilever plc* (1996) demonstrates the difficulty in confining this concept merely to procedure as opposed to the substance or merits of a case. By s 3(2) of the Income and Corporation Taxes Act 1988, a trading company can set off losses against profits so as to reduce its tax liability. A time limit of two years applies, but with power in the Inland Revenue to extend the time limit, although this was not used. Unilever and the Inland Revenue had, over some 20 years, adopted a procedure for dealing with the company's liability whereby the company would estimate its profits and losses, submit a schedule, followed later by detailed accounts. The accounts were often outside the time limit, in one case, 15 months late. The Inland Revenue had not insisted on compliance until in 1989, without warning, it refused to accept Unilever's claim for losses of some £17 million. It was held that the Inland Revenue was prohibited from disallowing this late claim, given its own previous conduct. Its behaviour was so unfair as to amount to an abuse of power. For the first time, it appears that the court found in favour of the applicant for judicial review, on the basis that its legitimate expectation as to substance, £17 million, had been breached. How later courts treat this apparent development in the scope of this concept will be of great interest.

Substantive justice

Leaving procedural justice, we will move on to consider substantive justice. This concerns the content of a rule and measures it against a 'higher' or more fundamental set of principles, such as fairness, justice or morality. The natural law school would use as its measure principles of morality or divine law, whereas in a State with a written constitution this will be the yardstick against which ordinary law is measured. The constitution will contain those principles which are considered to be fundamental and worth preserving and there may, in addition, be a Bill of Rights, guaranteeing the rights of the citizen against the State.

In the UK, there is no written constitution, and law which has constitutional significance takes no special form and is not entrenched. However, now that the Human Rights Act 1998 gives effect to the European Convention on Human Rights, the courts will be able to give effect to its provisions once the Act comes into force in October 2000, and where an Act conflicts with the provisions of the

Convention, the court will be able to make a declaration of incompatibility. Occasionally, in the past, the courts had been willing to decide a case in such a way as to comply with the provisions of the European Convention by developing the common law. An illustration of this is the case of *Derbyshire CC v Times Newspapers Ltd and Others* (1993), where the House of Lords held that, at common law, a local authority had no right to sue in defamation, since this would place an undesirable fetter on freedom of speech. The Court of Appeal, in reaching the same conclusion, had referred to Art 10 of the European Convention.

Impartial application of legal rules does not of itself ensure substantial justice. It is the content of the rules and the extent to which particular circumstances are taken into account when a decision is made that ensure that a just result is achieved. In future, any court in the land will be able to rule on the compatibility of domestic legislation with the provisions of the Convention.

Remedial justice

What criteria are used to assess whether a just result is achieved? This depends on one's view of right and wrong. A distinction can be drawn between the theory of remedial justice and that of distributive justice. The former is concerned with the remedy provided for breach of a legal rule. The ordinary person looks to the judge or the legislator to provide a remedy where a wrong is committed. The judge adopts the 'reasonable man' test, once described as that of 'the man on the Clapham omnibus', to decide what the ordinary person would expect of the law. Use of the term 'remedy' implies resolution of a dispute, as in civil law where the wrongdoer pays compensation to the victim so as to put him or her into the position that he or she would have been in if the wrong had not been committed. However, 'remedy' should have a wide meaning, so as to include penalties imposed by criminal law on those found guilty of criminal offences.

It is in the area of sentencing that questions of justice most often arise and whether the penalty imposed matches the crime committed by the defendant. The aims of sentencing are most often said to be:

- punishment of the offender;
- deterrence of offender and of others who might be tempted to commit an offence; and
- rehabilitation of the offender.

It is difficult to assess the relative weight of each of these in any one offence, but a sense of justice suggests that there should be an element of proportionality so that an offender is not made a 'scapegoat' for others and that, as between different offences, a trivial offence is not treated more seriously than a less trivial one. However, determining the relation of one offence with others involves value judgments, as does judging the relative seriousness of different instances of one type of offence.

This is clearly illustrated by the debate which was initiated following the report in 1993 of the Committee of Inquiry, chaired by Lord Lane, which recommended the abolition of the mandatory life sentence for murder. In 1994, Lord Taylor, the then Lord Chief Justice, joined the debate and advocated that judges should have the widest range of sentencing options so as to accommodate 'out of the ordinary' cases. In place of the life sentence, the judge would be free to impose a penalty suitable according to the facts of each case and life would be reserved for the most serious types of murder. He opposed the introduction of minimum sentences, but Parliament has since passed the Crime (Sentences) Act 1997, imposing mandatory and minimum custodial sentences for serious offences.

The report criticises the involvement of the Home Secretary in deciding the length of term to be served by those found guilty of murder and suggests that justice would be best served by a more open approach, whereby decisions would be reached by a judge in open court. The House of Lords in *R v Secretary of State for the Home Department ex p Doody* (1993) decided that the Home Secretary was obliged to allow those serving mandatory life sentences an opportunity to make written representations as to the term to be served and to inform the prisoner of the judicial recommendations as to term. If the Home Secretary then decided to depart from such recommendations, he was obliged to give his reasons for so doing.

The involvement of the Home Secretary in sentencing is clearly demonstrated in the decision to impose a 15 year tariff on the killers of James Bulger. The trial judge recommended an eight year term for punishment and retribution, before which neither Thompson nor Venables (both aged 10 at the time of the offence) would be eligible for parole. The Lord Chief Justice increased this to 10 years and the Home Secretary, having taken account of the strong public feeling, increased it to 15 years. The Court of Appeal ruled that the Home Secretary has power to detain Thompson and Venables at Her Majesty's Pleasure but that, on the facts, he had misdirected himself in taking into account extraneous factors in setting the tariff. In *R v Secretary of State for the Home Department ex p Thompson and Venables* (1996), an appeal by the Home Secretary to the House of Lords on this question failed. The House of Lords held by a 3:2 majority that he acted unfairly when he treated the two youngsters in the same way as adult murderers, and raised the minimum term to 15 years. They ruled that the Home Secretary had the power to set a provisional tariff, but that it must be flexible to allow regular reviews. They also ruled that the Home Secretary acted improperly in taking into account public petitions.

In *Singh and Hussain v United Kingdom* (1996), the ECHR ruled that murderers under the age of 18 could not be held indefinitely 'at Her Majesty's

Pleasure' and that the judges' recommendations on the length of sentences should be complied with. Those representing Thompson and Venables relied on this case and submitted papers to the European Commission on Human Rights for review of the Home Secretary's power to detain both boys and his ability to ignore the recommendations of the court. The Commission recommended, and the ECHR ruled in December 1999, that the trial process in an adult court was unfair and that the Home Secretary abused his powers by imposing a 15 year tariff.

Distributive justice

Distributive justice is also referred to as 'social justice' and attempts to share out the 'good and the bad things' amongst members of society as equally as possible. The good things are, for example, wealth, power and freedom, and the bad are duties and burdens such as liability to pay taxes, to be subject to restrictions over one's property and limitations on freedom so as to permit a degree of freedom in others.

Social justice recognises that not all members of society have the same advantages, physically, socially or mentally, and so there has to be a redistribution of resources so as to achieve fair shares for all. The criteria employed to arrive at an apportionment of goods will often be subjective and depend on value judgments. Apportionment of benefits might be according to the same thing to all, but this can lead to unfairness, in the sense that each person has a different starting point and no account is taken of age, ability, intelligence, wealth, and so on. Apportionment might be according to merit or worth, or to need or to status, or according to legal entitlement but, whichever criterion is used, subjective factors come into play. For example, how should a person's worth be determined and how should need be defined? This is properly the province of policy, which Dworkin concluded was the role of Parliament to determine, not the courts.

The law is said to be a means to an end, and, for substantial justice to exist, not only must the procedures by which the law is applied be seen to be fair, but also the content of the rules, that is, the social ends to be achieved. The analysis of substantial justice brings us back to such questions as to the role of law in society and the relationship of law and morality.

Certainty and equality

In any discussion of justice, two concepts are of particular importance, namely, certainty and equality.

Certainty

Law needs to be certain in its scope and effect if people are to know how to order their affairs and to accord the law respect. However, the advantage of certainty must not be overemphasised, particularly with regard to substantial justice where a patently unjust law, no matter how certain in its terms or effect, will remain one which offends against principles of morality or notions of a 'higher' law.

Certainty can also easily slide into rigidity, with the effect that the law and legal system will fail to meet changing social needs. This was a major criticism of the common law and one which equity attempted to remedy. Once equity itself applied the doctrine of precedent, it too became more rigid and less able to adapt to meet changing needs. A balance has to be found between, on the one hand, certainty and, on the other, flexibility. Another aspect of certainty is that of law taking prospective effect rather than a retrospective effect. If law applies to future actions, those affected will be able to arrange their affairs in such a way so as to comply. With law which has a retrospective effect, actions which were legal when taken become, at a later date, illegal, and this is seen as anomalous unless very special circumstances necessitate a law having retrospective effect.

Equality

Equality has been described as the 'foundation of justice' and is expressed in such principles as 'everyone is equal before the law' and 'all persons are subject to the law regardless of race, colour, creed or rank'.

Allied with these principles is the notion that the courts and legal system should be available to all and that judges should be independent and impartial. Equality and justice, however, are not identical if equality is taken only to mean that all people are to be treated alike, for this fails to take account of differences in character, upbringing, status, education, and so on.

Discrimination on the grounds of age, sex, colour, etc, should not be tolerated, but recognition of human differences must be retained if justice, in its widest sense of fairness, is to be achieved. Some consider that in the interests of justice some individuals or groups should benefit from positive discrimination so as to even out the disadvantages experienced by such individuals or groups in the past. Others would see this as unfair and that promotion or preferment should be achieved only on merit.

Given that individuals or groups may discriminate against others in subtle as well as overt ways, the law has had to develop the notion of direct and indirect discrimination in an attempt to change attitudes and ensure fairer treatment of those who would otherwise stand little chance of success in employment, education, housing or other social activities.

English law has taken a limited view of discrimination, only recognising, until recently, discrimination on the grounds of sex and race. Other systems recognise age, sexual orientation, discrimination and harassment, in addition to sex and race. The Disability Discrimination Act 1995 goes some way to redressing the balance, but is drafted narrowly in comparison with the Sex Discrimination Act 1975 and the Race Relations Act 1976. Its main aim is to protect the disabled in areas such as employment, goods and services and the sale or rental of property. The legal profession and system is itself accused of discriminating against women and those from the ethnic minorities, with the result that much talent is lost to the legal profession and judiciary. Selection is often conducted secretly, and rarely will reasons be given for non-appointment. This is seen to fall far short of acceptable standards of openness and accountability, but awareness within the profession and judiciary has increased and conscious efforts are being made to improve accessibility. In recent years, the Lord Chancellor has not been exempt from allegations of discrimination, for example, Nicola Mackintosh, a solicitor, recently unsuccessfully sought judicial review of the changes made to the system of allocating legal aid contracts for representation of vulnerable groups, having been refused a contract.

Rawls' theory

We have now considered some ideas of justice, and before moving on to consider failings in the criminal justice system, brief mention must be made of Rawls' *A Theory of Justice*, published in 1971. Rawls analysed law on the basis that the rational person will pay for those things wanted badly enough. His theory rejects utilitarianism, which is based on maximising happiness, and constructs a social contract aimed at establishing principles of justice. Free and rational persons concerned to further their own interests adopt principles of justice which define the basis of their association. 'People in the original position' (POP) are shrouded in 'a veil of ignorance' when debating principles of justice. They do not know their sex, class, religion or social position or whether they are weak, strong, clever or stupid, or the State or period in history in which they exist. Unanimous agreement has to be reached on the general principles underlying their society and they are assisted only by elementary knowledge of science and human psychology. They are governed by rational self-interest, so that the worst condition in society will be the least undesirable of all alternatives. On 'lifting the veil', any one of the POP could be at the bottom of the social hierarchy. Rawls considers that there are two principles of justice, namely liberty and equality, and the POP select the former over the latter.

Liberty ensures an equal right to basic liberties. Equality has two parts:

- the just savings principle, which ensures that social and economic inequalities are arranged so as to be for the greatest benefit of the least advantaged;

- the principle of ensuring equality of opportunity.

POP prefer the first to the second.

Some of the main criticisms of this theory concern its artificiality and the assumptions underlying it. It leaves unexplained why the POP should select liberty before equality and why natural talents are to be treated as collective assets. It fails to take account of deserts, whereas, traditionally, a vital element of the notion of justice is 'just deserts', or apportioning blame or rewarding hard work or compliance with accepted standards.

Miscarriages of justice

We now move on to consider the idea of miscarriages of justice. This could arise in the context of the criminal law where those who have committed a crime are acquitted or are not brought to trial or because the innocent are wrongly convicted. It is generally accepted that the price of a fair criminal justice system will be the acquittal on a technicality of those who have committed criminal offences or because of a failure of evidence, whereas conviction of the innocent is never acceptable and, should it arise, speedy measures should be taken to rectify the injustice.

Justice also needs to be achieved in civil law where a plaintiff seeks redress for a wrong committed by the defendant. Both parties should have 'their day in court' and the claimant will seek compensation for the alleged wrong providing it is one recognised by the law as giving rise to liability.

Returning to the question of miscarriages of justice in criminal law, some fundamental principles of our system are the presumption of innocence, the use of juries in trials in the Crown Court, the prosecution having the burden of proving the defendant guilty beyond all reasonable doubt, the right for a defendant to remain silent during interrogation, albeit subject to the drawing of adverse inferences and trial and the discretion in the judge to exclude illegally obtained evidence. In the light of ss 34–37 of the Criminal Justice and Public Order Act 1994, permitting the drawing of adverse inferences, it has been argued that the presumption of innocence is no longer the effective safeguard against oppression that it once was. The Royal Commission on Criminal Justice recommended retention of the right of silence, but proposed limitations on the defendant's right to elect jury trial. The Commission was set up following some notorious miscarriages of justice, including the Guildford Four, the Maguire Seven, the Birmingham Six, the Tottenham Three and the Judith Ward and Stefan Kiszko cases. A more recent miscarriage of justice referred to the Court of Appeal was the Bridgewater Three (formerly Four), involving those found guilty of the murder of the newspaper boy, Carl Bridgewater, in 1978.

In *R v Secretary of State for the Home Department ex p Hickey and Others* (1994), it was held that, when the Home Secretary received a petition from someone wishing to have his case referred back to the Court of Appeal under s 17 of the Criminal Appeal Act 1968 and the Home Secretary made inquiries and obtained fresh evidence, he was required in fairness to disclose this to the petitioner. Judicial review was granted to the applicants, who included the Bridgewater Three.

The most serious failing in these cases was the fabrication of evidence by the police and the false confessions obtained as a result of duress. It was suggested that these cases, with the exception of the Tottenham Three, had all occurred before the coming into effect of the Police and Criminal Evidence Act 1984 and that this statute provided sufficient safeguards for the suspect during police questioning. However, much criticism has been made of the effectiveness of this Act and codes of practice made under it and in any event in the case of alleged terrorist offences (with which all but the Tottenham Three and Kiszko were concerned) the Prevention of Terrorism Act 1991 excludes many of the safeguards for the suspect provided by the 1984 Act. As was shown in the Guildford Four trial, this had been conducted scrupulously fairly and the injustice resulted from fabricated evidence.

Michael Mansfield QC, in *Presumed Guilty* (1993), argued that our accusatorial system should be replaced, up to the time of trial, with an inquisitorial system to ensure that the investigation of crime by the police was properly supervised by the judge, thereby seeking the truth rather than merely securing a conviction. The trial itself should retain the accusatorial approach so that the burden of proving guilt would rest with the prosecution and the judge would not take an active role in the trial process. Above all, the fundamental principles of the presumption of innocence and the right to silence should operate to ensure a fair trial. He suggested that we should return to first principles to ensure fair trials and the attainment of justice. Failings will always occur, but these should be rectified by an independent review body.

The right to silence has been curtailed and the Criminal Cases Review Commission was set up by s 8 of the Criminal Appeal Act 1995. The Commission commenced work in March 1997, taking over the functions of the Home Office to investigate suspected miscarriages of justice. It has yet to prove itself. Sir Frederick Crawford is the Chairman and there are 13 Commissioners, drawn from a wide range of backgrounds. They will consider cases dealt with by the magistrates' courts and Crown Court. After considering evidence presented, the Commission can decide whether further investigation is needed. It will appoint an agent to prepare a report but it has no powers of search, arrest or access to police computers or criminal records. Its agent may have such powers in their own right, for example, a police officer, in which case that person may gain access to information so as to prepare their report. On receipt of the report, the Commission will decide whether to refer the case for appeal and it will then be for the applicant to pursue his or her appeal.

As we have seen, the principle at the heart of the criminal justice system must be the acquittal of the innocent and conviction of the guilty if justice is to be attained.

The constitutional context

Nature and characteristics of the UK constitution

A constitution is the fundamental law of a State, usually in the form of a written, legally binding document which sets out the rights and duties of citizens and the State and which regulates the three arms of government – legislature, executive and judiciary. The UK has no written constitution (that is, no one document or series of documents setting out fundamental law). Instead, our constitution is to be found in the ordinary sources of law, including statutes, case law, custom and European Community (EC) law. In addition, constitutional rules are to be found in conventions (that is, unwritten rules by which those subject to them feel obliged to be bound). Conventions are not exclusive to systems with unwritten constitutions, but may well have a part to play in systems with written constitutions also. The UK is one of the few States to have an unwritten constitution; others are Israel and New Zealand.

Constitutional law defines the three types of governmental powers (legislative, executive and judicial) and the relationship between each of them and their relationship with the citizen. Administrative law deals with the controls over power, in particular the power of the executive, by the courts. Other controls are described as administrative controls, including the Parliamentary Commissioner for Administration.

Characteristics of the UK Constitution

The main characteristics of the UK Constitution will be considered, including its unitary nature, that it is unwritten, flexible, is based on the legislative supremacy of Parliament and has a constitutional or limited monarchy. In addition, it is noted that no strict separation exists between the legislative, executive and judicial powers.

Unitary

The UK remains a union of England, Wales, Scotland and Northern Ireland, governed in part by the Westminster Parliament, but with devolved law making and executive powers to the Scottish Parliament, and executive powers to the National Assembly of Wales. Devolution was granted by the Scotland Act 1998 and the Government of Wales Act 1998, following referenda in 1997 in favour of devolution. Scotland had its own legal system before devolution, based on the Roman law tradition.

The question of devolution of legislative and executive power to Scotland and of executive power to Wales arose in 1979, but was answered in the negative by means of a referendum in each country. Another question concerning the Union is the relationship of the UK, in particular Northern Ireland, and the Irish Republic in the light of the Anglo-Irish Agreement entered into in 1985 and the later agreement brokered by the US Senator George Mitchell to hand back power to Stormont. The Northern Ireland Act 1998 provided for devolution of powers to the Assembly in Stormont. Early in 2000, after only a short time, power was to be returned to the Westminster Parliament, by means of legislation, following failure to decommission arms by the paramilitary groups. Further moves to devolve powers to other groupings include the election of a Mayor for London and the demands for greater power to be moved to the English regions. Unions can be compared with federations, as in the USA, where legislative functions are exercised centrally by Congress and regionally by State legislatures. Confederations such as Switzerland are formed by alliances between independent regions.

Thus, legislative and other power can reside at the centre or be devolved to the parts. This question is very much in point when considering the position of the UK as a member of the EC and, in particular, following the passage of the European Communities (Amendment) Act 1993 through Parliament, providing for the ratification of the Treaty on European Union 1992 (the Maastricht Treaty). It is too early to say how far along the road to full European union we have moved, but legal and political sovereignty has moved from the UK to European institutions and this was a process recognised from the start of membership. It is likely that the Treaty of Nice will be signed in the summer of 2000, giving effect to the Charter of Fundamental Rights, which will move the Community much further towards the concept of a European 'superstate', or European Union of States.

Unwritten

As already mentioned, the UK has no one document or series of documents setting out a fundamental law against which the legality of actions by organs of government can be measured. Written constitutions tend to be entered into following revolution or colonial occupation. The UK might well have set up a written constitution following the Glorious Revolution of 1688, but the Bill of Rights of 1689 merely attempted to settle the feud between Crown and Parliament and establish Parliament as the supreme law maker. It did not attempt to create a fundamental law of State and citizen. What is more, it takes the form of an ordinary statute which, like any other, can be repealed at any time. This applies to all our constitutional law – it can be altered at any time by Parliament.

Flexible

The notion of flexible constitutions is closely linked with the earlier one of unwritten constitutions, but written constitutions may be flexible, in that they are easily changed or contain no entrenched provisions as to the method by which changes can be made. The legal theory of the UK Constitution is that the Queen in Parliament can change any law at any time. The reality is somewhat different, in that political restraints may apply, and in any event UK membership of the EC restricts the doctrine of parliamentary supremacy.

Supremacy of Parliament

The supremacy of Parliament doctrine arose out of the 17th century conflict between Crown and Parliament, and provides that Parliament can legislate on any matter and the courts cannot review the legality of legislation. The courts are merely the interpreters of legislation and have no role as a 'constitutional court', and so are unable to strike down legislation as being unconstitutional and void (*Pickin v BRB* (1974)). However, the power of interpretation can be a wide one and, under the European influence, the UK courts are taking a broader approach to statutory interpretation than they have done in the past. No doubt the role of the courts will change once the Human Rights Act 1998 comes into effect in October 2000, and it is notable that all domestic courts will be able to apply the European Convention.

Ultimately, Parliament must decide on matters of policy and how the law should change, but, nevertheless, the courts have residual power to make law. A court asked to interpret a statute must look at the intention of Parliament as expressed by the words of the Act. If that Act expressly or impliedly conflicts with an earlier Act, the court is obliged to apply the later Act. This can be put another way, namely, that Parliament is not bound by its predecessors but can enact law afresh, and the courts are obliged to apply the later law.

Two issues are of major importance:

- UK membership of the EC;

- whether supremacy applies both to content and 'manner and form' of legislation.

So far as EC membership is concerned, the UK signed the Treaty of Accession in 1972 and this was given effect to by the European Communities Act 1972. Of particular importance is s 2(1), (2) and (4). The constitutional position is that the royal prerogative was used to sign the treaty, in order to give effect to it and all other EC law in domestic law, Parliament passed the European Communities Act 1972 which could then be applied by the courts. The European Communities Act 1972 was amended in 1986 to give effect to the Single European Act (a European treaty) and further amended by the European Communities (Amendment) Act 1993 to give effect to the Maastricht Treaty.

Strict legal theory would allow the repeal of these statutes, although political reality would deny this. In any event the question of direct repeal has never come before the courts, but in cases of implied conflict the courts have construed statutory provisions in such a way as to avoid conflict with EC law. The nearest we have come to a direct conflict is *R v Secretary of State for Transport ex p Factortame (No 2)* (1990) and *R v Secretary of State for Employment ex p Equal Opportunities Commission* (1993).

In *R v Secretary of State for Foreign Commonwealth Affairs ex p Rees-Mogg* (1994), Lord Rees-Mogg, the former Editor of *The Times*, asked the Queen's Bench Divisional Court for judicial review under RSC Ord 53. The case raised the interesting question of whether the exercise of the royal prerogative had been given effect to fully by Parliament. If it had not, the question arose as to whether the courts could strike the statute down. The answer depended on the second issue mentioned above.

Traditionally, the courts have not questioned the process by which Bills have become law. All that a court inquires into is whether it has passed all its stages and received the royal assent. The formula recited at the start of all Acts confirms this. By Art 9 of the Bill of Rights, proceedings in Parliament cannot be impeached or questioned in any court or other place outside Parliament. Parliament is not only not bound by its predecessors as to content, but also as to manner and form, and the courts have no means of challenging the legality of changes. The challenge to the European Communities (Amendment) Act thereby failed.

In this context, the Parliament Acts 1911 and 1949 deserve mention. The first limited the power of the House of Lords to delay legislation introduced in the House of Commons to three sessions or up to two years following the second reading in the Commons. The result of using this Act would be that a Bill that had passed all stages in the Commons but which on reaching the Lords was amended could become law on receiving royal assent once the time limit had been met. The Parliament Act 1949 itself purported to limit the power of delay further, from three to two sessions and from two years to one, and was passed into law by the Parliament Act 1911 procedure.

Learned writers, including Hood Phillips (in Jackson, *Constitutional and Administrative Law*, 8th edn, 1998), suggest that the Parliament Act 1949 is not an Act at all, not having been passed by Queen, Commons and Lords. Only the War Crimes Act 1991 has been passed under the Parliament Act 1949 procedure and no challenge in the courts has ever been made as to the legality of the Parliament Act 1949. The reason given for the Parliament Act 1949 not being valid is that it concerned a constitutional change and such changes can only be effected in the time honoured way. It was not suggested that the European Communities (Amendment) Act 1993 had not passed into law in the time honoured way – Queen, Commons and Lords – since, clearly, both Houses of Parliament voted in favour of its provisions. The question for the court was whether the Act gave effect to the Maastricht Treaty. The court held that it had.

Constitutional doctrines

Separation of powers

Taken to the extreme, the separation of powers doctrine would prevent any government taking place. However, some separation of the legislative, executive and judicial powers is warranted. Indeed, the independence of the judiciary from the other two branches of government is essential. This doctrine, as stated by the 18th century jurist, Montesquieu, required separation of persons, the absence of control or interference by one organ with the exercise of another's functions and one organ not exercising the functions of another.

This doctrine is given formal recognition in most written constitutions. For example, in the US Constitution, the President has executive power, the Supreme Court has the judicial power and is capable of questioning the legality of State and federal laws, and Congress, made up of Senate and House of Representatives, has legislative powers. The UK Constitution neither formally nor otherwise recognises such a doctrine. The epitome of the reverse is the office of Lord Chancellor, who fulfils roles in all three areas as Speaker of the House of Lords, head of the judiciary and as an executive with a seat in the Cabinet. The position had shown signs of strain when Lord McKay was Lord Chancellor, in particular, given the challenges by The Law Society under RSC Ord 53 of the cuts in legal aid funding brought into effect by statutory instrument. The case of *R v Lord Chancellor ex p Witham* (1997) held that the decision of the Lord Chancellor to abolish fee exemption and remission in the High Court was unlawful. This illustrates the potential conflicts of interest in the exercise of judicial, executive and legislative functions. The court stated that there is a constitutional right of access to the courts which the executive cannot abrogate unless specifically authorised to do so by Parliament. Laws J said: '... the right to a fair trial, which of necessity imports the right of access to the courts, is as near to an absolute right as any which I can envisage.' This case has great significance for the doctrine of the rule of law, as well as that of the separation of powers.

Although this is the most important area of overlap, there are others, including the royal assent to Bills (by convention not refused); the administration of justice in the name of the Crown; and the House of Lords, both as a legislative chamber and the highest appeal court (by convention, only the Law Lords make judicial decisions).

The rule of law

The rule of law is an elusive concept, but one which is often invoked by lawyers and politicians in support of the notion that no one should be above the law and that decisions should be reached in accordance with law. Coke's doctrine stated that Crown and government are subject to law, and in his time the ultimate source of 'good' law was God. In modern times, the doctrine has been taken to mean that the executive power should act in accordance with law and not arbitrarily or by discretion. However, this doctrine does not sit easily with that of sovereignty of Parliament, in that a strong government would be able to pass whatever laws it wished, subject, of course, to practical limitations and those now applicable as a result of EC membership. At the extreme, the spirit of the doctrine of the rule of law can be lost, in that law could be used as an instrument of oppression.

Dicey, in *The Law of the Constitution*, noted three aspects:

• all men and women are subject to the law;

• all are equal before the law;

• constitutional rules are judge made.

Much criticism has been levelled against Dicey's analysis, notably that the last point bears little relationship to the others and does not truly reflect reality, and that the second point fails to recognise that the law confers wide powers on, for example, the police and other officials.

This notion has been confirmed in the historic House of Lords judgment in *M v Home Office and Another* (1993), where the court affirmed the decision of the Court of Appeal in finding the former Home Secretary Kenneth Baker in contempt of court for failing to comply with a court order not to deport a foreign national pending the outcome of judicial review proceedings. The House of Lords stated that the Crown and government ministers are subject to law.

Constitutional conventions

Unlike custom, conventions are not law, and so their breach does not give rise to legal action. They are, nevertheless, rules which are treated as binding by those affected by them. Breach may cause a constitutional crisis and may result in change in the rules or resignation or censure of the offending party. Conventions develop over time and help to 'oil the wheels' of the constitution. They not only assist the workings of unwritten constitutions, but may be found in written constitutions where otherwise the rules would have to change by a formal procedure. Conventions are not mere habits or practices: they are ways of behaving which have stood the test of time, but which, given changing circumstance,s may change or cease to have effect.

Some examples are the royal assent to Bills; individual and collective ministerial responsibility; the so called Salisbury convention, whereby the House of Lords does not delay or refuse to pass a Bill approved by the House of Commons except where the Bill involves a significant constitutional or national issue; and the powers of the Queen to decide whether to dissolve Parliament at the request of the Prime Minister or to take alternative action.

The use of conventions comes into its own when things do not go to plan, as so easily could have happened during the course of the European Communities (Amendment) Act 1993. Could the House of Lords have delayed the Bill pending the outcome of a referendum? Would the Queen have had to agree to the request for dissolution of Parliament if the vote of confidence called by the Prime Minister on 23 July 1993 had not been successful?

Judicial independence

The independence of the judiciary from interference by the executive is a fundamental principle of the UK constitution. Written constitutions usually guarantee this principle and elevate the judiciary so that the judges can question the legality of not only executive action, but also legislation.

With increasing frequency, we are seeing our judges questioning executive actions by way of the judicial review procedure and, more recently, by way of holding a government minister liable for contempt of court. However, judicial review does not empower the courts to challenge the merits of a decision, but only ensures that the correct process has been used or that there has not been an abuse or excess of power. A fundamental change in the role of the judiciary would have to come about to permit the judges to challenge the merits of executive action, and even more fundamental changes in the constitution would be needed if judges were to be able to question the validity of legislation. By the Human Rights Act 1998, the courts will not be able to pronounce a statute invalid, but only that it is incompatible with the provisions of the Convention. However, the judges are aware of the concept of proportionality, which will be available to them under the Convention, and by this means, judicial review may in future be used to call into question the merits of government decision making.

By s 11 of the Supreme Court Act 1981, all High Court and Court of Appeal judges (other than the Lord Chancellor) hold their offices during 'good behaviour', subject to a power of removal by the monarch on an address by both Houses of Parliament. By s 6 of the Appellate Jurisdiction Act 1876, Lords of Appeal in Ordinary (the Law Lords) hold office during good behaviour, subject to a power of removal on the address of both Houses of Parliament introduced in the House of Commons. Thus, an office holder can be removed where he or she has misbehaved in respect of the office or other cause and thereby has forfeited the confidence of the both Houses. In addition, the Crown could remove a judge without an address of both Houses where official misconduct or neglect of official duties is proved, and probably where convicted of a serious offence.

By the Judicial Pensions and Retirement Act 1993, a retirement age of 70 for senior judges is imposed. Formerly, Law Lords and judges of the Supreme Court retired at 75, and circuit judges at 72. The change has been phased in, and did not apply to those already in post at the time of the change. Judges' salaries are charged on the consolidated fund, and so are not reviewed by the House of Commons annually. Salaries may be increased by Order in Council.

Circuit judges may be removed by the Lord Chancellor for incapacity or misbehaviour under s 17(4) of the Courts Act 1971, and, by s 21(6), a recorder may be removed for incapacity or misbehaviour or failure to comply with the terms of appointment. Magistrates may be removed by the Lord Chancellor if he thinks fit, but convention dictates that this can only be for good cause. The Justices of the Peace Act 1979 provides for the keeping of a supplemental list of justices no longer entitled to exercise judicial functions. This may be due to age or infirmity or for neglect of duty. When a justice of the peace reaches the age of 70, his name must be placed on the list.

Governmental powers

Traditionally, governmental powers are divided into legislative, executive and judicial powers and, as has already been mentioned, there is no strict separation between them. Each will be considered in turn, together with the main overlaps, in particular the office of Lord Chancellor, who performs roles in all three areas.

The legislature

The legislature is made up of the House of Lords (the Upper Chamber), the House of Commons and the Queen, who, by convention, does not refuse royal assent.

The House of Commons has some 651 members, elected by universal adult suffrage in one of the parliamentary constituencies by way of the 'first past the post' system. The Representation of the People Acts disqualify persons under 21, peers of the realm, Church of England clergy and bankrupts, for example, from sitting as an MP. A number of MPs are at risk of losing their seats, should they be made bankrupt following the Lloyd's financial losses. The House of Commons has two main functions – passing legislation and control of the executive. The doctrine of parliamentary supremacy and the procedure for the passage of Bills has already been noted.

Control of the executive takes different forms, principally by way of financial control. The executive demands money to carry out its policies and the House of Commons grants it (this is known as 'supply') and provides 'ways and means' (taxation and public money) to meet these demands. The Queen's Speech at the start of a new parliamentary year sets out the Government's proposed legislative programme and public expenditure proposals. Public expenditure is scrutinised by the House of Commons (the House of Lords can only consent). The expenditure is granted by way of annual Appropriation Acts for the financial year. The Opposition has 20 days for debate on the Government's financial estimates and matters of policy and, pending the passing of the Appropriation Acts, continuity is ensured by way of the Consolidated Fund Acts.

The Speaker acts as an impartial arbiter who keeps order in the proceedings of the House and ensures that its rules of procedure (standing orders) are complied with. The Speaker may certify a Bill to be a Money Bill under the Parliament Act 1911 and has a casting vote.

The House of Commons jealously guards its powers of financial control over government (no taxation without representation (*AG v Wilts United Dairies* (1922); *Bowles v Bank of England* (1913)). Other means of control are by way of debates, Prime Minister's Question Time and the Select Committees, which scrutinise the work of government departments and have power to call for 'persons, papers and records'. Select Committees must not be confused with Standing Committees, whose main role is the scrutiny of Bills at the committee stage.

The House of Commons (and, to a lesser extent, the House of Lords), under Art 9 of the Bill of Rights 1688 and as the High Court of Parliament, also claims various rights and privileges so as to assert its freedom from the courts, the executive and others. At the start of a new Parliament, the Speaker, in an ancient ceremony, claims freedom of speech, freedom from arrest, freedom from molestation, freedom to regulate proceedings, the right to punish for contempt and the right to regulate its own composition. 'Contempt' is a broad concept and can be invoked not only against outsiders who offend the rules of the House, but also its members, whether they be MPs or ministers.

Conduct both inside and outside the House is regulated, and the Select Committee on Standards and Conduct, set up as a result of the Nolan Committee on Standards in Public Life 1995, replaces the former Select Committees on Parliamentary Privilege and Procedure and on Members' Interests and establishes the Commissioner on Standards and Conduct. These procedures aim to improve the conduct in public affairs of both MPs and ministers, following scandals such as 'cash for questions', personal failures and allegations of 'sleaze'.

The Government is committed not only to constitutional reform, but also to reform the workings of the House of Commons. From 21 May 1997, Prime Minister's Question Time was moved from a 15 minute slot on both Tuesday and Thursday to a single 30 minute slot on Wednesday. Simplification of the customs and practices of the House is promised and, with the passage of the Human Rights Act 1998, it may be time to remove the ancient privileges of the House of Commons (and Lords) so as to ensure a modern democratic Parliament.

Before the House of Lords Act 1999, the House was made up of Lords Temporal and Spiritual, the former comprising some 750 hereditary peers, 300 life peers created by the Life Peerages Act 1958, and the Lords of Appeal in Ordinary. The latter were the Archbishops of Canterbury and York, Bishops of London, Durham and Winchester and 21 senior bishops of the Church of England.

Despite the many critics who had advocated its abolition or reform and greater curbs on its powers, the House of Lords, as an unelected chamber, continued in place, acting as a check on government and initiating Bills that would stand little chance of being promoted in the House of Commons. Under the 1999 Act, a Royal Commission was set up under the chairmanship of Lord Wakeham to consider how the House should be reformed, and this reported in January 2000. The report, 'A House for the Future', recommended that the new chamber should have 550 members, most of whom should be appointed by an independent committee. No one party should have a majority and a 'significant minority' would be elected from the regions of the UK. No agreement was reached as to how many members would be elected, or the system to be used. Names for the new chamber and the members were to be 'left to evolve'. The Government spokesperson in the Lords, Baroness Jay, on publication of the report said that time would be needed for consideration and that no timetable had been set for its implementation. A joint committee of both Houses to examine the recommendations has yet to be set up. The first stage of reform took place late in 1999 when the hereditary peers, other than some 92 (who were given a temporary stay in the Weatherill Compact), were stripped of their powers and removed from the House. Critics of the way in which the Government has attempted to reform the House of Lords suggest that the removal of the hereditary peers without any replacement will result in no reform taking place for at least 30 years, given that the life peers retain their seats for life.

The executive

The executive is a broad term, the meaning of which is determined by context. It can refer to the Crown, the PM, Cabinet, civil servants and government departments. The Crown and those acting as servants or agents of the Crown derive power both from statute and the royal prerogative, which is the residue of discretionary powers at any time in the hands of the Crown. The political prerogative powers concern both domestic and foreign affairs. We have mentioned examples of the former, in particular, the power of the Queen, at the request of the Prime Minister, to dissolve Parliament. Another example is that exercised in the name of the Queen by the Home Secretary, namely the prerogative of mercy. Use of this power is illustrated in the case of *R v Home Secretary ex p Bentley* (1993), below.

So far as foreign affairs are concerned, the prerogative powers are most clearly shown by the process by which treaties are entered into. The Crown signs a treaty and commits the UK to the obligations of the treaty in international law. So far as domestic law is concerned, it is usual for effect to be given to the treaty by way of legislation. The European Communities Act 1972 and its later amendments gave effect in domestic law to the obligations entered into on the accession of the UK to membership of the EC.

The extent to which the courts can question the exercise of the royal prerogative was clearly shown in *Council of Civil Service Unions v Minister for the Civil Service* (1984) (the *GCHQ* case), where the head of the civil service banned unions at the Cheltenham Headquarters without consultation, despite a legitimate expectation on the part of the workforce. Providing the issues were justiciable, the court, by a majority of three to two, said *obiter* that the prerogative was subject to judicial review. On the facts, a plea of national security by the Government, which was accepted by the court, prevented it from going further.

A more recent case concerning review of the direct exercise of the prerogative is the case of *R v Home Secretary ex p Bentley* (1993). In the *GCHQ* case, it should be remembered that the case concerned an instruction given in the exercise of a delegated power (by way of Order in Council) under the prerogative.

In July 1993, the former Editor of *The Times*, Lord Rees-Mogg, sought to challenge, by way of judicial review, the provisions of the European Communities (Amendment) Act 1993 (giving effect to the Maastricht Treaty). In the result, although leave was granted, the application was refused and no appeal was heard. The court concluded that the issues involving the exercise of the royal prerogative in entering into treaties and the passing of legislation was outside its remit.

Not to be confused with treaties involving the EC/EU is the European Convention on Human Rights, signed but not given domestic effect in the UK until the Human Rights Act 1998 was passed. Although this only comes into force in October 2000, the courts are already taking more notice of its provisions and have, in some instances, already found that the common law is able to recognise the existence of rights found in the Convention. In future, the judge will be able to apply the provisions of the Convention to domestic legislation, whenever passed.

The judiciary

The courts are unable to question the legality of legislation, but the Queen's Bench Divisional Court has a supervisory jurisdiction over inferior courts and tribunals and can declare delegated legislation *ultra vires*. Decisions by public bodies are also subject to review, on the basis that the powers by which such decisions have been made have been abused or exceeded.

A fundamental issue concerning the constitutional position of the judiciary is that of independence from the other arms of government, in particular, the executive. It is a well espoused principle that our judges are not only independent but also impartial in the way in which they reach decisions. One means of testing this would be by way of the doctrine of separation of powers, but we have seen that this doctrine is not well developed, in particular with regard to the position and role of the Lord Chancellor.

We have already mentioned the Supreme Court Act 1981 and the Appellate Jurisdiction Act 1876 concerning removal of superior judges and the charge on the consolidated fund for salaries. Judges are also immune from suit for things said during the course of a trial and, by ss 108 and 109 of the Courts and Legal Services Act 1990, this has been extended to include magistrates. Full immunity from civil action applies for matters within their jurisdiction, and also to matters outside their jurisdiction, providing they act in good faith.

The Contempt of Court Act 1981, regulating interference with the course of justice and failure to comply with orders of the court, as shown in *M v Home Office and Another* (1993), is also important in maintaining the independence and authority of the courts.

Those who flout the authority of the court may be found to be in contempt and liable to imprisonment for up to two years. The case of the father who took his son out of the jurisdiction of the court against a court order and was sentenced to 18 months' imprisonment on his return illustrates the power of the court. However, this was later reduced on appeal. The press risk being made liable for contempt for sensationalising reports of a trial, resulting in their being likely to prejudice a fair trial, and it is not only in notorious trials such as those of Fred and Rosemary West where such a risk arises.

The cases of *R v Schot* and *R v Barclay* (1997), involving two jurors who asked the judge for advice due to their difficulty in reaching a verdict, clarifies the law on when jurors may be in contempt of court and the role of the judge in assisting the jury.

Judicial review

This is properly the subject of administrative law, whereby the court reviews the exercise of public powers. Under the Woolf reforms to the civil justice system, this procedure, formerly found in RSC Ord 53 and s 31 of the Supreme Court Act 1981, has been revised and is now found in the Civil Procedure Rules 1998 (as amended).

Unlike on an appeal, where the court can impose its own decision, judicial review allows the court only to question the process by which a decision was reached. The court does not question the merits (that is, the substance) of the decision, but must be satisfied that the decision was reached in accordance with prescribed procedure, or the rules of natural justice, or that the decision maker had power to make the decision.

Given that the UK has no written constitution and that the doctrine of the sovereignty of Parliament still applies in matters not governed by the EC, the judges cannot question the validity of legislation. However, they may review the way in which statutory (and, in limited circumstances, the prerogative powers) are exercised by, for example, Ministers of the Crown and local authorities.

The case of *R v Panel on Take-Overs and Mergers ex p Datafin plc* (1987) established that judicial review may also be available against private bodies exercising public powers. The principles by which the judges have asserted their power of review are founded in the common law, and the cases in which the citizen has successfully challenged public decision making demonstrate the creativity of the courts in curbing excess or abuse of power.

Where the words of a statute are clear and unambiguous, the doctrine of the sovereignty of Parliament prevents the courts from doing other than giving effect to the words used. Where the words used are open to interpretation, the courts may, and, it may be argued, should, interpret the words used to give effect to accepted common standards and in accordance with the expectations of citizens.

Constitutional theory provides for no formal separation of powers and, given the doctrines of parliamentary sovereignty and the rule of law, the executive owes responsibility for the exercise of its power to Parliament. The reality suggests that Parliament is often not an effective check on the workings of the executive, and so it is vital that the courts exercise powers of review, albeit that this will be impossible where statutory provisions are clear and unambiguous. This limitation has resulted in calls for fundamental constitutional change by way of a written constitution and Bill of Rights. The Human Rights Act 1998 will go some way towards answering these calls.

An applicant for judicial review must apply for permission to a High Court judge. This is granted at the judge's discretion, provided the applicant has an arguable case, can show *locus standi* (a relevant interest in the outcome) and that the case is not misconceived or otherwise frivolous or vexatious. Proceedings must be brought promptly, and this usually means within three months from the date on which grounds arose. Extensions are at the judge's discretion. If leave is granted, the application for judicial review is made to the Queen's Bench Divisional Court. If refused, the applicant may appeal to a High Court judge or to the Court of Appeal. Even if an applicant is successful in obtaining permission to bring a claim, this does not mean that the court will, on hearing the case, grant the remedy asked for. In *R v Lord Chancellor ex p The Law Society* (1993), The Law Society challenged the decisions of the Lord Chancellor to amend the legal aid rules. Leave was granted, but the court refused the relief sought.

The remedies available are the prerogative orders of certiorari (quashing an *ultra vires* decision or one made in breach of the rules of natural justice or where there is an error of law); prohibition (an interim order prohibiting the taking of proposed action where *ultra vires* or breaches of natural justice are alleged); and mandamus (an order enforcing public duties). In addition, a declaration (an order stating the legal position where *ultra vires* and breaches of natural justice are alleged) or an injunction (a discretionary remedy which is not available where an alternative statutory remedy is available) may be granted.

A major shortcoming is the inability of the court to award damages against public bodies. This can only be done where the aggrieved party can rely on a private law right in contract or tort.

The ancient and now rarely used writ of habeas corpus is still available against public bodies (and others) who unlawfully detain a person. The court can call the captor before it to account for the detention.

The House of Lords' decision in *R v Independent Television Commission ex p TSW Broadcasting Ltd* (1992), which concerned an application for the renewal of a broadcasting licence by TSW for the South West region, illustrates when an application for judicial review will be successful. Parliament had not provided an appeal procedure from the decisions of the Commission, and Lord Templeman stated that 'the courts were not to invent an appeal machinery'. The court endorsed the statement of principle in the cases of the *GCHQ* case (1984) and *Associated Provincial Picture Houses Ltd v Wednesbury Corp* (1947) that judicial review was only available where it was shown that there had been 'illegality, irrationality or procedural impropriety'. Proof merely of a mistake on the part of the decision maker was insufficient, and it was not for the court to substitute its view of the case for that of the decision maker.

Lord Diplock, in the *GCHQ* case, stated that 'illegality, irrationality or procedural impropriety' were the well recognised grounds for judicial review. He queried whether a fourth ground had been developed, namely, 'proportionality'. This concept derives from continental legal systems and ensures a reasonable relationship between the end to be achieved and the means used to achieve it. Sir John Donaldson, in *R v Secretary of State for the Home Department ex p Brind* (1990), doubted that this was a separate ground and suggested that it was part of '*Wednesbury* unreasonableness' or, as it has in recent years been called, 'irrationality'.

An inherent danger of the court adopting the principle of proportionality is that it will attempt to test the merits of a case, with the result that it would substitute its decision for that of the public body. However, this principle will no doubt be used by the UK courts as a result of the Human Rights Act 1998, bringing the provisions of the European Convention on Human Rights into effect.

Brief mention must be made of each of these three grounds: illegality may be proved, for example, where the decision maker has purported to exercise a power he or she does not have; where he or she has misdirected him or herself in law or where he or she has used a power for an improper purpose; or where he or she has failed to take into account all relevant considerations.

The *Wednesbury* case concerned a condition attached to the grant of a cinema licence, preventing those under 15 from being admitted on Sundays. This was held to be lawful, but Lord Greene's statement of principle has been often quoted and included four propositions. These are that the decision maker should: consider all relevant matters; disregard all irrelevant matters; when exercising a discretion, properly direct him or herself in law; and act reasonably.

Procedural impropriety may take one of three forms. The first two are often referred to as the rules of natural justice (or, in a purely administrative context, procedural fairness), namely, the rule against bias and the right to a fair hearing. The third is of much more recent origin and is referred to as a 'legitimate expectation'. The scope of this principle has not yet been settled, and it is unclear from the case law whether it is merely a means of ensuring a fair procedure or whether it goes further and ensures that a particular decision will be reached. The danger with the second proposition is that the court would be exercising an appeal function, rather than one of review.

In the *GCHQ* case, the trade union would have had a legitimate expectation of being consulted about the proposed ban if it had not been for the defence of national security. This was a legitimate expectation of being consulted which had arisen from previous conduct.

In *R v Secretary of State for Home Department ex p Khan* (1985), an order of certiorari was granted against the Home Secretary, quashing his refusal of an entry certificate for a Pakistani child whom Khan wished to adopt. Khan had relied on a Home Office standard form letter, setting out the criteria to be satisfied for an adoption to be successful. The Home Secretary applied other criteria without first giving Khan a hearing, so as to put forward reasons why the adoption should go ahead. If the Home Secretary was to resile from the undertaking in the letter, he was obliged to allow Khan an opportunity to make representations.

In *AG of Hong Kong v Ng Yuen Shiu* (1983), it was held that, where the Government announced a policy of repatriation and stated that each case would be considered on its merits, it could not order the removal of Ng without first giving him a hearing so as to allow him to put forward any grounds which might have allowed him to stay.

Thus, where a public body makes a promise or a statement, or accepts an undertaking, or acts in accordance with a regular procedure, this may give rise to a legitimate expectation in those affected that decisions will be made in accordance with the statement or practice or that changes will be notified and those affected will have an opportunity of making representations.

In the case of *R v Home Secretary ex p Bentley* (1993), the applicant sought judicial review of the Home Secretary's refusal to recommend a posthumous free pardon for her brother. He did so on the basis that it had been the long established policy of successive Home Secretaries only to grant a free pardon where the person in question was both morally and technically innocent of the crime. The Home Secretary had concluded that there was no evidence in this case for such a conclusion. The Queen's Bench Divisional Court of the High Court made no formal order, but invited the Home Secretary to reconsider the matter and to exercise the prerogative by the grant of a conditional pardon in recognition that an injustice had occurred.

The court was not willing to question the established policy of Home Secretaries in setting the criteria for exercise of the prerogative, but considered that there had been an error of law by the Home Secretary in failing to consider whether to grant a conditional pardon where clearly, imposition of the death penalty had been wrong.

Another case which illustrates the use and scope of judicial review is that of *R v Secretary of State for the Home Department ex p Doody and Others* (1993), in which the respondents to the appeal to the House of Lords, who had each been sentenced to mandatory life sentences for murder, sought review of the Home Secretary's refusal to supply information as to how the dates fixed for the first review of their cases had been arrived at. It was held that such prisoners were entitled to submit representations in writing to the Home Secretary before he decided the first review date, and that prisoners should be informed of the judicial view as to the period to be served. Where the Home Secretary decided to depart from the judicial view (and the court held that this was possible), he was obliged to give reasons to the prisoner for so doing. *Dicta* in the case illustrates the relationship between the judiciary and the Home Secretary, in respect of both sentencing policy and judicial review of administrative decisions.

Three points are of particular note:

- it was stressed that sentencing was regulated by a statutory scheme which vested power in the Home Secretary to decide release dates in such cases. The Home Secretary was able to delegate these powers and, in the exercise of his discretion, he took into account the judicial view, but was not required to do more. The judges did not have a role as advisers or otherwise, and the Home Secretary was free to depart from the judicial view, provided he gave his reasons for so doing;

- as stated by Lord Mustill, the present law did not recognise any general duty to give reasons in administrative decisions, although it was clear that, in appropriate circumstances, such a duty would be implied;

- it was not for the courts in a judicial review case to attempt to make fundamental changes in the relationship between the State and a prisoner. Although procedural differences existed between mandatory and discretionary life sentences, any change in policy was for Parliament.

The House of Lords has now considered this area again in *R v Secretary of State for the Home Department ex p Hindley* (2000). It was held that the Home Secretary was required to conduct periodic reviews in relation to a life prisoner whom he considered should serve a whole life tariff for retribution and deterrence.

Administrative controls of power

An aggrieved citizen may decide not to resort to court action against a public body, or such action may be inappropriate. An alternative is to have recourse to the Parliamentary Commissioner for Administration (PCA), the Local Government Commissioner or the National Health Service Commissioner, depending on whether the complaint relates to maladministration at central, local or health service level.

By the Parliamentary Commissioner Act 1967, the PCA or Ombudsman investigates acts or omissions by public bodies specified in Sched 2, provided the conditions in ss 4 and 5 are met. These provide, *inter alia*, that the allegation must be one of maladministration and a written complaint must be made to an MP within 12 months of knowledge of the complaint. Reference must be made by the MP with the consent of the complainant to the PCA, and no alternative remedy would be available before a court or tribunal, or that it is unreasonable to resort to such remedy. Schedule 3 excludes investigation of health service matters, foreign relations and armed forces matters, for example.

The Ombudsman has the powers of a High Court judge, can call for documents (except Cabinet papers), and has full powers over conduct of the investigation, which is held in private. Two major shortcomings must be noted: the Act does not define maladministration, but this has been taken to include such things as delay, bias, incompetence, neglect and inattention; and no formal system of remedies exists, merely the report and recommendations made by the PCA. The PCA reports annually to Parliament and, where maladministration is found, a special report is prepared. From time to time, general reports are submitted.

Another means open to the aggrieved citizen is to seek redress by way of a tribunal. The work of tribunals is supervised by the Council on Tribunals under the Tribunals and Inquiries Act 1992. The Franks Committee Report 1957 recommended the setting up of a review body to monitor the constitution and workings of administrative tribunals. It is an advisory body and does not handle complaints from individuals. It submits annual reports to Parliament.

Supervision of the Parliamentary Commissioner can, in theory, be by way of judicial review, as was shown in the case of *R v PCA ex p Dyer* (1994), when the court said that the Parliamentary Commissioner Act 1967 vested wide powers in the Ombudsman, but his decision not to investigate a particular claim of maladministration could be the subject of judicial review.

Subsequently, the case of *R v PCA ex p Balchin* (1997) supports this, although in *R v Parliamentary Comr for Standards ex p Al Fayed* (1997) the court held that the work of the Parliamentary Commissioner for Standards was not subject to judicial review, as it involved the internal workings of the House of Commons.

The cases of *R v Secretary of State for the Home Department ex p Hargreaves* (1997) and *R v IRC ex p Unilever plc* (1996) have already been mentioned, but the most important application for judicial review, both generally and constitutionally, for many years has been *R v Secretary of State for the Home Department ex p Fire Brigades' Union and Others* (1995). The Fire Brigades' and other unions sought judicial review on behalf of their members, who were often the victims of crime and who had to rely for compensation on the State funded Criminal Injuries Compensation Scheme. The leading judgment was that of Lord Browne-Wilkinson, and Lords Mustill and Keith dissented.

In 1964 a criminal injuries compensation scheme was set up and run by the Criminal Injuries Compensation Board under royal prerogative powers. In 1988, ss 108–17 of the Criminal Justice Act codified the scheme but s 171(1) stated that the provisions were only to come into force on a day to be appointed by the Home Secretary by way of statutory instrument. In the meantime, the non-statutory scheme was to remain in force. In 1993, a White Paper identified the need to cut costs, and it was decided not to implement the Criminal Justice Act 1988 and to repeal it sometime in the future. In the meantime, a new tariff scheme would be brought into effect under the prerogative powers. The unions challenged this decision and the majority of their Lordships held that the Home Secretary's power to bring the Criminal Justice Act 1988 into force was coupled with a duty to keep under review whether or not to bring the provisions into force. The prerogative powers continued to exist, but the court held that it would have been an abuse or excess of power for the Home Secretary to exercise the prerogative in a manner inconsistent with the duty to keep the statutory provisions under review.

Lord Browne-Wilkinson stated the constitutional principles clearly:

> It is for Parliament, not the executive, to repeal legislation. The constitutional history of this country is the history of the prerogative powers of the Crown being made subject to the over-riding powers of the democratically elected legislature as the sovereign body. The prerogative powers of the Crown remain in existence to the extent that Parliament has not expressly or by implication extinguished them. But under the principle in *AG v De Keyser's Royal Hotel Ltd* (1920) ... if Parliament has conferred on the executive statutory powers to do a particular act, that act can only thereafter be done under the statutory powers so conferred: any pre-existing prerogative power to do the same act is *pro tanto* excluded.

Lord Browne-Wilkinson posited the question of its effect if the Act had specified that it would come into effect one year after the date of the royal assent instead of, on the facts, giving the Home Secretary discretion to appoint a date. Lord Browne-Wilkinson said that the decision would be the same. During that year, the prerogative power would remain exercisable, but would not discontinue the non-statutory scheme and in its place introduce a tariff scheme.

This is certainly the most important of many applications for judicial review which have been brought against the Home Secretary in recent years. It demonstrates the willingness of the judiciary to question the legality of decision making by one of the most powerful government ministers.

THE NATURE OF LAW

Classification of law

- Criminal and civil law.

- Substantive and procedural law.

- Public international and municipal law. The latter can be subdivided into:
    - civil (private) law;
    - public law (which includes criminal law);
    - private international law (which regulates conflicts between the private or civil laws of different States).

Rules

- 'A norm or guide regulating social conduct', breach of which may result in a fine, imprisonment or some sort of censure.

Rules have four characteristics:

- guide or lay down standards of behaviour;

- normative and either prescribe or proscribe conduct;

- imperative and require compliance;

- provide justification for a decision or course of action.

Law as a system of rules

- Law is imposed by the State or those who have authority to impose sanctions or penalties for breach.

Four elements should be taken into account when considering the nature and characteristics of law:

- its role in society and the purposes served;

- the reasons why law is obeyed;

- its relationship with morality;

- its relationship with justice.

Law and morality

- Cases involving moral issues: *Airedale NHS Trust v Bland* (1993); *R v Secretary of State for the Home Department ex p Doody* (1993).

Law and justice

- Justice is an ideal towards which the law should aim.
- Formal (procedural justice) and substantial justice (fairness of the content):
  - doctrine of the rule of law – *M v Home Office and Another* (1993).

Certainty and equality

- Certainty has to be balanced with flexibility.
- Law should have prospective (not retrospective) effect.
- Runciman Royal Commission Report on Criminal Justice 1993.
- Criminal Cases Review Commission, set up under s 8 of the Criminal Appeal Act 1995.

The constitutional context

- Constitutional principles: *R v Lord Chancellor ex p Witham* (1997); *R v Secretary of State for the Home Department ex p Fire Brigades Union and Others* (1995).

Governmental powers

- Legislature – the House of Commons, House of Lords and Parliament.
- Executive – the Crown, Prime Minister, Cabinet, civil servants and government department.
- Judiciary.

Judicial control of power

- Judicial review – RSC Ord 53 (see now CPR); s 31 of the Supreme Court Act 1981.
- Remedies – prerogative orders of mandamus, certiorari and prohibition; injunction, declaration and damages.

Administrative control of power

- Commissioners (Ombudsmen) regulate maladministration:
    - Parliamentary Commissioner for Administration (Parliamentary Commissioner Act 1967);
    - local government Commissioners;
    - National Health Service Commissioner.
- Tribunals and the Council on Tribunals (Tribunals and Inquiries Act 1992).

CHAPTER 2

THE SOURCES OF LAW

Introduction

'Source' refers to the place where the law is found. Judges need to be aware of what the law is – in order to apply it in reaching a solution to a dispute to be decided – and so too do legal advisers: barristers, solicitors and other legal professionals – who, faced with a client with a legal problem, will need to offer advice on the basis of what the law is, and may well have to predict the chances of success, should a dispute go to court.

The need to find the law is not confined to the legal professional. The law student will also need to find the law so as to apply it in reaching a reasoned solution to problem questions and in attempting essay questions. The lay person may also need to find the law, not only as litigants in person, but also in acting on behalf of others. Increasingly, technology is making access to legal materials much easier. Very few aspects of life are not in some way governed by law.

Distinguishing between sources of law

A distinction is drawn between literary and historical sources of law. Literary sources are the official written sources of law, such as law reports and the Queen's printer's copy of a statute. Historical sources emphasise the development of the law, for example, in the 13th century, the rise of equity or, in the 19th century, the increasing use and importance of statute and delegated legislation.

At the present time, the importance of European Community (EC) law is increasing in importance in relation to domestic law, whereas customary law is no longer of any great general importance. This is not to suggest that a person or group whose rights or duties are governed by customary law can ignore it, only that, in a complex society, custom is of decreasing application to the majority of people.

Another way in which sources can be distinguished is that of principal and subsidiary sources. The former refer to the most important and authoritative sources of law, which includes legislation, delegated legislation, case law and EC law. The latter refer to those sources which are of little general application, and include custom, Roman law, ecclesiastical law and books of authority, such as Bracton's *Treatise on the Laws and Customs of England* (13th century). Other famous and highly authoritative books include Coke's *Institutes of the Laws of England* (1628) and Blackstone's *Commentaries on the Laws of England* (1765).

The tradition which developed whereby the courts only made use of the works of deceased authors no longer applies and the works of writers still alive may now be referred to by counsel in arguing a case. An example is that of *Archbold's Pleading, Evidence and Practice in Criminal Cases*, to which courts may be referred to assist in applying rules of procedure, evidence, or the substantive law in criminal cases. This possibly now includes textbooks, at least those where the author is a recognised expert, such as Glanville Williams or Smith and Hogan in criminal law, and a court may be referred to such books so as to assist it in deciding a case.

We will concentrate on the principal sources, but, so far as subsidiary sources are concerned, custom will be briefly mentioned. As a source of law, custom is the oldest, originating from pre-Norman times, and which led to the development of the common law. In modern society, there is little place for customary law, in that it is unwritten and passed from one generation to the next by word of mouth. However, on occasion, a dispute comes before the court and one of the parties calls upon alleged custom to aid their case. It is for the court to decide the existence and extent of the alleged custom by applying various tests. In a county court judgment in 1990, an injunction was granted to New Forest commoners (those who had rights to graze their animals in the forest) against the National Trust over the size and depth of ditches dug by the Trust around the common land. The commoners were able to prove the existence of their right to free access and use of the commons and that this had been interfered with by the Trust in making ditches.

A distinction is made between general and local customs, but both must satisfy a number of tests and, in addition, local customs must be proved to have existed from 'time immemorial'. In *R v Oxfordshire CC and Others ex p Sunningwell Parish Council* (1999), the House of Lords stated that proof of a custom of using a village green for sports and pastimes required an inference of fact that this customary right had existed from time immemorial (which is deemed to be 1189). Most general customs have been incorporated into legislation or case law. Mercantile law, or commercial law, as it is more commonly called today, is a good example, where the law governing commercial transactions developed from the customs of merchants.

The tests used by the courts to establish the existence of custom include certainty, continuity, reasonableness, consistency and legality. As we have already mentioned, a local custom must be proved to have existed since time immemorial. The case of *Mercer v Denne* (1905) illustrates that, in practice, time immemorial is treated as having been proved where a local custom is shown to have existed within living memory of the oldest resident of the area: fishermen had used a beach for drying their nets, and residents could recall such use as far back as 70 years. The landowner attempted to prevent the fishermen from using the beach, but a presumption was raised in their favour which the landowner could not rebut. In *Simpson v Wells* (1872), W alleged a customary right to obstruct a public footpath and called upon an Act of 1361 to support this claim. This in itself rebutted any presumption that the alleged right had been established before 1361.

Legislation

Legislation takes the form of an Act of Parliament or 'statute'. A Bill becomes law after a formal process in both Houses of Parliament and receipt of royal assent. The Queen in Parliament is described as the supreme law maker and the doctrine of supremacy of Parliament ensures that no other body can pass law in conflict with that of Parliament and that the courts cannot question the validity of Acts of Parliament. As we shall see later, this doctrine is now subject to UK membership of the EC and, thus, European law can take precedence over domestic law as a result of the acceptance by the UK courts of rulings from the European Court of Justice (ECJ).

Another radical change has come about as the result of the UK incorporating the European Convention on Human Rights into domestic law by the Human Rights Act 1998. The Act takes effect in England as of October 2000 (and the Scotland Act 1998 implemented the Convention in Scotland with effect from June 1999), but the courts were being referred to its provisions many months in advance of this. Its effect will be that any court will be able to compare domestic legislation, passed at any time, with the Convention and make a finding as to its compatibility. To safeguard the doctrine of supremacy of Parliament, no court will be able to declare a domestic Act invalid, only incompatible, and it will then be for Parliament to amend the offending legislation.

Public Bills (initiated by the Government or a private member of Parliament) usually commence life in the House of Commons and some *must* do so, for example, those concerned with finance and which are referred to as Money Bills. The raising or spending of revenue is the traditional province of the elected representatives of the people and is one means by which Parliament keeps a check on the executive.

Those starting in the House of Commons, once they have passed all stages, move on to the House of Lords, where a similar procedure (although different terminology often applies to the stages of the process) must be complied with before the Bill receives the royal assent. By convention, this is automatically granted and, since Queen Anne's reign, the royal assent has not been refused.

In strict legal theory, the monarch may refuse to assent, but the unwritten conventional rule of the constitution has evolved whereby refusal would involve the monarch in political debate, and this is not acceptable in a constitution with a limited or constitutional monarchy. Since the clash between the monarch and Parliament in the 17th century, it has become a convention of the constitution that the Queen remains outside political debate. By the Parliament Acts 1911 and 1949, the power of the House of Lords to delay or initiate Bills is limited, as this is seen as a threat to the supremacy of the elected chamber to make law.

After many years of debate, reform of the composition of the House of Lords has finally been made by the House of Lords Act 1999, although this Act merely sets out the principles of reform and provides for the establishment of a commission to review the options, following the removal of the hereditary peers. Lord Wakeham's Commission suggests a mixture of appointed and elected peers. In recent years, the House of Lords have asserted their delaying powers over controversial measures proposed by governments of both political persuasions, some notable examples being the reduction in the age of consent for homosexuals and the Welfare Reform Bill. Debates in the House of Lords, sitting as a legislative chamber, have also been lively over attempts to ban hunting with hounds, reform of the criminal justice system, reform of the House of Lords itself and the suggested repeal of s 28 of the Local Government Act 1988, prohibiting the promotion of homosexuality in schools. Lord Wakeham had little to say regarding the retention of the Lords of Appeal in Ordinary as peers in the legislative chamber, and it is an anomaly whereby the Law Lords can engage in debate.

A notable illustration of the workings of both Houses is provided by the passage of the Bill to give effect to the Treaty on European Union 1992 (the Maastricht Treaty). The Bill took some 12 months to pass all stages in the House of Commons successfully and it was suggested that the Government faced defeat in the House of Lords. In the result, the Bill passed all stages in the Lords.

Other notable Acts include the Courts and Legal Services Act 1990, the Criminal Justice and Public Order Act 1994, the Environment Act 1995, the Criminal Appeal Act 1995, the Criminal Procedure and Investigations Act 1996 and, more recently, the Access to Justice Act 1999.

A public Bill which gave rise to much debate, both inside and outside Parliament, was the Sunday Trading Bill (which became the Sunday Trading Act 1994). This repealed the Shops Act 1950 (30 earlier Bills had failed to do so). Of the three options for reform, partial de-regulation, permitting limited opening between 10 am and 4 pm for large shops, was chosen following a free vote at the committee stage. This was conducted by a committee of the whole House (and not the more usual procedure of a Standing Committee) so as to reflect the strength of feeling engendered by the change in policy. The other options were to retain regulation or to allow full deregulation, but only moderate change was thought necessary.

The procedure for public Bills

The procedure for public Bills is as follows. Assuming that the Bill starts in the House of Commons, it will start with a formal first reading to announce its title and its aims. This is followed by the second reading, where its main principles are brought to the attention of the House and a debate follows. The Bill then passes to a Standing Committee (or, if it is of fundamental constitutional or national importance, to a committee of the whole House, as mentioned above), where its provisions are looked at in detail, often line by line. As the committee reflects the political balance of the House, the Government will ensure that the Bill passes this stage without major amendment. Limitations may be placed on the amount of time to be devoted to particular provisions and some may not be discussed at all. In theory, discussion of the detailed provisions of a Bill at committee stage is an important parliamentary check on the executive, and such discussion will be made public by the press and in the parliamentary official journal, called *Hansard*. However, in practice, a government intent on passing legislation and which has a sizeable majority can ensure safe passage of its Bills.

The outcome of the committee stage is then reported to the House – referred to as the report stage – and this is followed by the third reading, at which no changes can be made to the principles of the Bill. On being passed, the Bill goes to the House of Lords, where it will go through a similar procedure. If amendments are made, and this is usual, as was shown during the passage of the Criminal Justice and Public Order Bill, for example, it will have to be reconsidered by the House of Commons. A compromise may be reached, but, if this is not possible, the Commons has the final say. The powers of the House of Lords to introduce Bills and to delay government measures was curtailed by the Parliament Acts 1911 and 1949, and it remains open to what extent a reformed House of Lords, under the House of Lords Act 1999, will in future apply itself to challenging legislative changes proposed by government. It is generally recognised that a second chamber serves a vital function in a democratic State, but the hereditary principle has detracted from this.

In addition to the traditional procedure, an alternative, known as the Jellicoe Committee, or 'fast track', procedure exists. This allows technical law reform arising from the need to consolidate legislation or codify complex legislation and case law to be referred to the Special Public Bill Committee of the House of Lords (the Jellicoe Committee), which examines the provisions of a Bill in depth following receipt of evidence from the public. Amendments may be proposed only by peers and only members of the committee may vote on amendments. This is largely an untried procedure, but it aims to speed up the passage of legislation for which parliamentary time might not otherwise be found. The Family Homes and Domestic Violence Bill, which the Government withdrew in October 1995, illustrates the use of the procedure. However, the Bill contained such controversial measures (it attempted to extend the rights of cohabitees to those of spouses) that the fast track procedure was found not to be suitable. Attitudes continue to change, and this area is once again in the spotlight as being a prime subject for reform, but, given its controversial nature, this should be achieved through the Government promoting legislation in the House of Commons.

Private Bills are those promoted by individuals or groups for their own benefit or which relate to a locality or region. Some examples illustrate the point: the Prices Patent Candle Company Ltd Act 1992 was passed to give wider powers to this trading company; the Cattewater Reclamation Act 1992 provided for the purchase and development of waste property in an area of Plymouth; the Tamar Bridge Act 1998 provided for extensions to be built in the width of the existing bridge; the Avon Weir Act 1992 provided for the construction of a weir on the River Avon; and the British Railways Act 1992 provided for the acquisition of land in Kent to serve the channel tunnel. In 1999, the City of Westminster Act was passed to regulate street trading in that borough, and University College and Imperial College of the University of London both passed Acts to permit them to acquire other institutions.

The procedure for private Bills involves a first, second and third reading in both the House of Commons and Lords and also consideration of its provisions by a committee. Amendments may be made in either House, but, when agreement is reached, the Bill passes into law.

Private Bills should not be confused with Private Members' Bills. The former concern a private, local or regional matter, whereas the latter are of a public nature but are promoted by a private Member of Parliament. As the Government controls the timetable of the House of Commons (and, in practice, this also applies in the House of Lords), private Members have very little time at their disposal to promote Bills. In addition, they rarely have the benefit of parliamentary drafters who are skilled in the preparation of government Bills. Bills of a controversial nature may have to be left to the private Member or be promoted first in the House of Lords, particularly where the Government has a small majority or a heavy legislative programme.

At the beginning of a new session of Parliament, a ballot is held and the 20 private Members who are successful may introduce a Bill. Those with the first 10 places in the ballot may recover some of the expenses of promoting a Bill from the Government. Competition is usually very fierce and Members may be lobbied by interest or pressure groups to promote a Bill for them. There are usually many more Members wishing to promote legislation than places available, and those unsuccessful in the ballot may either make use of the Ten Minute Rule, under Standing Order 19 of the House, which permits a Member to put down a motion at the start of public business on Tuesdays and Wednesdays for leave to introduce a Bill or use the procedure by which government Bills are promoted.

Some notable examples of Private Members' Bills include the Abortion Act 1967, which was promoted by David Steel, as he then was, the Video Recordings Act 1984 and the Indecent Displays (Control) Act 1981. It is not merely sectional interests on which members may seek to promote legislation, rather, matters of general public interest may become law in this way. In 1994, the Merchant Shipping (Salvage and Pollution) Act was promoted by the former MP for St Ives, David Harris, who came 15th in the ballot used to allocate the Bills to receive parliamentary time. This aims to improve the law of salvage by offering salvors an extra bounty if they prevent or reduce the risk of marine pollution when a ship is in danger and to speed up rescue operations and avoid a repetition of the Penlee lifeboat tragedy in 1981. On the other hand, Michael Fabricant introduced a Ten Minute Rule Bill in 1992, designed to prohibit the practice of adding service charges to restaurant bills. It received little government support and did not pass into law, but illustrates that, although such Bills rarely become law, a private Member who feels strongly about a matter may raise public awareness, and that, in time, the Government may be persuaded to promote legislation. Alternatively, the private Member may gain sufficient support so as to promote a Bill at a later date.

Two other noteworthy Private Members' Bills are the Activity Centres (Young Persons' Safety) Act 1995, which was introduced by David Jamieson with the aim of preventing a similar tragedy to that of the Lyme Bay canoe accident, and also the Sale and Supply of Goods Act 1994, introduced by David Clelland to amend the implied terms as to quality and fitness for purpose of goods in the Sale of Goods Act 1979.

Of more recent note is the Bill introduced by Michael Foster to ban the use of hounds for hunting. This did not become law and the Government was unable to offer parliamentary time for passing legislation banning hunting. The Government still insists that its policy is to have legislation to ban hunting with hounds brought forward in the near future by way of a Private Member's Bill. Ken Livingstone has subsequently been successful in the ballot and proposes to promote a Private Member's Bill. On the question of animal welfare, Anne Clwyd intends to promote the Welfare of Broiler Chicken Bill, which has been drafted by the charitable organisation and pressure group Compassion in World Farming. This illustrates the unpredictable nature of ensuring changes in the law and that matters of crucial importance may not be tackled by the government, but left to the initiative of Members, who are often prompted by constituents or those with an interest in seeing change.

A more recent example follows the success of Judy Owen, who successfully took the Professional Golfers' Association to an employment tribunal for sex discrimination when she was sent home from work for wearing a trouser suit. Robert Walter MP is promoting a Bill to prevent private clubs, such as golf clubs, from discriminating against women by only allowing them entrance or use of facilities at certain times. The Bill is unlikely to be successful, but it will bring to public attention the fact that, at present, it is lawful for clubs such as the Pall Mall and Carlton Clubs in London, as well as schools such as Eton and Harrow, to exclude females.

Legislation is one of the principal sources of law, and an aspect of the doctrine of supremacy of Parliament concerns the role of the courts. The court is said to be merely the interpreter of legislation, and it cannot declare legislation to be invalid or unconstitutional. This, together with the other aspects of the doctrine, is now subject to EC law having precedence over domestic law, following the decisions in *Factortame* (1990) and *Francovich* (1992), where EC matters are in question.

Legislation is usually prospective in effect, that is, it applies in the future and will be given effect by the courts when called on to apply the law in resolving a dispute or when imposing criminal liability. A long established presumption is that, in the absence of express contrary provision, an Act is not to have retrospective effect. This is an important principle, particularly in criminal law, as a person should not face prosecution for an act which, when it was done, was lawful.

Delegated legislation

An Act may take the form of an enabling or parent Act. This may also be referred to as a 'framework' Act, as it sets out only the general aims to be achieved. This empowers others, such as a government minister or local authority, to make law by way of delegated legislation, so as to fill in the detail. In the case of a minister, it will take the form of rules, regulations or orders. The composite term is 'statutory instruments'. In the case of local authorities, it is 'bylaws'. By the Pollution Prevention and Control Act 1999, the Secretary of State for the Environment, Transport and the Regions is empowered to give effect to the Act by way of regulations and this, in turn, is to give effect to the UK's obligations under the EC Directive on Integrated Pollution Prevention and Control. For such a major piece of legislation, it is very short and one of the major criticisms that the House of Lords made was its skeletal nature and the vast discretionary powers vested in the Secretary of State to bring it into effect. It is increasingly common for the Government to have legislation passed by Parliament, vesting in it wide discretionary powers, but the House of Lords warned of the dangers and how the courts would attempt to check executive abuse of power in *R v Secretary of State for the Home Department ex p Fire Brigades' Union* (1995).

It became well recognised as long ago as the 19th century that Parliament had neither the time nor the expertise to legislate in minute detail in all areas considered to be in need of reform, so that delegation was necessary. Parliament remains supreme, in that it legislates on the general principles only, leaving the fine detail to the delegate. In addition, Parliament asserts control over the passage of statutory instruments in some cases, by way of a positive procedure whereby the rules, regulations or orders are placed before the House and a resolution in favour must be passed if the statutory instrument is to take effect. In the majority of cases, however, a negative procedure is adopted, which allows the statutory instrument to become law by way of resolution without objection or discussion by Members of Parliament.

The validity of an enabling Act cannot generally be challenged in the courts, as we have already noted, but the validity of delegated legislation can, by means of the doctrine of *ultra vires*. This doctrine assumes that Parliament may grant whatever power to make law that it chooses, but that the power granted to the delegate is thereby limited and must be complied with. If the delegate exceeds or abuses the power granted, the Queen's Bench Divisional Court of the High Court can declare an action of a delegate *ultra vires* and void.

A citizen aggrieved by the actions of a delegate (a local authority, public corporation or government minister) may seek redress by way of judicial review or may attempt to use *ultra vires* as a defence to a civil claim or a prosecution for breach of the delegated legislation. Authority for the former is to be found in *Bromley LBC v GLC* (1983), the so called 'fair fares' case, and, for the latter, in *Bugg v DPP* (1993). In *Bugg*, the court suggested that procedural *ultra vires* would arise as the result of a defect in the procedure by which the bylaw became law, and this properly should be dealt with in the Queen's Bench Divisional Court. Substantive *ultra vires* would arise where the delegated legislation failed in its terms to give effect to the purposes of the legislation, and any court would be able to decide such an issue. The case of *Boddington v British Transport Police* (1998) overruled *Bugg*, and the House of Lords stated that there was no distinction between substantive and procedural *ultra vires*, with the result that a person aggrieved by delegated legislation could either wait to be sued or prosecuted for its alleged breach or take charge of the matter and seek judicial review.

Another type of delegated legislation is an Order in Council. This refers to an order of the Privy Council, but the power to make such an order may originate from Parliament, whereby a minister is authorised to make such an order, or from the royal prerogative, where the Queen (or a minister to whom she has delegated power) makes such an order.

A good illustration of the use of the prerogative is in the *GCHQ* case (*Council of Civil Service Unions v Minister for the Civil Service* (1985)), where the prerogative power was delegated to the Minister for the Civil Service (who happened also to be the then Prime Minister, Mrs Thatcher), who banned unions at the Government Communications Headquarters without first consulting the employees. The House of Lords found on the facts that the ban was warranted on the grounds of national security and that no consultation was thereby required. The Law Lords, however, stated that the prerogative power would, in suitable cases, be subject to judicial review and that here, if national security had not demanded a ban, the employees would have had a legitimate expectation to be consulted before a decision was reached which adversely affected their terms of employment.

Delegated legislation has increased in use and is unlikely to decrease greatly. It has the advantages of speed, lower cost and use of the delegate's expertise in formulating detail, leaving Parliament to address itself to policy and general principles. There are notable disadvantages, however – in particular, the limitations on effective control by Parliament and especially the increasing use of a negative procedure whereby delegated legislation is approved in the absence of dissent.

The citizen is presumed to know the law, but, in reality, this is impossible, given the hundreds of statutes and thousands of statutory instruments passed each year. The citizen may either resort to the courts to challenge an allegedly *ultra vires* exercise of power or attempt to defend proceedings for breach of delegated legislation, but this will be both costly and time consuming.

We have already noted that the courts can challenge the validity of delegated legislation, but not that of legislation itself, on the basis of the sovereignty of Parliament doctrine. This is not to say, however, that the courts do not have an important function with regard to legislation.

The judge interprets the meaning to be placed on statutory provisions relied on when a case comes to court for settlement. Statutory provisions are not always unambiguous and may be interpreted narrowly or widely, and this gives a judge potentially great power in determining the future scope of the law. In interpreting statutory provisions, the judges add to the body of case law and this may assist future courts in deciding disputes.

The judges have formulated rules of practice, which are to be found in case law, to assist them in giving meaning to statutory provisions when those provisions form the basis of a dispute to be decided. These rules of interpretation, or construction, as they are sometimes called, will be considered in Chapter 6, together with the impact of the Human Rights Act 1998.

Judicial precedent

We will now move on to consider the other main source of law, namely, case law, which is the other main source of law within the English legal system (a common law based system as opposed to a Roman law or codified system). 'Common law' in this context refers to the system of precedent or *stare decisis* and not simply to decisions made by the old common law courts. Thus, it includes both the decisions of common law and equity.

Historically, precedent developed from the decisions of the common law courts and, from the 14th century, were supplemented by the decisions of the Court of Chancery. Common law became uniform throughout the country, and was applied to all. It is said to have developed from local customs which applied at the time of the Norman Conquest. Judges travelled throughout the country on circuit, dispensing justice. On their return to Westminster, which was traditionally the central location of the English courts, the judges compared the customs which they had applied in resolving disputes.

Over the centuries, a uniform law was moulded and established by means of the doctrine of *stare decisis* (let the decision stand). Judges were obliged to follow the decisions of superior courts and this ensured a degree of both certainty and fairness. This is a rather romanticised view of how the common law developed, but it is one which is entrenched. However, it has to be remembered that the nature of feudal society was one based on a hierarchy, at the top of which the King held absolute power, including the administration of the law. Rather than the common law emanating from the customs and mores of the common people, it is probably more true to say that it became a uniform law, applicable to all, to ensure the continued place of the monarch at the top of the hierarchy.

As a developed system of law, the common law became rigid and unable to meet new demands on it, in that it became over-reliant on fixed forms and failed to develop writs to meet new needs. Its very strengths of certainty and uniformity became its weaknesses. One of its strengths was that, once a plaintiff established his case, he would be entitled to compensation in the form of money damages.

In the 14th century, the Court of Chancery was founded by the Lord Chancellor. This dispensed equitable remedies to those either denied a remedy at common law or who had been granted an unsatisfactory remedy. Equity operated by way of maxims and its remedies were discretionary. These maxims were wise sayings and included the following:

- 'equity is but a gloss on the common law' – this denotes the idea that the common law was a complete system, whereas equity was a collection of concepts based on the principle of achieving fairness;

- 'equity looks to the intent rather than the form' – it is the substance of a matter which is important, rather than the means by which an end is achieved;

- 'he who comes to equity must come with clean hands' – a wrongdoer should not expect the court to assist him;

- 'equality is equity' – fairness between parties to a dispute should be aimed for;

- 'delay defeats equity' (*laches*) – a party should not expect the court to assist him if he has failed to act expeditiously;

- 'equity acts *in personam*' – this is against the person, so that the court would supervise the carrying out of an order, for example, by imposing an injunction.

The maxims illustrate the workings of equity and the fact that it was not a complete system in its own right, but attempted to fill in the gaps left by the common law. Equity was based on fairness, and its remedies were awarded only at the discretion of the court, which had to be satisfied as to the *bona fides* (the good intentions) of the plaintiff.

Equity originated from the Lord Chancellor, who was a cleric described as the Keeper of the King's Conscience, that is, he acted as the King's confessor. One of the early criticisms of equity – that 'equity varies with the length of the Chancellor's foot' – illustrates that, in the early days, equity reached decisions without reference to past cases and took a flexible approach in an attempt to achieve fairness and justice between the parties to a dispute.

Increasingly, equity remedied some of the defects of the common law, notably those of rigidity and over-reliance on the system of precedent. By the 15th century, equity and common law were rivals and it was only in the *Earl of Oxford's Case* (1615) that it was declared that, where there was a conflict, equity would prevail. It was not until the major reforms of 1873–75 in the Judicature Acts that this was put into statutory form and the administration of equity and common law were merged. Litigants could, from this time, seek both common law and equitable remedies in all courts, although it was necessary to ask for an equitable remedy, otherwise it would be assumed that common law damages would be sufficient.

In addition to equitable remedies such as rescission, injunction and specific performance, equity created concepts unknown at common law. Two important examples are mortgages and trusts.

Equity looked to the substance of a transaction rather than merely the form it took, and so, unlike the common law, equity would inquire into its purpose. In the case of a mortgage, this allowed a lender to take security for the loan over an item of property owned by the borrower. It did not allow the lender any greater rights over the property than those which protected his security. When the loan was repaid, the property used as security reverted to the borrower. Similarly, if the lender called in his loan and took possession of the property used as security, which he then sold, any surplus proceeds of sale were to pass to the borrower.

Trusts allowed the ownership of property to be transferred to one person for the benefit of another. So, for example, where a parent wished his son to have the benefit of a piece of land but the son was under age, the parent could transfer ownership to a trusted person (or, in the case of land, at least two people) to hold in trust for the benefit of the son. On reaching full age, it would then be usual for the trust to come to an end and for the trustee to transfer the property to the son (the beneficiary) for his own use. The common law did not recognise such interests as trusts, with the result that, at common law, the owner who purported to transfer property on trust would find that legal title passed to transferee outright and the intended beneficiary would have no claim.

Having outlined the origins of common law and equity and mentioned that their administration was merged as a result of the Judicature Acts 1873–75, it is now necessary to say more about the workings of precedent. Two factors are important in the development of precedent: the notion of a hierarchy of courts and the accurate and efficient reporting of cases. A court higher in the hierarchy has greater jurisdiction than a court lower in the hierarchy, and its decisions will be more authoritative in the interpretation of the law and in its application to the facts in a dispute.

It follows that the decision of a higher court and the reason or reasons for that decision will be binding on a later court lower in the hierarchy which is asked to decide a case on similar facts. On the other hand, decisions of courts lower in the hierarchy can only be of persuasive authority for courts higher in the hierarchy. A decision of the Court of Appeal does not bind the House of Lords, but the latter may take notice of a decision of the Court of Appeal concerned with similar facts. A similar rule applies to the decisions of Scottish and foreign courts, which are only of persuasive authority in English courts. Increasingly, the English courts are being referred to decisions of Commonwealth and US courts as a means of providing guidance in the resolution of disputes.

No mention of persuasive authority would be complete without reference to *obiter dicta* (things said by the way). Where, in the course of giving judgment, a judge makes comments not directly relevant to the dispute in question, such comments are described as *obiter dicta* (*obiter dictum*, in the singular). No matter what the place in the hierarchy of the court in which such statements are made, or of the court to which such statements are referred, such statements can only ever be persuasive authority.

In addition to hierarchy, the other element in the development of precedent is the system of reporting cases, that is, recording decisions so that they can be referred to by counsel in a later case concerned with similar facts. There are many examples of law reports, some specialised, for example, *Lloyd's Reports*, concerned with insurance and shipping matters, others general in nature, such as the *All England Law Reports*, the *Weekly Law Reports* and the most authoritative, the *Law Reports*, produced by the Incorporated Council of Law Reporting.

In addition to traditional law reports, lawyers are increasingly resorting to databases to retrieve case decisions. The most well known of these is LEXIS, which allows an authorised user access to the database containing case reports from the UK, the European Community, the Commonwealth, the USA and other jurisdictions.

It does not follow that a decision which is not reported is not a precedent. There have been instances where a decision is not reported for some time, and then only when its full significance is appreciated. Thus, counsel may well cite a case to a court which has not been reported and the court will take notice of it by way of oral evidence by counsel who appeared in the case. Lord Diplock in *Roberts Petroleum v B Kenny* (1983) and Lord Donaldson, the then Master of the Rolls, in *Stanley v International Harvester* (1983) attempted to discourage counsel from citing unreported cases from LEXIS, in particular those which demonstrated no great novelty or authority.

Only about one-10th of the decisions of the higher courts are reported and, in any event, there may well be a time lag in a court reaching a decision and its being reported in full. Various law reports offer only a summary of the decision reached (for example, the *Times Law Reports*; the *Student Law Review*). The advantage of this lies in the speed from the date of decision to the date on which it is reported.

Previous reported decisions may assist the lawyer asked to advise his client or the judge having to reach a solution in a dispute. When consulting a law report, there are several essential elements that must be identified. Not only the facts of the earlier case must be reported, together with the decision reached by the court, but also the *ratio decidendi* (that is, the reason or the reasons for the decision).

The court, in reaching its decision, may attempt to state the law by making a *per curiam* statement. However, it may not always be so clear for a later court asked to apply a previous decision. Its interpretation of the *ratio decidendi* of the earlier court permits a later court either to develop the law or restrict its scope. A later court will have to assess the degree of similarity and dissimilarity between the facts of the case it is asked to decide and those of the earlier case. If the judge in the later case finds no significant dissimilarities and is bound by the earlier decision, then the earlier decision will be applied. If the earlier decision is only persuasive authority, the judge can use his discretion to decide whether or not to apply the earlier decision. However, where the earlier decision is a binding precedent, the judge may be able or willing to distinguish the facts of the earlier case from those of the case he is asked to decide, and so avoid applying what would otherwise be binding on him. The advantage of distinguishing is that the law can develop to meet changing needs. Its disadvantage lies in over-use and the drawing of minute differences, leading to uncertainty in the law.

The doctrine of precedent as applied in the courts

The House of Lords is, as a general rule, bound by its previous decisions. This ensures a degree of certainty, by which legal advisers stand a better chance of predicting the likely outcome of cases. The House of Lords has, on many occasions, stated that if it wrongly interprets the law, it is Parliament's place to amend the law by way of legislation.

By the 1966 Practice Statement, the House of Lords stated that it would depart from its previous decisions 'where it appears right to do so'. This has been used rarely, but the case of *R v Shivpuri* (1986) illustrates that the House of Lords may decide that one of its earlier decisions had been wrongly decided. *Shivpuri* overruled *Anderton v Ryan* (1985), where it was held that it was not an offence to attempt the legally impossible. In *Shivpuri*, the defendant was convicted of an attempt at dealing in and harbouring a prohibited drug. In fact, the substance was harmless, although the defendant thought that he had in his possession a drug. As he had intended to commit the offence and had done an act more than merely preparatory to the commission of the offence, liability was proved.

Other examples where this power has been used include *R v Secretary of State for the Home Department ex p Khawaja* (1983), which overruled *R v Secretary of State for the Home Department ex p Zamir* (1980); *R v Hancock and Shankland* (1986), overruling *R v Maloney* (1985); and *Murphy v Brentwood DC* (1990), overruling *Anns v Merton LBC* (1978). The House of Lords is not bound by a decision reached *per incuriam* (that is, through carelessness in overlooking a relevant statutory provision or earlier decision). Decisions of the House of Lords bind all lower courts, provided statute has not overruled the decision and, in the case of a decision reached on the grounds of public policy, provided it remains socially appropriate.

The Court of Appeal (Civil Division) binds all inferior courts and, as a general rule, is bound by its own decisions. Three exceptions were noted in *Young v Bristol Aeroplane Co* (1944):

- the Court of Appeal can choose between two conflicting decisions of its own;

- the Court of Appeal is bound to follow a later House of Lords decision which conflicts with an earlier Court of Appeal decision but which does not expressly overrule it;

- the Court of Appeal is not bound by one of its own previous decisions which was taken *per incuriam* (failure to take account of a statutory provision or relevant case).

The position of the Court of Appeal has not always been so settled, as illustrated in the case of *Davis v Johnson* (1979), where Lord Denning (then Master of the Rolls) expressed the view that the Court of Appeal should be free to overrule one of its previous decisions where it was seen to be wrong. On appeal, the House of Lords reprimanded the Court of Appeal for this view and suggested that only the exceptions in *Young v Bristol Aeroplane* were available. The Court of Appeal, unlike the House of Lords, should not be able to disregard its previous decisions, other than where one of the three known exceptions applied. Section 3 of the European Communities Act 1972 may require the Court of Appeal not to apply a previous decision of its own which conflicts with EC law or a later decision of the ECJ. As a result of the Human Rights Act 1998, from October 2000, UK courts have to apply the decisions of the European Court on Human Rights, which bind all UK courts.

This brings into question why we have two appeal courts. On the one hand, in theory at least, litigants are free to look to the House of Lords for an authoritative statement of the law, although, owing to cost and delay, few cases reach the House of Lords. On the other hand, if the Court of Appeal was free to overrule its earlier decisions (although this might lead to uncertainty) it would provide litigants with a shorter and cheaper route to settlement.

As a result of the reforms in the Judicature Acts 1873–75, the Supreme Court of Judicature was set up, comprising the Court of Appeal and the High Court of Justice. The House of Lords as a court was abolished. However, by the Appellate Jurisdiction Act 1876, the House of Lords was once again made the highest appeal court and the reference to 'supreme' was one only in name. Now that reform of the House of Lords as a legislative chamber is proceeding, it may be timely to reconsider its role as the highest appeal court. Furthermore, a pressing need for a supreme court that is a constitutional court may well appear now that the Human Rights Act 1998 is in place. In the light of *R v Bow Street Metropolitan Magistrates ex p Pinochet Ugarte* (1998), in which Lord Hoffman overlooked the need to disclose his associations with the charitable arm of Amnesty International where the main organisation had been invited to put its case for the extradition to Spain of Colonel Pinochet, it became clear that not only the issue of judicial bias needed to be addressed, but also the future role of the House of Lords as the highest appeal court.

The Court of Appeal (Criminal Division) applies the rules of precedent less strictly than the Civil Division, on the basis that each case is to be treated on its merits. In *R v Gould* (1968), it was stated that the court is bound by its previous decisions, subject to the 'interests of justice'. The court will follow an earlier decision, even if thought to be wrong, if it results in the liberty of the defendant.

The High Court is bound by decisions of the House of Lords, the Court of Appeal and the divisional courts, but not by its own decisions. The Crown Courts, county courts and magistrates' courts are also bound by the decisions of the higher courts, but not by their own decisions. In the case of the divisional courts, where the supervisory jurisdiction is exercised in civil or criminal matters, the court is not bound by its own earlier decisions, but in appeals 'by way of case stated' in criminal matters, as a general rule, it is bound, unless the liberty of the defendant is at stake.

Insofar as the decisions of higher courts are concerned, the divisional courts are bound by the decisions of the House of Lords and Court of Appeal, except the Divisional Court of the Queen's Bench Division, where appeal lies direct to the House of Lords.

Strict application of the rules of binding precedent can lead to rigidity in the law. Several devices exist which allow the law to be developed, and a judge who is otherwise bound by an earlier decision may avoid applying it. One such device is that of 'distinguishing' the facts of the present case from that of an earlier decision which would otherwise be binding. Caution is needed, however, otherwise artificial differences might be used to justify not following decisions of a higher court. Distinguishing permits the law to be developed to cover new situations, but, at the same time, it may create uncertainty as to future developments.

Another device is to declare that an earlier decision was made *per incuriam* and that the law as stated in the earlier decision is incorrect. In *Rakhit v Carty* (1990), this was taken a step further when the Court of Appeal (Civil Division) held that it was not bound to follow a previous decision which was itself based on the authority of an earlier decision which had been made *per incuriam*, in that it had failed to take account of a relevant statutory provision. Russell LJ referred to the rule in *Young v Bristol Aeroplane Co Ltd* (1944) and the limited exceptions to that rule referred to in *Young and Morelle Ltd v Wakeling* (1955) and *Williams v Fawcett* (1985), whereby the Court of Appeal is permitted to depart from one of its earlier decisions if that decision was made *per incuriam* or 'in rare and exceptional cases' which involve 'a manifest slip or error'.

The Court of Appeal was not declaring that a precedent binding on it was *per incuriam*, but that the precedent which appeared to be binding on it had followed a decision which was itself *per incuriam*. The Court of Appeal felt free to rectify the position some eight years after the first decision had been made. It is unlikely that this will be used often.

The law may also develop where, on an appeal, previous authority binding on the lower courts is overruled. The rule or principle will be restated by the higher court correcting the error fallen into by a lower court. This may result in the appeal being successful, in which case the decision of the lower court is reversed.

The common law also develops as a result of later courts interpreting the scope and effect of binding precedent. It will not always be clear what the *ratio decidendi* of a case is, particularly in decisions of the House of Lords, where, although there may be agreement as to the decision itself, their Lordships may differ as to the reasons for the decision. A later court may find that what was considered to be the *ratio* of an earlier decision is too wide, with the result that it will be only of persuasive authority. Where a later court is faced with several conflicting decisions of the same level, it will have to choose between them. In other cases, what would otherwise be a binding precedent is found to be wrong or obscure or have been overruled by statute, with the effect that the court asked to apply the precedent is not bound to do so.

Apart from such devices, judges have generally considered that they have a limited role to play in making law. They are the interpreters of the law, and should not usurp the role of Parliament. The legislature is empowered to enact policy as the elected representative of the people. The role of the judge is limited to making law piecemeal, as and when cases come before the courts for solution.

Judges are not elected but appointed, and should not concern themselves with deciding between competing interests other than where the law (either in the form of statute or case law) already establishes where the line is to be drawn. We consider more fully the role of the judge in the development of case law in Chapter 6.

It now remains to consider the impact on domestic law of membership of the EC, which, for some purposes, from September 1993, became the EU, following ratification of the Treaty on European Union 1992, usually referred to as the Maastricht Treaty. This was given domestic effect by the European Communities (Amendment) Act 1993. Further changes have been brought about by the Amsterdam Treaty 1997.

European Community law

The UK joined the European Economic Community, the European Coal and Steel Community and Euratom in 1973, undertaking to establish a common market with the existing members to approximate economic policies by abolishing customs duties and trade barriers and ensuring free movement of persons, services and capital within and between Member States.

The Treaty of Accession was signed in 1972 and was brought into effect by the European Communities Act 1972. Similarly, the Single European Act 1986 was given domestic effect in the UK by the European Communities (Amendment) Act 1986, and 1993 saw the ratification of the Maastricht Treaty, which was implemented by the European Communities (Amendment) Act 1993 following some 19 months' discussion in Parliament. This Treaty had the effect of recognising Europe as a social and political, as well as an economic, community. The UK, however, did not ratify the Social Chapter in the Maastricht Treaty, but, in 1997 the Treaty of Amsterdam incorporated the Social Charter, as it had become, and the UK became a signatory. The Amsterdam Treaty has re-numbered previous Article numbers, so, for example, Art 177 of the Treaty of Rome, providing for a preliminary ruling by the ECJ, is now Art 234 of the EC Treaty.

Constitutional theory demands that an international treaty entered into by the Crown has no effect in domestic law unless and until it is given effect by legislation. Authority for this is to be found in the case of *Mortensen v Peters* (1906). This is an aspect of the doctrine of parliamentary sovereignty and, in legal theory, these Acts may be repealed by a later Parliament, with the result that the UK can be in breach of international law. The political reality is quite different, and any attempt to repeal this legislation would result not only in political crisis, but also call into question the position of the courts and whether the judges would comply strictly with the doctrine of parliamentary sovereignty or attempt to comply with law of the EC. At the present time, with the doctrine still in place, in so far as it gives effect to EC law, developments have shown the courts of the UK willing to give European law priority where there is a conflict with domestic law.

The institutions of the European Union

There are four main institutions of the European Union.

The Council of the European Union

The Council, which formerly was the Council of Ministers, is made up of one representative from each of the 15 Member States, usually the foreign minister, by the appropriate minister for the business to be discussed. For example, when agriculture is being dealt with, Britain would be represented by the Minister for Agriculture, Fisheries and Food. The Council is the principal decision making body and can conclude agreements on behalf of the Union. The presidency is rotated between each Member State on a six monthly basis. Decisions are reached in one of three ways: by simple majority; by qualified majority; or unanimously. Larger States have proportionately more votes.

The Council of Ministers must not be confused with the European Council, which was established in 1974 and was given formal recognition under the Single European Act 1986. This consists of heads of government and foreign ministers who meet in 'summit' at least twice a year, as provided for under Art 2 of the Single European Act. This is not one of the institutions of the Union and does not have general decision making power.

The European Commission

The Commission is the executive body likened to a 'civil service'. There are at present 20 members drawn from Member States, but not equally. Commissioners swear an oath of allegiance to the Union and each takes responsibility for a subject. Its main function is the preparation of proposals for new legislation and the formulation of policy.

The European Parliament

The Parliament, formerly called the European Assembly, has 626 members, directly elected by Member States for a five year term. Members sit in party groupings, not according to State. The involvement of the Assembly in law making was increased under the provisions of the Single European Act 1986. This is known as the 'co-operation procedure'. The Assembly can accept, reject or amend proposed legislative changes and it has a power of veto over the Commission's budget proposals. It can also dismiss the Commission on a two-thirds vote, but these powers have not yet been used.

The European Court of Justice in Luxembourg

The ECJ interprets EC law and its application to Member States and other bodies. The Court follows the Roman law tradition, in that no reliance is placed on precedent (although decisions of the Court bind the courts of Member States). An inquisitorial approach is followed, and no dissenting opinions are given. Counsel make written submissions and the Court reaches a preliminary decision through Advocates General. In *Grant v South West Trains Ltd* (1998), the claimant sought equal treatment for her same-sex partner as an employee with a spouse or heterosexual partner. The Advocate General recommended to the ECJ that Art 6 of the Equal Treatment Directive could extend to same-sex couples, but the Court rejected this view.

A president is appointed by fellow judges and each Member State sends one judge to the Court. The 15 judges are assisted by nine Advocates General. Reference may be made (and, in the case of Member States' final appeal courts, reference must be made) under Art 234 of the EC Treaty (formerly Art 177) for a preliminary ruling as to the meaning or effect of Union law. The case of *Bulmer v Bollinger* (1974), in which Lord Denning MR laid down four guidelines as to whether a reference was necessary and six guidelines for the exercise of the discretion by other than a final appeal court, remains instructive as to the use of Art 234, although it has been refined by later cases.

In 1989, the Court of First Instance was inaugurated, with the aims of easing the burden of the ECJ and speeding up the hearing of cases.

Use of Art 234 necessitates adjournment of a case in the domestic court pending the interpretation of EC law by the ECJ. The delay may be several years and this, of course, increases costs for litigants.

The application of European Community law

So far as application of European law within Member States is concerned, the view of the ECJ and the views of domestic courts have not always been identical. The UK courts are bound by the doctrine of sovereignty of Parliament and, whilst the UK is a member of the Union, European law is given effect under the European Communities Act 1972 and subsequent legislation. The ECJ has, on many occasions, stated that European law takes precedence over domestic law. Authority for this is to be found in *Costa v ENEL* (1964), the *Internationale* case (1970) and *Van Gend en Loos* (1963).

On 19 June 1990, the ECJ again ruled that European law was to take precedence over domestic law in what has become known as the 'Spanish Fishermen' case, which involved the provisions of the Merchant Shipping Act 1988. In *R v Secretary of State for Transport ex p Factortame Ltd and Others (No 2)* (1990), the House of Lords granted interim relief to the applicants by suspending the provisions of the 1988 Act.

A distinction has been drawn between directly applicable and directly effective provisions, although this distinction is not always made clear in the judgments of the ECJ. Regulations are directly applicable and bestow rights on individuals under Art 249 of the EC Treaty. No further measures need be taken by Member States to bring regulations into effect. On the other hand, directives are binding only as to the result to be achieved and Member States are free to choose the form of implementation, subject only to a specified timetable.

To be directly effective, a directive must meet three conditions:

• first, the provision must be clear and precise in its scope and application;

• secondly, it must not be conditional;

• thirdly, there must be no room for a Member State to exercise its discretion in implementing the directive.

If a directive meets these conditions, but otherwise is inadequately implemented by a Member State, an individual can still rely on its terms in the domestic courts. This is known as 'vertical direct effect', in that an individual can look to his or her government for a remedy.

Authority is to be found in *Marshall v Southampton and SW Hants AHA* (1984), which concerned the compulsory retirement age of 65 for men and 60 for women. It was held that the Equal Treatment Directive had been broken and that this could be relied on, as the employer was an organ of the State. An issue then arose as to whether direct effect could apply for the benefit of individuals who wished to bring claims not against the State, but against another individual or private body. This became known as 'horizontal direct effect'. The cases of *Von Colson* (1983) and *Marleasing SA v La Commercial Internacional* (1989) show that the ECJ used Art 5 of the Treaty of Rome (now Art 10 of the EC Treaty) to get round the difficulty, with the result that States (including domestic courts) must take 'all appropriate measures' to fulfil European obligations.

A further breakthrough was made in *Francovich v Italy* (1992) when the ECJ held that Francovich should be awarded damages against the Italian Government despite the directive in question having been found to be insufficiently precise to be directly effective. Further developments have now been seen concerning State liability to pay damages to individuals. In *R v Secretary of State for Transport ex p Factortame Ltd (No 4)* (1996) and *Brasserie du Pêcheur SA v Federal Republic of Germany* (1996), it was held that Member States can be made liable in damages to an individual for legislation that is incompatible with European law. In both cases, treaty provisions were in question.

In *Van Gend en Loos* (1963), Art 12 of the Treaty of Rome (now Art 25 of the EC Treaty) was held to have vertical direct effect, and this ruling was soon applied to other treaty provisions which satisfied the conditions above.

Horizontal direct effect of treaty provisions was recognised in *Defrenne v Sabena* (1975). In *R v Secretary of State for Transport ex p Factortame Ltd (No 5)* (1997), it was held that there was no right to claim punitive damages in respect of the breaches of EC law by the UK Government passing the Merchant Shipping Act 1988, which precluded Spanish trawler owners from registering to fish in UK waters. So far as decisions, recommendations and opinions are concerned, only decisions are binding and may have direct effect.

When considering the attitude of the English courts to the application of European law, two points are worthy of note. First, the use of Art 234 of the EC Treaty for the making of a preliminary reference for the interpretation of a European provision. As we have already noted, the landmark case was that of *Bulmer v Bollinger* (1974), in which Lord Denning MR laid down guidelines to assist the court in deciding whether or not to make a reference. In his judgment, he stated that the House of Lords, as the final appeal court, was under a duty to make a reference where one or both parties wished, providing it was necessary to do so on the basis of four guidelines. All other courts had a discretion and Lord Denning MR laid down six guidelines to assist a court with this question. Later cases have refined Lord Denning's statements and it may be that a court other than the House of Lords may be the final appeal court, in which case it will be under a duty to make an Art 234 reference.

The other point concerns the sovereignty of Parliament and how the English courts would deal with a clash between European law and domestic law. As we have already mentioned, European law is given effect by way of s 2(1)–(4) of the European Communities Act 1972, as subsequently amended. In strict legal theory, this legislation could be repealed and a conflict created with European law. Even whilst remaining members of the European Union, a clash between European and domestic law might arise. *R v Secretary of State for Transport ex p Factortame Ltd (No 2)* (1990) involved the suspension of s 14 of the Merchant Shipping Act 1988 pending the final determination of the issues. This case, together with *R v Secretary of State for Employment ex p Equal Opportunities Commission* (1994), involving the rights of part time workers under the Equal Pay Directive, illustrates the closest the UK has come to such a clash.

The question has often been posed as to how UK judges should react, and four possibilities have been put forward: they could follow the traditional doctrine of implied repeal and give effect to the later legislation; they could ignore such later legislation unless it expressly repudiated European law; the judges could apply a rule of construction and interpret UK law consistently with European law; or they could take a radical approach and apply European law.

In the light of the *Factortame* litigation and the ratification of the Treaty on European Union in 1993 and the Amsterdam Treaty in 1997, there is every likelihood that any clash between European and domestic law will be remedied not by the courts, but by amending legislation. Should legislation be passed in the future which repeals the European Communities Act 1972, as amended, this raises much more fundamental issues and the reaction of the judges would depend on their view not only of their role within the constitution, but, of the constitution itself.

Law reform agencies

The background to change

In considering the question of change and reform of the law, it is necessary to consider the agencies that facilitate change and the need for reform. Before looking at each of the main agencies, we will consider the need for change. If law is to meet the changing needs of society, it not only needs to adapt to social change, but must also anticipate change and, in some cases, mould and shape social habits and attitudes.

'Change' and 'reform' should, however, be distinguished, because reform implies change that is desirable and which improves the lot of members of society. Change, if it is too frequent and ill thought out, may outweigh any advantages in seeking reform. A fundamental tenet of law and of a developed legal system is the idea that there should be certainty in the legal rules and how they are applied, so as to allow those subject to them to arrange their affairs in such a way as to comply. The 1980s and 1990s saw much new legislation initiated by the Government to give effect to its policy of privatisation of public services and reform of many of the institutions of society, including the legal system and legal profession. The 19th century also saw many legal reforms, culminating in the Judicature Acts 1873–75.

Some notable examples from the last decade include the Environmental Protection Act 1990, the Environment Act 1995, the Courts and Legal Services Act 1990, the Criminal Justice Acts 1991 and 1993, the Criminal Justice and Public Order Act 1994, the Criminal Appeal Act 1995 and the Access to Justice Act 1999.

In the Queen's Speech of 1999, the Government included some 28 measures ranging from welfare reform, pollution control, the protection of wildlife and the countryside to criminal justice reform. The last century has been one where major social change has been brought about by legislation, in particular in the areas of health, education, housing and the working environment.

This is not to suggest that the only means by which legal change can be effected is by way of statute, for the courts too have a role to play in developing the law. Theirs is, however, a much more limited role, as we will see in Chapter 6.

Traditionally, the doctrine of the sovereignty of Parliament has limited the role of the courts and ensured that Parliament is the supreme law maker. The government of the day puts forward its legislative proposals and, providing it has a strong majority in the House of Commons, will expect to pass these into law. The courts will interpret the provisions contained in Acts of Parliament when and if a dispute arises concerning the meaning of the words used. The courts are also limited in developing the common law, and are generally reluctant to extend the boundaries of the law beyond established precedent. The advantage of this is that the law will have some certainty, but the disadvantage is that it may fail to take account of changing needs and attitudes. Policy is said to be the province of Parliament, and it will be for Parliament to promote major change in the law.

This is a relatively modern idea, for in the past the courts have taken it upon themselves to develop the law. This is clearly shown in the development of the law of tort, in particular the tort of negligence. However, some recent cases illustrate that the courts may yet demonstrate reforming zeal. For example, the case of *R v R* (1991), where the House of Lords recognised for the first time that a husband could be guilty of the rape of his wife and, in *Airedale NHS Trust v Bland* (1993), the House of Lords permitted the ending of treatment of a patient in a persistent vegetative state.

R v Brown (1993) also demonstrates the willingness of the courts to take into account the wider issues and see the need for the law to cover new situations. In this case, liability under ss 20 and 47 of the Offences Against the Person Act 1861 was imposed on those who had undertaken sado-masochistic acts in private. The European Court of Human Rights (ECHR) ruled in February 1997 in favour of the ruling that consent is no defence to sado-masochistic acts between adults in private.

On 30 March 1994, the Queen's Bench Divisional Court held that the rebuttable presumption that a child between the ages of 10 and 14 was incapable of committing a criminal offence was no longer part of English law. Lord Justice Mann said that the 'common law was not a system of rigid rules but of principles whose application might alter over time and should be renewed by succeeding generations of judges'. The court rejected three arguments for the retention of the presumption, namely, the decision would have retrospective effect, that change should only be made by Parliament or at least a decision of the House of Lords, and that the court was bound by the doctrine of *stare decisis*. The judge also said that the presumption 'had no utility whatever in the present era and ought to go'. On appeal by way of case stated, the House of Lords held that the *doli incapax* presumption remained part of English law and that, if change was to be made, this was for Parliament. This has now been passed into law by s 34 of the Crime and Disorder Act 1998, which removes the *doli incapax* rule so that criminal liability can attach at the age of 10.

Another area which demonstrates that the courts are taking into account the social context in which law exists and the fact that attitudes change is that of *Fitzpatrick (AP) v Sterling Housing Association* (1999), in which the House of Lords held that the appellant came within the definition of the deceased's 'family' in Sched 1(3) to the Rent Act 1977, and so was entitled to succeed to a statutory tenancy on the death of his male partner of 18 years, who had been the assured tenant of the respondent. The court also considered the question whether the appellant could have been entitled to a statutory tenancy under Sched 1(2) as the tenant's spouse, but held that this was not possible, as the statutory provision clearly referred to a heterosexual relationship. The court was careful to stress that, in deciding that the appellant was a member of the deceased tenant's family, it was only concerned with interpreting the language in the Act. In other contexts, 'family' could be interpreted differently. Reference was made to the decision in *Grant v South West Trains Ltd* (1998), in which the ECJ held that same-sex relationships were not to be treated as equivalent to marriage. This is a developing area where the barriers may yet be extended by the courts. Recent events, for example, requests by homosexuals to adopt children, suggests that the law – whether by statute or judicial decisions – will have to provide answers as to where the boundaries are to be drawn.

The government ban on homosexuals being members of the armed forces has been challenged in the ECHR, and the Government announced in January 2000 its intention to end the ban. Furthermore, the case of *Re W (A Minor) (Adoption: Homosexual Adopter)* (1997) held that s 15 of the Adoption Act 1976 did not preclude a single person from applying to adopt a child, even if in a homosexual relationship. The court was to consider all the circumstances, but the overriding consideration was the welfare and best interests of the child. In July 1999, Dame Elizabeth Butler-Sloss, President of the High Court Family Division, stated that gay couples could successfully adopt children. In the case of the homosexual couple who arranged for the birth of twins in America by a surrogate mother, the Home Secretary has granted the twins rights of indefinite stay in the UK, but without rights of citizenship. The question of adoption has yet to come before the courts.

Moving on to law reform agencies, the main body is the Law Commission, established by the Law Commissions Act 1965, and appointed by the Lord Chancellor with five commissioners, appointed for up to five years, and one consultant together with a legal support staff.

Two commissions exist, one for England and Wales and the other for Scotland. The Commission for England and Wales is chaired by a High Court judge and the members are solicitors and barristers, judges and academics. No lay representatives sit on the commissions. An annual report is laid before Parliament concerned with codification, repeal of obsolete and unnecessary Acts, reduction in the number of separate Acts (consolidation) and the elimination of anomalies.

The 1994 report concluded that, of the 30 reports published since 1983, only one in five have been acted on by Parliament. It also states that the law should be made as simple, fair and cheap as possible and that there are far too many faults and flaws. Much of the blame for the lack of effective reform is to be laid at the door of Parliament and its antiquated procedures, which are in urgent need of reform.

The Commission is charged with keeping under review the law of England and Wales, 'with a view to its systematic development and reform, including in particular the codification of such law, the elimination of anomalies, the repeal of obsolete and unnecessary enactments and generally the simplification and modernisation of the law' (s 3(1) of the Law Commissions Act 1965). The extreme breadth of jurisdiction is limited, in that the Commission may only work on topics approved by the Lord Chancellor. Its recommendations are, however, its own and are laid before Parliament. However, Parliament may decide not to give legislative effect to them and there is no duty in the Act on the Government to comment on such recommendations or on the decision to legislate or not. Many of the recommendations made in the past have been adopted, albeit in modified form.

Two areas which have been the subject of scrutiny by the Commission have seen its recommendations passed into law. The Unfair Contract Terms Act 1977 was passed as a result of the Commission's recommendations, and also in the area of family and matrimonial provision its recommendations have been given legislative effect. Its proposal for a draft criminal code has, however, not met with wide support. In the light of many serious miscarriages of justice, it might be argued that, rather than devoting its attention to codification of the criminal law, time and resources would have been better spent investigating and proposing reform of the criminal justice system. This is particularly true now that it has become clear that the Government has decided not to implement fully the recommendations of the Royal Commission on Criminal Justice. Of great concern is the removal of the right of silence of suspects and defendants on trial, contained in ss 34–37 of the Criminal Justice and Public Order Act 1994. Following the tragic death of Stephen Lawrence and the judicial inquiry under the chairmanship of Sir William McPherson, a retired High Court judge, the Law Commission has investigated the need to amend the double jeopardy rule, whereby a defendant, once convicted or acquitted of a criminal offence in a particular matter, cannot be re-tried. It has proposed that, where vital new evidence comes to light, a person should face re-trial. Certainly, the use of DNA samples may well provide such new evidence, but, at the same time, safeguards are needed to ensure that the system maintains fairness and justice, particularly where a long time elapses between the first trial and the emergence of new evidence.

A vital aspect of law reform is the process by which reform proposals are generated. An important preliminary to reform must be consultation with those affected by the proposals. This must include not only lawyers and judges, but also the general public and those whose interests would be affected. The Law Commission, under the chairmanship of Lord Scarman, developed the practice of issuing consultation papers (which became known as Green Papers, due to the colour of their covers). The Commission researches a topic, sets out possible courses of action and their implications, the law as at the date of the Green Paper and any relevant practice from other jurisdictions. This is then published, and responses are called for. An example is that of the Commission's consultation paper on administrative law, entitled *Administrative Law: Judicial Review and Statutory Appeals* (1993), in which the Commission considered the need for reform of the procedure for obtaining judicial review and the need for a general requirement for public decision makers to give reasons for their decisions.

Other bodies now also prepare Green Papers, including government departments. Another example is the Human Fertilisation and Embryology Authority, established under the Courts and Legal Services Act 1990, which called for the views of all interested parties on the issue of the use of foetal tissue in fertility treatments in 1993.

The Law Reform Committee

Another reform agency is the Law Reform Committee, made up of judges and practising and academic lawyers. This was set up in 1952 and took over the work of the Law Revision Committee which was set up in 1934. It deals with civil law matters referred to it by the Lord Chancellor and is under a duty 'to consider, having regard especially to judicial decisions, what changes are desirable in such legal doctrines as the Lord Chancellor may from time to time refer to the Committee'.

Some of the Acts which have resulted from its work include the Occupiers' Liability Act 1957, the Limitation Act 1939 and the Law Reform (Contributory Negligence) Act 1945. In 1966, its report, *Transfer of Title to Chattels* (Cmnd 2958), concluded that the interests of an innocent purchaser of goods should have precedence over those of the original owner and that the market overt exception to the *nemo dat* rule should be extended to cover all purchases from retail premises and auctions. This did not find favour with the Government in 1966, but, when Lord Renton put forward the Sale of Goods (Amendment) Bill in the House of Lords in January 1994, with the aim of abolishing the market overt exception, it was rejected by the Government pending publication of a Green Paper dealing with transfer of title. By the Sale of Goods (Amendment) Act 1994, the market overt exception to the *nemo dat* rule was abolished. This followed a campaign by the Council for the Prevention of Art Theft, which saw this loophole in the law as a 'thieves' charter'.

The Criminal Law Revision Committee

So far as criminal law is concerned, the Criminal Law Revision Committee oversees reform. This was established in 1959 as a Standing Committee and advises the Home Secretary of the need for reform. It is under a duty 'to examine such aspects of the criminal law of England and Wales as the Home Secretary may from time to time refer to the committee to consider whether the law requires revision and to make recommendations'. Notable reports led to the Suicide Act 1961, the Theft Acts 1968 and 1978 and the Criminal Law Act 1967. This committee has not been convened since 1985.

Royal Commissions and Advisory Committees

We have already mentioned the Royal Commission on Criminal Justice under Lord Runciman, which reported in July 1993. This was set up in 1991 in response to several miscarriages of justice, notably the Guildford Four and the Birmingham Six trials.

Royal Commissions are appointed by the Crown, on the advice of a minister who names a chairperson. Membership varies but reflects expert, professional and lay opinion. They have the aim of investigating a matter of public importance and take evidence and formulate recommendations. This may result in legislation following the usual process of Green Paper, followed by a White Paper containing the Government's proposals, followed by a Bill and finally enacted by statute. However, invariably, the recommendations are altered in part or are not adopted at all.

It is instructive to trace the sequence of events which resulted in the Courts and Legal Services Act 1990. The Benson Royal Commission reported in 1979 and was followed by the Marre Report, *A Time for Change*, in 1988. This was followed by three Green Papers which, in turn, were followed by the White Paper, *A Framework for the Future*. The Courts and Legal Services Bill followed and, after amendment, this was enacted in 1990 and brought into effect subsequently by means of regulations promoted by the Lord Chancellor.

The Lord Chancellor, through his Advisory Committee on Legal Aid, Working Parties on Legal Services and Contingency Fees, also proposes reforms. The report by Lord Justice Steyn for the Lord Chancellor's Advisory Committee on Education and Conduct recommended the abolition of the separate training of solicitors and barristers. The then chairman of the Bar, Robert Seabrook QC, published a consultation paper suggesting that reform was timely. It was proposed that the Bar should not retain the monopoly over the training of barristers and that there should be a common vocational training of barristers and solicitors. Since October 1997, the Bar Vocational Course is offered at centres outside London and at institutions within London, in addition to courses run by the Council of Legal Education.

Judicial inquiries

Another mechanism for reform is the judicial inquiry. Lord Justice Scott concluded his investigation of the Matrix Churchill ('arms to Iraq') affair and reported his findings in February 1996. It was suggested that reforms should be instituted, both in the issue of public interest immunity certificates under the Crown Proceedings Act 1947 as a result of the criticisms that were made of their use, and in the role of the Attorney General. To date, none have been instituted, but, as a result of the wide adverse publicity arising out of this case, it is likely that lessons have been learned.

Another notable inquiry was that of Lord Scarman into the Brixton riots in 1981, which led to the Police and Criminal Evidence Act (PACE) 1984. This was a tribunal of inquiry, regulated by what is now the Tribunal and Inquiries Act 1992, whereas the Scott Inquiry was an *ad hoc* inquiry, set up by the Prime Minister.

We have already mentioned the McPherson Report – a judicial inquiry – following the death of Stephen Lawrence, which made recommendations concerning coroners' inquests and the investigation of crimes by the police. Perhaps of most significance was the finding of 'institutional racism' endemic in the Metropolitan Police Force and the debate which has followed as to its significance for other institutions in society.

Much reform of the legal system itself arises out of reviews set up by the Lord Chancellor. Notably, the review of the civil justice system by Lord Woolf, which reported in 1996, has resulted in major reform of the civil justice system and effectively merged the administration of the work of the county courts and the High Court. More recently, the Lord Chancellor has appointed Auld LJ of the Court of Appeal to report on the workings of the criminal courts by the end of 2000. His brief is wide, with the aim of 'promoting public confidence in the rule of law'.

Private Members' Bills

When considering the means by which law reform may be achieved, the role of the private Member of Parliament should not be overlooked. If nothing else, a Bill promoted by a private Member may well publicise the issues and, even though not passed into law, may create an opportunity for law to be passed in the future. Lord Stallard introduced a Crime of Vagrancy (Abolition) Bill, which received its second reading in the House of Lords on 11 December 1993. This was not enacted, but its purpose was to repeal the Vagrancy Act 1824 (other than s 4, which prohibits indecent exposure in public), and thereby decriminalise begging and homelessness.

The progress of such Bills depends on the Government finding time for debate and providing they are not 'talked out' of time. This occurred with the Bill introduced by Dr Richard Berry in the House of Commons in March 1994, which had the aim of outlawing discrimination against the disabled. In the result, the Government introduced its own measure, which was enacted as the Disability Discrimination Act 1995.

There have been many notable Private Members' Bills, including the Abortion Act 1967, the Video Recordings Act 1984, the Defamation Act 1952 and the Indecent Displays (Control) Act 1981. Since the 1960s, major reforms in the law have been made on moral issues, including the Murder (Abolition of the Death Penalty) Act 1965, reform of the divorce law, abortion, suicide and homosexuality. So far as the latter is concerned, the age of consent was reduced from 21 to 18 as a result of Edwina Currie's amendment to the Criminal Justice and Public Order Act 1994. The present Government wishes to see this further reduced to 16, although the House of Lords warned that the Criminal Justice Bill 1998 would be put in jeopardy if that provision was included. It was subsequently included in the Sexual Offences (Amendment) Bill, but has yet to become law.

Pressure groups and legislation

The part played by pressure groups should not be overlooked in bringing the need for reform to the attention of the public and in lobbying MPs. For example, Liberty (formerly the National Council for Civil Liberties), Justice, the Howard League for Penal Reform, the Legal Action Group and the Statute Law Reform Society are bodies concerned with law reform. It is not always easy to distinguish 'pressure' and 'interest' groups. The former are those with a 'cause', such as prison reform, nuclear disarmament, protection of endangered species or divorce reform. The latter represent a body or group such as The Law Society, the Trades Union Congress, the British Medical Council, local authorities, the Royal Automobile Club or Automobile Association or the Confederation of Business Industry.

A recent Private Member's Bill, sponsored by Alan Beith, attempted to encourage energy conservation and had received the support of all the main conservation and environmental groups, including Friends of the Earth. However, the Government did not support the Bill (which would have imposed a duty on all local authorities to carry out an energy efficiency audit on all dwellings in their area), on the ground that it would have created an unnecessary burden on local authorities and increased costs on taxpayers. The Junior Environment Minister, Tony Baldry, talked out the Bill by tabling some 200 amendments. The Government assured the House of Commons that there were better ways of improving energy conservation and that Britain was on target to comply with the objectives agreed at the Rio Earth Summit in June 1992 on emissions into the atmosphere.

The issue of time and Government control of business in the House of Commons (and, to a lesser extent, in the House of Lords) is an important one, not only in relation to Private Members' Bills, but for legislation generally.

Governments in recent years have controlled business by such devices as the guillotine, which limits the amount of time devoted to debating the provisions of a Bill. This is not the only way in which poorly drafted legislation might result. Sometimes, the Government passes legislation to fill a gap or deal with an immediate problem. This was the case with the Insolvency (No 2) Bill 1994, which passed all its stages in one week from the announcement by the Secretary of State of the intention to introduce the Bill. The Act was passed to remedy the undesired effects of a judicial decision, but it is now feared that the Act itself will give rise to interpretation difficulties, not having been fully thought through. Other illustrations are the Dangerous Dogs Act 1991, the Offensive Weapons Act 1996 and the Knives Act 1997. Another controversial measure is the Pollution Prevention and Control Act 1999.

As we have seen when considering statutory interpretation, the courts will have a role to play in interpreting legislation and, following *Pepper v Hart* (1993), *Hansard*, the official journal of proceedings in Parliament, may be consulted in limited circumstances.

A distinction is usually made between 'codification' and 'consolidation'. The former involves re-writing a body of law (both statutes and case law), for example, the Sale of Goods Act 1893, the Theft Act 1968, the Bills of Exchange Act 1882 and the Partnership Act 1890. Consolidation involves reducing the number of statutes on a particular subject to a more manageable number. An example is the Employment Protection (Consolidation) Act 1978, which has, of course, now been supplemented by later Employment Acts, necessitating a new consolidating measure. The Consolidation of Enactments (Procedure) Act 1949 provides for consolidation measures. Increasingly, the Government seems little concerned with consolidation and even less with codification, with the result that the proverbial statute book is very cluttered.

The European context

Another means by which our law may be reformed is as a result of our membership of the European Union. A clear illustration, following the *Factortame* case, which demonstrates that European law takes precedence over domestic law, is the case of *R v Secretary of State for Employment ex p Equal Opportunities Commission* (1994), where the House of Lords held that the provisions of the Employment Protection (Consolidation) Act 1978, applying to part time workers, were incompatible with European Union law and that the Equal Opportunities Commission was entitled to judicial review, in the form of a declaration against the Secretary of State for Employment. The House of Lords decided that it was not necessary to refer the matter to the ECJ under Art 177 of the Treaty of Rome (now Art 234 of the EC Treaty), as it was competent to hear the matter itself.

Other areas which have been subject to the influence of European Union law and policy include the protection of the environment, pollution, and also regulation of companies, consumer and employee protection and quality standards for goods and services.

Reform may also be achieved as a result of the European Convention of Human Rights, especially now that this has been given binding effect in the UK by means of the Human Rights Act 1998 (in force October 2000). In the past, the continued failure of governments to ratify the Convention gave rise to calls for constitutional reform and the need for a Bill of Rights (and possibly a written constitution), enforceable through the courts of the UK, to protect the civil liberties of the citizen against governmental abuse of power. No such reform was forthcoming, given the arguments about the role of the courts and the doctrine of sovereignty of Parliament. However, following the general election in May 1997, the Labour Government announced its intention of bringing the Convention into effect in domestic law and to instigate constitutional reform. The Human Rights Act 1998 provides a compromise to the question of parliamentary supremacy by providing in s 4 that, if a court is satisfied that a provision in an Act is not compatible with a right under the European Convention on Human Rights, it may make a declaration of incompatibility. It will then be for the Government to bring before Parliament amending legislation, and this is provided for in s 10 and Sched 2 to the Act. Section 19 of the Act provides that a minister, in promoting a Bill in either House of Parliament, must, before the second reading, make a statement of compatibility or, if unable to do so, a statement that the Government nevertheless wishes the House to proceed with the Bill. This Act will no doubt give rise to much litigation, as parties to actions call upon the provisions of the Act to aid their case. It has been suggested that ss 34–37 of the Criminal Justice and Public Order Act 1994, amending the right to silence, will be questioned in this way. Furthermore, following a case in Scotland, where the Act is already in force, the independence and impartiality of sheriffs has been called into question and has been found to be wanting. When the Act comes into force in England, it may be that the role of the Lord Chancellor in all three areas of government – legislative, judicial and executive – may be called into question.

Some areas in need of reform

There are a number of other issues in need of legal reform, and this will necessitate one or more of the reform bodies referred to preparing proposals, and for Parliament then to pass legislation to give effect to them. It is unlikely that the courts will be able to effect such wide ranging reforms, given their traditional reluctance to involve themselves with policy issues other than in extreme situations or where traditionally Parliament has not passed legislation.

One issue which was the subject of debate for many years was the 'year and a day' rule in homicide. For a defendant to be prosecuted, it had to be proved that the victim died within a year and a day of the infliction of harm. The Law Commission proposed reform to take account of improvements in medical science and treatment, in particular the use of life support machines enabling patients to be kept artificially alive for long periods. The Law Reform (Year and a Day Rule) Act 1996 abolished the 'year and a day' rule. No proceedings for a fatal offence (murder, manslaughter, infanticide or any offence where an element is the causing of death, such as dangerous driving resulting in death) may be started without the Attorney General's consent if either the injury which is alleged to have caused death occurred more than three years before death or the defendant has previously been convicted of an offence in circumstances alleged to be connected with the death. Aiding, abetting, counselling or procuring a suicide is included in the definition of fatal offence.

The question of property rights for cohabitees – heterosexual and homosexual – was also referred to the Law Commission and the need to review the law in the face of the highest divorce rate in Europe and the fact that many couples decide not to marry. The Law Society, representing solicitors in England and Wales, endorses the view that the law governing homosexual couples should be identical to that of married couples. The Law Commission has also recommended that where, in a homosexual relationship, one partner is financially dependent on the other and that other dies, as the result of the negligence of another, the surviving partner should be able to claim damages for the tort of negligence.

We have already mentioned the Royal Commission on Criminal Justice, which made 352 recommendations for reform of the criminal justice system in July 1993. Sections 34–37 of the Criminal Justice and Public Order Act 1994 remove the right to silence and allow the court to draw adverse inferences from a defendant's silence. The then Government took the view that, on policy grounds, the judge should be able to comment on a defendant's silence during investigation where, for example, the defendant attempts to rely on information known to him or her earlier. The right to silence has been described as a 'criminal's charter', and it has been said that those who have nothing to hide have nothing to fear by answering police questions. It might be argued that this effectively dismantles the fundamental presumption that a person is innocent until proved guilty. This view was endorsed in *R v Condron and Another* (1997), but this case has been challenged in the ECHR (in *Condron and Another v UK* (2000)).

The reform proposed by the Royal Commission to create a criminal cases review body has been brought into effect by s 8 and Sched 1 to the Criminal Appeal Act 1995. The Criminal Cases Review Commission started work in March 1997.

As a result of the calling of the general election in May 1997, there was the need for Parliament to pass into law Bills in progress at that time. Some of the notable Acts passed at this time included the Firearms (Amendment) Act 1997, the Knives Act 1997, the Justices of the Peace Act 1997, the Criminal Evidence (Amendment) Act 1997 and the Police Act 1997. In the two years since the Labour Government came to power, the legislative programme has included constitutional reforms and freedom of information, the granting of devolution to Scotland and Wales, further restrictions on the use of handguns in the wake of the Dunblane tragedy, the possible imposition of a ban on hunting and the proposed right to roam in the countryside in the Wildlife and Countryside Bill.

Several other issues have highlighted the need for reform, for example, the question of selective abortion where a woman, pregnant with twins, decided to abort one and later gave birth to the other. Mandy Allwood also received much press attention when she became pregnant with eight foetuses but nature took its course and she lost all of them. The issue of surrogacy is also in debate where a surrogate mother decided to keep the child as her own and not hand it, when born, to the Dutch couple with whom she had agreed to act as surrogate mother for a payment of £12,000 for expenses. The donor of the sperm in such a case has no legal rights to the child. The position of the father of an unborn child has also come to public attention in the recent case in Scotland of the man who wished to stop the abortion of a 12 week old foetus which his estranged wife asserted that she had full legal right to do. In the event, the father decided not to appeal to the House of Lords, but this could open up the question for appeal in the future.

One other case which has demonstrated that the law may need reform is the case of Diane Blood, whose husband died in a coma without having given written consent for his sperm to be used. Although his sperm had been unlawfully obtained and could not be used by Mrs Blood in the UK, she was permitted to seek treatment in Belgium, where written consent is not required. The Court of Appeal ruled that the Human Embryology and Fertilisation Authority was right to withhold treatment, but had failed to take account of Mrs Blood's rights under EC law. The Authority was asked to reconsider its decision so as to take this into account. Having done so, the Authority acceded that Mrs Blood would be permitted to export the sperm to Belgium and to have treatment there. Other instances have since arisen where this Authority has refused consent for the use of sperm. Additionally, women who have had embryos frozen before undertaking cancer treatment have also questioned the right of the Authority to refuse its consent for their use. It has been suggested that legal regulation is required to prevent women who wish to continue with their careers from having embryos frozen so as to allow them to have a family later in life.

Conclusion

In conclusion, it can be seen from the above that reform of the law is often slow and piecemeal and that there is no one body charged with its reform and development. One thing that has become noticeable in recent years is that individuals or groups who wish to see reform of a particular area of law or the creation of law have become much more professional in their approach as to the means of achieving their aims. We have mentioned pressure and interest groups, and it is useful also to note the efforts of investigative journalists who highlight flaws and failings in the law. It is through publicity that public awareness can be increased and for a debate to take place as to what end should be achieved and by what means.

Given that law is not an end in itself, but rather a means to an end, it is right that not only lawyers and judges should be concerned with law reform, but also members of the public for whose benefit law exists. On a practical level, law reform is essential to remove clutter and to ensure that finding and understanding the law is as straightforward as possible.

In a common law system where there is no reliance on codes and which is based on judicial precedent, one of the major criticisms is that the law has become too complex, not only in substance, but also in form. Consolidating statutes should reduce this problem, but lack of parliamentary time is often mentioned as a reason for the few consolidating measures passed. The judges also have limited powers to reform the law, given their adherence to *stare decisis* and the fact that legislation is only interpreted when a dispute brings the meaning of a provision into doubt. We do not have a constitutional court with the power to measure legislation against the principles of a written constitution and thereby ensure that changes in the law are in line with the constitution. We have noted, however, that, in the past, many of the developments in the law arose as a result of judicial decisions and that this is still the case in special circumstances where the court feels compelled to break new ground on a serious issue rather than wait for Parliament to pass legislation. The judges are, however, guarded in the use of such power, often stating that Parliament determines policy as the representative of the general public and that the courts are ill-suited to this task. Residual power may, however, exist in the courts to reform the law in pressing cases and where parliamentary action is not likely.

THE SOURCES OF LAW

Distinguishing between sources of law

- Literary and historical sources.

- Principal and subsidiary sources:
  - principal sources – legislation, delegated legislation, case law and EC law;
  - subsidiary sources – custom, Roman law, ecclesiastical law and books of authority.

Legislation

- Public and private Bills should be distinguished.

- Private Bills must not be confused with Private Members' Bills.

- Private Members are subject to the Ten Minute Rule.

- Delegated legislation takes effect under enabling Acts. Challenging the validity of delegated legislation – judicial review procedure on the ground of *ultra vires*.

The doctrine of precedent

- Precedent develops as a result of the hierarchy of the courts and accurate and efficient law reporting.

- The hierarchy of the courts: House of Lords; Court of Appeal (Criminal and Civil Divisions); High Court and divisional courts; Crown Court; county courts; magistrates' courts.

European Community law

- UK membership of the EC: European Communities Act 1972; the European Communities (Amendment) Acts 1986 and 1993.

- Membership of the EC has implications on the doctrine of supremacy of Parliament (*Mortensen v Peters* (1906)).

The institutions of the European Union

- The Council of Ministers; the Commission; the Parliament and the ECJ.

- The Court of First Instance was set up in 1989 to ease the burden on the Court.

- Article 234 of the EC Treaty – preliminary rulings – guidelines in *Bulmer v Bollinger* (1974).

The application of European Community law

- ECJ's view: precedence of EC law over domestic law – *Costa v ENEL* (1964); the *Internationale* case (1970); *Van Gend en Loos* (1963); *R v Secretary of State for Employment v Equal Opportunities Commission* (1994).

- UK courts' view following *Factortame* and the European Communities (Amendment) Act 1993, despite the doctrine of parliamentary supremacy.

- Regulations are directly applicable: Art 249 of the EC Treaty.

- Directives may be directly effective; distinction between vertical and horizontal direct effect.

- *Marshall v Southampton and SW Hants AHA* (1984); *Von Colson* (1983); *Marleasing SA v La Commercial Int* (1989); *Francovich v Italian Republic* (1992).

- *R v Secretary of State for Transport ex p Factortame (No 4)* (1996).

- Treaty provisions may be directly effective (both vertically and horizontally) – *Van Gend en Loos* (1963); *Defrenne v Sabena* (1975)).

Law reform

- The Law Commission.

- Other reform bodies: Law Reform Committee; Criminal Law Revision Committee; Royal Commissions and Advisory Committees; judicial inquiries (for example, McPherson Inquiry into the death of Stephen Lawrence).

- The Human Rights Act 1998, incorporating the European Convention of Human Rights into UK.

CHAPTER 3

THE COURTS AND THEIR PERSONNEL

The court system

Classifying the courts

Although we often talk of 'the courts' as if to imply a uniform and precise group, this is not always the case. The courts comprise a hierarchy, within which each court has a separate jurisdiction regulating its powers, type of business and personnel. The hierarchy of the courts is best explained by way of a diagram.

Figure 3.1 sets out the structure of the civil and criminal courts with the avenues of appeal.

Figure 3.1

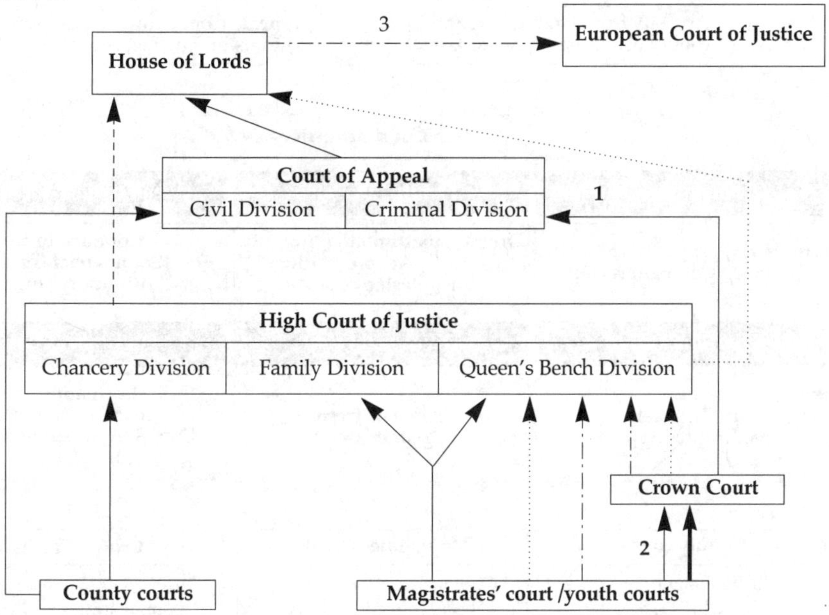

Key

➤ Main avenues of appeal	**1** Appeals against jury decisions only (Criminal Appeal Act 1968)
- - - ➤ Leapfrog appeal (Pt II of the Administration of Justice Act 1969)	
·········➤ Appeals by way of case stated (s 1 of the Administration of Justice Act 1960)	**2** Defendant can appeal against convictions and/or sentence if pleaded not guilty. If pleaded guilty, can only appeal against sentence
➤ Committals	
—·—·➤ Application for judicial review	**3** Article 234 preliminary reference

Figure 3.2 illustrates the types of business dealt with.

Figure 3.2

House of Lords	European Court of Justice
Appeals on points of law of general public importance with leave from Court of Appeal and High Court. Also civil appeals from Scotland and appeals from Northern Ireland	Article 234 applications for preliminary rulings on European Union law

	Judicial Committee of the Privy Council
	Appeals from Commonwealth States and some domestic tribunals

Court of Appeal	
Civil Division	**Criminal Division**
Appeals from High Court and county courts on points of law	Appeals from Crown Court jury trials on law/fact/sentence

High Court of Justice		
Chancery Division	**Family Division**	**Queen's Bench Division**
Trusts, tax, property, contested probate, Companies court	Divorce, matrimonial property, Children Act proceedings, uncontested probate	Contract, tort, Commercial court, Admiralty court
Divisional Court	**Divisional Court**	**Divisional Court**
IRC appeals, bankruptcy appeals	Appeals from magistrates' court	Case stated appeals from magistrates' courts and Crown Court supervisory jurisdiction

County courts	Magistrates' courts	Crown Courts
Small claims and fast track CPR 1998 £5,000 small claims limit £15,000 fast track limit	Civil jurisdiction – family licensing, council tax Criminal – summary trials and committals for triable either way offences s 51 of the Crime and Disorder Act 1998 Youth court	Jury trials, appeals from magistrates' courts Three tiers of court, four classes of offence

Figure 3.3 sets out the personnel of each court and is considered later in the chapter.

Figure 3.3

European Court of Justice
15 judges and nine advocates general

House of Lords
Lord Chancellor, Lords of Appeal in Ordinary, minimum three, usually five. 12 appointments

Judicial Committee of the Privy Council
Lord Chancellor and judicial office holders who are Privy Councillors

Court of Appeal
35 Lord Justices of Appeal

Civil Division
Master of the Rolls Lord Justices of Appeal

Criminal Division
Lord Chief Justice Lord Justices of Appeal *Puisne* judges

High Court of Justice
106 *puisne* judges

Chancery Division	**Family Division**	**Queen's Bench Division**
Vice Chancellor *puisne* judges	President *puisne* judges	Lord Chief Justice *puisne* judges
Divisional Court	**Divisional Court**	**Divisional Court**

County courts	Magistrates' courts	Crown Courts
Circuit judge District judge	Two to seven lay magistrates One stipendiary magistrate Justice's clerk	Puisne judges Circuit judges Recorders Magistrates – two to four to hear appeals only
	Youth court	

It is usual to classify the courts into those exercising criminal jurisdiction and those exercising civil jurisdiction. In the main this is useful, but some courts exercise both criminal and civil functions, for example, the magistrates' courts and the Queen's Bench Division of the High Court. The latter is primarily a civil court, but has an important supervisory jurisdiction in criminal matters by way of judicial review or case stated.

Courts can be classified according to whether they exercise appellate functions, or are first instance or trial courts. However, in the case of the High Court and the Crown Court, both functions are exercised, for example, the Crown Court may hear appeals from magistrates' courts and try indictable (the most serious) offences. Courts can also be classified into superior and inferior courts. The former include the Crown Court, the High Court, the Court of Appeal and the House of Lords, which have unlimited jurisdiction. The latter include the magistrates' courts and the county courts, which have limited jurisdiction, in criminal matters according to the seriousness of the offence, and in civil matters according to the track to which the claim is allocated. The High Court exercises a supervisory jurisdiction over inferior courts and tribunals and, for this purpose the Crown Court, when exercising its appellate jurisdiction, is also subject to supervision by the High Court.

When considering the composition and structure of the courts, it is also useful to note the role of the European Court of Justice (ECJ) in interpreting European law and hearing preliminary references made to it by domestic courts under Art 234 of the EC Treaty (formerly Art 177 of the Treaty of Rome). UK courts are now bound by decisions on the European Convention on Human Rights, following its incorporation into UK law by the Human Rights Act 1998. From October 2000, it is no longer necessary for litigants who wish to rely on the provisions of the Convention to petition the European Court of Human Rights (ECHR), as all domestic courts will be bound to apply the provisions of the Act giving effect to the Convention.

The part played in the administration of justice by tribunals is also worthy of note, as is the role of specialist courts such as coroners' courts, the Judicial Committee of the Privy Council, the Court of Protection and the Restrictive Practices Court. We will now take each court in turn and consider its role in the hierarchy.

The House of Lords

The House of Lords developed from the *Curia Regis* (King's Council), and dates from Norman times. It is the highest appeal court in the UK: appeals come from Northern Ireland, England and Wales and Scotland; although, in the case of Scotland, only in civil matters.

The Appellate Jurisdiction Act 1876 provided for the appointment of salaried life peers to hear appeals. These are known as the Law Lords, but their full title is that of Lords of Appeal in Ordinary. Their number has gradually been increased to the present maximum of 12. Lay peers may not participate in the judicial sittings of the House and, by convention, when the Law Lords participate in debates concerned with controversial non-legal matters, they do so in a personal capacity.

So far as appeals from England and Wales are concerned, the House of Lords in its judicial capacity hears appeals from the Court of Appeal (Civil Division) on points of law of general public importance, but leave is required from the Court of Appeal or the House of Lords' Appeals Committee.

By ss 12–15 of the Administration of Justice Act 1969, a leapfrog procedure is provided, allowing an appeal from the High Court, in its capacity as a trial court, directly to the House of Lords. The trial judge has a discretion to certify a point of law of general public importance concerning the construction of legislation or the effect of a binding precedent. Permission of the House of Lords is required and both parties must consent.

In criminal cases, the prosecution or the defence may appeal from the Court of Appeal or the Queen's Bench Divisional Court under s 33 of the Criminal Appeal Act 1968, providing the leave of the House of Lords or the court below is obtained and a point of law of general public importance is certified by the lower court and either court is satisfied that the case should be considered by the House of Lords.

Decisions of the House of Lords are binding on all other courts and, until the Practice Statement of 1966, the House of Lords considered itself bound by its own previous decisions. It now departs from such a decision where it sees fit to do so, for example, where a past decision is found to be *per incuriam*, although this power is exercised with caution so as ensure a measure of certainty in the law.

The House of Lords is no longer the supreme legal authority in European Union matters. A reference under Art 234 to the ECJ will determine the application of European law, and this was clearly demonstrated in *R v Secretary of State ex p Factortame and Others (No 2) (1990).*

The Court of Appeal

The Criminal Appeal Act 1968 abolished the Court of Criminal Appeal and provided for the establishment of Civil and Criminal Divisions. The former hears appeals on questions of law from the High Court and on law and fact from the county court. If an appeal is successful, the court may reverse the lower court's decision, amend it, or order a retrial. The Court of Appeal comprises the Lord Chancellor, Lord Chief Justice, Master of the Rolls, President of the Family Division and the Vice Chancellor, together with 35 Lord Justices of Appeal.

The Criminal Division hears appeals from decisions of the Crown Court in its capacity as a trial court. It has no part to play in appeals from magistrates' courts or Crown Court appellate decisions. An appeal from the Crown Court may be against conviction or sentence and concern law or fact. By s 1 of the Criminal Appeal Act 1995, all appeals against conviction and sentence must either have leave of the Court of Appeal or a certificate of fitness for appeal from the trial judge before an appeal can be made. Section 2 requires the Court of Appeal to allow an appeal against a verdict under s 12 (insanity), conviction under s 1 of the 1968 Act, or finding of disability, if it thinks that the conviction, verdict or finding is 'unsafe'.

Section 3 of the Criminal Appeal Act 1995 repeals s 17 of the Criminal Appeals Act 1968, which permitted the Home Secretary to make a reference to the Court of Appeal following a conviction on indictment or on a finding of not guilty by reason of insanity.

Section 36 of the Criminal Justice Act 1972 provides for an Attorney General's reference on a point of law to the Court of Appeal following an acquittal of a defendant for an opinion on the point of law in question. The acquittal will not be disturbed, but the point of law can be clarified. Leave is not required.

Sections 35 and 36 of the Criminal Justice Act 1988 provide for a reference by the Attorney General to the Court of Appeal for a review where he considers that an unduly lenient sentence was passed. This is only available for indictable offences or an either way offence specified by an Order of the Home Secretary (of which there has been none made to date). Leave of the Court of Appeal is required. The Court of Appeal may quash the sentence and replace it with any appropriate sentence, up to the maximum available in the Crown Court, and a further reference to the House of Lords is possible. The case of *R v Harnett (AG's Reference (No 60 of 1996))* (1997) is authority for the proposition that the Attorney General may make a reference in respect either of a sentence which he considers unduly lenient or one which is too severe in his estimation.

Decisions of the Court of Appeal bind all lower courts. In civil matters, the Court of Appeal is bound by the House of Lords and its own previous decisions, unless one of the exceptions in *Young v Bristol Aeroplane Co Ltd* (1944) applies or where there is a conflict with EC law or a later conflicting decision of the ECJ. In criminal matters, the court will depart from its earlier decisions when it considers that it is in the interests of justice to do so, as stated in *R v Gould* (1968).

Major reform of civil court appeals and composition of the Court of Appeal (Civil Division) will come into effect in 2000 under ss 54–65 of the Access to Justice Act 1999. As mentioned in Chapter 7, the Bowman Report recommended changes in the constitution of the Court of Appeal (Civil Division) and in its jurisdiction to hear appeals. Following the Woolf reforms of the procedures in the High Court and county court, it was felt that appeals to the Court of Appeal should be reformed so as not to waste the benefits to be obtained from this streamlining of procedure. Section 54 provides that rules of court are to be prepared, requiring that permission to appeal to the county court, High Court and the Civil Division of the Court of Appeal should be obtained. Only limited exceptions will permit appeals without permission. Where permission is refused, an appellant may be permitted by rules of court to apply again for permission. By s 55, there will normally only be one level of appeal, except where the Court of Appeal considers it should hear an appeal because the case raises an important point of principle or practice or some other compelling reason is shown. Similarly, the Master of the Rolls or a lower court can pass such a case to the Court of Appeal to hear an appeal. The Lord Chancellor is empowered under s 56 to make an order to vary the appeal routes so that appeals go to the lowest appropriate level, after consulting with the Heads of Division – the Lord Chief Justice, Master of the Rolls, President of the Family Division and the Vice Chancellor of the Chancery Division. Any order will be subject to an affirmative resolution of the House of Commons. Section 57 states, however, that those cases which merit it should be heard in the Court of Appeal. By s 59, the usual number of three judges able to hear appeals can be varied so that a court may sit with one, two or more judges.

Divisional courts of the High Court

Divisional courts exercise the appellate function of the High Court. Each division of the High Court has a divisional court. Thus, the Queen's Bench Divisional Court hears appeals from the magistrates' court and the Crown Court by way of case stated and judicial review.

Section 111 of the Magistrates' Courts Act 1980 provides for an appeal by way of case stated where an error of law or an excess of jurisdiction is alleged. If prosecution or defence allege some illegality in the trial or appeal process, application is made for judicial review under RSC Ord 53 (see now the Civil Procedure Rules).

Some tribunals, including the Solicitors' Disciplinary Tribunal, may also have a right of appeal. An appeal by way of case stated involves the magistrates' court or Crown Court setting out their findings of fact and prosecution or defence, applying to the Queen's Bench Divisional Court for a determination of a question of law in dispute. Sections 61–65 of the Access to Justice Act 1999 permit judicial review applications, appeals by case stated and others to be heard by one High Court judge, instead of a divisional court of two or more judges. Complex cases will continue to be referred to a divisional court.

By s 54 of the Criminal Procedure and Investigations Act 1996, a 'tainted' acquittal can be quashed. This occurs when a convicted defendant is later convicted of conspiring to pervert the course of justice by interfering with the jury at the first trial.

The Family Divisional Court hears appeals from the magistrates' courts on matrimonial matters and the Chancery Divisional Court hears appeals from the county court in bankruptcy and tax matters.

Appeals are heard by two or three judges of the appropriate division. Decisions act as precedents for future cases, except in magistrates' courts, where an appeal against acquittal by the prosecution by way of case stated ensures the setting of clear legal precedent and the avoidance of backlogs.

In civil matters, the divisional courts are bound by their own decisions and the decisions of the higher courts. In turn, their decisions bind the High Court in the appropriate division and all lower courts.

An appeal by way of case stated lies to the House of Lords under s 1(1)(a) of the Administration of Justice Act 1960, providing leave is obtained and a point of law of general public importance is in question. This provision is amended by the Access to Justice Act 1999 to allow appeals from one High Court judge, instead of a divisional court.

By s 18(1) of the Supreme Court Act 1981, criminal matters are not to be dealt with on appeal to the Court of Appeal, but directly by the House of Lords under s 1 of the Administration of Justice Act 1960.

The High Court

The High Court, together with the Court of Appeal and the Crown Court, make up the Supreme Court of Judicature. As we have noted, the High Court is made up of the Queen's Bench, the Chancery and the Family Divisions.

In November 1999, the Lord Chancellor sought parliamentary permission to increase the number of High Court judges from 98 to 106. By far the biggest division is the Queen's Bench, with over 60 *puisne* judges. The Queen's Bench Division is the busiest, trying large numbers of cases in contract and tort, particularly personal injury claims. It has a residual jurisdiction over all cases which are not dealt with by the other divisions.

The Commercial Court was established by the Administration of Justice Act 1970 as a separate court. Within this division, the judges are empowered to act as arbitrators. In addition, there is an Admiralty Court.

As we have noted before, this division exercises a supervisory jurisdiction over inferior courts and tribunals and regulates the actions of public bodies by way of judicial review. The prerogative writ of habeas corpus and the orders of certiorari, prohibition and mandamus may be granted in appropriate circumstances.

The Chancery Division deals with contested probate matters, trusts, mortgages, bankruptcy, company and partnership, sales of property and taxation matters. In addition, there is a separate Patents Court and a Companies Court.

The Family Division has jurisdiction over matrimonial matters, including dissolution of marriage, wardship, adoption and guardianship of minors. It also deals with uncontested probate matters.

The High Court is based in the Strand in London, but in addition sits in some 15 regional centres, and the judges of the High Court travel on circuit to the regions.

The Crown Court

The Courts Act 1971 abolished Quarter Sessions and Assizes and replaced them with the Crown Court, which tries indictable offences and triable either way offences where the defendant elects jury trial rather than summary trial in the magistrates' court. Regarding the former, trial of adults in the Crown Court has traditionally followed committal proceedings in the magistrates court, but s 51 of the Crime and Disorder Act 1998 has abolished committals for trial for indictable offences, and they will in future be dealt with only in the Crown Court. During 1999, pilot schemes have operated in some courts to monitor this change.

There may be a tactical advantage for a defendant electing trial by jury in the Crown Court. This is most often used in cases of theft where the defendant, or his or her defence counsel, may feel more confident of an acquittal before a jury compared with a case-hardened magistrate. The Runciman Royal Commission recommended in 1993 that the right of the defendant to elect jury trial should be limited, but this was not included in the Criminal Justice and Public Order Act 1994. In the Narey Review of Delay in the Criminal Justice System, published by the Home Office in April 1997, four options were identified. These were to retain the defendant's right of election for jury trial as it is, or to reclassify offences into indictable or summary offences, or to remove the defendant's election when he/she is charged with an offence similar to one for which he/she has been earlier convicted, or to abolish the right of election. This last option took two forms: either only the magistrates should be able to decide the trial venue after hearing representations by the defence and prosecution; or where, failing agreement by both sides, the magistrates decide on the trial venue. The Home Secretary has presented to Parliament the Mode of Trial Bill, in which it will be for the magistrates only to decide on trial venue, after hearing representations by both sides. These proposals have been the subject of much criticism from The Law Society, the Bar Council and others.

By the Criminal Justice Act 1988, the right of the defence to make challenges of potential jury members (known as the right to a peremptory challenge) was removed, with the result that the defence can now only make challenges by showing good reason. The Crown can, however, make challenges to potential jurors by asking a juror in waiting 'to stand by for the Crown'.

The Supreme Court Act 1981 regulates the Crown Courts' work. Crown Courts also have limited civil jurisdiction, mainly in licensing matters. The Crown Court also hears appeals from magistrates' courts and has the power to sentence defendants tried summarily for offences triable either way where the sentencing powers of the magistrates' courts are insufficient. This is governed by s 38 of the Magistrates' Courts Act 1980, as amended by s 25 of the Criminal Justice Act 1990. It applies to defendants aged 18 or over where the magistrates are of the opinion that the offence, or combination of offences associated with it, are so serious as to warrant a greater punishment than is within their power, or that a term of imprisonment longer than the court can impose is necessary to protect the public from serious harm where a violent or sexual offence has been committed by a defendant aged 21 or over.

Magistrates, two to four in number, may sit in the Crown Court to assist the judge in an appeal from the magistrates' court, but, so far as committals for sentence are concerned, their right to sit has been removed. This was thought necessary given the changes in procedure under s 49 of the Criminal Procedure and Investigations Act 1996, whereby defendants must plead guilty or not guilty before the decision is made as to trial venue. A defendant who pleads not guilty to a triable either way offence and who is then tried summarily and found guilty, and the defendant who pleads guilty, face being committed for sentencing to the Crown Court. The result has been that magistrates have been sentencing in more serious cases in the Crown Court than in the past, when more serious triable either way offences were committed for trial in the Crown Court. The problem with this was that many of those defendants, on being committed for trial, at the last moment changed their pleas to guilty.

The Access to Justice Act 1999 places appeals from the Crown Court by case stated to the High Court on a statutory basis for the first time.

The county court

County courts are governed by the County Courts Act 1984 as amended, and are presided over by a circuit judge, who normally sits alone. There are 539 of these, and some 250 county courts exist in England and Wales, administered by 337 district judges. Section 74 of the Courts and Legal Services Act 1990 removed the office of Registrar, and this was replaced by that of district judge with effect from 1 January 1991.

The county court is a local court which traditionally had a limited jurisdiction, determined by way of geographical area and the value of the claim. The High Court and County Courts Jurisdiction Order 1991, made under ss 1 and 120 of the Courts and Legal Services Act 1990 by the Lord Chancellor, abolished many of the financial limits on county court jurisdiction, and stipulated higher limits in some cases, laying down criteria for determining where proceedings were to commence, be tried and enforced. Most claims below £25,000 and equity and probate matters up to £30,000 were to be tried in the county court. Personal injury claims up to £50,000 and claims of between £25,000 and £50,000 not involving complex law or fact could also be tried in the county court, as could straightforward claims over £50,000 which had been started in the High Court and transferred to the county court.

The small claims procedure was used for claims up to £3,000 in value (or up to £1,000 for personal injury claims) in value unless the court decided the case was too difficult. For claims in excess of £3,000 (or £1,000 in personal injury claims), this informal procedure could still be used if either party wished and the court approved.

The jurisdiction of the county court and the High Court is now governed by the Civil Procedure Act 1997 and Rules 1998 (as amended). The county court has unlimited jurisdiction in tort and contract and the High Court can hear personal injury claims of £50,000 or more, other claims worth more than £15,000, where statute provides, and where a specialist matter is listed in one of the specialist courts in the High Court, for example, the Commercial Court. As a result of the Woolf reforms of the civil justice system, cases are assigned to the small claims track, the fast track or are multitrack cases, the procedures of the county court and High Court having been merged. More will be said about the litigation tracks in Chapter 7. The small claims procedure provides an informal procedure where a party appears in person or is assisted by a layperson. It is not usual to have legal representation and, in any event, costs for legal representation are not awarded. It is an alternative to the formal and more expensive county court trial. Most small claims involve sale or supply of goods and services, debt or accident claims.

Section 11 of the Courts and Legal Services Act 1990 provides a framework for the removal of restrictions on lay representation in county court claims. By s 11(1), the Lord Chancellor is empowered to make orders removing any such restrictions on representation by laypersons, sometimes referred to as 'McKenzie friends' (from the case of McKenzie v McKenzie (1971)).

The magistrates' court

Magistrates' courts hear some 98% of all criminal cases and, in addition, have limited civil jurisdiction in matrimonial and licensing matters. By s 10 of the Courts and Legal Services Act 1990, provision is made for civil jurisdiction in family proceedings under the Children Act 1989.

Some 560 magistrates' courts exist throughout England and Wales, staffed by lay or stipendiary magistrates or, as they have traditionally been called, justices of the peace. The Access to Justice Act 1999 merges the metropolitan and provisional benches of stipendiary magistrates and stipendiaries are re-named district judges (magistrates' courts). In larger towns and cities, stipendiary magistrates sit alone to decide cases, whereas lay magistrates usually form a bench of three, but any number between two and seven may sit. They are advised by a clerk to the justices, but he or she can only offer advice as to the law and cannot assist the magistrates in reaching their decisions. In 1992, some 29,000 lay magistrates and 76 stipendiary magistrates had been appointed.

As we have already seen, offences fall into one of three categories:

- indictable;

- triable either way; and

- summary offences.

The magistrates' court can try summary offences and those which are triable either way where the defendant does not elect trial by jury in the Crown Court. Sections 31, 32 and 133 of the Magistrates' Courts Act 1980 set out the magistrates' sentencing powers. The maximum sentence which can be imposed for a triable either way offence listed in Sched 1 to the Magistrates' Courts Act 1980 and which is tried summarily is generally £5,000 and/or six months' imprisonment for any one offence. Triable either way offences not listed in Sched 1 are subject to a sentence of imprisonment of six months or the maximum period provided for in the Magistrates' Courts Act 1980, whichever is less; whereas the maximum fine that can be imposed is the greater of £5,000 or the amount provided for in the Magistrates' Court Acts 1980.

For summary offences, s 37 of the Criminal Justice Act 1982, as amended by s 17 of the Criminal Justice Act 1991, imposes a standard scale of fines, ranging from £200 to £5,000.

As already noted, s 38 of the Magistrates' Courts Act (as amended) provides for committal for sentence to the Crown Court. Magistrates are no longer able to sit in the Crown Court to assist the judge on committals for sentence.

In the case of indictable offences, the magistrates formerly held committal proceedings to examine the evidence against the defendant and establish whether a *prima facie* case had been made out by the prosecution, warranting jury trial in the Crown Court. By s 51 of the Crime and Disorder Act 1998, a person charged with an indictable offence will appear for the first time in the Crown Court. Pilot schemes are continuing to monitor the effects of this change.

Lord Runciman recommended in 1993 that all committal hearings should be abolished, but s 44 of the Criminal Procedure and Investigations Act 1996 (this repealed s 44 of Criminal Justice and Public Order Act 1994, which never took effect but, if it had, would have replaced committals with a transfer for trial procedure) provides a modified procedure so that only written statements, depositions and other documents and exhibits may be brought into evidence by the prosecution. A defendant is only committed for trial now where, at the outset, he has pleaded not guilty or following a mode of trial hearing in an offence triable either way, he elects for jury trial. The Mode of Trial Bill now before Parliament will remove the right of the defendant to elect jury trial and the decision as to venue will be the magistrates'.

A s 6(1) committal, or what used to be called an old style or full committal, will now involve the reading aloud of written statements and (at the court's direction) a summary of statements not read out.

A s 6(2) committal, or what used to be called a new style or paper committal, will involve no consideration of prosecution evidence on the basis that all evidence is in writing, the defendant is legally represented and does not wish to submit that the evidence is insufficient to try the defendant.

Appeals from magistrates' courts lie to the Crown Court against sentence only where the defendant pleaded guilty, and against both conviction and sentence where he or she pleaded not guilty (s 108 of the Magistrates' Courts Act 1980). Appeals also lie to the Queen's Bench Divisional Court by the prosecution or the defence for judicial review or by way of case stated. By ss 61–65 of the Administration of Justice Act 1999, appeals to one High Court judge in place of two divisional court judges will be allowed in routine matters. Section 60 of the Administration of Justice Act 1960 is also amended to allow appeals heard by one High Court judge to go to the House of Lords.

Magistrates also try cases in youth courts, formerly juvenile courts (renamed by s 70 of the Criminal Justice Act 1991), against those under 18 years of age (s 68). By s 34 of the Crime and Disorder Act 1998, the *doli incapax* rule has been abolished, with the result that children from the age of 10 can be made liable in criminal law. This will be considered fully in Chapter 9.

By s 24(1) of the Magistrates' Courts Act 1980, a juvenile must be tried summarily except in the case of homicide; where he or she is jointly charged with an adult who is to be tried on indictment and the magistrates consider it is in the interests of justice to commit them both for trial; or the juvenile is 14 and is charged with an offence punishable with 14 years' imprisonment or more.

The presumption is that juveniles are to be tried summarily in the youth court, but, in limited circumstances, a juvenile may be tried in an adult's magistrates' court, for example, where he is jointly charged with an adult or proceedings started on the basis that he was an adult.

There are several important differences between a youth court and an adult magistrates' court. The former should sit at a different time and place from the ordinary court; the general public should be excluded; the bench must have three magistrates, one of whom should be a woman; reporting restrictions apply to details of the case and those involved; and the conduct of the proceedings is less formal. Amendments have been made by the Youth Justice and Criminal Evidence Act 1999 and these will be considered in Chapter 9, together with the power for magistrates to award anti-social behaviour orders under the Crime and Disorder Act 1998.

One of the most notorious cases to come before the courts in recent years was the trial of two 10 year old boys, Thompson and Venables, for the murder of the toddler James Bulger. At their trial in the Crown Court, both boys were sentenced to be detained at Her Majesty's pleasure with a recommendation that each serve a minimum of eight years to meet the requirement for punishment. The Lord Chief Justice then increased this to 10 years, and the

Home Secretary then increased the term further to 15 years. His decision was challenged by way of judicial review under RSC Ord 53 (see now the Civil Procedure Rules).

The Court of Appeal held in *R v Secretary of State for the Home Department ex p Venables and Thompson* (1996) that, although the Home Secretary has power to decide the tariff, on the facts of this case, he took into account extraneous factors, including public opinion, and must now reconsider the process by which he made his decision. In June 1997, the House of Lords held by a 3:2 majority that he acted unfairly when he treated the two youngsters in the same way as adult murderers and raised the minimum term to 15 years. They ruled that the Home Secretary had the power to set a provisional tariff but that it must be flexible to allow regular reviews. They also ruled that Mr Howard acted improperly in taking into account public petitions signed by 278,000 people and coupons from readers of *The Sun*. He should have ignored the 'high-voltage atmosphere of a newspaper campaign'. Lord Steyn added that such material was 'worthless' and incapable of telling him in a meaningful way the true state of informed public opinion based on all the material facts of the case.

Lord Browne-Wilkinson said the murder was a 'cruel and sadistic crime' which had given rise to much public concern and outrage. He backed the right of a Home Secretary to set a tariff to be served, but said it had to be flexible to allow him to reconsider the position in the light of the child's development and progress while in detention. He said Mr Howard had adopted a policy which totally excluded such factors from consideration during the tariff period:

> The unlawfulness lies in adopting a policy which totally excludes from consideration during the tariff period ... their progress and development, necessary to determine whether release from detention would be in the interests of the welfare of the applicants.

Any policy based on a tariff had to be flexible and should take into account retribution, deterrence and the welfare of the child.

The ECHR, late in 1999, in the *Thompson and Venables* case, ruled that trying children in an adult court was not lawful and that the Home Secretary had abused his powers, not only in this regard, but also in determining the tariff after taking into account public opinion. Substantial changes in the trial procedures for children and their detention are expected as a result of this decision. The ECHR applied their decision in *Singh and Hussain v UK* (1996), which concerned detention at Her Majesty's Pleasure and where it was held the Home Secretary did not have power to determine the tariff.

Other courts

At the outset, we mentioned some specialist courts, including the Judicial Committee of the Privy Council, Coroners' Courts, the Court of Protection and the Restrictive Practices Court. We will briefly consider each of these in turn.

The Judicial Committee of the Privy Council

The Judicial Committee of the Privy Council consists of all Privy Councillors who hold (or have held) high judicial office, including the Lord Chancellor and former occupants of this office, the Law Lords and Commonwealth judges.

Usually, five members sit to hear appeals from those few Commonwealth countries which have retained a right of appeal. It also hears appeals from Ecclesiastical Courts and domestic tribunals, including the General Medical Council. Its decisions are not binding either on itself or other UK courts, but are of great persuasive authority.

Coroners' Courts

Coroners investigate by way of inquest the cause of death where that death has been sudden, violent or unnatural. The death of prisoners, those in police custody and mental patients will also be investigated and a reason established for the cause of death.

The coroner, who must be a barrister, solicitor or medical doctor of at least five years' standing, may be assisted by a jury. Where it is suspected that death resulted from, for example, murder or manslaughter, poisoning or a road accident, a jury must be summoned.

The identity of the deceased is then established, and also the place and time of death. Various verdicts may be returned, including death by natural causes, misadventure, suicide or unlawful killing. Coroners are not able to return a verdict implicating any person in the murder or manslaughter of a deceased.

A case in point is the verdict of unlawful killing returned in connection with a serious road accident at Sowerby Bridge in Yorkshire, when several people were killed by a lorry that went out of control. The verdict can be used as evidence in any criminal prosecution brought by the Crown Prosecution Service (CPS) or a private individual, and in civil proceedings in the tort of negligence by relatives. The public judicial inquiry conducted by Sir William McPherson into the death of Stephen Lawrence in London in 1993 recommended that legal aid should be available to victims or their families to cover their representation at inquests and advance disclosure of documents as of right should be made to those parties who are allowed to attend an inquest. The inquiry highlighted many failings in the system of criminal justice, in particular the investigation of crime by the police, the abuse of the double jeopardy rule and the existence of what was termed 'institutionalised racism' in the Metropolitan Police Force. More will be said of these findings in Chapter 8.

Coroners also inquire into the ownership of property which is found and appears to have no owner. Gold, silver, coins, bullion and plate which have been hidden by someone unknown with the likely intention of returning to collect the hoard was formerly called treasure trove and, since the Treasure Act

1996, is now known simply as treasure. This, by default, passes into the ownership of the Crown. An inquest determines whether such items are treasure or were abandoned or lost, in which case the finder or the owner of the land or property on which they are found may have some claim to them.

The Court of Protection

The Court of Protection aims to protect and administer the property of those who are incapable of managing their affairs, owing to mental illness. The Mental Health Act 1983 provides for the appointment of judges of the Chancery Division to oversee the workings of the court. It is usual for close relatives of the patient to be appointed receiver of the property, which is then managed for the benefit of the patient. It also has power to administer the estates of those who die intestate (without a will) under specified values.

The Restrictive Practices Court

The Restrictive Practices Court investigates restrictive trading agreements between manufacturers of goods and those who provide services. The court is a superior court of record and its personnel are *puisne* judges of the High Court appointed by the Lord Chancellor, one judge from Scotland and one from Northern Ireland. They are assisted by up to 10 lay assessors, who are appointed by the Queen on the Lord Chancellor's recommendation and who have special knowledge or experience in industry.

One judge and two lay assessors sit to decide cases. Matters of law are decided by the judge. The lay assessors assist with questions of fact. The legislation with which the court is concerned includes the Restrictive Trade Practices Act 1976 and the Resale Prices Act 1976, as well as Arts 81 and 82 of the EC Treaty.

The personnel of the courts

Introduction

We have already mentioned in passing some of the personnel of the courts, but here we will treat each in greater detail and consider some of their roles. It will become clear that reference to the judges is not to a homogeneous group, but rather a disparate collection of individuals who work at different levels.

Two issues are of particular importance: the question of the selection and appointment of judges and their suitability for the roles performed; and the role of the judge in making decisions and in developing the law to meet changing needs. The first will be mentioned here, and the second in Chapter 6.

Lords of Appeal in Ordinary

Lords of Appeal in Ordinary are more usually referred to as Law Lords and, on appointment by the Queen on the Prime Minister's advice, become life peers. Prior to the Courts and Legal Services Act 1990, barristers of at least 15 years' standing, *puisne* judges in post for at least two years and Lords Justice of Appeal were eligible for appointment. Schedule 10 to the 1990 Act amends s 6 of the Appellate Jurisdiction Act 1876 so that those with the advocacy qualification will be eligible, based on rights of audience, for appointment.

It is usual for Lords Justice of Appeal to be appointed. They sit in the House of Lords and can perform both a judicial and a legislative function and are also members of the Judicial Committee of the Privy Council. There are at present 12.

The Lord Chancellor

More is said of the Lord Chancellor's office later, when we consider the judicial officers, but it is useful to note here that the Lord Chancellor, or, to give him his full title, the Lord High Chancellor of Great Britain, ranks eighth in the order of precedence after the Queen and this denotes the status of his office as being the head of the English judiciary, President of the Chancery Division of the High Court and of the House of Lords in its judicial capacity. He is a political appointee, and so, following the general election on 1 May 1997, Lord Irvine of Lairg succeeded Lord MacKay of Clashfern as the new Lord Chancellor.

He is appointed by the Queen on the Prime Minister's advice and performs functions in all three branches of government. In addition to being the head of the judiciary, he is a member of the Cabinet and is Speaker of the House of Lords. He sits in the Judicial Committee of the Privy Council and he advises the Queen on the appointment of *puisne*, circuit judges and recorders and appoints magistrates.

The Lord Chief Justice of England and Wales

The occupant of the Lord Chief Justice's office ranks next in importance to the Lord Chancellor and is appointed by the Queen on the advice of the Prime Minister and, on appointment, is made a life peer. He is head of the Queen's Bench Division of the High Court and the Criminal Division of the Court of Appeal. The present occupant is Lord Bingham.

The Master of the Rolls

The Master of the Rolls is also appointed by the Queen on the advice of the Prime Minister and is head of the Civil Division of the Court of Appeal. He is responsible for the admission of solicitors to the Roll of the Supreme Court. The present occupant is Lord Woolf.

Lord Justices of Appeal

Lord Justices sit in both divisions of the Court of Appeal and are appointed by the Queen on the advice of the Prime Minister. At present, there are 35 in number. Formerly, they were appointed from barristers of 15 years' standing or from High Court (puisne) judges, but s 71 and Sched 10 to the Courts and Legal Services Act 1990 provide for appointment from those with a 10 year High Court qualification or from judges of the High Court.

Judges of the High Court

High Court judges are also known as *'puisne'* judges (in the sense that they are not superior court judges) or justices of the High Court and are appointed by the Queen on the Lord Chancellor's advice. Formerly, barristers of at least 10 years' standing were eligible, but s 71 and Sched 10 to the Courts and Legal Services Act 1990 provide for appointment from those with a 10 year High Court qualification or from circuit judges in post for at least two years. There are at present 106 High Court judges assigned throughout the three divisions, and they hear the most serious offences in the Crown Court.

Circuit judges

These are appointed by the Crown on the advice of the Lord Chancellor, and formerly were barristers of at least 10 years' standing or recorders in post for at least five years. Section 16(3) of the Courts Act 1971 has been amended by s 71 and Sched 10 to the Courts and Legal Services Act 1990, and provides either a 10 year Crown Court or county court advocacy qualification. Recorders remain eligible and office holders, such as district judges and chairs of industrial tribunals, are eligible for appointment upon having been in post full time for at least three years. Circuit judges serve in the Crown Court and county court.

Recorders

Recorders are part time judges who sit in the Crown Court and who are appointed by the Crown on the advice of the Lord Chancellor. Formerly, barristers or solicitors of at least 10 years' standing were eligible, but, by s 71 and Sched 10 to the Courts and Legal Services Act 1990, appointment is based on a 10 year Crown Court or county court advocacy qualification. On appointment, a recorder is required by the Courts Act 1971 to sit for not less than one month each year.

District judges

District judges are appointed by the Lord Chancellor from solicitors of at least seven years' standing, and were formerly known as county court registrars. Section 74 of the Courts and Legal Services Act 1990 created the new title of district judge with effect from 1 January 1991.

Eligibility for appointment is now governed by s 71 and Sched 10 to the Courts and Legal Services Act 1990, which provides for a seven year general advocacy qualification. His or her main function is to act as a clerk in charge of the administration of the county court and operate the small claims arbitration procedure. In addition, he or she is empowered to decide other cases where the parties agree and where a point of law is not in question. Where the law is in dispute or the facts complex, the claim is decided by the county court judge.

Magistrates

As we have seen, magistrates are either unpaid voluntary appointees who form a bench of between two and seven members, or are stipendiary or paid magistrates who sit alone to decide cases in courts in London and other large cities. Part V of the Access to Justice Act 1999 reforms the organisation and management of the magistrates' courts, amending the Justices of the Peace Act 1997. As already noted, the metropolitan and provisional benches will merge and stipendiary magistrates will become known as district judges (magistrates' courts). A senior district judge (chief magistrate) will be appointed. The Lord Chancellor will be able to remove magistrates for 'incapacity or misbehaviour' and have the power to appoint deputy district judges (magistrates' courts). Part V also amends the provisions regarding the role of magistrates' clerks, whose primary task is to advise the magistrates of the law, but who will have administrative duties delegated to them by a new Justices' Chief Executive which will oversee the Magistrates' Courts Committees.

Lay magistrates can claim expenses for travelling, loss of earnings and subsistence, and are usually not qualified in the law. They are appointed by the Lord Chancellor under s 6 of the Justices of the Peace Act 1979, as amended by the Justices of the Peace Act 1997 (which consolidates the provisions of the 1979 Act and the Police and Magistrates' Courts Act 1994) and various disqualifications apply, for example, undischarged bankrupts. In practice, others will not be appointed, including those over the age of 60 and those convicted of serious offences.

Two main criticisms are made of the appointment process: namely, that it favours appointment of the socially better off; and that it fails to accommodate the ethnic minorities.

The Lord Chancellor attempts to maintain a political balance, as well as a balance between the sexes. The ratio of males to females is about 3:2. There is also the need to attract younger people to seek selection. Local advisory committees advise the Lord Chancellor, and they are assisted by area sub-committees, whose members' names remain secret. Within one year of appointment, the newly appointed magistrate must undertake a training course in sentencing aims and practice, criminal law and evidence and the role of the court clerk and others.

Magistrates are required to sit at least 26 times a year and, in practice, most sit more frequently and thereby acquire experience and training whilst performing their role. Section 6 of the Justices of the Peace Act 1979 also provides for the removal of magistrates by the Lord Chancellor where circumstances demand, for example, where they are convicted of a serious offence. By s 8, a magistrate's name may be placed on the supplemental list and as a result he or she will not be able to sit in court, but will be entitled to retain the title of justice of the peace and carry out minor functions such as the witnessing of documents. This will be done if a magistrate becomes unfit to carry out judicial duties and on reaching the age of 70 (or, in the case of those who have held high judicial office, the age of 75).

Sections 13 and 31 formerly provided for stipendiary magistrates to be appointed by the Queen on the recommendation of the Lord Chancellor from barristers and solicitors of at least seven years' standing. The Courts and Legal Services Act 1990 replaces eligibility by status with advocacy qualification. Retirement is at the age of 70, unless the Lord Chancellor permits an extension to the age of 72, and removal can be ordered for misbehaviour or incapacity.

Magistrates are appointed for a commission area, and outside London this is equivalent to a county. In London there are six commission areas. Magistrates must reside within 15 miles of their commission area unless the Lord Chancellor otherwise directs. Each commission area is divided into petty sessional divisions and each division has a court. A magistrate is assigned to a court by the Lord Chancellor and this is usually the division in which he or she resides or works. Section 19 of the Justices of the Peace Act 1979 provides for the appointment of a magistrates' courts committee made up of magistrates from each division to oversee administrative matters and the appointment of magistrates' clerks under s 26.

Section 26 has been amended by the Courts and Legal Services Act 1990 to provide for advocacy qualifications as defined in s 71(3). Magistrates' clerks were appointed from barristers or solicitors of at least five years' standing or who had at least five years' experience as an assistant to a magistrates' clerk. The Justices' Clerk (Qualifications of Assistants) Rules 1979 provide that an assistant cannot act as a clerk in court unless qualified as a barrister or solicitor or having undergone specified training.

Section 117 of the Courts and Legal Services Act 1990 amends s 28 of the Justices of the Peace Act 1979 to enable rules to be made under s 144 of the Magistrates' Courts Act 1980 for the delegation of the duties and powers entrusted to a magistrates' clerk to his or her deputy or assistant.

The clerk performs two main roles, namely, court administration and advising the magistrates on the law. Clerks are not empowered to make decisions for or on behalf of magistrates, but can only offer advice as to the relevant law or powers of sentencing. In *R v Uxbridge Justices ex p Smith* (1985), it was held that the clerk could offer advice to the magistrates after they had retired to consider their decision, but should not attempt to advise them on their decision.

Terms of employment

All those mentioned above, except magistrates, district judges, circuit judges and recorders, hold office 'during good behaviour' and may be removed from office by the Crown following an address to both Houses of Parliament. Salaries are paid out of the consolidated fund and are fixed by statute. This ensures that judges of the superior courts are independent of the executive. The Judicial Pensions and Retirement Act 1993 makes provision for the retirement of all judges at the age of 70, whereas previously retirement was at 75 for High Court judges and 72 for circuit judges (with the possibility of an extension for a further three years). This change is to be phased in and will not affect any judge presently in post.

Selection and effectiveness

Having discussed the structure of the courts, their functions and the personnel of the courts, we should consider the issues arising from the appointment and selection of the judges and the effectiveness of the judge in developing the law to meet changing needs.

Selection and appointment

So far as the selection and appointment of judges are concerned, we have seen that judges are not a homogenous group, and a distinction can be made between judges of the superior courts, appointed by the Queen on the advice of the Prime Minister, and those of the inferior courts, appointed by the Lord Chancellor.

Some critics question why it is that the Prime Minister should have any involvement in appointments; there is an inherent danger that the judiciary may be manipulated by a strong Prime Minister and government to serve its political goals. Furthermore, appointment by the Lord Chancellor is not without its critics, and it has on many occasions been proposed that the office of Lord Chancellor be replaced by a Ministry of Justice.

The former Lord Chancellor, Lord MacKay of Clashfern, showed the potential, if not actual, conflicts in interest between legislative, executive and judicial functions which he performs. His zeal for reforming the courts, legal services and the provision of legal aid and advice brought him into conflict with The Law Society, the General Council of the Bar and others concerned with the legal system.

On the question of the independence of the judiciary, the means by which members of the judiciary can be removed from office is also important. As we have noted, superior court judges hold office during good behaviour and can only be removed by a joint resolution of both Houses of Parliament. Even where independence is prized (albeit not guaranteed by a written constitution), this will not ensure that the decisions made are impartial.

There is usually no question of blatant bias in the sense of bribery or corruption, but rather the suggestion that the composition of the judiciary is such that judges are drawn from a narrow section of society and give effect to the moral and other values of that group. Judges are seen as establishment figures who are remote from, and who have little understanding of, the pressures and motives of the general population.

The counter-argument suggests that the very fact that members of the judiciary are remote and have undergone training and gained experience means that wise and well considered decisions can be made. It is inevitable that some mistakes are made, but these should be quickly remedied by way of an appeals system and ultimately by means of a review body independent of the judiciary.

The debate continues with suggestions that there should be greater opportunities for appointment from the ethnic minorities and from women. To speed up the process some would like to see positive discrimination in favour of these two groups, but to date this has been rejected in favour of appointment on merit and the dismantling of many of the barriers to entry to the judiciary.

Helena Kennedy QC, in *Eve Was Framed* (1922), describes the average British judge as white, male, conservative, Oxbridge and public school educated, and between the ages of 60 and 65. She quotes statistics prepared by the Lord Chancellor's Department for March 1991 to the effect that 'only one judge out of 550 was black' and only 'one Lord Justice, two High Court judges and 19 circuit judges were female'. She highlights the often subtle prejudice and stereotyping that abound in the judiciary and that those who suffer in consequence of this are not only women and those from the ethnic minorities, but also those who do not fit into traditionally accepted social groups, such as homosexuals, gipsies, the unemployed and vagrants.

Traditionally, members of the judiciary have been drawn from the ranks of barristers, with very few exceptions. Judges have been appointed following secret deliberations between the higher ranks of the judiciary, the Lord Chancellor and the Prime Minister. Reasons are not given for non-appointment, as is the case with the appointment of barristers to Queen's Counsel. However, this is set to change, following Pt III, ss 71–76 of the Courts and Legal Services Act 1990, as amended by the Access to Justice Act 1999, which permit those with an advocacy qualification based on rights of audience granted by an authorised body to seek appointment.

In June 1993, the first solicitor, Michael Sachs, was appointed the first High Court judge from outside the Bar under these provisions. Sections 27–33 of the Courts and Legal Services Act 1990, which permit solicitors rights of audience in the higher courts having obtained advocacy certificates, will no doubt increase the numbers of solicitors who in future seek appointment to the judiciary.

The Bar Conference in 1993 highlighted the secrecy and non-accountability of the appointments system and speakers suggested that this leads to allegations of discrimination and loss of confidence. Calls were made for published selection criteria and for set targets for the appointment of women and those from the ethnic minorities.

Positive discrimination was rejected and full confidence in the present selection process, managed by the Lord Chancellor's Department, was expressed by Sir Thomas Legg, Permanent Secretary at the Department. He attempted to justify the wide but confidential consultation process, in that it ensured that those who were consulted would make valuable contributions.

It was noted that the then Lord Chancellor had made proposals for reform in July 1993, including progressive introduction of the use of open advertisement for judicial vacancies, better forecasting and planning of numbers and expertise of judges, more specific job descriptions and the qualities looked for, further encouragement to women and ethnic minority applicants, the involvement of suitable lay people in the selection process and progression towards competition for posts at the lower levels.

In 1992, Justice, the all-party, independent law reform body, published a report of a committee chaired by Robert Stevens which recommended the creation of a judicial commission to oversee judicial appointments, training and the maintenance of high standards. The then Lord Chief Justice, Lord Taylor, rejected such proposals, suggesting that the present system was satisfactory and that any such change would undermine the independence of the judiciary. Following publication of the Royal Commission Report on Criminal Justice, he agreed that judges should become more interventionist so as to ensure advocates gave shorter speeches during trials, thereby reducing costs and delay.

In 1978, the Judicial Studies Board was established following the publication of Lord Bridge's working party report with overall responsibility for judges' training. On appointment, one week's formal training takes place, and visits are arranged to a prison and a young offenders' institution, an interview with a probation officer and one week shadowing an experienced judge. Refresher courses are offered on a voluntary basis to assist judges in keeping abreast of changes in the law.

Comparisons can be drawn between our system and that in European States and the USA. Not only is the training more rigorous, but the notion of a career judge pervades most other jurisdictions. This is unlike our system, which has traditionally seen the appointment of judges only from the ranks of barristers. In France, for example, judges are appointed and trained 'on the job', and training lasts from four to six years. In the USA, many of the judges are elected, so selection is conducted in public, with public participation, where the criteria for appointment are clearly stated. It may be too much to suggest that we should move from an appointment to an elected system, but proponents for reform suggest that the appointment system must become more open and accountable if the judiciary is to become more representative of society. Objective criteria open to public scrutiny can ensure that the most able candidates for appointment not only present themselves, but become appointed.

Many critics of the present system would welcome assurances that change will evolve, but do not wish to see revolutionary changes. Given the involvement of judges in crucial areas of everyday life, both in the criminal law and in areas such as judicial review, it is vital that the appointment of members of the judiciary, training and discipline be seen to be more open and subject to scrutiny.

Professor Griffiths, in *The Politics of the Judiciary* (5th edn, 1997), analysed the social class origins of the judges from 1820–1968 and concluded that the overwhelming majority of members were drawn from the upper and middle classes and were invariably male, middle aged and public school and Oxbridge educated.

His study is no doubt dated, but there are more recent studies. For example, in a survey conducted by the *Solicitors Journal* in March 1992 of the general public in six major towns, some 65% considered that judges are out of touch with everyday life. Some 79% considered that there should be more women judges and 69% that judges should be appointed to reflect ethnic mix. Some 47% thought that judges should retire at 65 and 23% at the age of 60.

Tony Gifford, a barrister, published research in 1986 which confirmed the narrow social background of the judges, and studies by the Lord Chancellor's Department confirm the minority representation of women and ethnic minorities. In addition, in a study commissioned by the Bar Council and the Lord Chancellor's Department in 1992, sexual discrimination at the Bar was shown in obtaining pupillage, conduct of interviews and the types of cases handled.

Recent cases suggest that some judges are out of touch with general feeling. Thus, Judge Prosser sentenced a schoolboy rapist in Gwent to a three year supervision order and ordered compensation of £500 to his victim for 'a good holiday to help her get over the trauma'. This was subsequently overturned on appeal. Ian Starforth Hill QC referred in one case to the eight year old victim of a sexual attack as 'no angel' and in another case imposed a conditional discharge on two men who had unlawful intercourse with a 13 year old girl. Judge Raymond Dean was reported in the press as having told a jury trying an allegation of rape at an Old Bailey trial that 'when a woman says no, she doesn't always mean it'.

In March 1997, it was reported in the press that Judge Crawford, sitting at Newcastle Crown Court, had made an offensive remark and that the Lord Chancellor had written to him, rebuking him for his unacceptable remark of a racist nature. The judge apologised for what he described as a 'regrettable slip'. In 1999, the Lord Chancellor and the Lord Chief Justice issued guidelines to the judiciary, entitled *The Equal Treatment Bench Book* and published by the Judicial Studies Board, outlining acceptable behaviour and speech with regard to race, culture and ethnicity. It is planned to issue further guidelines on disability issues, gender, sexual orientation, litigants in person and children. It was denied that this was an exercise in political correctness, preaching or moralising. Its aim is to inform and assist members of the judiciary when making decisions. At the same time, Sir Leonard Peach was appointed to review the use of 'secret soundings' in the appointment of members of the judiciary. He reported to the Lord Chancellor on 3 December 1999 after 'An Independent Scrutiny of the Appointments Processes of Judges and Queen's Counsel in England and Wales'. His main recommendation was the setting up of the Judicial Appointment Commission to investigate grievances and complaints, to undertake audits of the appointments processes and to recommend changes.

In the face of these and many more instances reported in the press, a radical overhaul of the appointments system was called for. Justice, as long ago as 1972, proposed the creation of an appointments committee to advise the Lord Chancellor. At present, the Lord Chancellor exercises an almost absolute discretion, based on such factors as professional ability, experience, standing and integrity, sound temperament and physical health, and regardless of sexual or ethnic origin, political affiliation or religion. He obtains evidence of these qualities confidentially from members of the judiciary and outside observers. Critics suggest that this is inward looking and favours those candidates who fit the preconceptions and stereotypes of those already in post. Furthermore, the system is not open to scrutiny and is subjective in nature.

In an attempt to make recruitment more fair and open, the first advertisements for district and circuit judges were made in September 1994, following an announcement by the then Lord Chancellor, Lord MacKay. It was recognised that the judiciary under-represented women and ethnic minorities, and that they were to be encouraged to apply. A new selection procedure by a panel, including a layperson, would select those of 'intellectual ability and sound judgment ... integrity, fairness and an understanding of people and society'.

This under-representation remains a serious drawback of our system and was commented on in June 1996 in a report by the Parliamentary Home Affairs Select Committee entitled 'Judicial Appointments Procedures', but this rejected positive discrimination and an open competitive appointment process for senior judicial appointments. The report also, *inter alia*, recommended that senior judges should no longer be appointed by the Prime Minister.

When considering the constitutional position of the judiciary (see Chapter 1) and the judicial function (see Chapter 6) it is important to take account of the independence and impartiality of the judges. Independence usually denotes freedom from oppressive or overbearing government, but may include others who attempt to compromise free and independent decision making. It is a well known constitutional doctrine to which our judges subscribe, and they are jealous to assert their independence. We have seen safeguards to protect this in how judges are appointed, retained and dismissed. Their impartiality is also of great importance, but we cannot afford to be complacent in assuming either that independence guarantees impartiality, or that the judges today always act impartially.

Certainly, Lord Hoffman in *R v Bow Street Metropolitan Magistrates ex p Pinochet Ugarte (No 1)* (1998) has done a major service in heightening awareness of the risks. The litigation involving the request by Spain for the extradition of Colonel Pinochet to stand trial for crimes of torture and genocide have been widely covered in the press. The House of Lords permitted Amnesty International to appear before it to suggest reasons why extradition should be allowed. Lord Hoffman (and his wife) had associations with the charitable arm of that organisation, but failed to disclose this to his fellow judges or to counsel for the parties in open court. In the event, Pinochet's lawyers asserted that this failure to disclose and to stand down gave rise to apparent bias. The House of Lords agreed and, in an unprecedented move, declared the judgment void and proceeded to rehear the request for extradition before a court with seven Law Lords. In the event, the Colonel was held not to have sovereign immunity and could face extradition, but only in connection with crimes that could be proved to have taken place after the treaty governing such crimes had come into effect in 1988. Lord Hoffman was found to have a direct interest in the outcome of the proceedings to which Amnesty International had been made a party. Unlike the case of *Dimes v Proprietors of Grand Junction Canal* (1852), no financial or proprietary interest existed, but the court held that he should have stood down unless, having disclosed his interest to all the parties, those affected had waived their right so as to permit him to continue to act in a judicial capacity.

It was stressed that there was no suggestion that Lord Hoffman was actually biased, merely that his interest in the charitable arm of Amnesty International gave rise to apparent bias. Where a direct interest exists, this gives rise to automatic disqualification. Where no such direct interest exists, the judge may nevertheless have to disclose factors which could give rise to a real danger of bias, as in *R v Gough* (1993). It will then be for the parties to decide whether or not to object. If they object, the judge would then have to consider the objection and decide whether or not to recuse (stand down). In the words of Lord Bingham in *Locabail (UK) Ltd v Bayfield Properties and Another* (2000): 'He would be as wrong to yield to a tenuous or frivolous objection as he would to ignore an objection of substance.' The case of *ex p Pinochet* was analysed and applied in the case of *Locabail* in the Court of Appeal. This case concerned five applications, only one of which was successful. That concerned a barrister QC who had sat as a recorder in a personal injury case. The defendant asserted that the recorder was a well known author and practitioner in this field and his views showed a real danger of bias against the defendant. The other cases concerned a solicitor QC acting as a deputy judge, who it was said was either automatically disqualified or there was a real danger of bias because his firm had acted for a company which had claims against the husband of one of the defendants and for the liquidator of a company which the husband had controlled; an application to an industrial tribunal against the Inland Revenue for sexual harassment and racial discrimination where the tribunal chairman had been employed by the Revenue in a junior post some 20 years before; and an unsuccessful application for judicial review in connection with the renewal of a bookmaker's permit where the judge was a director of family companies which had let properties to the bookmakers and associated companies. Lord Bingham CJ, giving the judgment of the Court of Appeal, said: 'It would be dangerous and futile to attempt to define or list the factors which might or might not give rise to a real danger of bias.' Each case would have to be decided on its facts and this could include the nature of the issue to be decided. Religion, ethnic or national origin, gender, age, class, means or sexual orientation of the judge could not give rise to objection. Nor could it generally be based on his social, educational, service or employment background or history, nor that of his family, previous political associations, membership of social or sporting or charitable bodies, Masonic associations, previous judicial decisions, extracurricular utterances in textbooks, lectures, speeches, articles, interviews, reports or responses to consultation papers.

With the increasing 'politicisation' of the judiciary as a result of the Human Rights Act 1998 and the changing attitudes to the effect of EC law on UK law, no doubt questions of impartiality will be of relevance. Furthermore, the warnings of 'institutionalised racism' in the police in the MacPherson Report on the death of Stephen Lawrence should not be taken literally to apply only to that institution. Others in society may well need to be subject to scrutiny.

Judicial officers

In this section, we shall consider the roles of the Lord Chancellor, the Attorney General, the Solicitor General and the Director of Public Prosecutions (DPP).

The Lord Chancellor

As we have already noted, the Lord Chancellor carries out roles in all three branches of government. He is head of the judiciary and is President of the Supreme Court. He is a member of the Cabinet and is the Speaker of the House of Lords.

The constitutional position of the office of Lord Chancellor has come into question, given the political controversy over cuts in legal aid provision, reform of the courts and the legal profession and major constitutional reform. The Lord Chancellor has faced challenges by way of judicial review on the question of legal aid provision. Although these were not successful, the court held that The Law Society had a sufficient interest in bringing the claim and a legitimate expectation to be consulted before changes were brought about. Other challenges have concerned the award of legal aid franchises and contracts and the imposition of court fees. In *R v Lord Chancellor ex p Witham* (1997), W, an unemployed businessman on income support, successfully challenged the Lord Chancellor's decision to abolish fee exemption and remission in the High Court. Witham wished to issue a writ for libel (for which legal aid is not available) but could not afford the £500 court fee. It was held that the action of the Lord Chancellor operated as an absolute bar for many seeking judicial redress. Access to the courts is a constitutional right which can only be abrogated by the executive specifically authorised to do so by Parliament.

Subsequently, the rules governing fees have been altered to allow discretion in the court to waive the fee and for those in receipt of State benefits not to be required to pay fees. This case and the others demonstrate the strength of feeling that cost-cutting is at the root of the reforms, albeit that the professed aim of the Access to Justice Act 1999 is to ensure the best use of resources in providing legal services for all. They also illustrate the potential conflict which can arise between the political and judicial functions performed and warned against in the doctrine of separation of the legislative, judicial and executive powers. In recent years, calls have been made for a Ministry of Justice to replace the office of Lord Chancellor, which has existed for centuries, in an attempt to ensure a more effective separation of powers. No doubt the role of the Lord Chancellor will again come into question when the Human Rights Act 1998 comes into effect in October 2000.

The Attorney General

The Attorney General is a political appointee, like his deputy, the Solicitor General. Traditionally, he has been appointed by the Queen from the ranks of barristers, but since the passing of the Courts and Legal Services Act 1990 this is not a requirement. He represents the Crown in civil cases and as prosecutor in important criminal cases such as serious breaches of the Official Secrets Acts. Some prosecutions cannot commence without his consent and others, for example, a private prosecution, may be terminated by his entering a *nolle prosequi* (an order not to proceed). He is head of the English Bar and supervises the work of the Director of Public Prosecutions. He is also principal legal adviser to the Government, particularly on issues of international and constitutional law.

The Attorney General represents the public interest, for example, in cases where a public nuisance is alleged. The case of *Airedale NHS Trust v Bland* (1993) is instructive, in that the Attorney General was represented as *amicus curiae* (friend of the court) and submitted that it would be in the best interests of the patient for treatment to cease.

The former occupant of the office, Sir Nicholas Lyell, was called to give evidence before the judicial inquiry into the 'arms to Iraq affair', chaired by Scott LJ. The advice dispensed to government ministers in connection with their signature of public interest immunity certificates issued under s 28 of the Crown Proceedings Act 1947 has been questioned, and members of the Opposition called for his resignation. Scott LJ reported in February 1996 and criticised the use of public interest immunity certificates and recommended that their use in criminal cases in the future should be limited.

The Solicitor General

As already noted, the Solicitor General assists the Attorney General in the carrying out of his functions and acts as his deputy in his absence or when a vacancy occurs. The Law Officers Act 1944 (which permitted him to act as the Attorney General's deputy in specific instances) has been repealed by the Law Officers Act 1997, which allows them to agree when he is to act as and when they think fit. Like the Attorney General, this is a political appointment and despite the title, the Solicitor General has traditionally been appointed from the ranks of barristers. In *R v Solicitor General ex p Taylor* (1995), the applicant sisters sought judicial review of the decision of the Solicitor General (who acted in the absence of the Attorney General) not to pursue contempt proceedings against sensationalist newspaper coverage of their trial for the murder of their father. The court held that the office of Attorney General was constitutionally unique and was not subject to judicial review. Despite the competing public interests of freedom of speech and the right to a fair trial, this case is authority for the proposition that it is for the Attorney General to decide on how these are balanced.

The Director of Public Prosecutions

The Prosecution of Offences Act 1985 radically altered the system of prosecutions in England and Wales by establishing the Crown Prosecution Service (CPS) and in redefining the powers of the Director of Public Prosecutions. It is the responsibility of the Director of Public Prosecutions, the present occupant of the office being David Calvert-Smith, to co-ordinate prosecution policy and oversee the running of the independent prosecution service. Since the passing of the Prosecution of Offences Act 1985, it is the Director of Public Prosecutions who decides which cases are to be prosecuted. Recent case law demonstrates the extent to which the courts will regulate the Director of Public Prosecutions in the use of his powers. In *R v DPP ex p Manning and Another* (2000), the Court of Appeal required him to give reasons for his refusal to prosecute in a case involving a death in custody. On the other hand, in *R v DPP ex p Kebeline and Others* (1999), it was held that, in a case where the Director of Public Prosecutions's consent was required for a prosecution to go ahead, this was not subject to judicial review.

The police are charged with the investigation of crime and, on completion of their investigations, the file must be handed to the CPS for a decision to be made as to whether a prosecution is to be brought.

The CPS is established in regional centres, each with a chief Crown Prosecutor who is assisted by Crown Prosecutors. Much criticism has been made of the lack of efficiency of the CPS and of the many decisions not to proceed with a prosecution or where a prosecution has commenced but no evidence is offered at the hearing, with the result that the case fails.

In February 1997, the Lord Chancellor and his designated judges (under s 17 of the Courts and Legal Services Act 1990) approved, subject to limitations, The Law Society's application for rights of audience to be extended to employed solicitors in the higher courts. Employed solicitors are those employed by organisations, local government and companies, including those employed by the CPS. The Administration of Justice Act 1999 amends these provisions so as to allow employed solicitors rights to appear in the higher courts if qualified to do so and regardless of any professional rules preventing them.

The recent announcement by the Director of Public Prosecutions, David Calvert-Smith, that Harold Shipman, the former GP who has been found guilty of murdering 15 of his patients, will not face more prosecutions, even though the police have evidence implicating him in more murders, demonstrates his role in the bringing of prosecutions. He has decided that information which is in the public domain would prevent Shipman from having a fair trial, if a case were to be brought to trial.

The layperson and the law

Lay magistrates

The magistrates' court deals with 98% of all criminal cases, at least initially. In 1992, some 566 magistrates' courts sat in England and Wales, staffed by 29,450 lay magistrates (stipendiary magistrates numbered 76). In 1990, some 95% of all offenders were sentenced in the magistrates' courts. Two to seven lay magistrates sit at any one time (although usually there will be a bench of three). Special rules apply in youth courts (formerly called juvenile courts) whereby at least one in three magistrates must be female. The court is also required to sit on different days and in a different place and restrictions on reporting will be imposed.

The Lord Chancellor appoints magistrates on the recommendation of the Magistrates' Commission. Retirement is at the age of 70 years. We have already considered the jurisdiction and powers of the magistrates and the role of the clerk. Here we will confine our comments to some of the criticisms that are made of lay magistrates.

Magistrates are often said to be 'case-hardened', and it is said that a defendant might be advised to elect for jury trial at the Crown Court where he or she is accused of a triable either way offence such as theft. Such a defendant, represented by a good counsel, may well be acquitted, whereas the likelihood is that trial summarily in the magistrates' court would result in conviction. Magistrates may also be seen to be too much under the control of the court clerk, but, of course, this may only be as it seems and, in any event, a clerk is not permitted to make a decision for the magistrate, but only to offer advice as to the law.

As Professor Zander has pointed out, the perception of defendants as to the differences in treatment between the magistrates' courts and the Crown Court may well vary with what actually happens. Research suggests that Crown Court judges impose tougher sentences, but defendants perceive magistrates as case hardened and that trial in the Crown Court is more likely to result in acquittal, or at least a lighter sentence.

Another criticism is that a bench of three magistrates will comprise two less senior magistrates and one more experienced magistrate, who acts as chairman. The chairman will have the casting vote, and the other two may defer to what they see as his or her better judgment. It is often pointed out that lay magistrates have relatively little knowledge of law, evidence and procedure and, moreover, little training. Over-reliance on the court clerk may result from the inability of justices to reach a decision taking into account complex provisions.

Magistrates are also drawn from a narrow social background and some have described them as 'do-gooders' who, for want of other things to fill their time, fulfil this public role. Allied with this is the criticism that magistrates are 'middle aged, middle class and middle minded', and that, in all, the system encourages the provision of justice on the cheap.

On a more positive view, some of the advantages of encouraging people to come forward to serve as justices include the following: the system is cost effective, and if paid personnel were to be employed or the role of the magistrates' court was to be dispensed with, the administration of criminal justice would at best become long and expensive and at worst would grind to a halt. The lay magistrate offers a different perspective from that of the professional judge, and may well have a better appreciation of fact. Magistrates are required to sit at least 26 times a year and average attendance is greater. At the same time, a magistrate who regularly sits over several years will no doubt build up a vast amount of experience in the working of the court and the criminal justice system. The magistrate is assisted by a trained professional, the clerk, and this ensures consistency and accuracy in decision making.

The Runciman Royal Commission (which reported in July 1993) recommended that in either way offences where the defendant can at present elect for jury trial, the defendant should no longer have that right. If the CPS and the defendant agree as to the mode of trial, this would determine the question. If the defence does not agree with the view of the CPS, the matter should be referred to the magistrates to determine the mode of trial. Legislation should lay down the criteria to be considered by the magistrates when deciding this question. As already noted, following the Narey Review, the Mode of Trial Bill proposes that it will be for the magistrates alone to decide on trial venue.

The Commission recommended the abolition of committal proceedings and also the reclassification of offences into those triable summarily by the magistrates (summary offences) and those triable in the Crown Court before a jury (indictable offences). The latter has not been taken up, but s 51 of the Crime and Disorder Act 1998 will remove committals for indictable offences and the Criminal Procedure and Investigations Act 1996 amends the procedure in committals for trial on triable either way offences.

The Justices of the Peace Act 1997 reformed the workings of the magistrates' courts and the role of the court clerk. The Lord Chancellor was given power to merge or adjust the number of Magistrates' Courts Committee areas, with the aim of reducing the number by about a half to between 50 and 60. Each new area is headed by a chief justices' clerk, appointed on a five year fixed term performance-related contract. New appointments of justices' clerks will also be on fixed term contracts and subject to the approval of the Lord Chancellor. Appointment of Chairpersons of Committee Areas are also subject to the Lord Chancellor's approval.

The Lord Chancellor's Department, in promoting these changes, stressed that, in its view, there was no threat to the independence of justices' clerks, but magistrates and their clerks protested as the reforms were seen on the one hand to increase bureaucracy and cost and on the other to compromise the independence of clerks and the trust which exists between magistrates and their clerks. The Administration of Justice Act 1999 now provides for the appointment of a Justices' Chief Executive and the merging of the provincial and metropolitan stipendiary benches.

Coroners

The office of coroner was established in 1194, and since that time the powers of the coroner have been successively narrowed until, today, their main functions are the holding of inquests into suspicious deaths within their area and into the status of property alleged to be a treasure as defined in the Treasure Act 1996 (replacing the more limited treasure trove). Coroners can be assisted by a jury of between seven and 11 persons and a majority verdict is acceptable, providing that no more than two jurors dissent.

Coroners are appointed by the local authority in whose area they serve and can only be dismissed by the Lord Chancellor for misbehaviour. On average, some 180,000 deaths are referred to coroners in any one year and, of these, some 20,000 result in inquests. Coroners have an important role to play in recommending improvements in safety standards and their findings may give rise to criminal or civil proceedings.

Lay assessors

Lay assessors are employed in the wide range of tribunals which have been established by statute to supplement the work of the courts in adjudicating disputes involving an aggrieved citizen and an administrative agency of the State. Some examples include national insurance tribunals, rent tribunals and industrial injuries tribunals, and these are more fully considered in Chapter 5. Lay assessors may assist in the deliberations of the Restrictive Practices Court, which sits as a superior court of record, comprising a High Court judge and two laypersons.

The Admiralty Court within the Queen's Bench Division, presided over by a High Court judge, also relies on the assistance of two nautical assessors (members of Trinity House) who are competent to advise on technical maritime matters.

By s 14 of the Courts and Legal Services Act 1990, s 63 of the County Courts Act 1984 is amended so as to enable district judges and circuit judges to appoint expert assessors. Section 14(2) provides that in any proceedings a judge may, on the application of a party to the proceedings, summon an expert assessor who is a person 'of skill and experience in the matter to which the proceedings relate' and who may be willing to sit with him and act as an assessor. Power also exists for the judge to summon such a person in the absence of an application by either party in prescribed proceedings, as defined by s 119(1), to be provided for by regulation. District judges have similar powers, but only in prescribed proceedings.

Another area where lay assessors may assist a judge in reaching a decision where complex matters arise is in criminal fraud trials. Suggestions have over the years been made that juries are unsuitable to decide issues of fact in such trials; also the need for judges to be assisted by those expert in financial matters was made clear in the Blue Arrow and Guinness fraud trials in 1992. The Roskill Committee on fraud trials, which reported in 1986, recommended the use of assessors in place of juries in complex criminal fraud trials.

The jury

In considering the issue of the role of the layperson in the administration of justice, it is the use of the jury, particularly in criminal trials in the Crown Court, that fires the imagination and gives rise to much debate as to its effectiveness. The main role of the jury is as an arbiter of fact. A recent illustration of this is in the civil case of *Ward v Chief Constable of West Midlands Police* (1998), in which it was held that a civil jury's role was to make specific findings of fact so as to enable the judge to make the final decision on liability in law. The jury depended on being properly directed by the judge as to the law and the issues involved. Failure to properly direct the jury would make the judge's decision on liability unsafe.

The jury has been described as 'a bastion of freedom' and has great constitutional significance. In a paraphrase of the words of Lord Hewart CJ in *R v Sussex JJ ex p McCarthy* (1924), 'justice should not only be done, but be seen to be done', that is, the jury plays its part in ensuring openness and fair play. It might be argued that use of the jury in criminal trials is one of the fundamental pillars of a free society, and is of the same order of importance as the presumption of innocence and a right to remain silent before and during trial.

Blackstone described the jury as 'the bulwark of our liberties', and Lord Devlin in *Trial by Jury* (1966) as 'the lamp which shows that freedom lives'. On the other hand, some suggest that the jury has little, if any, useful part to play and that, for those unfortunate enough to be called upon to serve on a jury, it is an unwelcome public duty from which few are exempt or can be excused, although compensation is paid for travelling, subsistence and financial loss.

Juries are rarely used nowadays in civil trials, although the most notable type of trial, namely defamation, where juries are used, has received much criticism, given the large amounts of damages awarded by juries in recent years. Some examples include civil claims by Jeffrey Archer, Lord Lindley, Esther Rantzen, Sonia Sutcliffe and Koo Stark. By s 8 of the Courts and Legal Services Act 1990, the Court of Appeal has a rule making power to substitute awards of damages by a jury where that is found to be excessive. In *Rantzen v Mirror Group Newspapers Ltd* (1993), the Court of Appeal held that the court's power under s 8 'to substitute for the sum awarded by the jury such sum as appears to the court to be proper' where a jury award is excessive or inadequate should be exercised in a way consistent with the European Convention of Human Rights. On the facts, the jury award of £250,000 was reduced to £110,000. Much of the criticism of the amounts of jury awards has resulted from comparisons between the awards of damages made in personal injury cases and those in defamation claims where the former, relatively, have been much lower.

By the Administration of Justice (Miscellaneous Provisions) Act 1933, civil courts have a discretion to order the use of a jury where either party requests one in cases of defamation, malicious prosecution, fraud and false imprisonment, unless there is good reason for not having a jury, for example, where the case will involve scientific investigation or prolonged examination of documents.

Civil juries in the county court comprise eight persons, whereas in the High Court the jury has 12 members and majority verdicts are acceptable.

The main use of juries is in trials on indictment in the Crown Court where the jury has the function of deciding the guilt or innocence of the defendant. Jurors take an oath or affirm that they will 'faithfully try the defendant and give a true verdict according to the evidence'. Where a juror has specialised knowledge concerning the background of the case and communicates this to other members of the jury, the jury should be discharged, as this amounts to new evidence which the defendant cannot challenge. The case of *R v Fricker* (1999) is authority for this proposition and underlines the rule that a jury should only take into account evidence that is put before the court.

Twelve persons aged between 18 and 70 (those aged 65 and over may be excused under s 119 of the Criminal Justice Act 1988, which amends the Juries Act 1974) are selected at random from the electoral register. Those aged 18 who are registered as an elector and who have been resident for five years are liable for jury service.

A distinction is made between exemption and excusal from jury service. The former allows those involved with the administration of justice, such as judges, barristers and solicitors, and others including clergymen, police officers and the mentally disordered, to be exempt, whereas the latter permits those who would find attendance at court difficult, to seek the permission of the court clerk to be excused. Those away on holiday or business or who have some other good reason, for example, doctors and members of the armed forces, must apply to the court clerk to be excused from the jury summons. Those with certain past convictions are disqualified, as are those who have been on probation during the previous five years.

Those who attend are empanelled and become jurors in waiting. A juror in waiting may be challenged for cause by the defence if, for example, the person is known to the defendant or has knowledge of the case. 'Cause' is defined by a Lord Chief Justice's Practice Direction of 1972 and must be a good reason for a juror in waiting not being sworn in to sit on the jury to try that particular case. It follows that such a person may be called on to remain in the precincts of the court and to sit on a jury trying another case. By s 118 of the Criminal Justice

Act 1988, the peremptory challenge was abolished. This permitted the defence to challenge up to three jurors in waiting without any reason. It was most often used to challenge those dressed smartly, on the assumption that such an individual would be more likely to convict a defendant accused of theft or burglary. In trials involving offences against a woman, it was usual for the defence to use its peremptory challenge to ensure representation of women on the jury. The prosecution can ask jurors in waiting 'to stand by for the Crown' and no limitation exists on the number of times it can be used.

The jury appoints a foreman from among its number to announce its verdict and to keep order during its deliberations following the trial when it goes into secret session. A unanimous verdict may be announced or by a 10:2 majority, providing the jury has deliberated for a minimum of two hours. Section 17 of the Juries Act 1974 (as amended) provides that a 10:1 majority verdict may be given if only 11 jurors sit, or a 9:1 majority if 10 jurors sit. The minimum number of jurors is nine.

The jury is the arbiter of fact whereas the judge is the arbiter of law. At the conclusion of the trial the judge sums up the evidence to the jury and may direct the jury to acquit or convict. The judge is not empowered to order a jury to pronounce one way or the other, as was clearly shown in the trial of Clive Ponting in 1985. Ponting was accused of offences under s 2 of the Official Secrets Act 1911 arising out of disclosures in the press on the sinking of *The Belgrano* during the Falklands conflict. The judge directed the jury to convict, but this was ignored by the jury, who acquitted the defendant on all counts. This is known as 'jury equity' and an illustration is to be found in the case of *R v Kronlid and Others* (1996), where three women had broken into a British Aerospace factory and caused estimated damage of £1.5 million to a jet fighter. The jury acquitted the defendants of charges of criminal damage under the Criminal Damage Act 1971. In their defence, the defendants, members of a peace group, wished to disarm the jet so as to prevent its use by Indonesia, which, they believed, was suppressing the people of East Timor.

These so called perverse verdicts by juries can be illustrated by other cases, for example, the acquittal of Cynthia Payne in 1987 on charges under the Sexual Offences Act 1956 of controlling prostitutes. Another is that of Stephen Owen in 1992, who was charged with the attempted murder of the lorry driver who had killed Owen's 12 year old son. The driver was sentenced to 18 months' imprisonment, but served only 12 months, and this, together with aggravating features of the running down, resulted in Owen shooting the driver. Despite overwhelming evidence, the jury acquitted Owen.

By s 10 of the Juries Act 1974 (as amended), provision is made for the discharge of a jury or of an individual juror. A jury can be discharged, for example, where the defendant's previous convictions are disclosed, or other information which might prejudice a fair trial.

Matters of law are for the judge and where counsel wishes to query a question of law, the judge will order the jury to retire whilst that matter is dealt with. By s 122 of the Criminal Justice Act 1988, if a question arises as to whether the defendant has previously been tried for the offence for which he appears before the court (*autrefois acquit* or *autrefois convict*), this is a matter of law for the judge to decide in the absence of the jury. Individual jurors may be discharged at the discretion of the judge, for example, for illness, wrongful conduct or contact with the defendant.

Several issues concern the selection and effectiveness of juries in criminal trials. First, selection is conducted secretly, as is the way in which they work. By s 8 of the Contempt of Court Act 1981, jury members are under a duty not to disclose what happened during the course of the deliberations. This is an absolute duty which prevents research into the workings of the jury. This not only applies to those who would like to research into the workings of the jury, but also the press and (as a recent case shows) the trial judge. As to the press, *R v Wood* (1995) states that 'fairness demands that pressure should not be put on jurors in a particular case by the press or anyone else'. As to the judge, in *R v Schot* and *R v Barclay* (1997), on an appeal to the Court of Appeal, it was doubted whether the trial judge should have sought clarification of a note he received from the jury stating they were unable to come to a decision owing to their 'conscious [*sic*] beliefs' and asking his advice. Following receipt of a second note, the judge asked for the names of the jurors involved, which he should not have done. On being informed that two jurors (including the foreman) were involved, the judge discharged the whole jury. He then held both jurors to be in contempt of court and sentenced them to 30 days' imprisonment. In fact, they only served one day, but the Court of Appeal held that each appellant should have been dealt with differently and that the judge had made an error of judgment. There was a real danger of bias and the judge could have discharged the appellants and sought a majority verdict. The following statements of principle were confirmed: s 8(1) of the Juries Act 1974 applies to the court as well as everyone else; conscientious objection to jury service was not an exemption but came within s 9(4), permitting discretionary excusal; a properly empanelled juror was not accountable for anything said or done in discharge of the office; a juror was neither punishable for contempt for returning a perverse verdict, as in *Bushell's Case* (1670), nor indictable for breaking the oath; and a juror who 'wilfully would not find for either side' should be fined, again as in *Bushell's Case*.

Lord Runciman recommended that suitable research should be conducted and that s 8 should be amended so as to permit research into the influence that jurors with criminal records may have on verdicts. To date, this has not been adopted. His other recommendations included:

- removal of the exemption for clergymen and members of religious orders, providing instead a right to be excused;

- in exceptional cases, the prosecution or defence should be able to apply for selection of a jury to include up to three people from ethnic minorities and that either the prosecution or the defence should be able to argue that one or more of the three should come from the same ethnic minority group as the defendant or the victim;

- writing materials should be provided as standard and the judge should explain to the jury at the start of the trial the extent to which they might ask questions and that they have a right to take notes.

Another issue is that concerning the intimidation of jury members (usually referred to as 'jury nobbling'). Lord Runciman recommended that every effort should be made to protect jurors from intimidation. Sensitive cases should be assigned to courtrooms where the public gallery cannot be used for such purposes. For example, members of the public present will not be able to catch the eye of members of the jury. The Criminal Justice and Public Order Act 1994 follows this recommendation and provides for a new offence of witness and juror intimidation, and we have mentioned earlier s 54 of the Criminal Procedure and Investigations Act 1996 in respect of tainted acquittals.

Another issue is that of jury vetting, whereby the prosecution seeks to check on, and then exclude from jury service, those who are considered undesirable. The Attorney General issued guidelines on jury checks in 1980 (revised in 1988), which recognised the following general principles:

- jury members are to be selected at random from the panel. The Juries Act 1974 lists those disqualified from, or ineligible for, jury service. The prosecution should only seek to exclude a member of the panel in open court by a request to stand by for the Crown or, if necessary, to challenge for cause;

- corrupt and biased jurors are provided for by way of majority verdicts and the provision that an unqualified person who sits on a jury commits an offence. Such persons can be removed following searches by the police of criminal records;

- further safeguards are needed to ensure the administration of justice where national security and terrorist cases are involved. In such cases, it is permitted for the police to make a limited investigation of the panel to see whether any have criminal records.

The Attorney General can, in addition, authorise that Special Branch records be searched following an application by the Director of Public Prosecutions by way of authorised checks. Following such a check, a right to stand a juror by for the Crown should only be used if there is strong reason to believe that the juror in waiting might be a security risk or susceptible to improper approaches or be influenced in arriving at a verdict by way of improper influences. Prosecuting counsel has a discretion whether or not to disclose the nature and source of such information. Where a juror is not asked to stand by for the

Crown but is believed to be potentially a risk to the defence, the latter should be given a general indication as to the reason why he may be inimical to their interests. As already mentioned, the question of secrecy as to the deliberations of juries is of great concern and ensures that the debate concerning the effectiveness of the jury in reaching decisions is hampered.

By s 8 of the Contempt of Court Act 1981, it is an offence to 'obtain, disclose, or solicit any particulars of statements made, opinions expressed, arguments advanced or votes cast by members of a jury in the course of their deliberations in any legal proceedings'.

This effectively prevents any intrusion on the independence of the jury, but, as noted by Professor McConville, its secrecy suggests that it 'is a source of weakness, making it vulnerable to charges of stupidity, capriciousness and bias'. In an article entitled 'Shadowing the jury' ((1991) 141 NLJ, pp 1588, 1595), Professor McConville describes the research conducted with the co-operation of the Lord Chancellor's Department by Twenty Twenty Television, *Inside the Jury*, where shadow juries sat alongside actual juries and whose deliberations were observed. In all respects, the shadow juries emulated the conditions of the actual juries and this was also reflected in the similarity of the verdicts. Of the five trials shadowed, agreement as to verdict was reached in four and, in the other, the actual jury convicted whereas the shadow jury failed to reach a verdict. Professor McConville suggests that we have every reason to be confident in the quality of decision making by juries, and that on the evidence of this experiment, the jury 'would survive any examination of its workings'.

In October 1994, Stephen Young won a retrial after conviction for two murders when it came to light that four of the jurors, who were wavering about the verdict, used a Ouija board to call up the spirits of the victims in an attempt to elicit from them who had killed them. This took place in a hotel room, and not the jury room, but this still amounted to a material irregularity in jury deliberations, as jurors must confine themselves to consideration only of the evidence presented to the court. Consideration of the evidence only may be a daunting task and one which may necessitate many hours of deliberation by a jury. Not only is this true in complex fraud trials, but also those involving serious sexual charges and trials of serial killers, such as Peter Sutcliffe, Rosemary West and Harold Shipman.

Use of the jury, particularly in trials on indictment in the Crown Court, is likely to be retained, as it is considered that findings of fact should be decided by more than one person. Also, it is considered important to have the involvement of the layperson in the administration of justice, as it retains public confidence and provides a balance between the interests of the State and of the individual.

However, many criticisms have been made of the jury, and some of these were addressed by the Royal Commission on Criminal Justice. The facilities afforded to jurors are often rudimentary. For example, paper and pencils are not always provided and members of the jury may be overawed by the judge, counsel or simply the occasion. Jurors receive no training for their task and they may be young or inexperienced. They may also be unwilling participants and be either unable or unwilling to participate fully. They may well have to assimilate long and complex evidence or that which is harrowing or unpleasant. Members of the jury may be swayed by the persuasive arguments of counsel and, in some cases, such as shoplifting, the defendant may elect for jury trial on the advice of counsel who considers that acquittal is more likely in the Crown Court. Should the Mode of Trial Bill become law, the defendant's right of election for jury trial will be removed in triable either way offences.

The trial judge has discretion to decide on its merits whether to allow disabled persons to sit as jurors. In a case in June 1995, a deaf man was refused permission to sit as a juror by an Old Bailey recorder. In 1999, the Lord Chancellor stated that the law permitting a trial judge discretion to refuse a profoundly deaf person from sitting as a juror and have the assistance in the jury room of a translator should be reviewed, as there may well be situations where a deaf or blind person would not be so incapacitated as to be prevented from serving on a jury. An application had been made by Mr McWhinney, as head of the Royal Society for the Protection of the Deaf, for a ruling that this should be allowed, but the trial judge refused his application. Only 12 jurors are allowed in the jury room and the Juries Act 1974 permits no exceptions.

Other disadvantages include the threat of intimidation and the possibility of corruption; undue leniency; unrepresentative composition and the cost to the State of reimbursing juror expenses. We have mentioned above the secrecy which surrounds the workings of the jury system and the disadvantages this causes for effective research and possible reforms.

However, in a reserved judgment, the Court of Appeal (Criminal Division) in the case of *R v Andrews* (1998) held that questioning potential jurors by means of a questionnaire to see whether they were biased should be avoided, other than in the most exceptional circumstances. The defendant had been accused of stabbing her boyfriend at the roadside and considerable publicity had implicated her in the crime. Oral questioning was also to be avoided, as this, like a questionnaire, was of doubtful efficacy and could be counter-productive. Reference was made to the exceptional circumstances noted in the *Attorney General's Guidelines on the Exercise by the Crown of its Right of Stand-By* (1989) 88 Cr App R 123.

THE COURTS AND THEIR PERSONNEL

The court system

- The High Court:
  - Queen's Bench Divisional Court;
  - Chancery Divisional Court;
  - Family Divisional Court;
  - specialist courts, such as the Commercial Court.

- The Crown Court:
  - indictable offences and triable either way offences where the defendant elects jury trial;
  - Supreme Court Act 1981;
  - appellate jurisdiction and the power to sentence defendants tried summarily for offences triable either way – s 38 of the Magistrates' Courts Act 1980 (as amended).

- The county court:
  - small claims procedure;
  - Civil Procedure Act 1997; CPR 1998.
  - civil cases: small claims, fast and multi-tracks.

- The magistrates' courts:
  - jurisdiction of the court in criminal matters – trial of summary offences; offences triable either way where the defendant does not elect jury trial;
  - committal proceedings;
  - sentencing powers of magistrates – ss 31, 32 and 133 of the Magistrates' Courts Act 1980; s 37 of the Criminal Justice Act 1982 (as amended by s 17 of the Criminal Justice Act 1991);
  - appeals to Crown Court and Queen's Bench Divisional Court;
  - role of magistrates in the youth court (formerly the juvenile court).

The personnel of the courts

- Judges
  - selection and appointment;
  - Lords of Appeal in Ordinary;
  - Lord Justices of Appeal;
  - High Court judges;
  - circuit judges, recorders, district judges and magistrates;
  - offices of Lord Chancellor; Lord Chief Justice and Master of the Rolls;
  - Access to Justice Act 1999.
- Judicial officers
  - Lord Chancellor, Attorney General and Director of Public Prosecutions (DPP);
  - DPP subject to judicial review? *R v DPP ex p Kebeline and Others* (1999); *R v DPP ex p Manning and Another* (2000).

The layperson and the law

- Lay magistrates.
- Coroners.
- Lay assessors.
- The jury:
  - Juries Act 1974;
  - s 118 of the Criminal Justice Act 1988;
  - relationship of judge (arbiter of law) and jury (arbiter of fact);
  - trial of Clive Ponting as perverse decision;
  - rules for the discharge of juries and recommendations for reform;
  - jury intimidation ('nobbling') and vetting distinguished;
  - Attorney General's *Guidelines on Jury Checks*;
  - case law – *R v Schot and R v Barclay* (1997); *R v Andrews* (1998).

CHAPTER 4

THE PROVISION OF LEGAL SERVICES

Introduction

In this chapter, we will consider the how the legal profession developed into a divided one in which barristers were the specialist advocates who, acting on the instructions of a solicitor, prepared opinions, drafted court documents and, if necessary, represented the lay client in court. The solicitor was the general practitioner who met the lay client, offered advice, drafted documents, such as contracts and wills, and if the law was in dispute referred the matter to counsel, the barrister, for an opinion on the law and the chances of success if the matter went to court. We will also consider the fundamental changes coming about in the profession as a result of the Courts and Legal Services Act 1990 and the Access to Justice Act 1999, in particular the breaking of the Bar's monopoly on advocacy. Other providers of legal services will be considered, including 'administrative agencies' such as the Citizens Advice Bureaux and the changes which will come about as a result of the Access to Justice Act 1999 to provide an integrated scheme, rather than the piecemeal one which has developed over the years. Of major concern has been the rapid increase in the costs of funding legal services and we will look at the present schemes available and how the vision for change of Lord Irvine, the Lord Chancellor, will change the system of funding. The drive towards the use of alternative dispute resolution (ADR) (see Chapter 5) and insurance provision and the use of 'no win, no fee' agreements will all have an impact on a person's access to legal services and it is certain that, in future, the State will not be responsible for funding legal services to the extent it has done in the recent past. Despite vast sums having gone into funding legal services, an unmet need was recognised to exist. Unless the 1999 Act provisions for change prove to be effective in ensuring that those with legal problems can solve them by seeking advice or information or ultimately going to court, this unmet need will only increase. As was said in *R v Lord Chancellor ex p Witham* (1997), it is essential in a civilised society for people to have access to legal services.

The legal profession

The traditional divide

Traditionally, we have had a divided legal profession in England and Wales. Legal practitioners have trained and practised either as solicitors or barristers. The titles solicitor, attorney and proctor originally denoted non-advocates who conducted preparation of cases in the Chancery, common law and the

Ecclesiastical and Admiralty Courts respectively. Barristers were apprentices-at-law, and those with rights of audience in the superior courts were known as serjeants-at-law. Reforms were made by the Judicature Acts 1873–75, resulting in the division between barristers and solicitors. The Law Society, as the governing body for solicitors, was incorporated in 1831 and received its royal charter in 1845. The General Council of the Bar is the governing body for barristers.

The barrister has been seen by some to be the senior member of the profession, advising and representing the client in court only on the recommendation of a solicitor. There were some 9,500 barristers in independent practice in 1999, of which about one-third were women. Of the 1,000 or so Queen's Counsel, under 100 are women.

The solicitor is often described as the general practitioner of the profession, advising the client direct, preparing documents on the client's behalf, such as wills and contracts, and representing the client only in the lower courts. Solicitors are the 'office' lawyers, to be found in any high street or business quarter of towns and cities, and who since 1985 have been able to advertise the types of services offered. There are some 60,000 solicitors in private practice, according to Law Society figures for 1999. In all, some 95,000 solicitors have their names on the roll, of which 75,000 hold practising certificates. About one-third of these are women, and about one-half are aged over 40.

Legal executives are a body of legal professionals in their own right who work in solicitors' offices. Traditionally, they were referred to as solicitors' 'managing clerks', but in recent times they have had much more responsibility for their own work, usually in the areas of matrimonial, conveyancing and probate matters. They have their own governing body, the Institute of Legal Executives.

The relationship between barrister, solicitor and client is governed by rules of etiquette, many of which have been, and no doubt will be, further relaxed following the reforms under the Courts and Legal Services Act 1990 and the Access to Justice Act 1999. One of the purposes of the rules was to maintain the division and the monopolies of both sides of the profession, for example, the barrister maintained a monopoly over rights of audience, that is, the right to represent clients in all courts.

Legal professionals are not only found in private practice; barristers, solicitors and legal executives also work in industry, the civil service, local government and organisations such as the Crown Prosecution Service (CPS).

The role of the barrister

The primary function of most barristers was to act as advocates, and this craft was learnt largely 'on the job' during one year spent in pupillage (under the supervision of an experienced barrister) and, following call to the Bar, by appearing in magistrates' and county courts. During the first six months of pupillage, the pupil expects to be closely supervised by the pupil master and assists the latter by reading instructions from solicitors, drafting documents and accompanying the pupil master to court. In the latter six months, the pupil might be permitted to take cases on his or her own behalf and work with much less supervision.

The barrister receives written instructions, known as a brief, from instructing solicitors, which may involve any one or a combination of three things: it may require simply advice as to the appropriate law to be applied to the facts outlined in the brief; it may require the drafting of a document; or it may require representation by the barrister in court.

Not all barristers spend the majority of their time in court or preparing for trial. Those at the Chancery Bar, for example, spend much of their time receiving instructions from solicitors to offer advice on points of law concerning disputed wills or rights on intestacy, transfers of property or rights under trusts and settlements. The result is a detachment from direct contact with the client and the needs of running a business.

Barristers operate as sole practitioners, unlike solicitors, who usually form partnerships, in what are known as sets of chambers. These are offices where the barrister takes a tenancy of a room and pays for the privilege of having the services of a clerk to chambers. Most are located in London near the Inns of Court and the law courts. The four Inns of Court (Gray's Inn, Lincoln's Inn, Inner and Middle Temples) are the only surviving Inns (there were many others dating back to the 14th century).

For some years, the provincial Bar has been developing, with barristers setting up chambers in modern offices outside London, and no doubt this will continue apace with the changes brought about by the Courts and Legal Services Act 1990. Barristers are now able to advertise their services and to come increasingly into direct contact with clients, in particular professional and corporate clients.

Training of barristers

Following the academic stage of training, a student seeking call to the Bar is required to join an Inn and dine in hall on 12 occasions. Each Inn is governed by senior members known as Benchers, who are often judges, who regulate conduct and discipline. Traditionally, the Inn was not only a place of work, but where barristers lived, and this is thought to be one reason for the continuation of dining, to ensure the perpetuation of the customs and traditions of this side of the profession.

The academic stage involves a law graduate or student (who has passed the Common Professional Examination or a Diploma in Law, offered at a recognised institution), taking a full time one year course at the Council of

Legal Education in London, leading to the Bar final examinations. Having completed the examinations and dining, the student applies for call to the Bar by his or her Inn of Court. With effect from September 1997, the Bar Vocational Course was offered for the first time outside of London. Several provincial centres have had their courses validated. The question of cost and the inconvenience of having students travelling to London to dine on 18 occasions was resolved when it was announced that, with effect from October 1997, this would be replaced by an educational programme involving lecture evenings or residential weekends or one day lectures, with the aim of making travelling to London more worthwhile. Dining terms have now been reduced to 12. The Lord Chancellor's Advisory Committee on Legal Education had questioned the need for any dining requirement, but this has not been given effect.

Distinctive features of the Bar

Barristers can be of two ranks, the senior, known as Queen's Counsel, and the less senior, known as Juniors (although this has nothing to do with age). Those who have been in practice and who consider the time is right may apply to the Lord Chancellor's department for the change in title and status. Application is made each year and not all will be successful at the first or later attempts. No reasons are given for refusal and deliberations are conducted in secret. An applicant who is successful is entitled to have 'QC' after his or her name, may be assisted in court by junior counsel, and is entitled to wear a strip of silk on his or her gown whilst in court. This has given rise to the reference to 'taking silk' by a barrister appointed as a QC. The other consequence of appointment is that the QC is more able to choose the cases he or she wishes to take and is not so strictly bound by the 'cab-rank' rule, which provides that a barrister should be ready and willing to take any case of a type with which he or she is familiar passed to him or her by the clerk to chambers.

The barrister has for some two centuries been extremely visible when appearing in court due to the robe, wig, wing collars and black attire required as standard dress. This is only one area which demonstrates that the legal profession is steeped in history and tradition and that the pace of change is often slow. However, a debate was generated in 1992 as to whether wigs and robes should be disbanded and, although this was settled in October 1993 in favour of retention of wigs and gowns, the question re-emerged following the ending of the barristers' monopoly over rights of audience in December 1993. In October 1993, a joint statement by the Lord Chancellor and Lord Taylor, the then Lord Chief Justice, confirmed that judges and members of the legal profession should retain wigs and gowns. Interestingly, when the Law Lords sit to hear appeals in the House of Lords, only counsel appear in wigs and gowns.

A consultation paper in 1992 received responses from 520 organisations and individuals, 67% of which were in favour of retaining daily court dress. Only 15% favoured total abolition of all formal dress. It was thought that the authority and status of the court, the law and the profession were assured by maintenance of formal dress. The question was then posed as to whether solicitors who obtain advocacy certificates under ss 27–33 of the Courts and Legal Services Act 1990 should wear wigs and black gowns or retain their traditional court dress of grey gowns. Representatives of the Bar opposed adoption by solicitors of court dress traditionally worn only by barristers (and this is the position today), although some in the profession still wish to see all formality removed.

The barrister has traditionally had an honorarium arrangement with instructing solicitors and only met the lay client in the presence of the instructing solicitor. This was binding in honour only, with the result that a barrister was unable to sue for his or her fees and, in some cases, solicitors or their firms were blacklisted for consistent failure to pay fees promptly. Section 61 of the Courts and Legal Services Act 1990 permitted barristers to enter into legally binding contracts for the provision of their services. In other respects also, the 1990 Act and the Administration of Justice Act 1999 have made changes to modernise the legal profession and place it on a business footing.

With the changes in the rules of audience brought about under the 1990 and 1999 Acts, in time, the exclusive monopoly of barristers to form the ranks of the judiciary will decline. This will not only change the composition of the judiciary, but will bring into question what is expected of the judge and people's perception of the role of the judge. One question that will no doubt arise will be possible conflicts of interest between the need to be impartial and possible conflicting interests between those involved in a case to be tried and a firm or company or past or present clients or their associates. This issue was raised in *Locabail (UK) Ltd v Bayfield Properties Ltd* (1999).

The role of the solicitor

Like the barrister who has a monopoly over advocacy, the solicitor had various monopolies, including land transactions (conveyancing), probate (the preparation of wills and the handling of estates on a person's death) and the right to conduct litigation.

The Administration of Justice Act 1985 abolished the conveyancing monopoly and established licensed conveyancers able to compete with solicitors in the conduct of the purchase and sale of property. Sections 34 and 35 of the Courts and Legal Services Act 1990 established the Authorised Conveyancing Practitioners Board to develop competition and supervise authorised conveyancing practitioners. Section 53 permitted the Council for Licensed Conveyancers to become an authorised body for the purposes of granting advocacy rights and rights to conduct litigation.

Conveyancing had been the 'bread and butter' work of the majority of small to middle sized firms of solicitors, and with its loss came calls for the abolition of the barristers' monopoly over rights of audience. The monopoly over probate matters was removed by ss 54–55 of the Courts and Legal Services Act 1990, and the right to conduct litigation by s 28.

Solicitors have always had rights of audience in the lower courts, that is, the county and magistrates' courts, and, in limited cases, solicitors have had a right to appear in the Crown Court, for example, on an appeal from the magistrates and in certain Crown Courts designated by the Lord Chancellor, such as Truro in Cornwall, where in the past the cost and delay of having counsel travel from London or the provincial Bar could be prohibitive. This is preserved by s 67 of the Courts and Legal Services Act 1990, which substitutes a new s 83 of the Supreme Court Act 1981.

Solicitors also had limited rights to appear in the High Court, but usually only in chambers (the private rooms of the judge concerning matters which were not to be dealt with in open court, such as applications concerning children). In the case of *Abse and Others v Smith* (1986), a libel action involving the MP Cyril Smith, it was stated that a solicitor would be permitted to appear before the High Court to read out a prepared statement, but was not entitled to present arguments to the court. It was the role of the barrister to present contentious issues to the court.

The governing body of solicitors, The Law Society, performs two roles. (Not all solicitors are members of the Society, but those in practice are under an obligation to obtain and renew a practising certificate and contribute to the indemnity fund to cover claims brought by clients for malpractice.) The Society not only provides social facilities for its members, but also by regulations made under the Solicitors Act 1974 (as amended), provides for the education and training of students, the discipline of all solicitors and the fees and scales of remuneration of solicitors.

Another change brought about by the Courts and Legal Services Act 1990 permitted the establishment of multidisciplinary and multinational practices (s 66). By s 66, all statutory and common law prohibitions on barristers and solicitors in England and Wales entering into partnerships with other professionals (such as accountants or taxation specialists) or foreign lawyers are removed, but The Law Society and the Bar Council may make rules prohibiting or restricting their members from entering into such practices.

Traditionally, solicitors in private practice have been restricted to operating as sole practitioners or in partnership with other solicitors. As we have seen, this has now changed, in so far as those who can enter into partnership with solicitors. By s 90 of the Courts and Legal Services Act 1990, s 9 of the Administration of Justice Act 1985 is amended to provide for contributions to the Compensation Fund (maintained by The Law Society to meet claims from clients who have suffered at the hands of a dishonest solicitor) from incorporated bodies, with the effect that solicitors are now able to form limited companies.

Training of solicitors

Training to become a solicitor involves completion of the academic stage, by way of law degree or non-law degree and Common Professional Examination or Diploma in Law, completion of the professional stage by way of a full time Legal Practice Course at a recognised institution, and the apprenticeship stage, formerly referred to as articles of clerkship but which is now referred to as the trainee solicitor stage, where practical experience is gained under the supervision of an experienced solicitor for two years.

Following qualification, the trainee is admitted to the Roll of Solicitors maintained by The Law Society and supervised by the Master of the Rolls. Non-graduates who have qualified as legal executives may enter the profession once they have become Fellows of the Institute of Legal Executives and have completed the Legal Practice Course. Where continuous legal employment is shown, The Law Society may waive the requirement that he or she undertakes traineeship.

Not all solicitors enter private practice; some take up appointments in the civil service, local government, the court service, for example, as magistrates' court clerks, and with the CPS.

Changing roles of barristers and solicitors – rights of audience

So as to avoid confusion, it is worth noting the distinction between rights of audience (advocacy) and the right to conduct litigation. The interpretation section of s 119 of the Courts and Legal Services Act 1990 offers assistance. The right to conduct litigation is the right to commence proceedings in any court and to have the conduct of matters which are ancillary to proceedings, such as entering an appearance on behalf of a client. Rights of audience permit one person to represent another in court. Usually, this will be for a fee, but, under s 11 of the Courts and Legal Services Act 1990, a person may be assisted by a friend or lay adviser, commonly referred to as a *McKenzie* friend (from the case of *McKenzie v McKenzie* (1971)). In *R v Bow County Court ex p Pelling* (1999), the Court of Appeal held that a litigant in person is only allowed a *McKenzie* friend if the judge is satisfied that fairness and the interests of justice require it. Pelling was refused access to a hearing in chambers (the judge's private room) without reason, and he sought judicial review of this refusal. The Court of Appeal refused his application on the basis that there was no right for a *McKenzie* friend to appear in chambers, whether paid or not.

In December 1993, it was announced that the Lord Chancellor and four senior judges (including the Master of the Rolls and the Lord Chief Justice) had, under ss 27–33 of the Courts and Legal Services Act 1990 and in accordance with s 17 of the Act, approved the application by the solicitors' governing body, The Law Society, for solicitors in private practice to be granted rights of audience in both civil and criminal proceedings in the House of Lords, the Court of Appeal, the High Court and the Crown Court. Section 17 sets out two objectives. The first deals with the development of legal services by providing new and better ways and wider choice of provider whilst maintaining proper and efficient administration of justice; and the second, the 'general principle', applies only to rights of audience and rights to conduct litigation. Such rights should be granted where the criteria provided in s 17(3) were met. These included appropriate education and training; membership of a recognised professional body; in the case of advocacy rights, that advocacy services would not be withheld on the grounds that a case is objectionable; the conduct, opinions or belief of the client are unacceptable to the advocate or any section of the public; or on any ground relating to the source of finance, such as legal aid.

This has been described as the principle of non-discrimination and applies to all advocates and those with rights to conduct litigation. Section 17(5) expressly permitted rules of conduct to be made by authorised bodies permitting their members to withhold their services where it would be reasonable in all the circumstances to do so (for example, where a proper fee was not offered). The authorised bodies referred to were The Law Society and the General Council of the Bar in relation to advocacy rights and The Law Society in relation to rights to conduct litigation. Section 29 of the Courts and Legal Services Act 1990 set out the procedures for application to the Lord Chancellor by other bodies for the grant of such rights.

The effect was to alter the traditional divide between solicitors and barristers by ensuring that barristers and solicitors would in future be able to compete in providing advocacy. This was much welcomed by The Law Society, but the General Council of the Bar, the governing body for barristers, stated that, although it was not adverse to fair competition, solicitors would have to ensure that clients were advised of their right to be represented by a barrister.

By March 1997, some 438 solicitors in private practice had acquired rights of audience in the higher courts. A further 170 applications were at that time in process. Of the 60,000 solicitors in private practice, those in criminal law practices largely dependent on legal aid funding, and those in commercial and financial city firms, are the most likely to apply and qualify for extended rights of audience, once they have taken the requisite tests and demonstrated relevant court experience.

Higher courts qualifications cover civil proceedings, criminal proceedings or both and are open to solicitors who have practised for three years and who have two years' experience of advocacy in the lower courts. They must demonstrate experience of higher court procedures, competency in a written test on evidence and procedure and complete the advocacy training course. Solicitors who are also barristers or part time judges may seek exemption from these requirements.

Also in 1997, The Law Society was successful when it applied for rights of audience for solicitors employed other than in solicitor's firms. Solicitors employed by the CPS were granted rights of audience subject to the three following exceptions: prosecuting solicitors in criminal proceedings committed for trial to the Crown Court; in civil proceedings in the higher courts in hearings to dispose of the merits of the case; and for local authorities in care proceedings. Individual employed solicitors would have to apply and satisfy the requisite tests and relevant court experience and be subject to any restrictions imposed on them by their professional bodies.

Part III of the Access to Justice Act 1999 amends the Courts and Legal Services Act 1990 in several important respects: the Lord Chancellor's Advisory Committee on Legal Education and Conduct becomes the Legal Services Consultative Panel; full rights of audience shall in principle extend to all lawyers; the procedures for authorising other bodies to grant rights of audience or to conduct litigation are reformed, as are those for approving changes to rules of conduct to allow the exercise of such rights; the powers of the Lord Chancellor to make rule changes are extended, and by Sched 5 he may amend the rules of authorised bodies so as to remove restrictions on rights of audience and rights to conduct litigation; the limitations placed on employed solicitors to act as advocates are removed, so that those employed by the CPS, for example, will be able to act as advocates, if otherwise qualified to do so; by s 40, the Bar Council and Institute of Legal Executives become authorised bodies, in addition to The Law Society, to grant rights to conduct litigation; by s 42, litigators and advocates owe duties first to the court and must act independently in the interests of justice, putting aside contractual or other interests. This is a crucial provision and ensures the independence of the advocate and that he or she is first and foremost an officer of the court.

Immunity from suit

By s 62, immunity from suit in the tort of negligence and breach of contract is extended to all those with advocacy rights, that is, covering the conduct of cases in court and the immediate preparation for trial. Thus, the immunity also applies to those who become authorised litigators under ss 27 and 28 of the Courts and Legal Services Act 1990 and to those authorised by the Lord Chancellor under s 11 to exercise rights of audience and to conduct litigation.

The common law established the immunity of barristers and the cases of *Rondel v Worsley* (1967) and *Saif Ali v Mitchell and Co* (1978) demonstrate that both barristers and solicitors, when acting as advocates, had immunity against claims in negligence. This rule has now been enacted under the above provisions. Not only is there immunity from civil claims, but the Legal Services Ombudsman is not empowered to investigate allegations of misconduct of proceedings or matters closely connected with this under s 22(7)(b) of the

Courts and Legal Services Act 1990, although in his first annual report in 1992, the first Ombudsman, Michael Barnes, who was appointed on 1 January 1991 (and re-appointed in 1994), criticised this immunity and stated that he wished to challenge the limits of his jurisdiction.

The liability of a solicitor for negligent advice is clearly shown in the cases of *Ross v Caunters* (1979), *White v Jones* (1995) and *Worby v Rosser* (1999). In *Kelly v LTE* (1982), the Court of Appeal held that an opposing client could sue a barrister for breach of duty and for negligent conduct of proceedings or preparation for trial. This will now apply to all who are authorised to conduct litigation or exercise rights of audience.

As we have seen, the traditional role of the solicitor has been that of the businessman offering legal services to lay and professional clients on a wide variety of legal, financial and other matters.

Contingency fees

By s 58 of the Courts and Legal Services Act 1990, those providing advocacy or litigation services are permitted to enter into a written contract for the fee to be payable 'only in specified circumstances', including where an action is successful. This section applied to barristers, solicitors and others offering services in personal injury claims, proceedings in the European Court of Human Rights (ECHR) or Commission and claims in insolvency. Changes have been made by ss 27–31 of the Access to Justice Act 1999 to extend the scope of the scheme in line with the major legal aid reforms which will be mentioned later. Such agreements have no effect where a client is legally aided and, if entered into before the legal aid certificate is issued, the agreement ceases to have effect on issue of a certificate.

The effect of such an agreement is that it provides for 'no win, no fee', but the fee will be the normal rate charged for that type of work uprated by a maximum of 100% to cover the risk to the lawyer of having no fee if the case is lost.

Complaints against barristers and solicitors

In the past, much criticism has been made of the complaints procedures and in particular the lack of remedies available to a client aggrieved by the actions of a barrister. In December 1993, the Bar Council set up a standards review body with lay membership to oversee the quality of service, fees, and to provide an overhaul of the complaints procedure. Shoddy standards and poor court performance were also considered. Michael Barnes, the then Legal Services Ombudsman, in his 1995 report (published in June 1996), reviewed the Bar Council's present complaints system and noted that a new system would come into effect in 1997. He welcomed the award of compensation up to £2,000 to lay clients for poor service but was disappointed that this only applied to cases where financial loss could be proved. He hoped that it would be extended in future to cover distress and inconvenience. The Professional Conduct Committee of the Bar Council hears complaints against barristers and, in serious cases, these are referred to the Disciplinary Tribunal of the Inns of Court which has wide powers including suspending, fining up to £5,000 and striking off a barrister. No provision is made for the payment of compensation, although the tribunal may order that fees be repaid or forgone. A barrister may also be reprimanded or advised as to future conduct. As we have noted, barristers have immunity from claims in the tort of negligence for their conduct in court, but, as was shown in the case of *Saif Ali v Mitchell and Co* (1978), this does not apply to pre-trial advice.

Under ss 21–26 of the Courts and Legal Services Act 1990, the Legal Services Ombudsman, appointed by the Lord Chancellor, replaces the office of the lay observer and oversees the handling of complaints against both solicitors and barristers. By s 21(7) of the 1990 Act, the Ombudsman is prevented from investigating matters determined or being determined by a court, the Solicitors' Disciplinary Tribunal, the Disciplinary Tribunal of the Inns of Court, other tribunals specified by order of the Lord Chancellor and where immunity from suit applies.

So far as solicitors are concerned, an aggrieved client has several means at his or her disposal for obtaining redress, although it may not be straightforward, as was illustrated by the protracted litigation by Peggy Wood, whose claim against several firms of solicitors and The Law Society itself had continued for some 10 years. In *Wood v Law Society* (1995), the Court of Appeal held that The Law Society was not liable to Mrs Wood for failing to investigate a conflict of interest between her solicitor and the lender who repossessed Mrs Wood's property when she failed to repay the loan. The Law Society may have been incompetent and dilatory, but this was not the cause of Mrs Wood's loss. In recent years, the number of complaints have soared.

In 1986, the Solicitors' Complaints Bureau was established and funded by, but acting independently of, The Law Society. Formerly, all complaints were handled by The Law Society, but little trust between the profession and the public was engendered, given that The Law Society represents solicitors.

The Bureau had wide ranging powers to effect a solution, including conciliation, investigation and adjudication. If conciliation, which was voluntary and only appropriate where communication had not broken down, did not effect an amicable settlement, the more formal process of investigation could be resorted to. In serious cases, the Bureau would refer the case to the Solicitors' Disciplinary Tribunal, which has similar powers to the tribunal regulating barristers, including the power to fine, strike off and suspend. Its findings are published and it has recently been announced that it will conduct its hearings in public. Appeal lies to the Queen's Bench Divisional Court of the High Court. In September 1996, the Solicitors' Complaints Bureau was replaced by the Office for the Supervision of Solicitors (OSS), which aims to improve the complaints handling system so as to ensure the speedy handling of other than deadlocked or complex matters. Michael Barnes, in his 1995 report, continued to monitor the progress of the profession (both barristers and solicitors) in dealing with complaints. He issued a warning that, if significant improvement was not made, then The Law Society would lose its complaint handling functions. The Ombudsman was also critical of the compensation scheme offered by the Bar Council in respect of financial loss suffered by clients and suggested its further extension to those caused inconvenience or distress by poor service.

As we have noted, solicitors can be sued in the tort of negligence when not acting as advocates. *Ross v Caunters* (1979) concerned the negligent preparation of a will and it was held that the solicitor was liable in tort to a third party who would have inherited under the will if it had been properly drafted. The Bureau had set up a panel of solicitors who offer private clients alleging negligence on the part of their solicitor an initial free interview, followed by an investigation, leading to civil action in appropriate cases.

All solicitors (whether in private practice or paid employment involving the provision of legal services) must hold a practising certificate. This has been made clear by s 85 of the Courts and Legal Services Act 1990 amending s 1 of the Solicitors' Act 1974, which left the matter in doubt. Those in private practice are also required to contribute to the compensation fund and hold indemnity insurance to meet successful claims made against them for malpractice. The former provides a safeguard for clients whose moneys have been misappropriated by dishonest solicitors (or their staff) and where the loss cannot be recovered by any other means. The Law Society has complete discretion in making awards of compensation from this fund. As we have noted, the Legal Services Ombudsman oversees the handling of complaints, but a time limit of three months applies. By s 22(2), the Ombudsman may investigate the matter to which a complaint relates (that is, not only the complaint itself), but s 22(7) imposes restraints on the types of complaint investigated.

Many complaints arise out of questions over fees. The Solicitors' Practice Rules 1991 attempt to ensure that full information is given to the client about who is handling his or her case, progress, likely cost and what he or she should do if not satisfied with the standard of service. Solicitors' charges are usually costed according to time and complexity of the subject matter, and will be subject to VAT and include expenses (called disbursements) which the solicitor has incurred, for example, stamp duty or land registry fees.

A distinction is drawn between costs incurred on matters not involving litigation (called non-contentious matters) and costs incurred in litigation (contentious matters). In the former, disputes over the costs charged can be referred to The Law Society, whereas, in the case of the latter, the costs will be subject to the scrutiny of the court and a process formerly called taxation, and since the Woolf reforms called assessment. Costs are assessed to see whether the bill is a reasonable one. In non-contentious matters, the client should first of all query the bill but, if this does not result in agreement, he or she can request the solicitor to obtain a remuneration certificate from The Law Society, that is, a statement that the bill is a fair and reasonable one. If the client fails to pay the bill and does not request the solicitor to obtain a remuneration certificate, the solicitor can only sue on the bill following service of a formal notice of the client's right to such a certificate and for the bill to be assessed by the court. On receipt of this notice the client has only 28 days within which to request the solicitor to obtain the certificate. This must be done at the solicitor's expense in all cases. The Law Society may confirm or reduce the bill and a client who remains dissatisfied may then resort to assessment by the court.

A pioneering complaints scheme was announced early in 2000 by law firms in Devon to be operated by the Devon and Exeter Law Society. This local scheme will supplement the national scheme run by the Office for the Supervision of Solicitors (OSS), which has been the subject of much criticism. Complaints have risen since The Law Society introduced the 'rule 15 procedure', which compels law firms to inform clients of their right to complain from the outset, and backlogs have built up under the national scheme. The local scheme will handle complaints against its member firms which the firm cannot resolve. An independent lawyer will be appointed to investigate, mediate and recommend a solution. Clients who remain dissatisfied will then refer their complaint to the OSS.

Have the professions fused?

Having looked at the traditional roles of barristers and solicitors and some of the many changes made by the Courts and Legal Services Act 1990 and Access to Justice Act 1999, it is time to make some concluding remarks about the legal profession and its future development and the effects these changes might have on the future composition of the judiciary.

Given the important changes extending advocacy rights and rights to conduct litigation, and that solicitors now have the right to appear in the higher courts, the question as to whether we have a fused profession, or should have one, re-emerges. It might even be argued that we have fusion in all but name. It is perhaps instructive to look to Australia and New Zealand, where barristers have direct access to clients and can form partnerships with solicitors and other barristers. This recognises the functions performed by each, but ensures that barristers can acquire work in conjunction with solicitors, and not in direct competition with solicitor advocates.

Under the reforms here, we have retained an exclusive Bar where barristers are dependent on solicitors referring cases to them and where barristers and solicitor advocates will be free to compete with each other. Neil Addison of the Bar Council suggests that this arrangement will have to change if barristers are to survive. He suggests that we adopt a system similar to that in Australia and New Zealand, effectively fusing the professions, although the titles of 'solicitor' and 'barrister' would remain.

Some have suggested that the titles 'solicitor' and 'barrister' should be replaced by 'attorney' and 'advocate' respectively, in order to identify more clearly the type of work performed by each. The attorney would act as the desk lawyer, whereas the advocate would appear in court. Providing the qualifications and training had been completed for both functions, a fusion lawyer would be competent to both advise and represent the client in court, or at least firms could be established in which both types of professional would operate.

We have noted when looking at the appointment of judges that, by the provisions of s 71 of the Courts and Legal Services Act 1990, solicitors and members of other authorised bodies with advocacy qualifications based on rights of audience will be entitled to seek appointment to the judiciary, and this will no doubt have implications as to its future composition.

The progress of reform has been much slower and at times very controversial, certainly slower than The Law Society would have liked, with allegations that the Lord Chancellor was driven by political motives to cut costs, particularly in respect of the funding of legal services. This will be dealt with in the next section.

The funding of legal services

Background to the legal aid and advice schemes

The first State aided scheme to assist those unable to afford legal services was provided by the Legal Aid Act 1949, which set up the legal aid fund from which those who satisfied a means test could qualify for financial help to bring or defend civil and criminal claims. This Act was later amended by Acts in 1974, 1979 and 1982. A major overhaul was made with effect from 1 April 1989 by the Legal Aid Act 1988, which introduced a new framework which was intended to supersede all previous legislation. Before 1988, administration of the civil legal aid scheme and the legal advice scheme were vested in The Law Society, but as a result of the Legal Aid Act 1988 administration passed to the Legal Aid Board. Administration of the criminal legal aid scheme remains in the hands of the magistrates' courts and Crown Courts, with overall responsibility vested in the Lord Chancellor. Suggestions to transfer responsibility to the Legal Aid Board have not met with approval.

The Legal Aid Board therefore administers the legal advice and assistance scheme, including advice by way of representation (ABWOR) and the civil legal aid schemes under the supervision of the Lord Chancellor who, each year, issues regulations under powers conferred on him by the Legal Aid Act 1988.

In *R v Lord Chancellor ex p The Law Society* (1993), the following regulations were the subject of judicial review proceedings brought by The Law Society, which contended that they were *ultra vires* since they failed to promote the purposes of the 1988 Act: the Civil Legal Aid (General) (Amendment) Regulations 1993 (SI 1996/565); the Civil Legal Aid (Assessment of Resources) (Amendment) Regulations 1993 (SI 1993/788); the Legal Aid in Criminal and Care Proceedings (General) (Amendment) Regulations 1993 (SI 1993/789); and the Legal Advice and Assistance (Amendment) Regulations 1993 (SI 1993/790). The challenge by The Law Society was unsuccessful, and the regulations took effect, imposing drastic cuts in eligibility for legal aid and advice. Each April, the figures are revised by the Lord Chancellor.

England and Wales are divided into 13 areas, each with a legal aid office and an area committee made up of practising solicitors and barristers. The area office decides whether or not to grant assistance by applying a merits test and deals with the legal advice scheme. The area committee deals with appeals against the refusal of assistance. Means tests are conducted by the Legal Aid Assessment Office of the Benefits Agency of the Department of Social Security (DSS).

Parts I and II of the Access to Justice Act 1999 will make radical changes in the provision of legal services and their funding, and given the nature of the changes they will take some time to bring into effect. We will consider each of the three types of state assistance available under the Legal Aid Act 1988 (as amended), and then consider the changes made by the Access to Justice Act 1999.

The three main schemes available under the Legal Aid Act 1988 were: the legal advice and assistance scheme (commonly referred to as the green form scheme, from the colour of the form completed on the client's behalf by the solicitor); the civil legal aid scheme; and the criminal legal aid scheme. The eligibility limits mentioned below took effect on 12 April 1999.

Legal advice and assistance (the green form scheme)

This scheme is regulated by Pt III of the Legal Aid Act 1988 and regulations made thereunder each year by the Lord Chancellor. Preliminary advice, letter writing and applying for legal aid are covered. This scheme has been severely limited in scope, with the result that assistance with probate and succession matters, will drafting, conveyancing, undefended divorces and advice and assistance in court is available only in special cases. An applicant who satisfies a means test administered by the solicitor to determine financial eligibility will be entitled to two hours' free advice (three hours in undefended divorce proceedings) on matters of English law. Financial eligibility depends on disposable capital and income. The limits are set out below:

Capital limits from 12 April 1999

No dependants	£1,000
One dependant	£1,335
Two dependants	£1,535
Each additional dependant	£100

Income limits

Weekly income limit	£83
Weekly dependants' allowances	
Partner	£29.25
Dependants under 11	£20.20
11–16	£25.90
16–18	£30.95
19 and over	£30.95

On 12 April 1993, the contributions system was abolished and, as a result, a person is ineligible if income or capital exceeds the above limits. Reference to disposable capital and income indicates that certain expenses and allowances can be deducted from gross capital or income to arrive at the eligibility limits. In the case of income, the above allowances can be deducted together with sums covering rent, mortgage payments, fuel and living expenses. In the case of capital (such as savings, a house or a car), certain types of property are exempt, such as the main or only home, household furniture and tools of trade. Those in receipt of income support, income-based jobseeker's allowance, family credit or disability working allowance automatically qualify on income, but may be ineligible if disposable capital exceeds the above limits.

Under the green form scheme, assistance will only be free in very few cases. Where the actual cost of the work performed by the solicitor exceeds the contributions made, if any, the shortfall can be claimed by the solicitor from money or property recovered or defended for the client. This is what is known as a statutory charge and is imposed to ensure payment of legal fees. Some property is exempt, including the first £2,500 in matrimonial proceedings, maintenance payments, welfare benefits, the value of an owner-occupied house up to £100,000, furniture, tools of trade and one-half of a redundancy payment. Only where exempt property is recovered or defended or where no property is involved in the claim will the shortfall be met by the Legal Aid Board.

By the Legal Aid Act 1979, the green form scheme was extended to cover ABWOR. This permits the solicitor to prepare a case and represent the client in most non-criminal cases in the magistrates' courts, in county courts where authorised, before mental health tribunals, and where prisoners face disciplinary charges. In addition, applications under the Children Act 1989 are covered, as are some criminal matters. The legal aid area office exercises its discretion as to whether to make an award and a right of appeal lies to the area committee. In cases of urgency, the magistrates' or county court may grant assistance. Under this scheme, not only must financial eligibility be shown, but also that reasonable grounds exist for bringing or defending a claim. This is known as a merits test, which also applies in awards of civil legal aid.

The financial limits for ABWOR from 12 April 1999 are as follows:

Capital limits

No dependants	£3,000
One dependant	£3,335
Two dependants	£3,535
Each additional dependant	£100

Income limits

Upper weekly income limit	£178

Weekly dependants' allowances are the same as under the green form scheme.

Those on income support or income-based jobseeker's allowance automatically qualify on capital, and those on income support or income-based jobseeker's allowance, family credit or disability working allowance qualify on income.

Where disposable income exceeds £75 per week but does not exceed £178 per week, contributions are payable of a third of the excess of income over £75 throughout the proceedings. No contributions are payable if weekly disposable income does not exceed £75. Where a change in circumstances results, ABWOR may be withdrawn, as is the case where a claim is ill founded.

Family mediation pilot scheme

The pilot scheme covers advice and assistance for mediation in family matters where practitioners or organisations have contracted with the Legal Aid Board to take part. The ABWOR limits apply and it is non-contributory. For 1999–2000, the income limit is £178 per week; the weekly dependants' allowances are the same as the green form scheme and capital limits are as for ABWOR.

Civil legal aid scheme

This is regulated under Pt IV of the Legal Aid Act 1988 (as amended) and provides assistance for claims in the High Court and county court, the Lands Tribunal, the Commons Commissioners and the Employment Appeal Tribunal. Important exceptions are inquests, arbitration, tribunals and defamation claims. An applicant's eligibility is decided on two grounds – a merits test and a financial means test – by the Legal Aid Board area office and an assessment office of the DSS Benefits Agency respectively. As a general rule, both tests must be met if assistance is to be awarded. In proceedings under the Children Act 1989, however, the general rule is that neither test need be met.

Merits test

An applicant must show that he or she has reasonable grounds for bringing or defending the claim and that it is reasonable in all the circumstances to grant legal aid. In the event of doubt, a limited legal aid certificate may be granted, requiring authorisation by the Legal Aid Board of further work to be done. The criteria applied include whether the claim involves a question of law or fact, whether alternatives exist, such as resort to arbitration, the applicant's motive in wishing to bring or defend the claim and whether or not he or she can meet any claim made against him or her and whether some benefit would result from the claim.

Financial eligibility

This is based on disposable yearly income and disposable capital. Disposable income is that which is left after appropriate allowances and living expenses such as rent, mortgage payments and fuel are taken out of gross income. Disposable capital includes savings and other assets, excluding the value of an owner-occupied house up to £100,000, furniture and tools of trade. In calculating disposable capital and income, the value of property which is the subject matter of the proceedings is excluded. This will depend on whether it is in jeopardy as a result of the proceedings. If so, its value is excluded. Maintenance payments are taken into account in calculating eligibility.

Capital limits

Lower capital limit	£3,000
Upper capital limit	£6,750 (personal injury claims £8,560)

Special rules apply to pensioners, permitting some capital to be disregarded. Co-habitees and spouses are assessed on their joint income and capital, except where they live apart or have contrary interests.

Income limits

Lower income limit yearly	£2,680
Upper income limit yearly	£7,940 (personal injury claims £8,560)
Dependants' allowances per year	
Partner	£1,525

Dependant under 11	£1,053
11–16	£1,350
16–18	£1,614
19 and over	£1,614

Contributions are payable where disposable capital exceeds £3,000 and monthly contributions from income are payable where disposable income exceeds £2,680 in the amount of one-36th of the excess throughout the case. Those on income support receive free assistance.

When both tests are met, an offer of legal aid is made, which the applicant is free to accept or reject. An offer may be made subject to contributions, and no right of appeal lies to the area office against contributions ordered. On acceptance by the applicant of an offer, a legal aid certificate is issued. If the case later proves hopeless, the applicant's solicitor must report this to the area office which has a discretion to withdraw the certificate. Duties are owed to the Legal Aid Board by both the applicant and his or her solicitor to inform the area office of changes in circumstances, address, to co-operate fully and to pay contributions when due. As we have noted above in respect of the green form scheme, legal assistance is often not free, and a statutory charge may be imposed to pay for legal fees.

When considering civil legal aid, it is necessary to distinguish between the situation where the winner is legally aided and that where the loser is legally aided.

Winner legally aided

The general rule about payment of litigation costs is that 'costs follow the event'. This means that the loser will have to meet not only his or her legal costs, but also those of the winner. If the winner is legally aided, the judge will probably order the loser to pay all costs and, in theory, this will ensure that the winner will not have to meet any of the costs of the action. However, in practice this is not always the case, either because the loser fails to pay or no order is made by the court, or the loser disappears or becomes bankrupt. In any event, the loser will submit the question of costs to the court for taxation (now called assessment). This is a process whereby the costs are scrutinised by the court to see if they are of a reasonable amount. Only in rare cases will the loser have to meet the full amount of costs, leaving a small shortfall to be met from the winner's contributions, if any, or by way of the statutory charge over damages or property recovered. The result may be that the winner ends up with little or nothing, even where at the outset free legal aid was granted. Spouses should never litigate over family assets in excess of £2,500, which is the only exempt property under this scheme.

Loser legally aided

At the court's discretion, the loser may be ordered to pay a reasonable amount towards the costs of the winner. Usually this amounts to two contributions by the loser, but any shortfall has to be met by the winner by way of statutory charge. Any shortfall of the loser's costs is paid by the Legal Aid Board. The statutory charge cannot be waived, and only in exceptional circumstances can it be postponed.

In cases of emergency, for example, that of battered wives, cases involving children or eviction from property, an emergency legal aid certificate may be granted following a telephone application. A full application is made later and if the applicant turns out not to be eligible he or she will be liable for all costs.

Criminal legal aid scheme

Criminal legal aid is regulated by Pt V of the Legal Aid Act 1988 and provides assistance to those accused of criminal offences. Private prosecutions are not covered, so an individual who wishes to bring a private prosecution – for example, where they or a member of their family has been the subject of an offence and where the CPS decides not to prosecute – will be responsible for funding the case. In the event that the case is successful, an order for costs may be made out of public funds, but any shortfall will have to be met by the individual. As with civil legal aid, the applicant must satisfy both a merits and a means test, but the provisions of each are different.

Merits test

It must be shown that the application is desirable in the interests of justice. The criteria were set out in the Widgery criteria of 1966 and are now enacted in s 22 of the Legal Aid Act 1988. These include the complexity of the issues involved; the ability of the defendant to understand the proceedings due to inadequate knowledge of English; mental illness or disability; the need to trace or interview witnesses by the defendant or the need to cross-examine prosecution witnesses; the desirability of legal representation of the defendant so as to protect the interests of another, for example, a child when sexual abuse is alleged and the defendant would wish to cross-examine the child; and conviction likely to result in imprisonment or loss of livelihood.

Some 97% of Crown Court defendants are granted legal aid, but defendants in the magistrates' courts are only granted legal aid in serious cases, and this includes defendants committed for trial to the Crown Court.

Financial eligibility

The capital limit is £3,000 and the weekly income limit is £51. The weekly dependants' allowances are the same as for the green form scheme. Those on income support, income-based jobseeker's allowance, family credit or disability working allowance receive free legal aid. For those with disposable capital in excess of £3,000, contributions from capital are payable, and for those with a weekly disposable income in excess of £51, a weekly contribution from income of £1 for every £3 or part in excess is payable. Those aged 16 or over apply on their own behalf, whereas parents or guardians apply for those under 16.

The court has a discretion at the end of a case to order the defendant to pay additional costs, but the court must take into account the sentence imposed. No appeal lies against such an order, and even if the defendant is acquitted, he or she may be ordered to pay additional costs.

Duty solicitor scheme

This is regulated by Pt III of the Legal Aid Act 1988 and the Legal Aid Board Duty Solicitor Arrangements 1990. This scheme offers free legal advice to those questioned by the police at a police station or elsewhere, whether or not arrested. No means test or financial eligibility applies, and a suspect may choose either his or her own solicitor, or the 24 hour duty solicitor, or one whose name appears on a list retained by the police. This scheme also covers attendance at the magistrates' court and, by s 58 of the Police and Criminal Evidence Act 1984 and the Codes of Practice, suspects must be informed of their right to a solicitor under this scheme. In practice, trainee solicitors and others employed by solicitors often give advice under this scheme and concerns have been raised as to the poor standard of advice given.

Having described the main provisions of the State schemes, we need to consider the alternatives available, the main defects of the State schemes and the enactment of proposals for reform in the Access to Justice Act 1999.

Alternatives

Several private schemes have been set up over the years, the most well known being the £5 scheme operated by solicitors on a voluntary basis who offered 30 minutes of advice for £5 (or other stipulated sum). No limitations applied as to the number of solicitors consulted on a matter, but only advice could be obtained. This scheme has now been withdrawn. However, it is usual for solicitors to either offer free advice at clinics of one kind or another or for the first interview, or at least part of it, to be free of charge. In 1987, The Law Society established the Accident Legal Advice Service (ALAS) scheme, where volunteer solicitors offer free initial interviews to accident victims.

Another means by which legal services are provided free is through law centres. These are funded by local authorities in the main, although central government may provide some funding. Law centres are located in London and other large cities and employ solicitors on a full time basis, and the client receives free legal advice and representation. Law centres have seen severe financial pressures in recent years, and although popular with those in need of legal assistance, they have not always been popular with government, since their role has involved questioning social policy on matters such as housing, State benefits, family matters and employment rights.

Advice on legal matters and other problems may be sought from legal advice centres and the Citizens Advice Bureaux. The former offer advice, mainly on consumer or housing matters, and act as a referral agency, often in conjunction with the latter. The Citizens Advice Bureaux form a national scheme, offering free and independent advice on legal and other social matters. Most towns throughout the country have a Bureau, staffed by volunteers who undertake training courses to enable them to offer specific advice on social benefits, housing, family and employment matters. Since the recession, one of their main areas of work is in debt counselling. Solicitors offer their services on a voluntary basis in some bureaux on a rota basis.

In Chapter 5, we consider the alternatives to litigation which have received attention in recent years. It is a fundamental notion of a civilised State that an individual with a grievance, either against the State or another individual, should be able to obtain justice. Traditionally, this has been through the courts of law or by way of a tribunal. Given the adversarial nature of litigation and its high costs in both money and time, and in recent times the financial stringency applied to State funding, the need for alternatives such as mediation, conciliation and arbitration to arrive at solutions by agreement and reconciliation have increased. It is unlikely that such alternatives will replace traditional means of resolution, but certainly they are likely to be used increasingly where their effectiveness surpasses adjudication by the courts.

A traditional assumption has been that with adjudication in a court of law comes the need for professional representation. As we have seen earlier, this no longer simply refers to representation by barristers, but, under the reforms given effect to by the Courts and Legal Services Act 1990, rights of audience are extended to solicitors (and in future will be extended to those who are not barristers or solicitors but who satisfy the requirements of authorised bodies and demonstrate fitness to practise as advocates).

The Lord Chancellor may, by order, remove restrictions on those with rights of audience or rights to conduct litigation in specified county court proceedings. This extends the use of what has become known as a *McKenzie* friend, that is, a person able to sit in court and offer advice and support to a litigant in person.

Other voluntary initiatives include the Hoxton Legal Advice Service (LAS), which offers free legal advice to members of the public by part time volunteers, some of whom are qualified lawyers and some law students. Advice is offered on housing and employment matters, debt, taxation and consumer affairs and State benefits. Advisers refer those likely to be eligible for legal aid to local law firms, and for others the LAS offers advice and, at the court's discretion, represents clients in court.

Given the rising cost of legal services and the cost-cutting exercise in the provision of State funded legal aid and advice schemes, together with an ever increasing unmet need for legal services, alternatives have to be found if people's legal problems are to be dealt with.

By s 58 of the 1990 Act, lawyers could be paid on a 'no win, no fee' basis but, unlike the US system, not by way of a percentage of the damages awarded but on the normal hourly rate or fixed sum fee uprated by a maximum of 100% to compensate for the risk of receiving no fee should the case be lost. Both barristers and solicitors were covered and were paid only for winning a case. The Law Society recommends a voluntary additional cap on damages of 25%, and this has been widely accepted.

Those able to provide litigation and advocacy services could enter into a binding written agreement for a conditional fee. Lay representatives and others with litigation rights and rights of audience would also be covered by the provisions. However, s 58 only applied to personal injury claims, insolvency matters and proceedings before the ECHR.

Such agreements and the grant of legal aid were mutually exclusive, so that once legal aid was granted, the agreement ceased to have effect. However, their use provided the client with a wider choice when deciding whether to proceed with a claim. In *Thai Trading Co (A Firm) v Taylor* (1998), the court held that lawyers can agree to work for less than their normal fee if the case is lost. Where it is won, they should recover no more than their normal fee, except in those cases where a conditional fee agreement could be made.

In *Bevan Ashford v Yeandle (Contractors Ltd)* (1998), the court held that conditional fee arrangements can apply in arbitrations, regardless that this is not strictly court proceedings. The Conditional Fees Order 1998 extended the scope of conditional fee arrangements to all civil matters, other than family cases. In theory the use of 'no win, no fee' arrangements is an excellent way of ensuring that a person can undertake litigation; however, where a case is seen to be weak or of high risk, it is likely that it will be turned away. Until the 1999 Act changes come into effect, another off-putting feature was the high cost of insurance premiums and the uplift which could not be passed on to the loser. Sections 27–31 of the Access to Justice Act 1999 amend these provisions so that the court can order the loser to pay the winner's costs, uplift and any insurance premium paid.

Having considered the position of the client and the shortcomings of State provision, it is also necessary to consider the position of the provider of legal services. Fundamental change has been taking place as to the eligibility of those able to provide legal aid and advice under the State schemes. The Lord Chancellor put forward proposals to franchise the provision of legal services in 1992, and in 1993 suggested that its future lay in competitive tendering for franchises.

By 1993, the first franchises had been applied for by firms of solicitors who had satisfied the criteria laid down by the Board. In January 1994, the first franchises were awarded. Government policy was to cut the cost of legal aid, so it was proposed that franchises should in future be granted by way of competitive tendering, the lowest bidder being awarded a contract to supply legal services. The Legal Aid Board could award franchising contracts to firms of solicitors, advice agencies and law centres. Areas of work included family, crime, housing, debt, employment, personal injury, welfare benefits, contract and consumer matters and those relating to nationality and immigration. Franchisees derived several benefits from this system, including devolved powers to grant or extend advice and assistance; higher rates of remuneration in recognition of their providing accessible and 'quality assured' services and payment on account with six monthly payments thereafter.

Reform culminating in the Access to Justice Act 1999

Commentators have described the provision and funding of legal aid as in crisis and it is hard to accept the stringent cost-cutting on the one hand and on the other the drive towards encouraging the citizen to be more aware of his or her rights and to seek redress through the courts. The principles espoused by the 1948 legislation attempted to ensure that those who were unable to afford to bring or defend a legal claim would receive State funded assistance. In 1994, the Legal Aid Board published its management statement, in which it stated that the main objective of the legal aid system, the courts and the justice system as a whole was 'to resolve disputes and to assist people in pursuing their rights and understanding their obligations'.

In 1995, the Lord Chancellor's Department published its consultation paper, *Legal Aid: Targeting Need*, and this was followed in 1996 by the Government White Paper, *Striking the Balance: The Future of Legal Aid in England and Wales*. Its overall aim was to balance the 'needs of those seeking state assistance, the rights of unassisted opponents and the interests of the taxpayer'. The main proposals were as follows:

- to replace the open ended approach to resources with pre-determined budgets allocated to meet local needs within national priorities;

- to extend the scheme to other agencies, although solicitors and barristers were to retain the largest role;

- to introduce controls between providers and the Legal Aid Board with two types of contract – a fixed price for a specific service over a period of time and block contracts for an agreed price per case;

- to introduce a new test for legal aid eligibility, targeting the most deserving cases;

- to increase the potential liability of assisted persons contributing to their own and opponents' costs;

- to provide better information, have separate funds for expensive cases, to set up appeals and complaints procedures and monitoring of cases by the Legal Aid Board.

The possibility of extending conditional fees and the setting up of a test case fund for novel claims was also considered.

On the whole, the proposals did not meet with support. The Legal Action Group said that, if brought into effect, they would deny thousands of low income people access to legal advice, given that decisions to fund would be governed by availability of resources. The Law Society said that the proposals imposed arbitrary regional limits on legal aid and block contracts would result in a two tier system, one for the rich, and one for the poor.

The provision of legal aid was still the subject of debate following the White Paper, *Striking the Balance*. The general election in May 1997 and the change in Government continued the debate as to how best to reform legal aid provision. One thing remained clear, namely, that the ever-increasing cost of the legal aid budget and an increasing unmet need for legal services necessitated drastic action.

The Lord Chancellor has proceeded with the reforms, given the imperative of cutting the legal aid bill. The Access to Justice Act 1999 contains provisions for a radical overhaul in how legal services are provided and funded. The legal aid scheme and Legal Aid Board will be replaced by a Legal Services Commission, which will operate the Community Legal Service and the Criminal Defence Service. The former will replace civil legal aid and the latter criminal legal aid. The Community Legal Service will be funded by a Community Legal Service Fund and the Commission will be subject to orders, directions and guidance from the Lord Chancellor in the exercise of its powers. The Lord Chancellor will set priorities and the Commission will have a duty to ensure value for money and provision of a range of legal services. It will also have to ensure that a co-ordinated approach is taken to funding and providing legal services. Under s 2 of the 1999 Act, the Lord Chancellor will review the new system to see whether the Commission needs to be replaced, some time in the next few years, by separate bodies to administer the Community Legal Service and the Criminal Defence Service.

These reforms are very far reaching and depart radically from the present system, which has developed piecemeal and which has become extremely costly to administer. In 2000, the Legal Services Commission will take over the responsibilities of the Legal Aid Board and Sched 14 to the Act makes transitional provisions to cover the handover. The Commission will have a much wider role in respect of the Criminal Defence Service than the Legal Aid Board had over the provision of criminal legal aid, as this had been administered largely by the courts.

The Community Legal Service will manage the Community Legal Services Fund (replacing legal aid in civil and family matters) and this will cover both providers of litigation services, as well as alternatives, such as mediation. It will also co-ordinate plans to develop national, regional and local plans to identify needs and priorities and to match these with legal services provision. Community Legal Service Partnerships will be formed to act as fora for the co-ordination of funding, the provision of services and to prioritise need. The voluntary sector providers of services will be kitemarked so as to guarantee the quality of the service on offer to the public. By s 4 of the 1999 Act, the services provided from the range of providers will include advice and assistance, representation, ADR, provision of information and IT and the services of those in the voluntary sector. A fixed budget will be provided under s 5 of the Act, and the main aim will be to ensure the best value for the available funds in family and other civil cases. The Criminal Defence Service will be quite separate, with its own budget, and some civil matters are excluded, such as defamation, wills and conveyancing, other than the provision to individuals of information in these areas.

Many of the provisions replicate the legal aid scheme, but with time it will no doubt change if the use of legal expenses insurance and conditional fee arrangements expand. Eligibility limits will continue to be set by the Lord Chancellor before Easter each year, but s 8 replaces the merits test with a funding assessment which will take account of eight factors, including: the importance of the matter to the individual and his or her conduct; the prospects of success; availability of funds; the cost of funding and benefits gained; the availability of alternative services; and any other factors which the Lord Chancellor by order will require the Commission to consider. An underlying principle will be that mediation should be used in the settlement of family cases. At present, a legally aided person can be required to make contributions to the Legal Aid Board, and contributions will continue in place. By s 10, however, the Lord Chancellor will have two additional powers. He will be able to order a successful party to pay more than the cost of the services provided, or to mix public funding with a conditional fee arrangement. He will also be able to order repayment of the full cost of the service provided. Assisted persons will only have to pay the costs of an unassisted party to the extent that those costs are reasonable, and regulations may be made covering the award of costs against an assisted party.

The Criminal Defence Service will ensure provision of advice, assistance and representation in the interests of justice. It will enter into contracts with lawyers in private practice and salaried defenders in non-profit making organisations. By s 13(2), the Commission has a range of options for the provision of services in criminal proceedings, including through lawyers employed by the Commission. This raised fears that representation could not be guaranteed. However, s 14 imposes a duty on the Commission to fund representation for individuals who have been granted a right to representation under Sched 3 to the Act. Section 15 gives defendants a right to choose their representative, subject to limitations which can be imposed by regulation, for example, to subject specialists or those who have contracts with the Commission. The Commission will have power to assign a representative to a defendant.

At present, means testing is an essential part of criminal legal aid provision, although it is costly to administer. This will be abolished and, in its place, the judge will be able to order a defendant to pay some or all of the costs of his defence, at the end of a trial. To assist the judge, the Legal Services Commission can investigate the defendant's means.

From the above, it can be seen that these reforms are far-reaching and must be taken as a whole with the reforms of the civil and criminal justice systems, in particular the move away from reliance on litigation in civil disputes to ADR and negotiation. The changes are controversial, but made in recognition that, if the increasing unmet need for legal services is to be met and, at the same time, the legal aid bill is to be stemmed, change is inevitable. Alternative funding and alternatives to litigation have to be found and used and a co-ordinated approach, where priorities are set and value for money assured, must be adopted.

THE PROVISION OF LEGAL SERVICES

The legal profession

- The traditional divide is between barristers and solicitors.

- The governing bodies of solicitors and barristers; the role of lawyers in industry, local and central government and the court service.

- Part I of the Courts and Legal Services Act 1990 and Pt III of the Access to Justice Act 1999.

Complaining about the legal profession

- The methods by which complaints are handled against solicitors and barristers; proposals for reform.

- Sections 21–26 of the Courts and Legal Services Act 1990.

- Disciplinary procedures are regulated by the governing bodies – Bar Council; Inns of Court; The Law Society; Solicitors' Complaints Bureau, as replaced by the Office for the Supervision of Solicitors.

- Section 85 of the Courts and Legal Services Act 1990.

- Actions in negligence may be brought against those not acting as advocates. Many complaints relate to fees and the Solicitors' Practice Rules 1991 lay down procedures for handling complaints.

- Fusion of the legal profession.

- Courts and Legal Services Act 1990; Access to Justice Act 1999.

The funding of legal services

- Background to the Legal Aid and Advice Schemes.

- Legal advice and assistance (the green form scheme).

- Civil legal aid scheme.

- Criminal legal aid scheme.

- Duty solicitor scheme.

- Alternatives:
  - voluntary initiatives;
  - alternative dispute resolution;
  - extensions in rights of audience and the use of *McKenzie* friends.

- The effects of s 58 of the Courts and Legal Services Act 1990, as amended; the award of legal aid franchises to providers of legal services.

- Government White Paper, *Striking the Balance: The Future of Legal Aid in England and Wales* (1996); *R v Lord Chancellor ex p Witham* (1997), concerning court fees.

- Access to Justice Act 1999, setting up the the Legal Services Commission, to replace the Legal Aid Board.

- Private provisions for funding.

- Voluntary agencies will receive State funding and contracts will be awarded so as to meet the need for legal services.

CHAPTER 5

ALTERNATIVE DISPUTE RESOLUTION

Introduction

In this chapter, we will consider some of the alternatives available, or which are proposed, for the settlement of disputes, other than the traditional means by way of adjudication in a court of law. It has long been established that disputes may be settled by way of adjudication by courts of law and, in more recent times, by tribunals. Tribunals took on much of their present day importance following the post-war welfare state reforms. They were set up by statute to adjudicate disputes between the citizen and the State on such matters as welfare benefits, rates, taxation and land disputes. Some, including industrial tribunals, adjudicate disputes between individuals but where the State regulates the relationship of the parties by legislation, for example, pay and conditions of work, redundancy, maternity rights and unfair dismissal.

Tribunals may provide an alternative to a court of law, in the sense that statute may provide that a certain type of dispute shall be adjudicated on by a tribunal rather than a court. This should not, however, be confused with a concept from the USA and countries of the Commonwealth known as 'alternative dispute resolution' (ADR) and which is still in a developmental stage in the UK.

Alternative dispute resolution covers fora for the settlement of disputes by way of negotiation, conciliation, mediation and mini-trials (or a combination of some or all of these methods) and which emphasise settlement by agreement, rather than adjudication, where the emphasis is on finding in favour of one party and against the other. ADR may precede litigation as a way of establishing the common ground between the parties and the points on which they cannot agree. It must be noted that, in any dispute, litigation will usually be a last resort and legal advisers will attempt to negotiate a settlement.

It is now compulsory as a result of the Woolf reforms enacted in the Civil Procedure Act 1997, and given effect to by the Civil Procedure Rules 1998 (as amended), for the court as part of its case management function to encourage the parties to make use of ADR and to make this a viable alternative to litigation. The court has the power to halt proceedings either where the parties make a request or the court on its own initiative considers that ADR is appropriate, so as to allow the case to be dealt with by ADR. Although this is a recent development, the Commercial Court has for some time encouraged the use of ADR, and judges of this court have an established reputation of acting as arbitrators in disputes involving insurance, shipping and commercial matters.

In some disputes, settlement may not take place until just before or even after the case comes to court. This is known as a settlement 'at the door of the court' and has the advantages for the claimant (formerly plaintiff) that he or she does not have to prove his or her case before a court together with the attendant delay, cost and the possibility of losing the case and being responsible for not only their costs but those of their opponent. The advantages for a defendant may be similar, and another advantage is that no precedent will be set, and this is particularly useful for an institutional party such as an insurance company faced with a personal injury claim.

Terminology is not necessarily well defined and it is not always easy to distinguish between, for example, mediation and conciliation. The former involves an impartial independent third party who attempts to bring the parties to agreement but who does not put forward solutions. It is used in family disputes and is the less formal. Conciliation, on the other hand, may go further in an attempt to effect a reconciliation and a non-binding opinion may be given, as is the case with court conciliation schemes, which can then lead to a settlement.

Another means of settlement which can properly be included under ADR is arbitration. This is the most formal, and a decision is made by an umpire appointed with the agreement of both parties, which will be binding and is usually enforceable by the court. Given that arbitration is a well established means of settling disputes and results in an adjudication, albeit not by a judge sitting in that capacity, we shall first consider its main uses, then move on to consider the role of tribunals, and then consider the developing use of ADR. Other methods of dispute resolution will be considered briefly, including the increasing use of ombudsmen, in both commercial matters and in the relationship between public bodies and the citizen.

Arbitration

Both parties agree to submit to the procedure and decision of an arbitrator, who will usually be a person with both legal knowledge and specialist knowledge of the subject matter of the dispute. Arbitration is most often used in landlord and tenant disputes, commercial and shipping claims and where a contract provides that settlement shall be by way of arbitration. It is also used in the High Court, where judges of the Commercial Court can act as arbitrators under s 4 of the Administration of Justice Act 1970, having obtained the permission of the Lord Chief Justice that pressure of work in the High Court and Crown Court is not such as to prevent their availability.

The judge, when acting as an arbitrator, sits in private and in any place convenient to the parties. Conduct of the hearing is informal and the award is private, and so is not published as is a court judgment. The Arbitration Acts 1950, 1975 and 1979 have been replaced by the Arbitration Act 1996 which provides a new approach to ensure that the arbitration procedure is speedy, cost effective, informal and a proper alternative to litigation.

Arbitration was also used in the county court by way of the 'small claims procedure', but by Pt 29 of the Civil Procedure Rules 1998, this has become the 'small claims track' to which cases are allocated for a small claims hearing. Jurisdiction applies to claims not exceeding £5,000 (or £1,000 for personal injuries and housing disrepair cases). These were known for their informality and the willingness of the district judge to assist the parties. However, the recovery of costs was limited and legal representation was not promoted. These features remain, but under the new rules greater emphasis is given to paper adjudication and the parties may give notice of their intention not to attend the hearing. In claims in excess of these limits, this procedure is permitted where the court approves and the parties agree. However, the limitations on recovery of costs will not apply, subject to recovery of costs on the fast track level.

It is usual for some people to have the assistance of a *McKenzie* friend, or expert non-professional adviser, who offers a party to the proceedings support and advice. By the Lay Representatives (Rights of Audience) Order 1992, passed under ss 11 and 120 of the Courts and Legal Services Act 1990, lay representatives have rights of audience in small claims where the client they represent attends the hearing. More will be said about the small claims track in Chapter 7.

The advantages of arbitration are often said to be speed, cost, lack of formality, a binding decision which can be enforced by the court with the minimum of publicity and also the absence of a binding precedent for similar cases. However, in recent times, the cost, time and complexity of arbitration proceedings have certainly increased, but it remains a favoured option, for it is still relatively cheaper and quicker than litigation, particularly in commercial matters.

It is usual for parties to a contract to include a term known as a *Scott v Avery* clause, after the case of that name in 1856, stipulating that in the event of a dispute arising it will be referred to arbitration, and only if this is not successful will application be made to the court. This is permissible, unlike a provision which attempts to oust the jurisdiction of the court altogether, that is, prevent a claim from ever coming to court. For businesses, the main advantage of arbitration is that no binding precedent results, so that if more than one claim arises, each will have to be settled separately. It is worth mentioning here the work of the Advisory, Conciliation and Arbitration Service (ACAS), which is an independent body which promotes good industrial relations by way of the voluntary co-operation of employers, employees and their representatives. Its services are free and it comprises a council with a chairperson and members drawn from employers, trade unions and employees. The main functions it performs are to provide advisory and information services, conciliation in trade disputes, arbitration services at the request of both parties, mediation and conciliation in individual cases of complaint, for example, where unfair dismissal or discrimination is alleged. Arbitration awards made by ACAS are not binding in law, and normally attempts to settle a dispute by conciliation should be made before resort to arbitration.

The Arbitration Act 1996 was passed to ensure that the importance of commercial arbitration was recognised, and, in order to increase its use, reform of its procedures and rules was required. Section 1 of the 1996 Act sets out the general principles to be achieved, which include: the fair resolution of disputes by an impartial tribunal without unnecessary delay or expense; parties should be free to agree how their disputes are resolved subject to necessary public interest safeguards; and court intervention should be kept to a minimum. The role of the arbitrator is crucial and only where the arbitration process is found to be failing or where legal knowledge is required will the court intervene. Section 5 of the Act provides that the Act applies only to agreements in writing, not oral agreements. However, by s 5(3), where the parties agree in writing to use arbitration, this will be sufficient for the Act to apply.

The major novelty about the 1996 Act is that the parties are free to agree the procedures to be followed. Taken to the extreme, this could mean that strict legal rules are forgone in favour of commercial practice. In a competitive market place this could be important to a commercial organisation wishing to ensure that it continues doing business with those it takes to arbitration. Where there is a failure to agree, then the Act can apply. In order to achieve the general principles stated in s 1, s 33 provides that the arbitrator is under a general duty to act fairly and impartially and give each party a reasonable opportunity to state his or her case. Also, suitable procedures must be adopted and delay and expense minimised.

Where a binding arbitration agreement provides that litigation is not to be undertaken, the court can stay any proceedings initiated by one party under ss 9–11 of the Act. The court functions in the background but, for example, where there is a failing in procedure the court can order compliance.

Section 15 provides that the parties are free to agree on an arbitrator or a panel of arbitrators. Usually, these are drawn from experts in the area in question or from a trade association. The arbitrator will agree the procedures to be followed and the parties may be legally represented.

Two grounds of appeal against the decisions of an arbitrator are provided in ss 67 and 68 of the Act. The first deals with an allegation that the arbitrator acted without jurisdiction, and the second with an allegation of serious irregularity, such as failure to comply with the general duty in s 33. Section 69 permits an appeal on a point of law, but the parties can exclude this provision. The 1996 Act has reduced the right of appeal, and this again emphasises the shift away from court control of the arbitration process in an attempt to encourage commercial disputes to be dealt with in this way.

Tribunals

Since tribunals are so varied in composition, appointment of members, procedure and functions, it is not possible to provide a satisfactory classification. Many examples of statutory tribunals can be found, including the Social Security Appeals Tribunal, Medical Appeals Tribunal, mental health review tribunals, industrial tribunals, Pensions Appeal Tribunal, Immigration Appeals Tribunal, Agriculture Land Tribunal, the Lands Tribunal, Plant Varieties and Seeds Tribunal, Commissioners of Income Tax, VAT tribunals, rent tribunals and Data Protection Tribunal. As a general rule, tribunals comprise three members, one of whom is appointed chairperson and who is legally trained. The other two members are drawn from the area or areas of concern. For example, with industrial tribunals one member will have knowledge and experience as an employer, and the other as an employee. In some cases, as, for example, in the Lands Tribunal, one member sits alone.

Before looking more closely at some of the statutory tribunals, we must mention 'domestic' tribunals which regulate disciplinary matters of trades and professions and also sporting activities. Some examples include the General Medical Council, the Solicitors' Disciplinary Tribunal of the Law Society, the Inns of Court, the Jockey Club and the General Nursing Council. Some have been set up by statute or Royal Charter and others by way of contracts entered into between members and the association.

We will consider later the extent to which such tribunals are regulated by the courts. Statutory tribunals are subject to the supervision of the High Court whereby, if they act *ultra vires* or in breach of the rules of natural justice, the prerogative orders of mandamus, certiorari and prohibition will lie so as to correct the excess of power. In addition, a person aggrieved by the decision of a tribunal may seek an injunction or declaration of his or her rights, and where a private law right has been broken a claim for damages may be made.

As so many 'administrative tribunals' exist, we will consider the role of four administrative or statutory tribunals – social security tribunals; valuation and lands tribunals; employment tribunals (formerly called industrial tribunals); and mental health tribunals.

Social security tribunals

Procedure is governed by Sched 8 to the Health and Social Services and Social Security Adjudications Act 1983, amending the Social Security Act 1975. On refusal of a claim for benefit, such as employment benefit, by the Social Security Office, application is made to the local administration officer. Appeal lies to a local social security appeal tribunal with three members: two non-lawyers and a legally qualified chairperson. A further appeal lies to a Social Security Commissioner with leave. These are appointed from barristers or solicitors of not less than 10 years' standing and, since the Courts and Legal Services Act

1990, eligibility will be extended to those with rights of audience. Further appeal lies to the Court of Appeal with leave of the court or the Commissioner and then to the House of Lords.

The Lands Tribunal

Procedure is governed by rules made by the Lord Chancellor. Hearings are in public in various parts of the country and there is a right for claimants to be legally represented and to receive legal aid. Decisions are written and full reasons are given. The tribunal deals with valuations of property, for example, for compulsory purchase compensation claims. Appeal lies to the Court of Appeal on points of law. The tribunal is presided over by a President who will have held high judicial office or will have been a barrister of at least seven years' standing (or equivalent). Other members will either hold legal qualifications or have experience in land valuation.

Employment tribunals

Employment tribunals hear claims concerning contracts of employment, unfair dismissal, redundancy, equal pay and sexual and racial discrimination in employment. They are regulated by the Employment Tribunals Act 1996. The chairperson will have been a barrister or solicitor of at least seven years' standing appointed by the Lord Chancellor. The other two members will have expertise in employment matters, one as an employer and the other as an employee. They are selected by the President of Industrial Tribunals appointed by the Lord Chancellor from a panel compiled by the Secretary of State for Employment. Legal aid is not available, although it is on appeal to the Employment Appeal Tribunal. The legal advice scheme will permit initial advice to be given and a claimant may wish to have the assistance of a *McKenzie* friend during the tribunal proceedings.

The Employment Appeal Tribunal is a superior court of record which hears appeals on points of law. Appeals are heard by a High Court judge or a judge of the Court of Appeal and two or four appointed members with special knowledge or experience in employment. A majority decision may be made and hearings are usually in public, except where questions of national security or trade secrets are raised. Appeals lie to the Court of Appeal and then to the House of Lords. Leave is required in both cases.

The House of Lords' decision in *R v Secretary of State for Employment ex p Equal Opportunities Commission and Another* (1994) illustrates not only that, where domestic legislation (in this case, the provisions of the Employment Protection (Consolidation) Act 1978 concerning the rights of part time workers) conflicts with European law, the latter takes precedence, but also that a body such as the Equal Opportunities Commission has a sufficient interest in challenging legislation to seek judicial review. Mrs Day, the subject of the litigation, was not entitled to seek judicial review in her capacity as a private individual. Instead, she could have brought a private claim against her employer in the industrial tribunal, from which appeal could have been made to the Employment Appeal Tribunal; then the Court of Appeal; and then to the House of Lords, where appropriate.

Mental health review tribunals

The Mental Health Act 1983 permits the detention of persons in secure hospitals in certain circumstances. A person who considers that he or she is entitled to be discharged may apply for release to the above tribunal. The tribunal may order conditional or unconditional discharge. The tribunal is staffed by a chairperson, who must be legally qualified, and two other members, one of whom must be a medical doctor and the other a person considered by the Lord Chancellor to be suitable in the light of his or her knowledge or experience. Where a restricted patient does not apply for release, those who have charge of him or her are under a duty to do so at prescribed frequencies and, in any event, the Secretary of State has power to refer cases to the tribunal. With effect from 11 April 1994, the advice by way of representation (ABWOR) scheme has been extended to cover all applications to this tribunal. This is available regardless of means.

Domestic tribunals

As we have already mentioned, domestic tribunals, such as the General Medical Council, regulate the standards of members of the trades, professions or activities and enforce the rules amongst their members. In law, domestic tribunals are treated as private associations based on contract and so are not subject to the prerogative orders granted under the judicial review process. This was established in the case of *Law v National Greyhound Racing Club* (1983) and subsequently followed in *R v Football Association Ltd ex p Football League Ltd* (1993), where it was held that the Football Association was a domestic body whose powers derived from private law and that, in general, it was not susceptible to judicial review.

However, it has been recognised that the courts do have a limited jurisdiction over domestic tribunals. Thus, the court may grant a declaration of rights, as in the case of *Lee v Showman's Guild of Great Britain* (1952). Alternatively, the court may grant an injunction to ensure that an association interprets its rules and applies the rules of natural justice correctly. The courts have prohibited the wrongful expulsion of members, refusals to admit to membership, refusals to admit women and restrictions improperly placed on members.

Prior to 1986, the law was quite clear and judicial review would be available where an organisation derived its powers from statute or the royal prerogative.

If the source of power was from a contract entered into between the organisation and its members, the courts only had a limited jurisdiction. In *R v Panel on Take-Overs and Mergers ex p Datafin* (1986), the Court of Appeal decided that this body was susceptible to judicial review even though its powers were not derived from either statute or the prerogative. The panel exercised public functions in the City of London and these functions gave rise to public law consequences. Thus, in addition to the source of power, it was essential also to consider the nature of the functions performed. In later cases, however, the courts have retracted from this bold approach and have emphasised the need for the public function to have some relationship with government.

In *R v Chief Rabbi ex p Wachmann* (1992), the court stated that judicial review was only available where the source of the public function was the Government. This was followed in *R v Disciplinary Committee of the Jockey Club ex p Aga Khan* (1993), where it was held that, although governmental functions were performed, the club derived its powers from contract, and so judicial review was inappropriate. The case of *R v Insurance Ombudsman Bureau and Insurance Ombudsman ex p Aegon Life Assurance Ltd* (1993) comes full circle, in that the court held that, where power derives from contract, judicial review will not lie even where governmental functions are performed.

Two further cases illustrate the distinction between contractual source of power and that derived from statute or the prerogative. In *R v Visitors to the Inns of Court ex p Calder and Persaud* (1993), it was held that the visitors to the Inns (judges of the High Court who adjudicated in matters of discipline) were only subject to judicial review in limited cases, namely, where the visitor had acted outside his jurisdiction or had abused his power or had acted in breach of the rules of natural justice. This had long been established in educational institutions founded by charter or by way of contract or charitable trust, and further authority is to be found in *Page v Hull University* (1993), where a lecturer who had been made redundant claimed that under the university statutes he could only be dismissed for good cause and that none had been shown. The university visitor found that the dismissal was *intra vires*. It was held on the facts that there was no jurisdiction to hear an application for judicial review.

However, in *R v Manchester University ex p Nolan* (1993), which concerned a student who was alleged to have cheated at examinations, the statutory source of the powers of the university was noted (as a new university it was set up as a result of the Education Act 1988) and, despite contractual elements in the relationship of student and university, judicial review was available without the limitations placed on charter institutions. The anomaly has been commented on by Professor Wade and others, who suggest that it is time for reform in this area.

Control of administrative tribunals

We have already noted that tribunals may be controlled by means of the supervisory jurisdiction of the Queen's Bench Divisional Court. It has often been said that as tribunals are created by the State to adjudicate on disputes between the citizen and the State, there is a tendency for them to find against the individual.

In addition to the control by way of judicial review, control is also imposed by the Council on Tribunals, established as a result of the Franks Committee Report in 1957 by the Tribunals and Inquiries Act 1958. This Act has subsequently been amended by the Act of 1971, and both have been replaced by the 1992 Act of the same title.

The Council gives advice to the Lord Chancellor on the workings of administrative tribunals and reports to Parliament annually. It keeps under review the constitution and workings of tribunals and has power to examine rules of procedure used by a tribunal. The Franks Committee Report concluded that the system of administrative justice should achieve the aims of 'openness, fairness and impartiality' and, if these were to be achieved, tribunals should give reasons for their decisions (so as to facilitate appeals in appropriate cases) and a right of appeal should exist to the High Court or Court of Appeal.

Following the Franks Report, chairmen of tribunals are selected by the Secretary of State from a panel of persons appointed by the Lord Chancellor. It is usual for chairmen to be legally qualified. Legal representation is usually allowed, but a major drawback is the lack of legal aid availability except in the Employment Appeal Tribunal and the Lands Tribunal. The ABWOR scheme has, however, now been extended to hearings before the Mental Health Review Tribunal. Hearings are normally in public unless, for example, the interests of national security are paramount. Although the rules of evidence are relaxed, it is usual for all documents to be disclosed to the other side and reasons for the decision are given at the request of the parties. Appeal lies to the High Court or where statute provides to the Court of Appeal.

It is useful to mention here the role of inquiries, which are also governed by the Tribunals and Inquiries Act 1992. In some areas of administration, notably town and country planning and compulsory purchase of land, no right exists for an aggrieved individual to have resort in the first instance to a court or tribunal. Statute – and in the case of planning provisions, this is the Town and Country Planning Act 1990 – provides for an administrative appeal to the Secretary of State, who appoints an inspector to conduct a public local inquiry into the grievance. It might be that an applicant for planning permission has been refused consent by the local planning authority for his or her area or, having been granted permission, has had conditions attached which the applicant finds unsatisfactory. The inspector hears evidence and then prepares a report for the minister, who then makes a decision. Only then does a right of appeal lie to the High Court and, in some cases, it may be appropriate to seek judicial review of a planning decision where it is alleged that the decision maker acted *ultra vires* or in breach of the rules of natural justice.

It is usual where major developments are planned, for example, highways or an airport, for the Secretary of State to call a public inquiry so that all those who have some interest in the proposed development have the opportunity to air their views. It is not only residents of an area which is the subject of a proposed major development who may put forward their views, but also those who represent interests which may be adversely affected, such as environmental and conservationist bodies, for example, Friends of the Earth, the National Trust or the Council for the Conservation of Rural England.

Advantages and disadvantages of administrative tribunals

Before concluding our discussion of tribunals, it is necessary to sum up briefly with some of their main advantages and disadvantages. Following the post-1947 governmental intervention into social welfare and administration, a need arose for quick and cheap means of adjudicating disputes. The courts were not considered suitable to handle the detailed provisions of such legislation and delegated legislation and, in any case, could not have coped with the volume of claims. Tribunals offered a means of adjudication in an informal setting where the rules of evidence were relaxed and, compared with the courts, were cheap, quick and located locally. They also provided knowledge and expertise from those selected for their connection with the subject matter in dispute.

Tribunals are primarily concerned with the proof of fact and are not bound by previous decisions, although, in applying the law, they must take account of superior court decisions. Tribunals are firmly embedded into dispute resolution, but they are not without criticism either generally as a system or in relation to particular tribunals or decisions. One criticism is that they tend to find in favour of the government view, although this should be checked by the supervisory jurisdiction of the High Court and the Council on Tribunals. Another criticism is the lack of legal aid, and a further criticism is that there is neither a uniform procedure regulating all administrative tribunals, nor one appeal procedure.

It has been suggested that there should be established an Administrative Court to hear all appeals from tribunals and replace the present jurisdiction of the High Court and Court of Appeal. Some argue that resort to tribunals is justice on the cheap, particularly as there is no choice as to forum and that, consequently, tighter procedures should be instigated so as to ensure a high quality of decision making, including the automatic giving of reasons and legal aid. A criticism made in recent years has been that the idealism of the Franks Report has been lost and that tribunals are no longer so cheap, quick and informal as they once were, and that in fact they have become subject to delay and complex procedures, with no overall pattern of procedure or control.

The employment tribunals are a good illustration, where it may take up to a year for a case to be heard and, in some 22% of applications, parties are legally represented. This increases the chance of success for those represented, but the compensation awards are low and legal aid is not available. One other factor is the increased amount of legislation that has to be taken into account, emanating from the European Union and also precedent.

Alternative dispute resolution

In this section, we shall consider recent developments to encourage the use of non-adversarial procedures in the settlement of disputes, including mediation, conciliation and mini-trials. The most formal type of ADR, arbitration, has already been considered. On consulting a dictionary, this phrase is used to describe 'conciliation, mediation and mini-trial procedures for the resolution of disputes without recourse to litigation'.

It has been in use in the USA and Australia, Canada and New Zealand for some time and has found favour there in family and sporting disputes, and has been endorsed by the Lord Chancellor in the light of major criticisms as to the effectiveness of the civil justice system and the pressures on legal aid. A court decision offers certainty and finality (subject to rights of appeal), but these are often outweighed by delay, cost and the stress of undertaking litigation.

ADR attempts to involve the client in the process of resolving the dispute. It does not rely on an adversarial approach, but rather on reaching an agreement. Each case is decided on its merits without reference to previous cases, and the common ground between the parties can be emphasised rather than points of disagreement. It offers a confidential process and the outcome will not be published without the consent of both parties. Resolution of a dispute can be quicker and more straightforward and hearing times and places are at the agreement of the parties. As we have already noted, negotiation before undertaking litigation is a recognised procedure in an attempt to settle the matter amicably. However, it will be important for each party to preserve his or her position should litigation be unavoidable. It is usual to state that all correspondence is 'without prejudice' or 'without prejudice except as to costs', so that statements made during negotiation cannot be relied on by the opponent at the trial unless the recipient agrees.

Lord Woolf, in his interim report, suggested three reasons for having ADR:

- it contributes to 'the fair, appropriate and effective resolution of civil disputes';

- to increase awareness on the part of the legal profession and members of the public of the virtues of ADR in improving access to justice; and

- ADR can offer the courts lessons in terms of practices and procedures.

There was no suggestion by Lord Woolf that we should adopt the American practice of compulsory mediation. ADR was not to be compulsory either as an alternative or a preliminary to litigation. However, signs have not been positive that voluntary ADR is working. In the *New Law Journal* of 19 March 1999, pp 410–11, District Judge Trent referred to a comment by a colleague that ADR stood for 'Alarming Drop in Revenue'. He also referred to the central London county court pilot set up in 1996 for selected cases where both parties volunteered. Only about 5% of the parties referred to it took it up. Of these, some 62% settled at the first meeting.

For the first time, the Civil Procedure Rules 1998 impose a duty on the courts to encourage the use of ADR, and the parties are obliged to assist the court in this. Under these rules, litigants will be required to complete an allocation questionnaire, in which one of the questions requires the parties to say whether they are willing for a one month stay in proceedings, so as to allow settlement by way of ADR or other means. More will be found on these procedures in Chapter 7.

Mediation

This involves a neutral third party acting as a 'go-between' so as to facilitate co-operation and agreement. Where the relationship between the parties needs to be preserved, for example, in family disputes or those involving commercial matters, mediation ensures that the relationship is not soured, as it would be by litigation. It is a voluntary process and, should it fail, the parties will have preserved their positions. The procedure is informal and involves an independent third party discussing the matter in dispute with each party in separate rooms. The mediator is independent and assists the parties to negotiate with each other on points in dispute. Parties feel in control, and mediation is much used in the USA in family and corporate disputes. It can be used to settle priorities before the start of litigation or, in some cases, in place of litigation. However, its use presupposes a degree of co-operation between the parties, and one of the major criticisms is that, where parties are entrenched, mediation will not be appropriate.

Commercial mediation is used in the UK and has been promoted by companies such as International Dispute Resolution Europe Ltd, which predict that, before long, lawyers will adopt mediation, as it is being demanded by commercial clients who see its advantages as speed, cost, simplicity and the preservation of goodwill. Its mediators are lawyers with mediation training. The Centre for Dispute Resolution, founded in 1990 under the auspices of the Confederation of British Industry and commercial law firms, also offers commercial mediation. The National Association of Family Mediation and Conciliation Services offer mediation in family disputes. Some 57 local agencies offer support to those who wish to conduct their own negotiations and only refer to lawyers in an advisory capacity. Some 300 mediators throughout the country offer family counselling and legal advice. The mediators are trained solicitors and counsellors, and the aim is to arrive at a mutually agreed settlement.

Other organisations who offer mediation services or who provide information on ADR include the Family Mediators' Association, the UK College of Mediators, the Agency for Dispute Resolution and the Family Law Association set up by The Law Society. The National Family Mediation charity launched its own website in 1999, which sets out the benefits of mediation when dealing with disputes involving children, property and financial matters. Given the major change in culture following the Woolf reforms of the civil justice system, moving away from the emphasis on litigation as the main method of dispute resolution, law firms and the College of Law and other providers of legal education and training see the need to ensure that solicitors are trained in ADR methods. Many of the large City firms specialising in commercial work have seen the benefits of arbitration and are now offering mediation, conciliation and mini-trials as alternatives to, or as a preliminary to litigation, should ADR only resolve part or none of the dispute. A variation known as Med-Arb is also used in the USA. If both parties agree, mediation is used, with the option of resorting to arbitration where appropriate.

The Lord Chancellor published a Green Paper in 1993, proposing radical reforms in divorce law. The sole ground for divorce would be irretrievable breakdown, but only after 12 months' reflection time. Divorce settlement would be taken out of the courts and instead, family mediation centres would be established throughout the country. It would be compulsory for all parties to attend such a centre for an hour-long interview with the aim of saving those marriages which have not irretrievably broken down. The Lord Chancellor also indicated that the annual £180 million legal aid bill for divorce had to be reduced. Those who refused mediation could be denied legal aid.

Part I of the Family Law Act 1996 refers to the principles of supporting the institution of marriage and bringing those which have irretrievably broken down to an end, but minimising distress, promoting parental co-operation and ensuring costs are kept under control. A complex process has to be complied with before the divorce process is completed and an order made. This involves making a statement of marital breakdown and at least three months beforehand both parties must attend an information meeting. A period of reflection follows filing of the statement of marital breakdown of at least nine months (but this is extended to 15 months where there are children aged under 16 years). Before filing the statement, the parties must have been married for at least a year and, during this period, those on legal aid will be required to attend mediation unless their case is deemed inappropriate (for example, where violence is shown). Access to future State funding for marital services is made dependent on attendance at mediation.

This was a radical set of reforms which could not be given effect to immediately. Instead, a number of pilot schemes were established to test the take-up rate and effectiveness of mediation. Lord Irvine endorsed the principles behind this move and suggested that the Act would come into effect in 2000. The results of the pilot schemes were not supportive of the idea that people in family disputes, particularly on questions of property and money, were willing to forgo having a legal representative 'fight their corner'. On questions involving children, mediation appears more of an option, in that the law and most, if not all, parents, want to act in the best interests of their children. In mid-1999, Lord Irvine announced the postponement of the divorce law reforms and, in the face of academic and practitioner doubts as to the effectiveness of the reforms, it could be that, in time, they will be abandoned. The position remains that the Government still promotes the idea that mediation is a good thing in family disputes, but it will be for the parties to decide the extent to which they use such services.

Conciliation

Conciliation is a half way house between arbitration on the one hand and mediation on the other, the former being the most formal and the latter being the least formal. The conciliator offers a non-binding opinion, which may lead to settlement. In 1985, the Lord Chancellor's Department commissioned a report by the Conciliation Project Unit at Newcastle University to investigate the cost-effectiveness of conciliation in the county court and in the settlement of matrimonial disputes. The Civil Justice Review of 1992 highlighted the often costly and bitter litigation resulting in such disputes and recommended reform. However, it must be noted that, where ADR is used in conjunction with litigation, the result will be an increase in cost and delay in some cases.

Mini-trials

This is another practice much used in the USA to settle commercial disputes. Lawyers representing the parties present the arguments in the case to the parties themselves and a neutral adviser, who may be a judge or senior lawyer. In the words of the Beldham Report, this will enable the parties 'to assess the strengths, weaknesses and prospects of the case, and then have an opportunity to enter into settlement discussions on a realistic, business-like basis'. The neutral adviser has a vital role to play and may offer an opinion on the case, having knowledge or experience of the matter in dispute.

In 1992, the Hart Workshop at the Institute of Advanced Legal Studies held a debate on civil justice and its alternatives. Several points were made, including the fact that conciliation procedures first started to be used in the UK in the 1970s and that they had already been much used abroad, particularly in commercial disputes.

The aim of ADR is to facilitate settlement, whereas the aim of litigation is to obtain judgment. Judges are increasingly becoming involved with ADR, as are solicitors and barristers. This may well have the disadvantage of clouding the perception of their roles by the lay client. In addition, it will create tensions between lawyers and other professionals who might expect to offer services, such as counsellors and social workers. Proper training is essential, but to date little has been done to provide public funding for such services and, where litigation follows ADR, the costs of both will have to be met.

In 1993, a Practice Statement was issued by the Commercial Court on ADR, to the effect that parties should be encouraged to consider using ADR as an additional means of settling disputes. Judges of the Commercial Court cannot offer ADR, but the clerk to the court retains a list of bodies offering mediation, conciliation and other ADR services, although it would be for the parties or their legal representatives to approach such bodies. This has since been replaced by a new Practice Statement of 11 June 1996.

The Report of the Committee on Alternative Dispute Resolution, established by the General Council of the Bar and chaired by Lord Justice Beldham, was published in 1991 and supported the notion that the courts should embrace ADR in order to support the judicial process. This is a widely supported idea, and involves potential litigants undertaking ADR processes before resorting to litigation.

Several experiments have been conducted in the English courts. For example, in the divorce county courts, property matters and proceedings relating to children have been subject to pilot ADR schemes. There is no one pattern, but they range from meeting with the parties to draw their attention to the advantages of settlement to encouragement for further negotiations, leading to settlement. In some courts, the judge or court welfare officers act as mediators or refer the parties to an outside agency. In others a 'pre-trial' review is held, at which conciliation on property matters is encouraged, leading to settlement. The Beldham Report recommended that such preliminary procedures should generally be used in civil disputes and proposed that pilot projects be set up in both the county court and High Court. The scheme could be either entirely voluntary or, in suitable cases identified by the judge, mediation could be suggested. The mediator would be selected from lawyers with at least seven years' post-qualification experience.

At least two concerns have been identified with court-linked ADR, namely, the clouding of the perception of the roles of judges and lawyers and the position of weak parties who may find themselves manipulated by the other party and the mediator. Some would go so far as to say that compromise of a dispute is not as effective as allowing a person his or her 'day in court', and that ADR is a poor substitute for having one party win and the other lose in open court. The Beldham Report assumes that lawyers with long experience will make competent mediators, but this is unproven, and there would seem to be a serious conflict in the roles of a neutral adviser and that of a representative of a claimant. Certainly, following the Family Law Act 1996, although the proposed divorce reforms have been postponed, solicitors are now undertaking training as family law mediators, and, where the parties are able to settle amicably without one exerting undue pressure on the other, this is a useful alternative to litigation. The perception, perhaps, is that the process of mediation is cheaper, but in order to ensure that it is not less effective there may be a high financial cost in employing mediators with the right expertise. One of the real dangers of any type of ADR is that a strong, overbearing party may be able to browbeat a weaker party and where the real issues affecting them are not dealt with. Those with established expertise of ADR in various fields include social workers, accountants, family counsellors, architects and surveyors.

In concluding our discussion of ADR, we must note in passing the role played in settling disputes of administrative agencies such as the Citizens' Advice Bureaux, the Advertising Standards Authority, trade associations such as the Association of British Laundry Cleaning and the National Association of Retail Furnishers, and ombudsmen schemes such as the Estate Agents Ombudsman and the Office of the Banking Ombudsman.

Before leaving the issue of alternatives to litigation, it is worth mentioning another initiative by the legal profession to assist those who, for whatever reason, cannot resolve a dispute by the traditional routes. This is referred to as a *pro bono publico* (for the public good) service offered by members of the legal profession, solicitors and barristers, without fee. It involves legal advice at law centres or Citizens' Advice Bureaux, or advising charities or pressure groups. The Bar has set up its *Pro Bono* Free Representation Unit and solicitors have a *Pro Bono* Group, although notably the latter was a private initiative, not one from The Law Society.

In addition, some university law schools offer free representation units (FRU) which offer clinical legal education to its students by allowing students, under supervision, to offer advice, write letters and represent individuals in tribunals, such as employment and social security tribunals. It has been found that such services complement those offered by solicitors and other professional advisers, as those who are assisted by FRU would not otherwise make use of the professional provider.

Another method of solving disputes which is increasing in importance is the idea of an ombudsman. Ombudsmen ('grievance men') in the public administration field were set up as a result of the recommendations of the Justice Report in 1960. The Parliamentary Commissioner for Administration (PCA) and Local Government Commissioners were established under the Parliamentary Commissioner Act 1967 and the Local Government Act 1974 respectively to review maladministration in the conduct of public powers and duties. In 1987, the Health Services Commissioner was set up with power to review the workings of the National Health Service (NHS). Under ss 21–26 of the Courts and Legal Services Act 1990, the Legal Services Ombudsman oversees the workings of what was formerly the Solicitors' Complaints Bureau but is now the Office for the Supervision of Solicitors (OSS), which deals with complaints against solicitors not involving allegations of professional negligence. The ombudsman also reviews complaints against barristers and other professionals such as legal executives and licensed conveyancers. More can be found about this ombudsman in Chapter 4.

The first Prisons' Commissioner was appointed in 1994. This is an area where, increasingly, prisoners are asserting that their civil rights have been infringed by the prison authorities, for example, that they have been denied postal deliveries or that mail has been intercepted, or that they have been denied access to the press or that sanctions have been imposed unfairly. Such complaints may fall on deaf ears within the prison system, in the person of the governor, and so it was felt necessary to appoint an independent to investigate how such complaints are dealt with.

A more recent appointment is the Parliamentary Commissioner for Public Standards, following the Nolan Committee report on 'cash for questions' in the Commons. In the case of *R v Parliamentary Comr for Public Standards ex p Al Fayed* (1997), it was held that this commissioner was not subject to judicial review for the way in which he exercised his powers, as he was concerned with the internal workings of the House of Commons and this was a privileged area outside the scope of the courts. However, in *R v PCA ex p Balchin* (1997) it was held that judicial review would be available to scrutinise the way in which complaints by members of the public against public servants had been handled. It is important to note here that these cases concerned 'complaints about complaints', in that the aggrieved person refers a complaint against a minister or civil servant to the ombudsman, only to find that the method of investigation or the result obtained is unsatisfactory. This leaves the aggrieved person to seek judicial review of the way in which the ombudsman acted in the hope that the issue will be referred back to him and he will reconsider how to deal with the original problem.

The procedures vary for referral of complaints to the different types of ombudsman, but we will mention those regulating the PCA. This is provided under the Act of the same name passed in 1967 and provides for an 'MP filter', in other words, a person with a grievance must make this known to his MP, or another MP to whom he is referred, for the MP to decide whether there is a matter deserving of investigation. It may be that the MP will be able to offer assistance, leading to resolution of the question. If not, the MP then refers the matter to the PCA, who has wide ranging powers to investigate. In the terms of the Act, he can seek out 'persons, papers and records', although he does not have access to Cabinet papers, which are secret. He is authorised to investigate 'maladministration', which include such things as delay, bias, incompetence, neglect and inattention by a public official. Following his investigation, he will prepare a report, in which he will make recommendations. Should he make a finding of maladministration, he will advise the government department at fault to reconsider its position. Unlike the Parliamentary Commissioner for Northern Ireland, the PCA cannot enforce his recommendations through the courts. This, together with the MP filter, is seen as a serious flaw in the system. An improvement in its effectiveness is the willingness of the courts to oversee the working of the PCA by way of judicial review. This also increases the likelihood that, following an investigation by the PCA concerning controversial matters, the publicity generated by his investigation and report will go some way to ensuring that such matters do not occur again. This may provide little comfort, however, to those who have made the complaint and find that they cannot receive any compensation or other recompense as of right. The PCA in addition publishes an annual report to Parliament, and where he investigates a matter of national concern, he can submit a special report. He is, as his title suggests, an officer of Parliament and he owes duties to Parliament to keep the executive under scrutiny in its dealings with the citizen. A Select Committee of the House of Commons also monitors his work. The workings of the PCA have come to public attention recently over the operation of the Child Support Agency, and over the Channel Tunnel Link and how the route was to be allocated.

ALTERNATIVE DISPUTE RESOLUTION

Alternatives to court action

- The existing and proposed alternatives to adjudication as a means of settling disputes; the reasons for the shift towards finding alternatives and their advantages and disadvantages.

- Arbitration, tribunals and types of alternative dispute resolution (ADR).

Arbitration

- The appointment and functions of an arbitrator: small claims procedure; appointment of High Court judges from the Commercial Court – s 4 of the Administration of Justice Act 1970.

- The advantages of arbitration.

- *Scott v Avery* clauses.

- Advisory, Conciliation and Arbitration Service (ACAS).

- Arbitration Act 1996, which attempts to make the process more widely accessible, particularly for international users.

Tribunals

- Statutory tribunals must be distinguished from domestic tribunals.

- Supervisory jurisdiction of the High Court over inferior courts and tribunals.

- *R v Football Association Ltd ex p Football League Ltd* (1993); *Lee v Showman's Guild of GB* (1952); *R v Panel on Take-overs and Mergers ex p Datafin* (1986); *R v Chief Rabbi ex p Wachmann* (1992); *R v Disciplinary Committee of the Jockey Club ex p Aga Khan* (1993); *R v Insurance Ombudsman Bureau and Insurance Ombudsman ex p Aegon Life Assurance Ltd* (1993); *R v Visitors to the Inns of Court ex p Calder and Persaud* (1993); *Page v Hull University* (1993); *R v Manchester University ex p Nolan* (1993).

- Social security tribunals.

- The Lands Tribunal.

- Mental health review tribunals.
- Control of administrative tribunals.
- Advantages and disadvantages of administrative tribunals.

Alternative dispute resolution

- Mediation.
- Conciliation.
- Mini-trials.
- Other initiatives to investigate and encourage the use of ADR.

CHAPTER 6

THE JUDICIAL FUNCTION

Introduction

The main function of the judge is to reach a solution in a dispute by applying the law to the facts. As we have seen, the law is derived from various sources, the two principal ones being statute and case law. We describe our judicial process as an adversarial one, in which the judge is an arbiter dependent on the presentation of oral argument by counsel for each party. The judge waits to be persuaded by the strength of arguments put to him and, on the whole, does not intervene or conduct his own researches into the law, less so the facts. In reaching decisions, the judge may be applying an area of the law found in case law (past decisions of judges) or interpreting statutory provisions. A decision of the court in which a statute has been interpreted may in turn be used by a later judge and, in that sense, the decision may add to the body of precedent.

In this chapter, we consider how the judge applies case law and statute so as to arrive at a solution in a dispute or criminal case. We have already mentioned the main rules of precedent, including binding and persuasive precedent, *obiter dicta* and *ratio decidendi*, the hierarchy of the courts and the importance of accurate law reports. It is worth reminding ourselves here of the importance of such devices as distinguishing and the distinction between overruling and reversing. Where a court is referred to a past precedent which is binding on it, the court is expected to follow that precedent providing there is sufficient similarity between the facts of the case it has to decide and the one it is asked to follow. Where there are sufficient dissimilarities, in the estimation of the judge having to reach the decision, he will be free not to follow the previous authority. In other words, the later court distinguishes the facts of the case it has to decide from those of the previous authority. This gives the courts scope for innovation and allows the law to develop. However, its disadvantage is that it can be abused and result in 'hair splitting', leading to over-technicality and uncertainty. Where, for instance, the Court of Appeal is referred in argument to a previous persuasive authority (but which binds courts below the Court of Appeal, for example, the High Court), it may decide that it is not good law. In such a case, the court can overrule that precedent, by declaring that the rule or principle for which it is authority is wrong. The precedent may be of long standing and would have involved litigants whose legal position had been determined by earlier courts. It would be anomalous if those litigants many years later found that their positions altered. Thus, overruling refers only to changing the rule or principle on which a decision is founded and it takes effect prospectively, not retrospectively. In comparison, reversing refers to the situation where litigants appeal to a higher court and that court finds for the loser the first time round. Here, the position of the litigants is altered as the appeal court takes a different view of the facts, the law, or both from the lower court. Having distinguished overruling and reversing, it is important to note that where a higher court reverses the decision of a lower court on a different view of the law governing the facts in question, this different view may arise as the result of the higher court overruling a precedent binding on the lower court.

We will also consider the main rules of statutory interpretation, including the literal, golden and mischief rules. In addition, given the increasing influence of European Community law, we will consider the use of the purposive approach. Now that the Human Rights Act 1998 has incorporated the European Convention on Human Rights into UK law, it is likely that use of the purposive approach will expand and, in turn, this will have an effect on how UK statutes are drafted.

Judicial thought processes

Before considering how judges make use of precedent and interpret statutes, we will consider some of the mental processes that a judge may adopt in coming to a decision. Remember that trial judges give an oral judgment, but appeal judges pronounce not only orally but in written form, the essential components of the judgment being to establish the relevant facts, identify the decision reached and give a reason or reasons for the decision.

A matter that was explored more fully in Chapter 3 is the independence and impartiality of the judiciary, but it is necessary to make some mention of it here in the light of Lord Hoffman's judgment in *R v Bow Street Magistrates' Court ex p Pinochet Ugarte (No 1)* (1998). It is a fundamental tenet of the UK constitution that the judges will be independent of the executive and will make decisions grounded in law 'without fear or favour'. A clear exposition of the relationship of the courts, Parliament and the executive is to be found in the House of Lords' judgment in *R v Secretary of State for the Home Department ex p Fire Brigades' Union and Others* (1995).

In addition, it is important for those coming before the courts to be assured that the judge is impartial and acts without bias. These concepts complement each other, but where one is present, the other cannot be assumed to be present also. Until Lord Hoffman overlooked his associations with the charitable arm of Amnesty International in 1999, the question of the lack of bias, other than a direct financial interest, would be assumed. This complacency, however, resulted in the unusual situation of the House of Lords declaring its first judgment void and then rehearing the appeal with a differently composed court. Even more unusual was the second decision, in that the court refined its reasons for holding Colonel Pinochet liable for human rights abuses. Lord Hoffman did a particular service in heightening awareness that, although there certainly was no suggestion that he was in fact biased, it is the question of apparent bias requiring disclosure that causes the difficulty; and where shown to be direct, the judge should step down. Subsequent cases have come before the courts where allegations of judicial bias have been made and these were mentioned in Chapter 3 .

In arriving at a judgment, the judge must have gone through a mental process in which he listened to arguments from both sides, weighed up and assessed the strengths and weaknesses of the evidence and the legal sources to which he was referred, so as to come to a reasoned conclusion. Logic must play a large part here: we expect judges to be logical and to employ reason in their decision making. A distinction is often made between deductive and inductive reasoning and either, or a combination of both of these may be used. Both use a system of rules or principles, but their starting points are different.

Take two examples:

All women are female; Posh Spice is a woman; therefore Posh Spice is female.

Posh Spice is successful; Posh Spice is a woman; therefore all women are successful.

The first seems to do no more than state the obvious, and is an example of deductive reasoning. Providing the premises on which this formula are based are correct, the result can be proved. However, if they are incorrect, the formula proves nothing other than that the formula itself is correct. Thus, compare the following with the first example above:

All women are tall; Posh Spice is a woman; therefore Posh Spice is tall.

Clearly, not all women are tall and, in any case, it is a relative concept: what one person considers tall, another would say is short.

The second is an example of inductive reasoning, moving from the particular fact to the general proposition. Again, the form cannot be faulted, but the substance of the conclusion reached can. Posh Spice may be successful, although even that is debatable; she is a woman, but that does not mean that all women are successful. This type of reasoning is even less certain than deductive reasoning, in that it extrapolates from the particular to the general and there is no certainty that the general can be quantified or assessed to be seen to be correct.

Judges do not approach their task conscious of such categories; at least, there is no requirement that a judge makes clear what method he is adopting. Furthermore, in reaching a decision, more than one method may be used. With the deductive approach, the judge reasons from the general to the particular. A general rule or principle is established in previous cases and the judge in the present case deduces a solution to the problem before him by applying that general rule or principle to the facts of the case. In theory, this is the most used method of reaching decisions and perhaps the safest. All that a judge has to do is find a previous authority, locate the *ratio decidendi* and then apply it to the particular facts of the case he has to decide. However, it is by no means a foolproof means of reaching a decision. There may not be a ready authority within the range of similarity of facts and more problematic, the *ratio* of earlier authorities may not be clear or may be conflicting. In the House of Lords, it is usual to have five Law Lords to hear a case. They may all agree on the decision, but their reasons for so deciding may differ. The question for a later court having to apply that authority will be to establish what its *ratio* was. This in itself gives the judges scope for developing the law, as it is the later judge who can determine whether to expand or narrow a previous authority.

With the inductive approach, the judge moves from the particular (in the form of past cases, perhaps from which earlier courts have not seen any general principle applying) to the general. The later court is willing to find such a general rule or principle to explain the earlier cases and to rationalise them into a pattern. Once such a general rule or principle emerges, it will be for other courts to make use of it deductively. This may be an even more precarious method than the deductive approach. The judge will have to ensure that his starting point is sound and that the conclusions he draws are not simply accurate in strict logic.

Of the two methods, the inductive approach allows the judge the most scope for judicial law making, as is demonstrated by Lord Atkin's *dictum* in *Donoghue v Stevenson* (1932), when he established the 'neighbour principle'. This was revolutionary at the time and allowed the law to redress wrongs even where there was an absence of privity of contract. Once that principle became established, later courts have applied it deductively and it is what has been made of this general principle by later courts which has seen the law of negligence extend far beyond the factual situation before Lord Atkin. Another area of law which has been developed by the judges using inductive reasoning is the law of restitution. Lord Goff, both as judge and textbook writer, has contributed to the development of this area over many years. By way of piecemeal developments, we are gradually reaching a general principle which recognises that, where a person unfairly obtains a benefit from another, the law will hold him accountable. The judges had developed the law of tort and the law of contract, but there was a gap left where some individuals fell and for which the law of restitution may provide a remedy. Where a benefit is found to have unjustly enriched the recipient and neither the law of contract nor tort provides a remedy, then an order for its restitution may be available. By piecing together the cases decided over many years, Lord Goff in *Woolwich Building Society v IRC (No 2)* (1992) suggested that a general principle of restitution should be recognised. This case concerned the overpayment of tax and whether the Inland Revenue was obliged to refund the taxpayer with interest. The court held that in fairness, the taxpayer was entitled to a refund as of right plus interest where the mistake was made following the wrong interpretation of the law by the Revenue. It was not merely at the Revenue's discretion to decide to refund or not, but as the result of a legal obligation.

Another way in which a judge may reach a decision is by way of reasoning by analogy. Take the following example:

Cotton is a type of yarn used to make garments; wool is like cotton; therefore wool is suitable to make garments.

Compare the following statement:

Cotton is a type of yarn used to make garments; paper is like cotton; therefore paper is suitable to make garments.

In the first statement, a comparison is made between cotton and wool as being suitable to make clothes. Providing it is correct to assert that wool and cotton are sufficiently similar, the conclusion reached can be justified. The second statement demonstrates that if the premise on which the analogy is drawn is incorrect, then a false conclusion will be reached. Reasoning by analogy may appear to be a certain method of reaching decisions, but even here there is scope for discretion in comparing one thing with another.

This process is based on identifying the similarities between cases and their relevance and importance. The judge will have to assess the material similarities and dissimilarities in the facts of decided cases to which he is referred and the facts of the case before him. If sufficient similarity exists, then the judge will apply the previous authority to reach a decision on the facts before him. This process gives the judge scope to develop the law, as it is in the assessment of the degree of similarity that value judgments can be made. Elements of policy – the desirability or expediency of extending the rule or principle to a new factual situation – will no doubt play a part in the process.

In judge made law, the deductive approach is generally used, but sometimes a judge may attempt an innovation, or, as in the case of the celebrated former Master of the Rolls, Lord Denning, be known as an innovative judge, and make use of the inductive approach so as to develop the law in a particular area. This is not to say that such a method results in a judge making a decision by whim, but rather that he draws on rules and principles in morality or religion or from other jurisdictions to arrive at a decision. At other times, reasoning by analogy will be used. In the case of *Airedale National Heath Service Trust v Bland* (1993), the court was asked to decide whether treatment should be withdrawn from a patient in a persistent vegetative state. The courts were not able to draw on any previous binding authorities, but were referred to persuasive authorities from courts in Commonwealth jurisdictions. The House of Lords relied heavily on principles of morality to weigh up the competing beliefs in the sanctity of life and retaining a person's dignity in being allowed to die. At the other extreme, the case of *Bettinson v Langdon* (1999) demonstrates also that a judge may have no binding authorities on which to rely and, after argument from counsel for the parties, will have to reach a reasoned decision. This case concerned the rights of commoners to graze their animals on a common. It was held that, despite some 300 years of uncertainty on the point, the law permitted certain grazing rights to be 'in gross', that is, exist free of the ownership of land, with the effect that a commoner could sell the grazing rights to the highest bidder. The Court of Appeal took into account a myriad of persuasive authority to the contrary, but considered that public policy permitted such rights to be in gross.

Interpreting statutes

So far as statutory interpretation is concerned, it is more likely that the deductive approach or reasoning by analogy is used, as Parliament states the general rules to be applied. We will now move on to consider the role of the judge in interpreting legislation. This includes the interpretation of delegated legislation. We have already noted that the courts can challenge the validity of delegated legislation, but not that of legislation itself, on the basis of the sovereignty of Parliament doctrine. This is not to say, however, that the courts do not have an important function with regard to legislation.

The judge interprets the meaning to be placed on statutory provisions relied on when a case comes to court for settlement. Statutory provisions may be interpreted narrowly or widely, and this gives a judge potentially great power in determining the future scope of the law. In interpreting statutory provisions, the judges add to the body of case law, and this may assist future courts in deciding disputes.

The judges have formulated rules of practice, which are to be found in case law, to assist them in giving meaning to statutory provisions when those provisions form the basis of a dispute to be decided. The traditional approach has been for the judge to look at the words of the statute to be interpreted and, from the words used by Parliament, gauge the meaning intended by Parliament.

Jacqueline Martin in *The English Legal System* (1997) reminds us that Sir Rupert Cross (a well known jurist who wrote a textbook on statutory interpretation) suggested that the judge should make use of four steps in interpreting a statute and this was based on the literal rule of construction. The first step involves the judge looking at the context of the provision to be interpreted and applying the grammatical or ordinary or technical meaning of the words. Secondly, he can use his discretion to apply a secondary meaning if the first leads to an absurdity. Thirdly, the judge may read in words necessarily implied by the statute and may 'add to, alter or ignore words in order to prevent a provision from being unintelligible, unworkable or absurd'. Finally, to assist him, the judge may make use of intrinsic aids to construction and presumptions.

We will now consider the distinction between extrinsic and intrinsic aids to construction. Little use was made of the former when interpreting domestic legislation, for reliance was placed on finding the meaning of the words used from the words themselves. Notably, records of debates in Parliament were not consulted, as this was considered to be beyond the bounds of the court and could be argued to offend Art 9 of the Bill of Rights 1688, whereby proceedings in Parliament should not be questioned in any court or other place. In the case of *Pepper v Hart* (1993), the House of Lords held that reference may be made to parliamentary debates recorded in the official journal of proceedings (*Hansard*) when the court is asked to interpret a statutory provision which is ambiguous or obscure or leads to an absurdity providing the records consist of clear statements by a minister or another promoter of the Bill. This appears a tall order to fulfil, and is not such a radical innovation as at first thought. It is one which is unlikely to give rise to an 'opening of the floodgates'. Lord Mackay, the then Lord Chancellor (dissenting in the case), referred to the policy issues of permitting access to *Hansard*, including cost and delay in litigation.

In the case of *Massmould v Payne* (1993), decided only days after *Pepper v Hart*, Vinelott J found that, as there was no ambiguity on the face of the legislation he was asked to interpret, he could not make reference to *Hansard*. This was also adopted in the case of *Sheppard v IRC* (1993) by Aldous J. The court was confined to the words used in the legislation where on their face they appeared clear. It was not for the court to compare such words with the meaning attributed to words used during the course of parliamentary debate, even though it appeared that Parliament had intended a different meaning to be attached to the words used in the legislation. Thus, if the court concluded that the legislative words could mean X or Y, then *Hansard* could be consulted, but where the words only meant X, then *Hansard* was not to be consulted, even if, during Parliamentary debate, it was intended that the words meant Y. In *Van Dyck v Secretary of State for the Environment* (1993), which concerned the interpretation of a provision in the Town and Country Planning Act 1971, the Court of Appeal held that the provision was itself ambiguous, but that *Hansard* was not sufficiently clear as to the meaning to be attributed to the words used, and so was of no assistance to the court.

Despite this cautious approach, wider use of parliamentary speeches has been made, for example in the case of *Three Rivers DC and Others v Bank of England (No 2)* (1996), a judgment which reflects the continental approach to statutory interpretation. The plaintiffs sued the Bank of England, alleging that it failed to supervise the activities of the Bank of Commerce and Credit International, which resulted in their suffering financial loss. Their arguments depended on the general purpose of the Banking Acts 1979 and 1987, which, they asserted, imposed a supervisory role on the Bank of England in compliance with EC Directive 77/780. They further asserted that this purpose could be elicited from the parliamentary speeches during the second reading of each Act. The High Court held that, to ascertain the true purpose of the Acts, which were not giving effect to purely domestic legislation, it was permissible to consult parliamentary speeches. The case of *Pickstone v Freemans plc* (1989) was relied on.

Judges in continental jurisdictions view their role quite differently from that of the judge in a common law system. Case law does not develop by way of binding precedent, and legislative provisions are more concerned with general principle rather than precisely drafted provisions. The continental approach is known as the purposive approach, where the judge is not confined by the words used in a statutory provision but can consult extrinsic materials to assist him or her in finding the meaning intended by the legislator. The judicial role has greater scope and the judge can afford to be more dynamic in attaching meaning to statutory provisions.

Use of the purposive approach by the English courts has been limited, in that the judge is still governed in the first instance by the words used. If these are clear and unambiguous, they must be applied. Greater reliance on the purposive approach may well have two results: namely, that judges in future may make greater use of extrinsic aids to construction, and the style of drafting statutory provisions may become more like that used in continental systems. The courts have had to change their approach when interpreting provisions emanating from what is now the European Union, which are drafted in much more general terms. Here, the courts have the assistance of the European Court of Justice, to whom preliminary reference under Art 234 of the EC Treaty (formerly Art 177) may be made in specified situations.

Lord Scarman in *Shah v Barnet LBC* (1983) stated that an Act should be read as a whole in conjunction with any permitted documents so as to find the purpose or policy intended by Parliament. The court could not, however, interpret an Act so as to give effect to its own views as to policy or purpose. Lord Scarman said in *Duport Steels Ltd v Sirs* (1980) that:

> ... in the field of statute law the judge must be obedient to the will of Parliament as expressed in its enactments. In this field Parliament makes, and un-makes, the law: the judge's duty is to interpret and to apply the law, not to change it to meet the judge's idea of what justice requires.

He continued later that the judge should 'not deny the statute. Unpalatable statute law may not be disregarded or rejected, merely because it is unpalatable'.

In *R v Registrar General ex p Smith* (1990), the court held that an applicant who wished to obtain a copy of his birth certificate under the Adoption Act 1976 was not entitled to information which would have enabled him to obtain a certificate and thereby discover the identity of his mother, on the grounds that the absolute duty to supply such information was subject to a principle of public policy where there was a real risk of the commission of a serious crime by the applicant in the future against his mother. The court adopted a purposive approach in the face of clear and unambiguous legislative language, as it was felt that if the legislator had been confronted with such a situation it would have been obvious that no information should be revealed. Public policy demanded that all statutes, no matter when passed, be subject to this principle and not merely those passed after declaration of the principle by the court.

When interpreting legislation having purely domestic effect, the courts will no doubt continue to follow the traditional approach, namely, making use of intrinsic aids to construction subject to the limited application of the purposive approach and the use of extrinsic aids to construction. These include referring to an interpretation section within the Act, the long title of a public Act (or in old Acts, a preamble, as is still the case with private Acts which set out its objectives), the 'literal', 'golden', 'mischief' and *ejusdem generis* rules of interpretation and others. Also, reference can be made to the Interpretation Act 1978 and presumptions, for example, that legislation is presumed to have prospective effect in the absence of express words to the contrary.

We will consider each of these in turn, but before doing so it is worthwhile mentioning the case of *Fothergill v Monarch Airlines* (1980), in which the House of Lords was asked to interpret the word 'damage' and concluded that, although its use in the Carriage by Air Act 1961 was ambiguous, it was to be construed as including 'partial loss'. This Act was passed with the intention of giving effect to the Warsaw Convention 1929 (as amended) and the court held that *travaux préparatoires* (preparatory materials), including the minutes of meetings at which amendments to the treaty were negotiated, could be used to assist the court in construing ambiguities. In the result, the plaintiff was unable to claim for items lost from his suitcase when he failed to give the requisite notice, although he had done so with regard to damage to his suitcase.

When considering domestic statutes which do not attempt to give effect to international treaties or obligations entered into by the Crown, the courts have a much more limited role and traditionally are confined to construing the meaning of statutory provisions from the words used or by way of other recognised rules of construction and the use of presumptions. The starting point for the judge will be to apply a literal or grammatical meaning to the words used. This is known as the 'literal' rule. It may have unexpected results, as illustrated in *Whitely v Chappell* (1868), where an Act made it a criminal offence to personate 'any person entitled to vote at an election'. The defendant attempted to vote in the name of a deceased person, but it was held that no offence had been committed, as a deceased person was not a 'person' in a literal sense. Clearly, the intention of the legislature was to prevent abuses of the electoral system and, to rectify this shortcoming, amending legislation was passed.

It might be questioned whether the court could or should have addressed itself to the question of what Parliament would have done if it had considered the problem. In *ex p Smith*, as we have seen, the court referred to public policy to justify it making an absolute rule subject to the principle of public policy. In *Whitely*, the court made no attempt to 'second guess' Parliament and 'fill in the gaps' in the face of express words. In its view, to have done so would have usurped the sovereignty of Parliament and have had the result of creating uncertainty in the law.

In some situations, however, the court will not apply the literal rule where, in the time-honoured phrase, to do so would result in 'absurdity, repugnancy or inconsistency'. This exception to the literal rule is known as the 'golden' rule and is well illustrated by *Re Sigsworth* (1935), where a son who had murdered his mother was prevented from inheriting her property as her sole next of kin under the Administration of Estates Act 1925, on the grounds that it would be repugnant to allow him to do so. On first impression, it may be difficult to distinguish the reasoning in this case from that applied in *ex p Smith*, but it must be remembered that, in *ex p Smith*, the court was concerned not with past criminality, as in *Re Sigsworth*, but the possibility of future criminality and that the principle that a person should not profit from his or her own wrong was well recognised. It is therefore a question of degree, and in *ex p Smith* the court was willing to depart from the express words of the statute to a greater extent.

Should use of the golden rule not produce a reasonable result, a court may make use of the 'mischief' rule where appropriate. This was defined in *Heydon's Case* (1584) and involves the court posing four questions when attempting to interpret a statutory provision:

- what was the common law before the Act was passed?;
- what defect or mischief did the common law fail to remedy?;
- what remedy does the Act attempt to provide?;
- what is the reason for the remedy?

In *Gardiner v Sevenoaks RDC* (1950), a cave used to store films was held to be covered by an Act regulating safety measures in premises. The Act attempted to ensure the safety of places used for business purposes and, as the cave was so used, it was covered by the Act.

In *Gorris v Scott* (1874), a provision requiring the penning of sheep whilst on board ship, so as to prevent disease, was held not to apply to sheep washed overboard as a result of not being penned. This demonstrates the four questions above. The common law failed to prevent sheep becoming diseased when transported by ship. The mischief was the disease in such sheep. The statute provided that sheep were to be penned to prevent disease (but not their being washed overboard).

This rule involves the court in considering the purpose of the statutory provision which it is asked to interpret, but this is not the same thing as the purposive approach. The latter has a broader scope than the mischief rule, and at its widest may involve a court looking to the purpose of an Act even where the words used are not ambiguous. The purposive approach is still in a developmental stage in English law, although no doubt *Pepper v Hart* (1993) could well assist its further development.

The other rules of statutory interpretation only apply in specific circumstances:

- *ejusdem generis* ensures that general words which are preceded by particular words which form a class or genus are interpreted in accordance with the class words. Thus, in *Powell v Kempton Park Racecourse Co* (1899), Tattersall's open air racecourse enclosure reserved for bookmakers was held not to be subject to a provision prohibiting the keeping of 'a house, office or other place for betting purposes', as this referred only to covered accommodation;

- the *noscitur a sociis* rule provides that the meaning of a word is to be gathered from its context. Thus, in *IRC v Frere* (1964), the House of Lords held that 'interest' in the phrase 'interest, annuities or other interest' meant annual interest;

- *expressio unius est exclusio alterius*, roughly translated, means that where something is expressed it must be taken to exclude something else. *In R v Inhabitants of Sedgley* (1831), rates were to be charged on 'lands, titles and coal mines'. This expressly excluded rates being charged on any other type of mine.

The Interpretation Act 1978 or an interpretation section within the Act itself may offer the court some, albeit limited, assistance. The former provides, for example, that the masculine shall include the feminine unless a contrary intention appears and that the singular includes the plural and vice versa. Notable examples of the latter are s 118 of the Police and Criminal Evidence Act 1984 and s 119 of the Courts and Legal Services Act 1990.

Presumptions, already mentioned above, may assist the court in interpreting a provision. We have mentioned the presumption that legislation will normally have prospective effect. Other examples are that criminal liability is not imposed without proof of fault in the absence of express statutory provision (*Sweet v Parsley* (1969)); the Crown is not bound by statute unless named and as stated in *Pyx Granite Co v Minister of Housing* (1960); it is presumed that the court's jurisdiction to try a case is not ousted unless expressly stated. In *Davis v Johnson* (1979), the House of Lords noted that reference could properly be made by the court to Law Commission reports and those of committees and commissions appointed by the Government or Parliament to assess the need for law reform. Usually, such reports contain a detailed résumé of the law and the ways in which it might be reformed, and this may well assist the court in attempting to interpret a provision.

Some more cases which illustrate statutory interpretation include the following: in *Re Marr and Another* (1990), it was held *per curiam* (in the opinion of the court) that, where two sections of a statute conflict, the court should apply the purposive approach so as to arrive at a sensible meaning rather than arbitrarily giving the later provision priority. The so called 'rule of last resort' had become obsolete in respect not only of two sections of an Act, but also with regard to two sub-sections within a section; in *Waltham Forest LBC v Thomas* (1992), the defendant, who had resided with his brother prior to the brother's death, was entitled to protection under s 87 of the Housing Act 1985 as having succeeded to the brother's secure tenancy, albeit that they had only resided in that particular house some 10 days before the brother's death. By the terms of s 87, it was sufficient that the defendant had resided with his brother for 12 months before his death. It was not necessary that this was in the premises to which succession was claimed.

In *Knowles v Liverpool CC* (1993), the House of Lords affirmed the decision of the Court of Appeal in holding that the word 'equipment' in the Employer's Liability (Defective Equipment) Act 1969 could refer to a flagstone. K, a flagger, sued his employers for injuries sustained from a faulty flagstone. The word 'equipment' in this provision had been earlier interpreted to include a ship in the case of *Coltman and Another v Bibby Tankers Ltd* (1987), which involved the loss of *The Derbyshire*, a 90,000 ton cargo carrier.

It is by no means uncommon for the courts to be asked to interpret the meaning of one word, as further illustrated in *AG's Reference (No 1 of 1988)* (1988), where it was held that the recipient of inside information relating to a company's affairs who dealt in the company shares committed an offence of obtaining such information under the Company Securities (Insider Dealing) Act 1985, not only where he had procured it on purpose, but also where he had come by it without any positive action. The court was referred to the dictionary meaning of 'obtain', and to a White Paper which preceded the 1985 Act. In the light of the purpose of the Act, the court concluded that the word 'obtain' meant no more than 'receive', and that an unsuspecting person who came by such information would only commit an offence if he or she then dealt in the shares of the company to which the information related.

In *Wychavon DC v National Rivers Authority* (1993), the council was accused of an offence, under s 107 of the Water Act 1989, of causing the discharge of sewage into a river. The question on an appeal by the council was whether 'causing' included a failure to act promptly. It was held that 'causing' required a positive act, whereas 'knowingly permitting' pollution would cover a failure to act promptly. The court was referred to the dictionary meaning of 'causing' and noted that, in a penal section, if a word is capable of bearing more than one meaning, the one most favourable to the defendant must be adopted. In *National Rivers Authority v Yorkshire Water Services Ltd* (1995), the House of Lords re-affirmed their decision in *Alphacell Ltd v Woodward* (1972) on the issue of causation, stating that it is a question of fact in each case. It is an offence of strict liability and pollution is caused by carrying on an activity where a causal link is proved between it and the discharge. No negligence or fault need be shown and there is no requirement of knowledge on the part of the defendant. Some other cases which illustrate how words are interpreted include:

- *R v MAFF ex p Bray* (1999), where it was held that 'instrument' in s 5 of the Sea Fisheries Regulation Act 1966 did not include the vessel to which the instrument was attached. However, the section was sufficiently wide that a bylaw restricting fishing by reference to the size of the vessel was valid;

- *Anyanwu and Another v South Bank Students' Union and Another* (1999), where 'knowingly aided' in s 33 of the Race Relations Act 1976 was to be given a narrow meaning so that, where two paid executives of the student union were dismissed by the union, following their expulsion from the university by the Vice Chancellor, the university had not 'knowingly aided' the dismissal;

- *Fitzpatrick v Sterling Housing Association* (1999), where it was held that the partner of a deceased tenant was entitled to succeed to a statutory tenancy under the Rent Act 1977 as a member of the tenant's family. He was not entitled to succeed to a tenancy, however, as a spouse of the tenant;

- *Oxfordshire CC v Sunningwell Parish Council* (1999) involved the interpretation of s 22 of the Commons Registration Act 1965. It was held that, on an application for registration of a village green, the inhabitants did not have to prove that they knew or believed that they had a legal right to indulge in sports and pastimes on the green. The meaning 'as of right' in s 22 denoted a customary right to use the green, not a subjective state of mind of its users.

Cases of statutory interpretation come almost daily before the courts and the law reports in *The Times* are a useful source of such cases. In addition, the publication *Current Law* gives a list of case references showing the words and phrases which have received judicial interpretation.

Developing case law

We will now move on to consider the other main role of the judge, namely, developing case law. The declaratory theory of law states that judges do not make law, but merely declare what the law is and, as a consequence, the social characteristics and values of the judge are of no importance. The judge makes decisions founded on the statement of the law to be found in precedent or statute and has no power to make law or inconsistent decisions.

Both Bentham and Austin concluded that judges do in fact make law. Bentham described the common law as 'the product of Judge and Co', and Austin wrote that judges made law as a result of the implicit command of the sovereign. Bentham and Austin were 19th century positivists who were concerned with the law as it is rather than with how it ought to be. Neither attempted to deny that the law might have faults and, in the case of Bentham, he described the common law as 'dog's law', in that it was only after a wrong had been committed that a penalty would be imposed. However, the positivist school suggests a limited judicial role in making law, in that the judge should not attempt to usurp the role of Parliament and concern himself with policy issues. On the one hand, the declaratory theory suggests that the judge does not at any time or in any way make law, whereas at the other extreme, it is suggested that judges are a product of the society in which they live and work and as a result make value-laden choices when making decisions. This is not to deny their independence and impartiality, but rather to recognise that their backgrounds and past experiences will have some bearing on their decisions. It must be noted, however, that this takes no account of their training and experience, which instils objectivity and acts as a counterweight to personal influences.

It is surely a question of degree, rather than saying that judges do not at any time or in any way make law (the declaratory theory), or at the other extreme that judges are law makers in the sense of legislators concerned with ensuring its development in a particular way to meet certain goals. It is suggested that the better approach is to recognise that where there is no clear relevant rule in precedent or statute governing the question in dispute, the judge will develop the law by reference to principle or logical consistency and in so doing may resort to extra-legal matters such as morality, justice, expediency or social policy to justify his decision.

Judges are most often concerned with piecemeal development of the law rather than wholesale changes to effect their vision of how the law should respond to or shape major questions. Social policy in our age is left to Parliament as the representative of the people and to whom those concerned with or about reform in the law can lobby and make known their views. This is not to deny that judges have views on the purposes of law in general and particular laws, and of their own role in society, but these views should not have free rein, as judges are not elected and only deal with disputes as and when they arise.

The House of Lords' decision in *Cambridge Water Co v Eastern Counties Leather plc* (1994) illustrates the relationship of judge and Parliament. Lord Goff, delivering the main speech, said that:

> ... it did not follow from those developments [legislation imposing liability for environmental pollution on the basis of the 'polluter pays' principle] that a common law principle such as the rule in *Rylands v Fletcher* should be developed or rendered more strict to provide for liability in respect of such pollution.

In the result, it was considered appropriate that strict liability in *Rylands v Fletcher* (1868) should only arise on proof of foreseeability of damage.

The outcome might well have been different had Parliament not enacted the Environmental Protection Act 1990 and other legislation to give effect to European obligations, or if the decision had been made several years ago. The tort of negligence is largely regulated by the common law and continues to develop, albeit within bounds, for example, in the area of nervous shock claims.

This is illustrated in the House of Lords case of *Alcock v Chief Constable of South Yorkshire Police* (1992), involving claims arising out of the Hillsborough Stadium disaster, where *dicta* of Lord Wilberforce in *McLoughlin v O'Brian* (1983) were applied so that liability for nervous shock would only arise where such injury was reasonably foreseeable and other conditions were satisfied, including proximity of the relationship between the plaintiff and the defendant; ties of love and affection; proximity of time and space of the plaintiff to the accident; or its immediate aftermath. Lord Oliver warned against extending the law in a direction for which there was no pressing policy need and no logical stopping point, as this was the province of Parliament following public debate and representation as to where the line ought to be drawn. He considered the position of a mother who sees her son negligently walk in front of a car and who, as a result, suffers nervous shock. Proximity and foreseeability could be proved, but the policy of the law might prohibit a claim on the basis that the son had not acted tortiously towards his mother. He suggested even greater complexity might arise where the son had been 75% to blame and the car driver 25% to blame, and that such policy considerations should be tackled by Parliament, as is the case in Australia.

Subsequent litigation arising out of the Hillsborough disaster demonstrates the boundaries of the law drawn by the courts. For example, in 1998 it was ruled in the House of Lords' case of *White v South Yorkshire Police* that police officers who suffered severe mental trauma as a result of attending to victims were not entitled to compensation. This overruled the decision of the Court of Appeal in the case referred to as *Frost v South Yorkshire Police* (1997). The officers had not been placed beyond the normal call of duty and were not close enough to the scene of the tragedy. One had been on duty at the mortuary and the other five had assisted the injured, and none had been exposed to the risk of personal injury. Officers who had been in close proximity and who had carried out immediate rescue work of victims succeeded in their claims against South Yorkshire Police and the football club, liability having been conceded and their claims settled.

The House of Lords stated in *White* that, in fairness, their claims should be rejected and to extend the law would, in the words of Lord Hoffman, 'offend against an ordinary person's notion of justice', particularly when relatives and friends of those who had died and who had seen the tragedy unfold on television were not able to claim for their mental suffering. However, more recently, the courts have upheld the claim of an off-duty nurse who was at the stadium and who suffered mental trauma as a result of her sometimes futile attempts to help victims. The courts have to draw a line, one based on public policy, between the claims which can be allowed and those which are outside of the boundaries of fault. The House of Lords called on Parliament to reform the law governing claims for psychiatric harm.

In past times, courts may well have had the primary role in deciding the future course of the law, but in recent years judges have deferred to Parliament in many areas and emphasised the need for logical consistency and to decide similar cases alike. This rather begs the question as to what is meant by 'similar cases' and inevitably the judge has to make choices. However, the judge is not alone in his task. He is assisted in the adversarial system by the advocate, who presents a dispassionate view of the law and helps the judge in reaching a reasoned decision after weighing the available options. By reasoning from well established rules or principles, the integrity and independence of the judiciary is preserved. Binding precedent ensures continuity and certainty in the law, although it may lead to rigidity. The *ratio decidendi* depends on principle, but a later court may widen or narrow its application.

Other means by which the law may develop include the use of distinguishing previous cases on their facts, overruling and disapproving and holding that an otherwise binding precedent was decided *per incuriam*. The common law may need to be flexible where Parliament is slow to act. In areas involving moral issues, the judges may extend the law by prohibiting actions which they consider to be wrong. Should their view of what is right or wrong conflict with popular opinion, Parliament may well be called on to pass amending legislation. The House of Lords case of *R v Brown* (1993), involving prosecutions under ss 20 and 47 of the Offences Against the Person Act 1861 for sado-masochistic acts, illustrates the two opposing views that where legislation should prohibit socially undesirable behaviour, the courts should apply it, and it is for Parliament to rectify any error or omission. The alternative view taken by those who dissented was that the benefit of the doubt should lie in favour of the defendants and, if this was unsatisfactory, it was for Parliament to make such acts unlawful. In February 1997, the European Court of Human Rights ruled in favour of the House of Lords' decision and ruled that there had not been a breach of the Convention.

The policy issues involving questions of life and death were considered in *Airedale NHS Trust v Bland* (1993), when the House of Lords decided that treatment of a patient in a persistent vegetative state could lawfully be ended where it was shown that there was no hope of recovery. The court emphasised that euthanasia was prohibited by law and that, in cases such as this one, safeguards should be provided by the court and that all the issues should soon be considered by Parliament.

Professor Dworkin, in his writings on law and the legal system, disagreed with Professor Hart that law was merely a system of rules. Dworkin distinguished between rules, principles and policies which he called 'rules' and 'non-rule standards'. He rejected the idea that judges should, or do, make law, stating that they look for the soundest theory to assist them in deciding hard cases. The judge is concerned with the formulation of principle, whereas Parliament is concerned with policy. Principles must be weighed and may conflict, but they provide reasons for deciding a case in a certain way. Policy is a standard which sets out a social goal to be achieved. It is not the province of the courts. Dworkin referred to the New York case of *Riggs v Palmer* (1889) to illustrate the principle that 'no man should profit from his own wrongdoing', which was applied to reach a solution where a murderer claimed to be entitled under his victim's will. The rule allowing inheritance created uncertainty and it was held that it was overridden by the fundamental principle.

Principles may lead to the development of a rule, or alternatively a rule may lead to the formulation of a principle. We have referred to the cases of *R v Registrar General ex p Smith* (1990) and *Re Sigsworth* (1935) when considering statutory interpretation, and these illustrate the dilemma facing a court where a clear rule conflicts with a fundamental principle. The court in each case looked to the issue of policy and decided each on the basis of the principle. Should the courts overstep the limits of law making, it will be for Parliament to redefine the boundaries as to the future scope and effect of the law.

Professor Dworkin talked of the role of the judge in deciding 'hard' cases where no rule applied by which the judge was bound. As *ex p Smith* and *Re Sigsworth* demonstrate, this may be interpreted by the court to include a case where, although a rule applies, the judge prefers not to apply it on the grounds of unfairness or public policy. In this sense, the judge does make law and justifies his or her doing so by reference to principle or fairness. The result may be short lived, for, if Parliament passes amending legislation in specific terms, the course of the law may be changed.

In future, as a result of the Human Rights Act 1998, the courts will increasingly have to confront issues of public policy when deciding cases involving allegations of breach of the European Convention on Human Rights. Courts will not be asked to rule on the illegality of statutes, as this would conflict with the doctrine of the supremacy of Parliament, but will be able to make a declaration of incompatibility. The Lord Chancellor, when giving the Pilgrim Fathers Lecture in Plymouth in late 1999, commented on the likely effects that the Act will have on the role of the judge. He indicated that judicial reluctance in the past to recognise the doctrine of proportionality will in future be another means by which the judiciary will be able to question the actions of the executive. This is a continental doctrine, which ensures that the means by which an objective is achieved are proportionate to the objective. This concept is also much used in European Community law and, as both of these separate entities converge, the UK courts will no doubt adopt the methods and principles of European courts. It must be stressed that the European Community and the European Convention on Human Rights are still separate entities, the former with 15 members, the latter with 40 signatories.

It may be that, following the Human Rights Act 1998, calls for a constitutional court will be renewed and also for constitutional reform, in particular the role of the Lord Chancellor. In any event, the use of judicial review will no doubt increase to question the substance of government decision making by means of the concept of proportionality.

THE JUDICIAL FUNCTION

The role of the judge

- Judges' mental processes: deductive reasoning; inductive reasoning; reasoning by analogy.

- The declaratory theory states that judges do not make law, but this has lost favour and it is recognised that judges contribute to the development of law.

- The positivist views of Bentham and Austin.

- *Cambridge Water Co v Eastern Counties Leather plc* (1994); *Alcock v Chief Constable of South Yorkshire Police* (1992); *White v South Yorkshire Police* (1998); *R v Brown* (1993); *Airedale NHS Trust v Bland* (1993); *R v Registrar General ex p Smith* (1990).

Interpreting statutes

- Courts have no general right to challenge the validity of legislation (except where it conflicts with European Community provisions), but their ability to decide the meaning of statutory provisions when trying cases gives them potentially wide scope for developing the law.

- *Dicta* of Lord Scarman in *Duport Steels Ltd v Sirs* (1980) concerning the role of the judge in interpreting legislation.

- Narrow approach of judges: the words of statutory provisions.

- *Pepper v Hart* (1993), applied in *Massmould v Payne* (1993); *Sheppard v IRC* (1993); *Van Dyck v Secretary of State for the Environment* (1993).

- The purposive approach, used in continental jurisdictions and the European Court of Justice, applied in *Shah v Barnet LBC* (1983) and *R v Registrar-General ex p Smith* (1990).

- *Three Rivers DC and Others v Bank of England (No 2)* (1996): increasing willingness of the domestic courts to consult parliamentary debates when interpreting legislation.

- Use of extrinsic aids to construction: *Fothergill v Monarch Airlines* (1980).

- Literal or grammatical meaning of the word(s) used: *Whitely v Chappell* (1868).

- The golden rule.
- The mischief rule.
- Other rules:
  - *ejusdem generis* (*Powell v Kempton Park Racecourse Co* (1899));
  - *noscitur a sociis* (*IRC v Frere* (1964));
  - *expressio unius est exclusio alterius* (*R v Inhabitants of Sedgley* (1831));
  - Interpretation Act 1978.
- Presumptions:
  - prospective effect;
  - criminal liability not to be imposed without proof of fault in the absence of express provision (*Sweet v Parsley* (1969));
  - the Crown is not bound by statute unless named.

Developing case law

- Precedent/*stare decisis* (let the decision stand).
- Historical development of common law and equity and the different meanings of common law.
- Development and use of equitable maxims and concepts such as mortgages and trusts demonstrate the role of the judge.
- *Earl of Oxford's Case* (1615); Judicature Acts 1873–75.
- *Re Sigsworth* (1935) and *ex p Smith* (1990).
- Public policy; Human Rights Act 1998.

CHAPTER 7

CIVIL PROCEEDINGS

Introduction

It is worth mentioning some of the main features of the civil justice system. The underlying principle of any system, whether criminal or civil, must be the attainment of justice.

One means by which this can be assured is equality of access regardless of means. In addition to substantive rules of law, there must also be fair rules of procedure and requirement for proof of facts alleged. Ours is an adversarial system, likened to a battle between two adversaries, only one of whom can be adjudicated the winner. The judge is usually the arbiter of both fact and law and makes a decision following the presentation of evidence by oral testimony. The claimant (formerly the plaintiff) has the burden of proof, on a balance of probabilities (that is, more likely than not), and usually decisions are made in open court where the result can be published and to which members of the public can be admitted. A decision will be final, except where an appeal is permitted, and in some cases this may only be on questions of law or where permission is given.

Civil disputes involve a wide range of matters, including claims for faulty goods and services, trespass to property, personal injury claims and disputes over the ownership or disposition of property. Taking a case to court will be the last resort in the majority of disputes and this is just as well, if for no other reason than if everyone with a legal claim wished to litigate, the courts would be unable to cope with the demand.

When a case goes to court, there is more to the decision than just the substantive rules of law governing the parties. It will be essential to comply with the rules of procedure, such as use of the correct forms, within specified time limits, informing the other party or parties of information, payment of fees and so on. Also, rules of evidence will have to be satisfied, for example, the calling of witnesses, use of written statements and the admissibility of evidence. In civil claims the burden of proof rests with the claimant, who must prove his or her case on a balance of probabilities. The nature of litigation is adversarial, the parties 'do battle' and there will be a winner and a loser. The general rule is that the winner expects to have his or her costs paid by the loser as vindication that he or she is in the right. Under the Woolf reforms, we will see that the court has discretion to vary this rule when it considers it proper to do so.

Most claims are settled before they reach court and the legal representatives of both parties should try to negotiate a settlement from the outset. What was known as a letter before action and is now called a letter of claim is sent by the claimant or his or her lawyer, setting out the position and how it might be settled. This principle is not a new one and is endorsed by the Woolf reforms, which stress that litigation should be the last resort.

We are primarily concerned here only with rules of procedure, in particular, the changes that have come into effect as a result of the proposals for reform made by Lord Woolf in his Final Report, *Access to Justice – Final Report to the Lord Chancellor on the Civil Justice System in England and Wales*. These reforms, which came into effect on 26 April 1999 (W Day), signal the most important changes in civil procedure for many years and envisage a uniform procedure in all civil courts and a major shift in the powers and functions of the judges. At the centre of the reforms is the idea of case management which will allow procedural judges to organise and insist on a timetable in which proceedings are completed. This will take away much of the power of litigants (particularly those who are financially well off) from delaying and thereby increasing costs.

The Woolf reforms must been seen in context. The legal system and profession are also undergoing much change. The *Access to Justice Report* makes changes to the rights of audience, the provision of legal aid and 'no win, no fee' arrangements, increasing the use of alternative dispute resolution (ADR), including negotiation and settlement of disputes out of court. Some commentators have suggested in the press that the culture of litigation is out of date, given that for many years it has been seen to be very costly, slow and divisive. No doubt a place remains for litigation as an effective means of resolving some disputes, and the Woolf reforms will no doubt increase efficiency, but for others, alternatives, such as mediation, may well provide a better solution.

It is usual to conduct negotiations by inserting into correspondence the phrase 'without prejudice' or 'without prejudice except as to costs', so as to preserve the position of the writer and prevent the contents of letters being called in evidence without their consent.

It may be that ADR is available and allows the parties to settle the issue by agreement rather than resort to litigation. This takes various forms, as we have seen in Chapter 5, including arbitration, mediation and conciliation. It may have the advantages of speed and cost, and avoid the stress of appearing in court and preparing for a trial.

We have two courts with jurisdiction to hear civil claims at first instance, the High Court and the county court, and although this may appear cumbersome, it is due mainly to their historical development. The High Court was created by the Judicature Acts 1873–75 with originally five divisions: Chancery, Probate, Divorce and Admiralty, Queen's Bench, Common Pleas and Exchequer. The Common Pleas and Exchequer Divisions were merged with the Queen's Bench Division a little later, and in 1970 the Family Division was created from the Probate, Divorce and Admiralty Divisions. The county courts were created in 1846 as a system of small claims courts, dealing mainly with debt enforcement.

Although both have developed along different paths, differences have largely been ones of detail rather than substance, for example, differences in terminology, the forms used and the means by which judgments were enforced. The most notable difference was in the procedures used in each court – High Court procedure was regulated by the White Book or, to use its full title, the Supreme Court Practice and the Supreme Court Act 1981 (as amended), and the county court by the Green Book, otherwise called the County Court Practice and the County Courts Act 1984. In the High Court, a writ was used to start proceedings, whereas in the county court it was usually a default or a fixed date summons. The pace of litigation was very much in the control of the parties, or at least, the party with more financial clout, who would be able to invoke procedural rules to delay the proceedings.

These have now been replaced following the Woolf reforms of the civil justice system, which came into effect in April 1999. The Civil Procedure Act 1997 and the rules of practice and procedure, the Civil Procedure Rules 1998 (as amended), provide uniform procedures in both the County Court and the High Court and their jurisdiction is determined according to the allocation of cases to tracks – small claims procedure, fast track and multi-track. All but the last will usually be heard in the county court, whereas the last will normally be heard in the High Court, but may be heard in the county court.

Civil justice reform

By far the most important proposed reforms of the civil justice system last century were contained in the Final Report of Lord Woolf, published in July 1996, entitled *Access to Justice*. Lord Woolf was appointed by the Lord Chancellor in 1994 to review the rules and procedures of the civil courts in England and Wales in order to improve access and to create one set of procedural rules. Lord Woolf's Interim Report was published in June 1995. In an attempt to tackle delay and cost, case management is at the heart of the reforms. The court, through procedural judges, will be able to dictate the order and pace of proceedings (not litigants). Woolf was looking for short, effective, cogent and credible litigation.

Accompanying the Final Report was a set of Draft Civil Proceedings Rules, to replace the Rules of the Supreme Court and Rules of the County Court. By the Civil Procedure Act 1997, the Civil Procedure Rules Committee was established to introduce one set of procedures for all litigation in the High Court and county court.

Lord Woolf spent two years reviewing the system and concluded that delay, cost and complexity were its main faults. The interests of the litigant should be paramount and the most serious problem was that of costs. These were said to 'contaminate the whole civil justice system'. Alternatives to litigation were to be encouraged, one set of rules for High Court and county court should be adopted and cases should come to trial and be dealt with at trial faster.

Lord Woolf described his proposals as 'the new legal landscape' and hoped that they would become law in 1997 by way of legislation and statutory instrument. Sir Richard Scott was appointed Head of Civil Justice, responsible for bringing them into effect. The overriding objective of the reforms was to deal with cases justly, ensuring that parties were on an equal footing and that the saving of expense was taken into account.

The proposals have had their critics, notably Professor Zander, who in particular criticised the need for judicial case management. He asserted that the delays in the system did not arise from how 'lawyers played the adversarial game' but were as a result of the factors highlighted in research conducted by KPMG Peat Marwick for the Lord Chancellor's Department. This research suggested that delay resulted from the nature of the case; the parties; the judiciary; court procedure and administration; and external factors such as obtaining evidence, in particular, that of experts. Some delay resulted from legal representatives, but not as was suggested by Lord Woolf, whereby lawyers manipulated the procedural rules simply to get tactical advantages over opponents. Professor Zander was of the opinion that this fundamental change would be just as likely to increase costs, as lawyers would have to meet deadlines artificially imposed by the court and it would necessitate radical changes in culture.

Lord Woolf's Final Report, July 1996

The main recommendations were as follows.

At the heart of the proposals is the concept of judicial case management – litigation would be controlled by the court and not the parties. Timetables would be fixed and the judge would be more active in identifying the issues, deciding the order of treatment, disposing of issues which would otherwise cause delay and controlling disclosure of documents and the use of expert evidence.

Litigation should be the last resort – ADR should act as a filter and legal aid should be available. The court would encourage and facilitate this with power to stay proceedings to allow the parties to go to ADR either at their request or where the court considers it appropriate.

A three tier system should be adopted – small claims (up to £3,000, excepting personal injury claims); a fast track process for less valuable or complex cases (£3,000–£10,000); a multi-track process for all other claims. On receipt of a defence, a procedural (district) judge would allocate the case to the requisite track.

The fast track would be 'civil justice without the frills' in the words of Lord Woolf. Costs recoverable would be limited, and trials would be of limited duration (three hours or half a day, up to a maximum of one day). The procedural judge would set the timetable and make directions for trial, including expert's reports, witness statements and disclosure of documents. Costs would be limited to £2,500 excluding VAT and disbursements.

The multi-track would provide flexible case management so as to accommodate a wide variety of cases and complexity. Following the filing of a defence, a case management conference would be held and this would be followed by a pre-trial review some eight to 10 weeks before the trial date.

Preventative (as opposed to punitive) sanctions would be imposed to encourage parties and their advisers to comply with the new procedures. Defaulters would have to apply to the court for relief and the striking out of a claim would only be used as a last resort.

The pre-action protocol or Code of Practice is a new idea, which encourages negotiations with a view to early settlement of claims.

Parties should make contact earlier and exchange information with a view to settling the claim without the need for litigation.

Payments into court would be replaced by offers to settle – either party would be able to make an offer, before or after the start of proceedings. Orders for costs would depend on all the circumstances and at the court's discretion, but as a general rule, where the plaintiff (claimant) recovers the same or less at trial than the sum offered by the defendant, the defendant would be entitled to his or her costs from the date of the offer. Where the claimant recovers the same or more than his or her offer to settle, he or she would be entitled to an enhanced rate of interest on the sum recovered.

All actions would start with a claim form, the term 'plaintiff' would be replaced by 'claimant' and 'pleadings' would be replaced by 'statements of case' and 'defences'.

Experts would be employed by the court as independent advisers and where there is a conflict of expert opinion, a co-operative approach would be adopted, involving a joint investigation and a single report.

The appeal process should be simplified and a procedure adopted to allow the Treasury Solicitor or Official Solicitor to seek clarification of general points of law from the Court of Appeal or House of Lords.

Lay users of the system should be encouraged and rules of court and documents should be in plain English.

The main provisions of the Civil Procedure Act 1997 and Civil Procedure Rules 1998 (as amended)

The Civil Procedure Act 1997 came into force mainly on 27 April 1997 by the Civil Procedure Act 1997 (Commencement) (No 1) Order 1997 SI 1997/841.

Section 5 of the Act provided for a unified set of rules replacing the White and Green Books (in all courts, throughout the country). The Rules took effect on W Day, 26 April 1999. All courts closed on Friday 23 April 1999 (except for urgent matrimonial matters) to allow for final preparations for W Day and much time, effort and money has been spent on training court staff and judges. The courts will operate a computerised diary system so as to monitor the progress of cases and ensure compliance with deadlines. The procedural judge, on finding non-compliance, can impose sanctions. It is now the duty of the court to manage the pace of a case. Under the old system, this was dictated too much by the parties, or at least usually the stronger party, who could cause delay and expense as a result. This change is in furtherance of the overriding objective. Use of IT and the need to train staff, including judges, will necessitate that some delays are inevitable and no doubt it will be necessary to revise the Rules and practice directions from time to time.

Rule 1 sets out the overriding objective of the Rules. This is to provide a new procedural code to enable the court to deal justly with cases. In addition, various factors must be taken into account when exercising discretion, for example, the value and complexity of a case, the finances of the parties and allocation of scarce resources in dealing with the case and others.

Section 5 of the 1997 Act provides for the making by the Lord Chancellor of practice directions which supplement the Civil Procedure Rules and offer guidance to the parties on all aspects of the procedure. For example, Practice Direction 6 allows service of documents by electronic means and Practice Direction 7 provides special rules for land, hire purchase, mortgages and specific performance.

At the heart of the reforms is judicial case management which involves the procedural judge allocating a case to the appropriate track, maintaining a timetable and ensuring that the Rules, practice directions and pre-action protocols (only two have been issued so far, one in respect of personal injury claims and the other for clinical negligence claims) are complied with by the parties. In the case of *Mullan v Birmingham CC* (1999), it was held that the Civil Procedure Rules give the court wide powers of case management and it is permissible for a trial judge to allow a defendant to make a submission of no case to answer at the close of the claimant's case without requiring the defendant to elect not to call evidence in the event that his or her submission failed.

The two pre-action protocols cover clinical negligence and personal injury claims and, in the words of Lord Woolf's Final Report, 'build on and increase the benefits of early but well informed settlements'. They aim to encourage the parties to agree a settlement by ensuring that they have full information and, where settlement is not possible, to 'lay the ground for expeditious conduct of proceedings'. Those interested in this area, for example, The Law Society, helped in drafting the protocols and it is likely that more will be drafted in other specialist areas. An important element of the reforms is the need to foster co-operation between the parties to a dispute, rather than concentrating on its adversarial aspects. Each protocol sets out a recommended process which emphasises the need to consider the use of ADR or negotiation to settle the dispute.

Such reforms would be rendered worthless without the ability to impose sanctions on a party who fails to comply with the procedures. Sanctions include costs orders penalising the defaulting party, the striking out of a claim and refusal to grant extensions or reliance on documents filed late. It will be imperative for parties and their representatives to move away from the use of an adversarial approach at the outset. Instead, settlement of the claim or ADR should be considered. The court has power to stay proceedings either at the parties' request or on its own initiative where it considers ADR more appropriate. The parties will have to report back to the court within 14 days of the stay as to whether they wish to use ADR to settle the matter. The emphasis on keeping to a timetable comes from Lord Woolf's conclusion that cost and delay go together and must be avoided. In the *Practice Direction (Civil Litigation: Case Management)* (1995), time limits are to be set by the judge on speeches and cross-examination of witnesses; documents should be disclosed to the other side before trial and the issues in a case should be limited; reading aloud documents and law reports should be limited; and the judge's express permission is required to examine in chief. Failure to comply can, at the court's discretion, result in some costs of the delaying party not being recoverable.

Before commencing a claim, the claimant should send a letter of claim to the defendant with full details of the circumstances giving rise to the claim. This will form the basis of the court proceedings, although amendments may be made later. The defendant has 21 days in which to acknowledge receipt and to give details of the name of his or her insurers, where appropriate. He or she then has three months to investigate and either admit or deny liability. Where the defendant denies liability he or she must supply his reasons, together with any relevant documents identified in the pre-action protocols. To date, there are two of these, one for personal injury claims and the other for clinical negligence claims.

All cases are to start in the same way, in whichever court. For claims involving sums of money, either specified or unspecified, and non-monetary claims, these are started by the claimant issuing a Pt 7 Claim Form against the defendant. It will be usual for the claimant to ask for a stated remedy, but this need not be specified. The value of the claim dictates the track to which the case is allocated by the procedural judge. For claims involving a request for a court order, for example, approval for a course of action, the claimant issues a Pt 8 Claim Form and the case is automatically allocated as a multi-track case.

The claimant may include in the Claim Form, or attach to it or serve within 14 days of service of the Claim Form, a Particulars of Claim form. This is a concise statement of facts relied on, together with details of the damages and any interest claimed and any convictions of the defendant relied on and the claimant to establish liability in civil law. The claimant may also include any points of law relied on, the names of witnesses, but it is not necessary to state the legal nature of the claim.

The Claim Form, Particulars of Claim, the defence and any counterclaim, replies to defences and counterclaims, and third party claims are together called Statements of Case. The Statements of Case must contain a Statement of Truth and any deliberate untruths amount to contempt of court. This also saves the swearing of affidavits.

The Claim Form is served on the defendant, together with a Response Pack, a Form of Acknowledgment of Service, Form of Admission, Form of Defence and Counterclaim and an Allocation Questionnaire. If the Particulars of Claim is served after the Claim Form, the Response Pack accompanies the former. The defendant has 14 days in which to respond and, on failure to do so, the claimant may ask the court for judgment.

The defendant may respond by paying the sum claimed or by admitting the claim in whole or part or by filing a defence.

Alternatively, he or she returns to the court the Acknowledgment of Service, for example, where the defendant has changed his or her name or address or where he or she disputes the jurisdiction of the court.

It is no longer sufficient for a defendant simply to deny the claim, he or she must make a denial of each and every allegation made by the claimant in the Particulars of Claim. Reasons for denial are also required. Where a specific sum is claimed and the defendant admits it only in part it will be for the judge or the court staff to determine the process for settlement. If the defendant wishes to defend a claim for a specific sum, the case is automatically transferred to the defendant's local court. For claims for unspecified sums which are admitted in part, the case will go for trial after a case management process is gone through. Where the defendant files an Acknowledgment of Intention to Defend this will extend the time in which he or she has to file his or her defence to 28 days. If he or she then fails to file a defence, the court may order judgment in default.

When documents are prepared and lodged with the court for processing, the documents are said to be issued; where they are sent to the parties, they are served. The parties may serve documents personally, by electronic means, by post or by document exchange. Alternatively, the court can serve documents on the other party by first class post. This is deemed to arrive two days after the date of posting. If documents are returned to the court unserved, the court notifies the party wishing to have the document served and he or she then decides on the method of service.

When the defendant files at the court a defence, copies are sent to all parties together with an Allocation Questionnaire and Notice of Automatic Transfer (if appropriate). On return of the Allocation Questionnaire the procedural judges (in the High Court, a Master, and in the county court, the district judge) will allocate the case to one of the three tracks and notify the parties. The tracks are the small claims track; the fast track; and the multi-track. The Allocation Questionnaire asks the parties whether they wish to have a one month stay to attempt to settle the claim; which track they consider to be more appropriate; whether they have complied with the pre-action protocols and if not, why not; an estimate of costs incurred and the overall estimate of costs to date of the trial; their progress to date; and whether they need to rely on an expert witness. It provides an overview of progress to date and the parties at this time should make any applications to the court, for example, to add a third party or for summary judgment.

The small claims track: the financial limit for the value of claims with effect from April 1999 is £5,000 (except for personal injury and housing claims, where the limit is £1,000) – these are heard in the small claims court.

The fast track deals with claims with a value up to £15,000, with a transfer to multi-track possible once the court considers that the answers to an allocation questionnaire have been completed by the parties. Case management system applies. For the time being, fixed costs have been deferred. A 30 week timetable applies from commencement to trial. Practitioners must have a manual or computerised case management system, so as to meet deadlines. The county court hears these claims and, in the words of the Interim Report, p 41, allocation to the fast track aims to speed up the process and ensure 'equality of treatment between litigants even if they are of unequal means'.

The multi-track deals with all cases over £15,000 and complex cases under £15,000. The county court will hear all contract and tort claims and the High Court will hear personal injury claims over £50,000, other claims worth more than £15,000 where statute stipulates action to commence in the High Court, and claims concerning specialist matters such as commercial cases. No standard procedure will apply here, but instead a range of case management techniques will be used according to the circumstances of each case. These include case management conferences to allow the parties to take stock, that is, to check progress in respect of evidence, and make any amendments that need to be made to documents. If a party is represented, his or her representative familiar with the case must attend. Another is the pre-trial review which takes place after the listing questionnaire so as to decide a timetable for trial, bundles of evidence to be relied on and to agree an estimate of trial length. Again, a party's representative who is familiar with the case must attend.

The role of procedural judge involves identifying issues; deciding on the appropriate track; considering requests for transfer from one track to another; summarily disposing of issues; deciding on the order in which issues are resolved; the fixing of timetables and the limiting of documents to be disclosed by the parties; and the preparation of expert evidence. He will need to be proactive in identifying and restraining oppressive behaviour and in the use of sanctions against those parties who fail to meet deadlines. The requirement of a 30 week period from the date on which the claimant issues his or her Claim Form to the date set for trial may be over-optimistic, given that applications to postpone may be made and that the trial may only take place in a three week period.

An important aspect of the reforms in procedure are the rules providing for payments into court by the defendant and offers to settle the claim, which can be made by the claimant and the defendant. These provisions apply to the fast and multi-tracks. Their main purpose is to offer incentives to the parties to settle a claim without the need to litigate. If at the trial the claimant recovers in damages no more than the sum which the defendant has offered or paid into court, the court will order the claimant to pay the costs of the defendant which have been incurred from the date on which the claimant could have accepted the defendant's offer or payment. The court can also exercise a discretion to alter the normal 'costs follow the event' rule in other cases, by taking into account the conduct of the parties and their reasons for not settling the claim. Furthermore, where the defendant is held liable for more than the claimant has proposed in an offer to settle, the court has discretion to order the defendant to pay interest at no more than 10% above the bank base rate on the sum awarded from the date when the defendant could have accepted the offer.

The procedure for assessing the costs of the parties was formerly called 'taxation', but this is now called assessment and involves the court agreeing the amount of costs incurred, either at the end of the hearing or at a later stage, following a detailed assessment.

Court fees have also been reformed and together with the discretion in the court to impose sanctions for non-payment, payment will be made at the various stages of the procedure and on the basis that the courts must be self-financing, and so fees must cover the full cost of litigation.

Two other provisions are worthy of note. Increasingly, the relationship of time and expense have been recognised and so time spent reading documents in court and the use of over-complex language are to be resisted. The evidence which a witness intends to give contained in witness statements will have to be brief and expressed in ordinary language. If at trial a witness attempts to add to his or her witness statement, he or she will have to give good reasons. A controversial provision concerns the use of experts. Traditionally, each party to litigation would employ his or her own expert and again much time and expense was incurred, but Lord Woolf wished to see the courts move towards the use of only a single expert witness whose duty would be to the court to assist it on matters on which they were expert. This duty to the court would override any contractual or other obligations to the person appointing the expert.

Appeals

From the county court, appeals are heard by the Civil Division of the Court of Appeal and permission is required. From the High Court divisions and the Divisional Courts, appeals go to the Civil Division of the Court of Appeal on questions of law, fact or both and require four weeks' notice. From the Court of Appeal, appeals go to the House of Lords on points of law of public importance, with the permission of either court.

The Administration of Justice Act 1969 provides for a leapfrog appeal from the High Court to the House of Lords on points of statutory interpretation and precedent binding on the High Court, if both parties and the House of Lords agree.

We now move on to consider some of the main procedural steps in bringing Pt 7 and Pt 8 claims.

Part 7 claims

The claimant lodges with the court a Claim Form, containing or to which is attached a Particulars of Claim, fees and copies, requesting personal service, where appropriate. The court issues the claim and sends a Notice of Issue to the claimant, giving a claim number and date of service, if served by the court. Claim Forms must be served within four months of the issue of the documents by the court. The claimant must include in the Claim Form a statement that he or she believes that the facts stated are true.

If the court serves the Claim Form, it is sent with a Response Pack, which includes an Acknowledgment of Service, Form of Admission, Form of Defence and Counterclaim and an Allocation Questionnaire. This is served by first class post and it is deemed to be served two days after posting. If this fails, the claimant is sent a Notice of Non-Service and it is for him then to arrange service of the forms. If the claimant wishes to serve the documents, the Claim Form and Response Pack are sent to him or her and he or she files with the court a Certificate of Service within seven days of serving the claim on the defendant.

A claimant may issue and personally serve a Claim Form without a Particulars of Claim. If the Claim Form and Particulars are separate, the Particulars of Claim must be served within 14 days of service of the Claim Form. The Response Pack accompanies the Particulars of Claim and the latter must contain statements of truth.

The defendant must file a defence within 14 days from the service of the Particulars of Claim. If not able to do so, or he or she wishes to challenge the jurisdiction of the court, he or she must file an Acknowledgment of Service. The defendant then has 14 days from service of the Acknowledgment to serve a defence. If neither is filed, the court can order judgment in default, if the claimant makes a request for judgment. For specified sums, the court can make an order for judgment. For unspecified sums, the papers are referred to a Master of the High Court or a district judge, as appropriate, for case management directions for the assessment of the amount, and then the court enters judgment for an amount to be decided by the court. The order includes directions and hearing date and copies are sent to the claimant and defendant.

Where the defendant alleges that he or she is not liable on the claim, he or she may file a defence. A copy of the defence is served on each claimant. Alternatively, the defendant may allege that the sum claimed has been paid and the case is closed by the court if the claimant indicates that he or she does not wish to proceed. If the claimant fails to respond, the court stays the claim until such time as the claimant applies for the stay to be lifted. If the claimant indicates that he or she wishes to proceed, the court sends an Allocation Questionnaire to each party and treats the claim as defended. Where the defendant wishes to make a claim against the claimant, he or she can attach a counterclaim to the defence or, with the court's permission, can file a counterclaim after he or she has filed the defence with the court. For example, where the defendant is being sued for breach of contract for failure to pay £6,000 which he or she agreed to pay for carpets to be fitted, he or she can counterclaim to recover the costs of damage to his or her house caused by the carpet fitter.

A Right to Reply and Further Statements of Case are only permitted with the leave of the court. Amendments to Statements of Case, once served, are permitted with the leave of the court.

Where the defendant admits the claim in whole or part, the procedure varies according to the defendant's admission. For example, he or she may admit the whole claim for a specified sum and is permitted to request to make payment by instalments. On the other hand, the defendant may make a part admission in a claim for a specified amount which the claimant is willing to accept in satisfaction of the whole claim. If he or she is not, the proceedings continue with the issue of Allocation Questionnaires by the court. Where the sum of money claimed is unspecified, the defendant may offer an amount in satisfaction and if the claimant does not accept this sum, the court enters judgment for the claimant for an amount to be decided by the court following case management directions for assessment of the amount by the procedural judge. If, on a claim for an unspecified amount, liability is admitted, but no offer is made, the court enters judgment for the claimant for an amount to be decided by the court after case management directions to assess the amount.

Where a claim is treated as defended, Allocation Questionnaires are sent by the court to all parties for completion. On return of the Allocation Questionnaires to the court, depending on the extent to which the parties have completed them, the Procedural Judge, a Master in the High Court and a district judge in the county court, will allocate the case to one of the three tracks. A one month stay of proceedings may be ordered to allow the parties to attempt to settle the claim by the use of ADR.

For the small claims track, the district judge decides either to fix a date for the hearing or order a preliminary hearing to decide whether a hearing should take place or to strike out the claim or defence. Alternatively he or she can decide that a hearing is not necessary and if the parties agree, the claim is dealt with on the papers alone.

For fast or multi-track, the district judge or Master considers any representations regarding the trial venue and whether the claim is multi-track or a specialist list case which should be dealt with by the High Court. The claim is allocated to either the fast track or the multi-track, with directions and timetable to date of trial.

For fast track claims, a Notice of Allocation is sent by the court to all parties and this includes directions, the date for filing the Listing Questionnaire and trial period of three weeks.

For multi-track claims, a Notice of Allocation is sent by the court to all parties and this includes directions, the date of any case management conference or pre-trial review, the date for filing the Listing Questionnaire and trial period of one week.

Either party may apply for re-allocation if this was made on paper or appeal against an allocation made at the allocation hearing. The Listing Questionnaire is sent to the parties for return, with fee, within 14 days of service. For the fast track, on return of the Listing Questionnaire, the court serves a Hearing Notice confirming the trial date, trial venue, an estimate of the time and any further directions such as permission for oral expert evidence, the trial timetable and preparation of and filing of the bundle of documents to be produced at trial. For multi-track claims, the court serves a Trial Notice, once it has received the Listing Questionnaire, which fixes a trial date or week, trial venue, time estimate and any further directions for preparation for trial.

Part 8 claims

The claimant lodges a Pt 8 Claim Form, written evidence, copies for service on all parties and the fee with the court. The court issues the claim and sends a Notice of Issue to the claimant with a claim number and date of service. If the court is to serve the documents on the defendant, it sends the Claim Form, written evidence and Acknowledgment of Service to the defendant by first class post. If the postal service fails, the court then sends a Notice of Non-Service to the claimant, who must arrange service. If the claimant wishes to serve the documents personally on the defendant, then the court sends them to the claimant. Following service, the claimant returns to the court the Certificate of Service.

Within 14 days of the service of the Claim Form, the defendant should file at the court an Acknowledgment of Service, any written evidence on which he or she relies and serve copies of these documents on the claimant and any other party. He or she must state whether he or she is contesting the claim and, if seeking a different remedy, what that is. If the defendant fails to reply, he or she may attend the hearing, but will not be able to take part, unless the court gives permission.

In Pt 8 claims, it is essential for both claimant and defendant who wish to rely on written evidence at the hearing to file the claim form at the court and serve it on the other party, otherwise the permission of the court will be required.

Once the claim is issued, the court may give case management directions immediately, either on its own initiative or at the request of either party. The directions may set a final hearing date where this is convenient. In some claims, a hearing date is not required and, in those where it is, but it is not fixed on issue, the court will give directions for the disposal of the claim as soon as practicable after the Acknowledgment of Service is filed or order a directions hearing.

Implications of the reforms

Litigation will alter as a result of the reforms and research into the workings of the fast track is essential, although no government funding has been provided for this. Small claims made by individual litigants numbered 98,000 in 1997. There was an increase in limits in April 1999 to £5,000 (except for housing and personal injury). But, there is little, if any, support for litigants in person and Woolf's recommendation for advice agency duty representatives at busy court centres has not been pursued. Compare CAB funding and the Legal Aid Board; the increasing use of no win, no fee arrangements; the possible demise of State funded legal aid and the effects of the Access to Justice Act 1999.

Other implications of the reforms have been changes in terminology, that is, the loss of Latin expressions and, for example, the use of 'claimant' in place of 'plaintiff'; 'statements of case' in place of 'pleadings'; 'disclosure of documents' in place of 'discovery'.

Other proposed reforms of the civil justice system

Several themes have run through the various reports prepared in the last 20 years or so on civil justice reforms, notably the high costs of litigation, delay, procedural complexities, how family disputes are handled, whether the High Court and the county court should be merged, not simply so far as procedures are concerned, but also with regard to the judiciary, types of business and terminology. As long ago as 1969, the Beeching Royal Commission had rejected the idea of merger, suggesting instead a more efficient allocation of judges between the two courts so that important cases could go to appeal. This raised the question of what is important – high value claims may be straightforward, whereas a low value claim may involve a complex issue of fact, law or both – but no answer was provided. Following the Woolf reforms (Civil Procedure Rules), this question has re-emerged and the three stumbling blocks to merger identified in the Beeching Report may be close to resolution, now that the procedures of both courts have been merged. Woolf could not address these, as they were outside his terms of reference: the specialist jurisdictions of the High Court, such as the Commercial Court and applications for judicial review, should be retained; and the special status of High Court judges should be preserved, as should the rights of audience, leading to judicial appointment.

In 1983, the Lord Chancellor issued a Consultation Paper, in which he proposed to integrate the work of the High Court and the county court. The resulting court would be equivalent to the Crown Court in the court hierarchy. The civil jurisdiction of the magistrates' court was to remain unchanged. Alternatively, the identities of the High Court and county court were to be retained, but transfers of cases and allocation of judges between them was to be permitted. Lord Hailsham, the then Lord Chancellor, favoured the former option.

Lord Hailsham set up the Civil Justice Review in 1985 to investigate improvements that might be made in the machinery of civil justice – jurisdiction, procedure and court administration, reduction in delays, cost and complexity. Five areas were studied: personal injuries; small claims; the Commercial Court; the debt enforcement process; and housing cases. In each area, a consultation paper was prepared in 1986–87, setting out the options for reform and preferred solutions.

A further consultation paper followed in May 1986, which noted five criticisms of the present system: fragmentation and overlap of jurisdiction; lack of transfer facilities; less expertise owing to fragmentation; delay and expense; and different remedies in different courts. It was also noted that the system was too adversarial, too formal and the magistrates' court was associated with criminal cases. Three options were proposed: a revised structure; a unified court to replace the High Court and county court; and a wholly new court structure and judiciary.

In March 1987, the Lord Chancellor's Department issued a general issues paper identifying common problems and proposing changes in jurisdiction, procedure and administration. Three aims of the civil justice system were identified: a high quality of justice including fair procedures and adjudication methods; limitation of delay and cost, both to the parties and the court service, proportionate to the subject matter; and an effective system able to respond to the types of business, changing needs and convenience of the parties.

The paper recommended a single unified system to replace the High Court and county court. Two models were suggested: either a single civil court with two levels of judiciary equivalent to judges from the High Court and Court of Appeal; or a single court with an integrated judiciary. The Law Society supported the idea of a single unified court but the Bar did not, for, in its view, this would jeopardise barristers' monopoly over rights of audience. It was also suggested that the courts should work longer hours and have an extended legal year.

In June 1988, the Final Report was published and implemented by Pt I of the Courts and Legal Services Act 1990 and the High Court and County Courts Jurisdiction Order 1991. The High Court and county court were to remain separate, with no upper limit on county court jurisdiction. A lower limit of £25,000 for High Court cases was set, with all cases below £25,000 to be heard in the county court, except in matters of public law, specialised matters or where unusual complexity was involved. Cases of £25,000 to £50,000 were to be heard in either court. All personal injury cases were to start in the county court. Registrars were to be called district judges and their jurisdiction was to be increased to £5,000.

Thus, cases were allocated according to substance, importance and complexity. Generally, cases below £25,000 were to be heard in the county court; cases above £50,000 in the High Court; and those between £25,000 and £50,000 in either, depending on the above criteria and judicial availability. Personal injury claims were to start in the county court, unless above £50,000, and claims under £25,000 in the county court, unless transferred to the High Court on the above criteria. Claims under £25,000 commencing in the High Court were to remain there if these criteria were met.

Another recommendation of the Civil Justice Review which has come to nothing is the replacement of the Lord Chancellor's Department with a Ministry of Justice for Civil Matters (and of the Home Office for criminal matters).

The report of the Civil Justice Review also commented on the delays in litigation and, in 1993, the Heilbron Hodge Report, *Civil Justice on Trial: The Case for Change*, recommended 72 changes, also commenting on the delays and poor service to the litigant. It is this backdrop which led to the Woolf Inquiry in 1994 and the major reforms undertaken in the Civil Procedure Act 1997.

Another criticism concerns the arrangements for handling family disputes and the need for a family court. The Finer Committee as long ago as 1974 recommended a family court comprising three tiers of circuit judges, lay magistrates and registrars. Appeals on questions of fact from the first tier were to be made to circuit judges and two magistrates and reserved categories of work were to be allocated to High Court judges.

No changes have been made, largely due to the cost of implementing change. The High Court, county court and magistrates' courts retain jurisdiction in family matters. In 1989, the Children Act was passed (under the supervision of Lord Mackay), providing for concurrent jurisdiction between the magistrates' courts and the High Court, allowing for transfer of cases and uniformity by way of regulations. A separate Family Court was not introduced by Pt I of the Courts and Legal Services Act 1990, but by the Family Law Act 1996 mediation was made part of the divorce process following proposals of the Lord Chancellor's Green Paper in 1993. However, plans to bring the divorce reforms contained in this Act into effect were postponed in July 1999, so that use of mediation continues on a voluntary basis.

Another area for concern has been the role of the Civil Division of the Court of Appeal, where it has been felt that too many undeserving cases have come to the court and this has been wasteful of time, money and the expertise of the Lords Justices of Appeal. In 1998, Sir Jeffrey Bowman reported following his review of the court. Again, delay and expense were important factors and he recommended that the lower courts should shoulder more of the burden of appeals and that only cases involving important points of principle or a specialised area should go on appeal to the Court of Appeal. As a general rule, permission (formerly called leave) should be sought to bring an appeal, except in adoption cases, child abduction and refusals of habeas corpus. Sir Jeffrey Bowman's other recommendations took on board those made by Lord Woolf in his Interim and Final Reports on the civil justice system, in particular the use of judicial case management, strict procedural timetables, better access of litigants in person to information and the use of IT by judges and court staff. These and the emphasis on allocation of cases to tracks to ensure value for money and the best use of resources in the lower courts should not be lost on an antiquated set of procedures in the Court of Appeal. On the question of family appeals, a specialist committee under Thorpe LJ was set up and it reported in July 1998.

Several novel recommendations were made concerning the constitution of the Court of Appeal, which traditionally has comprised three to five Lords Justices of Appeal, appointed from those experienced as counsel with general knowledge of the law. The report recommended that it might be appropriate for some cases to be heard by a single judge. At other times, the court could benefit from the knowledge or expertise of academics or practitioners sitting as judges, and the use of judges with specialist knowledge of an area of law would be useful so as to dispose of backlogs in that area. This was followed by the Lord Chancellor's Consultation Paper, *Reform of the Court of Appeal (Civil Division): Proposals for Change to Constitution and Jurisdiction*, in 1998, which has now led to Pt IV of the Access to Justice Act 1999, and these provisions are mentioned in Chapter 3.

CIVIL PROCEEDINGS

General

- Litigation should be a last resort.

- The parties will be encouraged to settle out of court or by way of alternative dispute resolution (ADR).

- Letters of claim (formerly letters before action) and 'without prejudice' clauses.

- The historical differences between High Court and county court; the differences in terminology, forms and procedure.

- The replacement of the White Book governing High Court procedure and the Green Book governing county court procedure by the CPR 1998 (as amended); the Civil Procedure Act 1997.

- The main features of the civil justice system, including its adversarial nature and the burden and standard of proof.

Civil justice reform

Lord Woolf's Interim and Final Reports set out the main proposals for reform of the civil justice system and culminated in the Civil Procedure Act 1997 and the CPR 1998. They include:

- judicial case management;

- ADR should be encouraged and litigation should be a last resort;

- the adoption of three tiers – the small claims track, the fast track and the multi-track;

- the use of sanctions to encourage compliance with the case management timetable;

- the encouragement of settlement and negotiation by means of pre-action protocols and offers to settle;

- simplification in terminology, for example, replacement of 'plaintiff' with 'claimant';

- the use of experts by the court, rather than their appointment by one party.

The Civil Procedure Rules 1998

- A unified set of procedural rules in the High Court and the county court. The overriding objective is set out in r 1 and aims to ensure that cases are handled efficiently.

- Judicial case management.

- Pre-action protocols in clinical negligence and personal injury claims.

- Sanctions.

- Claim forms: Pt 7 form; Pt 8 form.

- Detailed provisions for the issuing and serving of documents, the forms which must be used and time limits.

- The allocation of cases to one of three tracks – the small claims track for claims up to £5,000; the fast track for claims up to £15,000; and the multi-track for cases over £15,000 or those which are unduly complex.

- The importance of settlement and negotiation; the rules permit either party to offer to settle the issue before trial.

- It is too early to assess the full implications of these reforms, but Lord Woolf hoped to create a 'new legal landscape'.

Other proposed reforms of the civil justice system

- The Civil Justice Review 1985 and subsequent developments, culminating in the Courts and Legal Services Act 1990 and the Access to Justice Act 1999.

- The recommendations of the Bowman Report concerning the role and constitution of the Civil Division of the Court of Appeal.

- Should the High Court and county court be unified?

- The reform of divorce law and the requirement for use of mediation in family disputes under the Family Law Act 1996 was postponed by the Lord Chancellor in July 1999.

CHAPTER 8

CRIMINAL PROCEEDINGS

Introduction

In this chapter, we will deal with trials in the magistrates' courts and the Crown Court, together with appeals and how miscarriages of justice are dealt with by the Criminal Cases Review Commission. We will also deal with the role of the Crown Prosecution Service (CPS) and, in outline, that of the police in investigating offences. Sentencing of offenders will be dealt with in Chapter 9.

We will also mention the major proposals for reform of the criminal justice system, noting those that have been brought into effect, and in passing, the recent appointment of Auld LJ by the Lord Chancellor to conduct a Criminal Courts Review.

The investigation of offences

The police are the chief agents of law enforcement, with extensive powers of arrest, to question suspects, to enter premises, to search persons and property and to seize property. In contrast, the citizen has very limited powers of arrest under s 24(4) of the Police and Criminal Evidence Act (PACE) 1984, but may be called on to assist the police in effecting an arrest or preventing the commission of an offence. The citizen also has a limited right to bring a private prosecution but the Attorney General may issue a *nolle prosequi* (no prosecution) to prevent it from continuing.

The prosecution, brought by the CPS under the Prosecution of Offences Act 1985, has the burden of proof (beyond all reasonable doubt). Sections 76–78 of PACE 1984 permit exclusion of evidence at the judge's discretion where it has been obtained unfairly. Involuntary confessions must be excluded.

Section 1 of PACE 1984 allows a person to be stopped and searched (although there is no general power) where a police officer reasonably believes he or she is in possession of stolen or prohibited articles. Section 60 of the Criminal Justice and Public Order Act (CJPOA) 1994 permits 'stop and search', in anticipation of violence, by a police officer in uniform who may stop a pedestrian and search him or her or anything carried by him or her or stop any vehicle and search it, the driver or passengers, for offensive weapons or dangerous instruments. The police officer does not have to have grounds for suspecting that a person or vehicle is carrying such items and he or she can seize any dangerous instruments and also any articles which he or she reasonably suspects to be offensive weapons. Authorisation is required by a superintendent or, where incidents involving serious violence are imminent, by a chief inspector or an inspector when a superintendent is unavailable. The authorising officer must have a reasonable belief that incidents of serious violence may take place in his or her area and that it is expedient to give authorisation so as to prevent them taking place. It is notable how vague these provisions are and the amount of discretion vested in the police. It will take time to see how the police use these powers. The Crime and Disorder Act 1998 amends s 60 to permit a police officer to insist on the removal of face coverings where their use is aimed at reducing the effectiveness of CCTV.

Once arrested, a person may be searched under s 32 if reasonable grounds exist for believing that he or she may present a danger to him or herself or others, for anything which might be used to escape or which might be evidence of an offence.

By ss 24 and 25 of PACE 1984 the police (and sometimes others) are empowered to arrest suspects. Arrest deprives a person of his or her liberty and may involve physical restraint or simply a restriction on freedom. Police wishing to question a suspect must effect an arrest unless the suspect voluntarily consents to assist them.

Section 24 permits an arrest by police officers and citizens for an 'arrestable offence', that is, an offence where the penalty is fixed by law or carries a penalty of at least five years' imprisonment or where statute so provides, for example, official secrets offences. Other offences covered are conspiracy, attempts and incitement.

As might be expected, police officers have wider powers of arrest than the citizen. A police officer may arrest a person committing, about to commit or whom he or she has reasonable grounds to suspect to be committing, about to commit or who has committed an offence. The citizen can arrest a person who is committing an offence or whom he or she has reasonable grounds to suspect to be committing an offence. Where an offence in fact has already been committed, a citizen can only arrest the person who has committed the offence or one whom he or she has reasonable grounds of suspecting has committed it. If he or she is mistaken and no offence has been committed, he or she can be sued in tort for wrongful arrest.

In *Walters v WH Smith* (1914), W had been reasonably suspected of having taken books from a station bookstall and was arrested. W insisted that he or she had no intention to steal and the jury believed him or her and he or she was acquitted of theft for lack of *mens rea*. W then sued WH Smiths for false imprisonment and succeeded. The citizen, if he or she is to arrest another lawfully, must not only have a reasonable suspicion, but also an offence must have been committed by someone, not necessarily the arrested person.

In *R v Self* (1992), X, a store detective, saw S pick up an item and then leave without paying. X went outside and arrested S, who resisted and assaulted both X and a passer-by who lent assistance. The jury acquitted S of theft for lack of *mens rea*, and so he or she was entitled to use reasonable force to resist arrest by X.

By s 25, a police officer with reasonable grounds of suspecting that a person is committing or who has committed a non-arrestable offence can arrest that person if he or she considers it impracticable to serve him or her with a summons because his or her name is not known, or he or she reasonably suspects that he or she has not given his or her true name or a satisfactory address or arrest is reasonably necessary to prevent injury or damage or the commission of a public decency offence or obstruction of the highway or for protection of a child or other 'vulnerable person'.

Arrests can also be made where a statute permits, such as the Prevention of Terrorism (Temporary Provisions) Act 1989, or where there is a common law breach of the peace, as in *R v Howell* (1981), 'whenever harm is actually done or is likely to be done to a person or in his or her presence to his or her property or a person is in fear of being so harmed through assault, an affray, a riot ... or other disturbance'.

Magistrates may issue a warrant for the arrest of a suspect. At the time of an arrest, reasonable force may be used under s 117 of PACE 1984 and s 3 of the Criminal Law Act 1967. Reasonable force may be used to resist an unlawful arrest, as seen in *R v Self* (1992).

Section 28 of PACE 1984 stipulates that the person arrested must be informed of the reason for arrest as soon as is practicable and until he or she is informed of this fact and the ground for arrest it is unlawful, except where he or she escapes before being told. Civil law remedies will be available for wrongful arrest including assault and battery and false imprisonment. In *Wheatley v Lodge* (1971), a deaf person was treated as having been properly arrested even though he or she was unaware of the arrest and the police officers did not know he or she was deaf.

No technical or precise language needs to be used in informing a person that he or she is arrested, as illustrated in *Christie v Leachinsky* (1947) and *Abassy v MPC* (1990), where A was arrested 'for unlawful possession' of a car.

On arrest, the police may wish to question a suspect and in order to do so must administer a caution. The wording of the caution has had to be revised, following ss 34–37 of the CJPOA 1994, where adverse comment can be made at trial where a defendant fails to mention either a fact on which he or she relies in his or her defence or one which he or she reasonably could have been expected to mention. In addition, this applies to failures after arrest to account for the presence of an 'object, substance or mark' or for his or her presence at a place where and at a time at which the alleged offence was committed.

No general power exists to enter private property, but the police may do so with the owner's consent. Reasonable force may be used to gain entry to effect an arrest under warrant or to arrest for an arrestable offence under s 17 of PACE 1984. This is also permitted to prevent a breach of the peace, to recapture a fugitive and to prevent serious injury or damage. *O'Loughlin v Chief Constable of Essex* (1998) is authority for the proposition that the police officer should inform the occupier as to the reason for entry, unless this is impossible, impracticable or undesirable.

Section 18 of PACE states that the police may enter and search premises occupied or controlled by a person under arrest for an arrestable offence if reasonable grounds exist for suspecting that there is evidence on the premises relating to the offence or to other arrestable offences connected with or similar to that offence. In contrast, s 32(2)(b) allows the police to enter and search the premises where the suspect is arrested, or where he or she was immediately before arrest, for evidence relating to any offence for which he or she was arrested. The scope of s 32 is much narrower than s 17 and is rarely used by the police.

Section 32 also provides that for arrests, other than at a police station, a police officer can search the arrested person, if he or she thinks he or she may be dangerous, or for anything which might be used for an escape, or which might be evidence of an offence. Only outer clothing may be removed, and dangerous items or evidence of an offence can be seized.

On arrest, a person's property can be searched if relevant to the alleged offence, and also his or her premises and premises where he or she was arrested belonging to another person. Evidence obtained during an unlawful search may be admissible at the discretion of the judge. Other Acts, such as the Theft Acts, permit magistrates to issue warrants to enter and search premises.

There is a duty to take an arrested person as soon as is practicable to a police station designated by the Chief Constable as one for detention of those arrested. A lone officer can take an arrested person to any station if he or she is dangerous, but within six hours the arrested person must be taken to a designated station. In *Dallison v Caffery* (1964), X was arrested in Clapton, taken 34 miles to Dunstable, where the alleged offence took place, then to a house to verify his or her alibi, then to his or her own house and, after seven hours, to a police station. In *Lewis v Tims* (1952), L was arrested by a store detective and was taken to the manager's office where she waited for one hour for the arrival of the manager, whose decision it was whether to call the police. The House of Lords held that this was a reasonable delay, as it demonstrated that the decision to proceed against a person was taken seriously.

At common law, the police cannot detain a person or insist on his or her answering questions without arresting him or her. *Rice v Connolly* (1966) is authority for the proposition that a citizen has no legal duty to assist the police. Section 29 of PACE 1984 confirms this, but the police are not under any duty to tell those 'helping them with their inquiries' that they have no legal duty to assist. There may be a moral or social duty, and in some cases there is a legal duty to assist the police, for example, s 1 of PACE 1984 or under the Road Traffic Acts.

Detention should only normally arise on arrest and then only for up to 24 hours (s 41 of PACE 1984). For serious arrestable offences (as defined in s 116 of PACE), this can be extended to 96 hours, subject to conditions. Section 116 defines 'serious arrestable offences' as those serious by nature such as murder, rape, kidnapping; those causing, intended or likely to cause serious harm to national security or public order or interference with the administration of justice, investigation of crime, death, serious injury, substantial gain or serious financial loss to the victim.

Extension must be shown to be necessary to get or preserve evidence and that the investigation is being conducted diligently and expeditiously. The following extensions apply:

- s 42 – police superintendent: further detention of 12 hours;

- s 43 – magistrates' court: a further 36 hours;

- s 44 – magistrates' court: a final 24 hours, making 96 hours in all.

Section 46 of PACE 1984 states that at the end of the time limit a suspect must either be charged with an offence, be set free or released on bail. If charged, a suspect should be brought before the magistrates, either the same day or the next day.

Part IV of PACE and the Codes of Practice (which replaced the Judges' Rules 1964) regulate the making of confessions, the giving of cautions, the right of the police to question a suspect, the defendant's right to remain silent, the taking of statements and the right of the suspect to be informed of his or her right to a solicitor under s 58.

The suspect has a right (and a right to be informed of this right) to have one named person informed of his or her arrest and whereabouts, without delay, unless it is necessary in the interests of the investigation or prevention of crime, and then only up to 36 hours in the case of a serious arrestable offence (s 56).

Evidence of identification may be obtained by way of an identification (ID) parade, fingerprints and photographs. Section 61 requires authorisation for the taking of fingerprints by a police superintendent when satisfied that reasonable grounds exist (or the suspect consents).

Sections 54 and 55 provide powers of search and intimate search respectively. Part IV, ss 54–59 of the CJPOA 1994 gives the police power to take intimate/non-intimate body samples, fingerprints, to retain samples and to search a suspect's mouth.

Section 76 (confessions) and s 78 (inducements): the former provides that a court shall not admit confession evidence unless the prosecution proves beyond reasonable doubt that it was not obtained by 'oppression of the person who made it' or is unreliable due to 'inducement by reward or threat'. In *R v Hudson* (1980), a 59 year old man of good character was detained for 108 hours, asked 700 questions and confessed after 105 hours. The court excluded this evidence. Section 78 gives the court a discretion to exclude evidence obtained unfairly, as in *R v Mason* (1987), where the police falsely told M and his or her solicitor that M's fingerprints were on a bottle used to carry inflammable liquid.

The case of *R v Smurthwaite* and *R v Gill* (1994) illustrates the discretion that the court has in holding evidence to be inadmissible. It was held that s 78 of PACE was to be given its natural meaning and the court was to have regard to the circumstances in which the evidence (relied on) was obtained and to exclude it, but only if it would have such an adverse effect on the fairness of the proceedings that the court ought not to admit it. Where evidence was obtained by entrapment or by an *agent provocateur* or by a trick, this did not of itself require the judge to exclude it. If, in all the circumstances, he or she considered that the means by which it was obtained would have an adverse effect on the fairness of the trial, he or she should exclude it. Fairness in this context referred to fairness to the accused and to the public. The judge should take into account all the circumstances, including whether the police officer was acting as an *agent provocateur* (that is, enticing the accused to commit an offence he or she would otherwise not have done), the nature of the entrapment, whether the evidence consisted of admissions to a completed offence or the actual commission of an offence, how active or passive the officers' role was in obtaining the evidence, whether there was an unassailable record of what happened or whether it was strongly corroborated. Suspects should not be questioned by undercover detectives in abuse of their role or deprived of the protections of PACE 1984 and the Codes of Practice. The judge should rule evidence obtained in this way inadmissible.

PACE 1984 introduced tape recording of police interviews, but these do not solve the problem of oppression, threats and so on before or between interviews. It is suggested that full video-recording of police stations will achieve that. Tapes can, however, remove disputes as to who said what during an interview. The fears over confessions remain, as, unlike Scottish law, corroborative evidence is not required. The changes in the right to silence by the CJPOA 1994 heightened these fears, because many miscarriages of justice have involved false confessions and fabricated evidence. In the case of the Broadwater Three, the miscarriage arose after PACE had become law.

Bail

The law of bail is now governed by the CJPOA 1994, as further amended by the Crime and Disorder Act 1998, and this, together with earlier amendments by the Criminal Justice Act 1988, the Criminal Justice Act 1991, the Bail (Amendment) Act 1993 and the Magistrates' Courts Act 1980, merely amends the original Bail Act 1976, without starting afresh.

There are two stages at which bail may be granted: by the police; or by the magistrates' court. The police (the custody officer) may refuse bail in specified circumstances or impose unconditional or conditional bail when conditions are necessary.

By s 27 of the CJPOA 1994; the custody officer may impose conditions of bail if necessary to secure that a suspect, following arrest but before charge, surrenders, does not commit an offence while on bail or does not interfere with witnesses or obstruct justice. Conditions as to residence at a bail hostel or for mental treatment may be imposed in addition.

Section 54 of the Crime and Disorder Act 1998 extends the powers of attaching conditions or security, including the requirement to attend for interview with a legal representative.

By s 28 of the CJPOA 1994, amending s 38 of PACE 1984, a suspect charged with an offence may be refused bail: where his or her name and address cannot be ascertained or reasonable grounds exist to believe those supplied are false; the custody officer reasonably believes the accused will fail to attend court; on arrest for an imprisonable offence reasonable grounds exist for believing that detention is necessary to prevent the commission of other offences or to prevent the accused from causing injury to another or loss or damage to property; where reasonable grounds exist so as to prevent interference with the administration of justice or the investigation of offences; or where it is reasonable to detain for the accused's own protection. Conditions may be varied by another custody officer at the same police station at the accused's request by s 27(3) of the 1994 Act, but either more or less favourable conditions may result. Application for variation may then be made to the magistrates' court under Sched 3 to the CJPOA 1994 and the conditions may be removed, varied or the accused remanded in custody.

By s 46A of the CJPOA 1994, where a person fails to answer police bail, for example, to attend the police station at an appointed time, he or she may now be arrested without warrant.

A defendant appearing at the magistrates' court for the first time still has the benefit of the presumption in favour of bail as per s 4 of the Bail Act 1976. The magistrates' courts not only deal with bail from the time of first appearance, but may confirm, vary or remove any conditions of police bail or remand a defendant in custody.

By s 25 of the CJPOA 1994, bail could be refused where the defendant was charged with or convicted of murder, attempted murder, manslaughter, rape or attempted rape, if previously convicted of such an offence or if the previous offence was manslaughter and a custodial sentence was imposed. This has been amended by s 56 of the Crime and Disorder Act 1998 to allow the grant of bail in these cases where the court or the police considers that exceptional circumstances justify it. This provision has now been the subject of challenge before the European Court of Human Rights (*Caballero v UK* (2000)).

Section 26 provides that a defendant need not be granted bail if the offence is indictable or triable either way and it appears to the court that he or she was on bail in criminal proceedings at the date of the offence.

If new information comes to light after the original police bail decision, the prosecution may apply to the magistrates' court to have bail revoked or for conditions to be imposed under s 30 for indictable or triable either way offences. By the Bail (Amendment) Act 1993, the prosecution may appeal against bail decisions for all types of offence.

The trial process

The procedure for summary trials and committals in the magistrates' courts and Crown Court trials is considered, together with the possible outcomes and differences.

The magistrates' court

The vast majority of all criminal cases start in the magistrates' court. They have two main roles in criminal cases: as examining justices to decide if the defendant should be committed for trial to the Crown Court (trial by jury); or by hearing the case summarily and making a decision.

Each case starts as a result of the prosecution (this is the CPS in most cases) laying an information, a statement of the alleged offence and the name of the accused. The information can be in the form of an oath, in writing or oral (unless statute stipulates a prescribed form).

The defendant may have been summoned to appear before the court following an information put before a magistrate or magistrates' clerk. This is most often used for motoring offences and the summons requires the defendant to attend court on a stated date (the return date).

Alternatively, a warrant may have been issued for the defendant's arrest following a written and sworn information against him or her. This is used for indictable and imprisonable offences or where the defendant's address is unknown or where he or she has failed to answer to a summons. A defendant may also appear as the result of a charge following arrest without warrant for an arrestable offence or offences under ss 24 and 25 of PACE 1984.

The magistrates have to decide whether the defendant is to be tried summarily or committed for trial to the Crown Court. This will depend on both the class of offence and the wishes of the defendant, prosecution and the magistrates.

In summary offences, the magistrates must try the case. Only in offences which are triable either way has the defendant any choice as to mode of trial. He or she has a right to elect jury trial in cases of theft, burglary and damage to property, as referred to in Sched 1 to the Magistrates' Courts Act 1980. This will change if the Mode of Trial Bill 1999, which provides that it will be for the magistrates to decide on trial venue, becomes law.

In offences triable either way, the magistrates must determine the mode of trial for adult defendants. By the Magistrates' Court (Advance Information) Rules 1985, the magistrates must satisfy themselves that a person who is subject to the rules is aware that he or she may ask for advance information before mode of trial is decided (or before plea for youths).

The prosecution is under an obligation to give written notice to the defence, setting out this obligation, and an address to which a request for information may be made. Service must be as soon as is practicable after charge or summons. Material parts of all written statements to be relied on by the prosecution must be given to the defence or a summary of all facts on which it is proposed to call evidence.

Withholding information is permitted where the prosecution is of the opinion that it might lead to intimidation or attempted intimidation of witnesses or the course of justice would otherwise be interfered with. Notice of this must be given to the defence and an adjournment may be ordered where the prosecution fails to comply with a request for information without good reason.

Section 49 of the Criminal Procedure and Investigations Act 1996 inserts a new s 17A into the Magistrates' Courts Act 1980, amending the mode of trial procedure. A defendant is required to plead guilty or not guilty to triable either way offences immediately before the magistrates decide on mode of trial.

If the defendant pleads guilty, the court proceeds to sentence or commit him or her to the Crown Court for sentence. If he or she pleads not guilty, or fails to enter a plea, the court decides on mode of trial. This aims to encourage defendants to be dealt with by the magistrates' court rather than the Crown Court, but it has been criticised for putting defendants under undue pressure to plead guilty without knowing the strength of the prosecution's case. In order to elect jury trial, defendants will have to enter no plea or a not guilty plea.

The magistrates must take account of the following matters: whether the offence appears more suitable for summary trial or trial on indictment; representations made by prosecution and defence; whether the offence is a serious one in the light of its circumstances; whether the sentence imposed by the magistrates would be sufficient in all the circumstances; and any other relevant circumstances.

Where the Attorney General or the Director of Public Prosecutions initiates a prosecution, he or she can require that trial is on indictment.

Where summary trial appears more suitable, the charge is read to the defendant and his or her right to elect jury trial is explained, together with the fact that if he or she is tried summarily he or she may be committed to the

Crown Court for sentence if the powers of the magistrates are insufficient. The defendant makes known his or her choice.

Where trial on indictment appears more suitable, the defendant is informed of this and may make representations for summary trial. However, the defendant cannot insist on summary trial.

Criminal damage

Special rules apply to a charge of criminal damage. If the value of the property exceeds £2,000, the offence is treated as triable either way. If it is less than £2,000, the magistrates treat the case as if it were triable summarily and the defendant cannot elect jury trial. The maximum sentence is three months' imprisonment or a fine of £2,500, and there is no power to commit for sentence to the Crown Court under s 38 of the Magistrates' Courts Act 1980. If the value of the property is in doubt, then the defendant is asked to consent to summary trial and if he or she does so it must be explained to him or her that he or she will be sentenced by the magistrates and cannot be committed for sentence to the Crown Court.

Committal proceedings

When magistrates act as examining justices, they have a duty to decide whether the defendant should be committed for trial to the Crown Court on indictment. In other words, the prosecution must establish a *prima facie* case against the defendant.

By Pt V of the Criminal Procedure and Investigations Act 1996, the procedure for committal proceedings has been amended. Section 5A–F have been inserted into the Magistrates' Courts Act 1980 and amend s 6 of that Act.

The only evidence that may be used in committals are written statements, depositions and other documents and exhibits served by or on behalf of the prosecution.

A s 6(1) committal (formerly an old style committal) now involves the reading aloud of written statements or, at the court's direction, a summary of statements not read out. No oral evidence can be called, but the defence may submit that there is insufficient evidence for trial.

A s 6(2) committal (formerly a new style or paper committal) involves no consideration of the evidence tendered by the prosecution. It must fall into the prescribed categories of written statements, depositions or other documents or exhibits. The defendant must be legally represented and should not wish to make a submission of insufficient evidence.

The magistrates decide whether to commit or not and, if committal is ordered, the application for legal aid, bail and costs are decided. In committing the defendant for trial to the Crown Court, several matters are taken into account, including the convenience for the defendant, prosecution and witnesses, the class of offence and the need to expedite trial.

There are four classes of offence, ranging from the most serious, for example, murder, tried only by a High Court judge, to the least serious, usually tried by a circuit judge or recorder, but power of the High Court judge to try must be taken into account in addition to the three tiers of Crown Court.

Summary trial

If the defendant pleads guilty, the magistrates then pass sentence. If he or she pleads not guilty, or there is some doubt as to the plea, the magistrates hear the evidence and decide guilt or innocence.

The order of events is as follows:

- the defendant's identity is checked by the clerk;

- the plea is entered;

- the prosecution opens its case by stating the charge and outlining the evidence;

- oral testimony and other evidence is given. Witnesses are examined-in-chief, cross-examined and re-examined if appropriate. The clerk makes notes of the evidence;

- the defence may submit no case to answer;

- assuming this is not accepted, the defence opens its case;

- the prosecution *may* call evidence in rebuttal on matters arising unexpectedly in the course of the defence case;

- the defence makes its closing speech;

- either the prosecution or the defence may address the court with leave. If one does so, the other has a right to do so also;

- the magistrates decide guilt or innocence;

- if the defendant is found guilty, the magistrates pass sentence.

For any one offence, the maximum penalty is generally six months' imprisonment and/or a fine of £5,000, although in some matters the fine can be much greater. For example, in some food safety cases and environmental pollution cases, the penalty can be as much as £20,000.

Guilty by post pleas

For summary offences punishable with not more than three months' imprisonment, a defendant may plead guilty by post, providing he or she has been served with the summons, statement of facts and an explanatory note and he or she sends to the court a written guilty plea. The court will take note of the statement of facts and any written comments of the defendant in mitigation. The defendant may be convicted and sentenced in his or her absence.

The Crown Court

The defendant must be present when arraigned (naming of the defendant, reading to him or her the indictment and a request as to how he or she pleads) so as to plead to the charge in the indictment (the formal document setting out the alleged offence or offences). The defendant may represent himself, seek the services of a *McKenzie* friend, or be represented by a lawyer (with or without legal aid). The right of a defendant to represent himself applies in all courts, but the case of *R v Edwards* (1996) highlighted the dangers of this in a Crown Court trial for rape. The defendant questioned the victim of the alleged offence over the course of six days, with very little interruption on the part of the judge. The victim felt traumatised as much by the questioning as the offence itself, the defendant was found guilty, and guidelines were sought to prevent this in future.

Sections 34–40 of the Youth Justice and Criminal Evidence Act 1999 restrict the defendant's freedom to personally examine alleged victims in sexual offences and children giving evidence in sex, violence, kidnapping, cruelty and neglect cases. Where a defendant is subject to this restriction and refuses to appoint counsel, the court may appoint a legal representative on his or her behalf to test the evidence in the interests of the defendant, and the court may order payment. The court can give jury warnings to the effect that the evidence may not be as fully tested as if the defendant's own representative had cross-examined the witness, but the jury should not draw prejudicial inferences from the fact that he or she has been prevented from cross-examining in person. By s 36, the court has power to restrict the defendant's right to other cases where it is satisfied that the circumstances of the case and the witnesses merit it and that this would not be contrary to the interests of justice.

The trial is in public with reporting in the press, unless restrictions apply as, for example, in official secrets trials or those where delicate personal matters are dealt with.

The jury is empanelled before the start of the trial, but remains outside the courtroom until the defendant is arraigned and has pleaded. This ensures the impartiality of jurors and challenges can then be made subject to conditions (noted in Chapter 3).

The prosecution opens its case, calls witnesses and the usual order of examination-in-chief, cross-examination and re-examination is followed. The defence then opens its case and the defendant may decide to give evidence on oath and on which he or she may face cross-examination by the prosecution.

The prosecution then sums up, followed by the defence. It is then the turn of the judge to sum up to the jury, after which the jury retires to consider its verdict. From amongst its number a foreman is appointed to deliver the verdict. Following a guilty verdict, the judge passes sentence, whereas if the defendant is acquitted, he or she is discharged. Each count on the indictment is tried separately and a separate verdict is given.

By Pt I of the Criminal Procedure and Investigations Act 1996, a statutory scheme of disclosure of evidence by prosecution and defence was introduced. This radically altered the rules of disclosure and for the first time the defence in Crown Court trials must make disclosure.

The prosecution must disclose all relevant unused material which might undermine its case. This is called primary prosecution disclosure. On application to the court, the prosecution may be allowed not to disclose material not in the public interest. Any material not disclosed but which is not sensitive should be referred to in a document supplied to the defence.

In Crown Court proceedings, the defence must provide a defence statement, disclosing in general terms the nature of the defence and particulars of any alibi relied on. In the magistrates' court, the defence may make voluntary disclosure. The prosecution must then make secondary disclosure to the defence of any additional unused material which might reasonably be expected to assist the defence as disclosed in the defence statement.

In a recent drugs trial, the judge stayed the proceedings on the basis that the trial could not be fair where the CPS had failed to disclose some 2,500 pages of evidence. This was followed by Attorney General Guidelines, stating that the prosecution must make good and proper disclosure of evidence. Critics of this Act and the Guidelines say that its inherent flaw comes from the requirement that a police officer has to put himself in the position of the defence lawyer in deciding whether or not evidence should be disclosed. No mechanism exists to question whether a police officer acts correctly. The Guidelines do not provide specific standards, only that the Codes of Practice should be complied with. The Law Society, *inter alia*, has been very critical of the disclosure rules and suggests that their use will give rise to serious miscarriages of justice.

Appeals

Section 1 of the Criminal Appeal Act 1995 amends the 1968 Act so that appeals against conviction, against a verdict of not guilty by reason of insanity or against a finding of disability on a question of law only must have leave of the Court of Appeal or a certificate of fitness for appeal from the trial judge before an appeal can proceed. These appeals are now made subject to the filter which used only to apply to appeals against conviction and sentence involving mixed questions of law and fact.

Section 2 provides that the Court of Appeal must allow an appeal against conviction under s 1, an appeal against a verdict of insanity under s 12 or an appeal against a finding of disability if it thinks that the conviction, verdict or finding is unsafe. This replaces the formula under the 1968 Act, applied by the Court of Appeals that the conviction, verdict or finding was unsafe and unsatisfactory.

Section 4 amends s 23 of the 1968 Act, retaining a general discretion in the Court of Appeal to admit fresh evidence of any witness where it is thought necessary or expedient in the interests of justice. In addition, the court must consider several criteria, including the extent to which the evidence is capable of belief, whether it affords any ground for allowing the appeal, whether it would have been admissible at trial and whether a reasonable explanation exists for it not having been adduced at trial.

Other powers of the Court of Appeal

Section 36 of the Criminal Justice Act 1972 provides for a reference by the Attorney General on a point of law to the Court of Appeal following acquittal for an opinion on the state of the law. This must not be confused with the power under ss 35 and 36 of the Criminal Justice Act 1988, whereby the Attorney General may refer an unduly lenient sentence to the Court of Appeal which may quash the original sentence and replace it with one considered appropriate, up to the maximum available in the Crown Court. In *R v Harnett (Attorney General's Reference (No 60 of 1996))* (1997), it was held that this power of referral applies also to sentences which are considered to be too severe. Following review by the Court of Appeal, either party may, subject to a Court of Appeal certificate and leave of Court of Appeal or House of Lords, refer the case to the House of Lords for an opinion on a point of law of general public importance.

Consideration of criminal appeals would be incomplete without mention of appeals by way of case stated, the rights of prosecution and defence to appeal to the House of Lords from the Court of Appeal with leave on a point of law under s 1 of the Administration of Justice Act 1960 and exercise of the royal prerogative of mercy by the Home Secretary. Section 133 of the Criminal Justice Act 1988 introduced a right for defendants wrongly convicted to seek compensation from the Home Secretary.

Youth court

Formerly called juvenile courts, youth courts deal with offenders aged up to 18 years inclusive (ss 68 and 70 of the Criminal Justice Act 1991). Special rules apply at the police station, during detention pending first appearance at court, courtroom procedure and sentencing. By s 24(1) of the Magistrates' Courts Act 1980, a juvenile must be tried in a youth court (or an adult magistrates' court if jointly charged with an adult) unless charged with homicide or charged jointly with an adult who is to be tried on indictment, and the magistrates consider it is in the interests of justice to commit both for trial, or the juvenile has reached the age of 14 and is charged with a grave offence.

Trial in the youth court necessitates that magistrates are drawn from a special panel and the court should sit in a room not used for an adult court in the previous hour. The public are not admitted and the magistrates should comprise at least one woman. Reporting restrictions apply unless reporting is necessary to avoid injustice and the procedure is less formal. There is no dock, and the magistrates sit at the same level as the juvenile, who is seated with his or her parents.

Amendments have been made by the Crime and Disorder Act 1998 and the Youth Justice and Criminal Evidence Act 1999, and more will be said about youth trials in Chapter 9.

Reform of the criminal justice system

The Royal Commission on Criminal Justice (chaired by Lord Runciman) reported in July 1993, and made 352 recommendations for improvements in the criminal justice system. The Commission took two years to report and followed some notable miscarriages of justice, including the Guildford Four, the Birmingham Six, the Maguire Seven, Judith Ward, the Tottenham Three and Stefan Kiszko.

These cases illustrated some very important failings in the system, including how easily convictions can be secured as a result of fabricated evidence, how vulnerable suspects are accused and found guilty of offences they have not committed, and the near impossible means by which wrong decisions can be rectified. The overriding conclusion was the inadequacy of the judicial process in detecting and dealing with major shortcomings arising during and as a result of the investigative process. The court and the jury can only be as good as the evidence put before it, given that ours is an accusatorial and not an inquisitorial system.

Thus, the due process of law (formal justice) usually remains above reproach but, where it is found wanting, an appeal may lie to the Court of Appeal to correct the error. The case of *R v Whybrow and Saunders* (1994) demonstrates failings in due process. The Court of Appeal held that, although the trial judge should prevent the trial from becoming protracted, he or she should not attempt to cross-examine the defendant or show disbelief of the defendant's evidence, since this would prevent the defendant from receiving a fair trial.

The essential failings in the system concern the collection of evidence and its disclosure (or lack of disclosure) to the court. What needs to be improved on are the mechanisms for ensuring that fabrication of evidence does not take place, and where it does, it is found out quickly. Commentators have suggested that we must reform our present system in order to have an independent investigative process charged with finding the truth rather than leaving the police to conduct the investigations alone.

Michael Mansfield QC in his book, *Presumed Guilty* (1993), proposed that the accusatorial system be retained, but that a judge should conduct an independent investigation along the lines of the French *Juge d'Instruction* into the truth, and not be concerned with finding evidence to prove a theory or hunch as to who committed the offence. The prosecution should also be obliged to reveal to the defence (if not the court) all evidence collected, whereas under the present system the prosecution need only disclose evidence on which it intends to rely at the trial. The risk that in some cases the guilty will go undetected may be an acceptable price of justice, but it is not acceptable that the innocent should be wrongly convicted. If this happens, then at least there should be speedy and effective means of rectifying mistakes.

Two fundamental principles lie at the heart of the criminal justice system, namely, the presumption of innocence and the right to elect trial by jury. Some would still add the right to remain silent when being questioned by the police and at trial, but now that ss 34–37 of the CJPOA 1994 permits the drawing of adverse inferences, it might be argued that this reduces the effectiveness of the presumption of innocence. Some major defects in the criminal justice system have been identified which lead to the acquittal of the guilty and the conviction of the innocent.

We have mentioned the role of the police in conducting investigations and the allegations of bias, presumption of guilt, stereotyping and targeting of those with records. This has led to calls for independent supervision of police investigations. The Police Complaints Authority has also been the subject of much complaint in failing to win the confidence of the public. The Crown Prosecution Service has not only been much criticised in failing to disclose all evidence in its possession, but also for its policy of initiating prosecutions and then in some cases offering no evidence on reaching trial.

The CPS was set up by the Prosecution of Offences Act 1985 and is under the general control of the DPP. The police investigate offences and then pass their file to the CPS, which can decide whether or not to initiate criminal proceedings. It also has the power to take over and discontinue cases started by others, such as trading standards officers.

From the outset, the CPS has been dogged with staff shortages, high staff turnover and low morale. In 1999, following the Glidewell Report in 1998, a new DPP was appointed to replace Dame Barbara Mills, and a drastic re-organisation took place so as to re-establish that police area boundaries and those of the CPS matched each other. Critics have poured scorn on this as demonstrating that the notion of independence from the police has been lost. Another worrying feature is the extension of rights of audience to solicitors in the CPS without restrictions from their professional body, although s 42 of the Access to Justice Act 1999 provides that advocates owe their first duty to the court and must act independently in the interests of justice. The setting up of a Criminal Defence Service under the Access to Justice Act 1999 will also raise concerns as to the position of the individual facing criminal investigation or charges.

By s 10 of the 1985 Act, the Code for Crown Prosecutors sets out the principles governing the work of the CPS and must be taken into account by the police when deciding whether or not to charge a defendant with an offence. It is fallacious to suppose that the law expects every criminal act to result in prosecution. Those involved in this decision have a great deal of discretion – the police in deciding whether to bring charges, and the CPS in deciding whether to prosecute. The CPS apply two tests in deciding whether to prosecute, namely, whether a realistic prospect of conviction exists, and whether prosecution is in the public interest. The former is described as the evidential test and depends on the reliability and admissibility of evidence. The latter considers such factors as the prevalence of that type of offence, whether it was against a public official, whether a weapon or violence was used, whether it was committed by a group, and the likelihood of a serious penalty. Such decisions depend on balancing carefully all the factors of each case, and it may be added that this is extremely difficult and time consuming. Very little, if any, judicial control exists over such decisions, and this can be clearly seen in such cases as *R v MPC ex p Blackburn* (1968), where it was held that the court should not attempt to regulate a Chief Constable as to the resources available in policing his or her area. Similarly, the judiciary can only use censure when faced with the CPS offering no evidence at the beginning or during the course of a trial.

Another area for concern is the collection and disclosure of evidence by the prosecution. The Forensic Science Service is a State-run monopoly, largely benefiting the prosecution, and it has been suggested that this should be made freely available to the defence. The need for this will no doubt increase, given advances in new technology and DNA profiling and wider police powers.

Other criticisms concern the ineffectiveness of the jury system, the need to reform the judiciary and legal profession and court procedures so as to ensure that it is a challenging forum in which to decide the guilt or innocence of an individual.

The creation of the Criminal Cases Review Commission by s 8 of the Criminal Appeal Act 1995 was long overdue, but it will be some time before its effectiveness can be assessed. Early indications suggest that it is already overburdened with cases and underfunded to do its job effectively. Moreover, the Criminal Procedure and Investigations Act 1996 seems to run counter to the need for openness in the trial process whereby decisions are left in the hands of the police as to the prosecution evidence to be disclosed in court. One of the first cases of long standing was that of *R v Home Secretary ex p Bentley* (1993), and in August 1998, it was referred back to the Court of Appeal and the conviction for murder was overturned. However, since then it has become apparent that many thousands of alleged miscarriages of justice are being processed by the Commission and, with the current changes in the criminal justice system, more will occur in time.

Recommendations of the Royal Commission on Criminal Justice

The main recommendations of the Royal Commission on Criminal Justice were as follows.

The decision whether a defendant should be tried by jury should rest with the magistrates, so as to ensure a more rational division of triable either way offences between the magistrates' court and Crown Court.

The right of silence in police stations should be retained; adverse inferences were not to be drawn; and the police caution on silence was to be retained, together with the direction by the judge at trial that the jury should not draw adverse inferences from a defendant's silence during investigation or the trial.

An independent review body should be set up to investigate alleged miscarriages of justice and to refer appropriate cases to the Court of Appeal. Section 17 of the Criminal Appeals Act 1968 (power to refer cases to the Court of Appeal) should be replaced by a review body, to be chaired by a person appointed by the Queen on the advice of the Prime Minister. Other members would be appointed by the Lord Chancellor. No appeal would lie from its decisions, nor would judicial review be available.

The Court of Appeal to be enabled to overturn unsafe verdicts and to order retrials where practicable – s 2(1) of the Criminal Appeal Act 1968 is to be redrafted, providing a single broad ground for a retrial or an appeal where a decision is or may be unsafe.

Pre-trial defence disclosure should be required and be subject to adverse inferences by the jury for non-disclosure.

Video surveillance of police custody suites and of police interviews of suspects should be introduced.

Committal proceedings should be abolished, but submission by the defence of 'no case to answer' should remain.

The defendant should have an enforceable right of access to forensic evidence held by the prosecution.

The judge should warn the jury regarding the dangers of uncorroborated confessions and the need for independent evidence.

Sentence discounting should be allowed – earlier pleas would receive higher discounts.

The guidelines issued in the Judith Ward case on disclosure of evidence by the prosecution should be narrowed.

Increased use should be made of DNA profiling by the police (for example, saliva samples).

A forensic science advisory council should be created and both prosecution and defence should have access to the public sector forensic laboratories.

Improvements should be made in standards for those attending to offer advice to police suspects.

The low level of fees for criminal work reflected on the quality of service required.

Prosecution counsel's opening speech should last no longer than 15 minutes, unless the judge gives leave. Opening speeches should be confined to an explanation of the issues in question.

The recommendations concerning juries have been mentioned in Chapter 3.

Reactions to the proposals

Generally, the recommendations have been said not to be far reaching enough, and unlikely to reduce significantly the risks of wrongful convictions. Outrage was expressed at the proposal to abolish the defendant's right to elect jury trial. This was seen as merely a cost-cutting exercise and not done in the interests of justice. The Mode of Trial Bill, currently before Parliament, will give effect to this proposal, if it becomes law. However, the proposals to retain the right of silence, appointment of an independent review body and the proposed changes in the functions of the Court of Appeal were welcomed, together with a mixed reception for most of the other recommendations.

In the result, the report was not followed by a Green or White Paper but by the Criminal Justice and Public Order Bill and the Police and Magistrates' Court Bill. Both became law in 1994, but the latter has since been consolidated with the Justices of the Peace Act 1979 into the Justices of the Peace Act 1997. The Criminal Appeals Act 1995 and the Criminal Procedure and Investigations Act 1996 also bring into effect other recommendations of the report. The Access to Justice Act 1999 makes further amendments.

Another means by which reforms in the criminal justice system should come about is the McPherson Report, published in 1999 following the stabbing of Stephen Lawrence. His or her parents, a year after publication, were not convinced that anything sufficient had been done to ensure that the same mistakes will not be made again. We have already mentioned, in connection with reform of the law in Chapter 2, some of the recommendations of the report, including amending the double jeopardy rule to permit a new prosecution after acquittal where fresh and viable evidence is presented and the need to tackle institutionalised racism in the police and other institutions. The recommendations concerning the Coroner's Court were noted in Chapter 3. Also of note is the need for the CPS to take into account the existence of racism when deciding whether or not to initiate prosecutions; also that the police should be subject to the Race Relations Acts and victims of crime and their families should be able to become parties in criminal proceedings so as to be kept informed of progress.

The Lord Chancellor has appointed Auld LJ to report on the workings of the criminal courts by the end of 2000. His terms of reference include a review of the practices, procedures and application of the rules of evidence in the criminal courts, so as to ensure that justice is delivered fairly. This is to be achieved by streamlining all processes, increasing efficiency and strengthening the effectiveness of relationships with outside agencies, taking into account the interests of those who use the courts, including victims and witnesses, so as to promote public confidence in the rule of law. Some of the matters which Auld LJ wishes to gauge opinion on are:

- the structure and organisation of the courts and distribution of work;

- composition of and use of juries and lay/stipendiary magistrates;

- case management, procedure, evidence and use of IT;

- service to and treatment of all users, attenders and offenders;

- liaison between the courts and criminal justice agencies, including victim support schemes; and

- management and funding.

CRIMINAL PROCEEDINGS

The investigation of offences

- Police and Criminal Evidence Act 1984 and Codes of Practice.

- *Walters v WH Smith* (1914); *R v Self* (1992); *Christie v Leachinsky* (1947); *Abassy v MPC* (1990); *Lewis v Tims* (1952); *R v Hudson* (1980); and *R v Mason* (1987).

- Limits on the admissibility of evidence: Prosecution of Offences Act 1985; *R v Smurthwaite, R v Gill* (1994).

Bail

- Right to bail under the Bail Act 1976, as amended by the Criminal Justice and Public Order Act 1994 and the Crime and Disorder Act 1998.

- *Caballero v UK* (2000) and s 56 of the 1998 Act.

The trial process

The magistrates' court

- The magistrates try cases summarily and act as examining justices for offences which may be committed to the Crown Court.

- The differences between indictable offences, offences triable either way and summary offences; procedure in determining the mode of trial for triable either way offences.

- The provisions of the Magistrates' Court (Advance Information) Rules 1985; provisions concerning criminal damage.

- The procedure for committal proceedings; modified procedure for committal proceedings under Pt V of the Criminal Procedure and Investigations Act 1996.

- Summary trial procedure; the provisions for pleading guilty by post.

Trials in the Crown Court

- Procedure, including the arraignment of the defendant, calling of the jury and the order of presentation of prosecution and defence and summing up by the judge.

- Appeals – s 2(1) of the Criminal Appeal Act 1995, amending the powers of the Court of Appeal.

- Other powers of the Court of Appeal:
  - s 36 of the Criminal Justice Act 1972;
  - ss 35, 36 and 133 of the Criminal Justice Act 1988;
  - s 1 of the Administration of Justice Act 1960.

Youth court

- Sections 68 and 70 of the Criminal Justice Act 1991.
- Section 24(1) of the Magistrates' Courts Act 1980.

Reform of the criminal justice system

- The background to the Runciman Royal Commission on Criminal Justice 1993; the distinction between miscarriages of justice arising from defects in the investigative process and failures of due process (*R v Whybrow and Saunders* (1994)).

- Proposals for reform and criticisms of the present system.

- The threat to the fundamental principle of the presumption of innocence.

- Recommendations of the Royal Commission on Criminal Justice; reactions to the proposals – the Criminal Justice and Public Order Act 1994; Police and Magistrates' Courts Act 1994; Criminal Appeal Act 1995; and Criminal Procedure and Investigations Act 1996 give effect to some of the recommendations. One of the most controversial provisions has been ss 34–37 of the Criminal Justice and Public Order Act 1994, removing the suspect's right to silence during police questioning and at trial.

- The McPherson Report in 1999 on the death of Stephen Lawrence.

- The appointment of Auld LJ to conduct a Criminal Courts Review in 2000.

CHAPTER 9

LEGAL LIABILITY

Introduction

Here, we will consider the concept of legal liability as compared with moral responsibility. The concepts of personality, status and capacity will also be considered, together with limitations on capacity due to age, mental state and the liability of corporations. Liability in criminal law and in the tort of negligence, together with the sanctions and remedies in criminal and civil law, will be mentioned. Other concepts such as strict and vicarious liability will be noted. We will start by considering the distinction between legal and moral responsibility.

Legal and moral responsibility

In this chapter, we are concerned with situations where the law imposes a responsibility on a person (either natural persons or, on the other hand, artificial or juristic persons, that is, corporations, such as a borough council, a bishop acting in his official capacity, a public limited company (plc) or a public corporation). In some cases the law imposes a liability on groups of persons, such as partnerships or associations, where loss, damage or injury is caused to another person or group.

It is useful to remind ourselves of the classification of law into civil and criminal – both can impose liability on persons, in different ways. The civil law, mainly the law of contract and tort, seeks to compensate a wronged person and put him or her back into the position he or she would have been in, if the contract had been performed, or the tort had not been committed. We talk of the claimant suing the defendant in damages (although other remedies may be available, as we shall see later, such as an injunction, an order of the court demanding that something is done, or not done). In criminal law we talk of an offence against society having been committed and the defendant or accused being prosecuted by an official body, usually the Crown Prosecution Service (CPS). The victim or his or her family may be called as witnesses at the trial, but will not usually receive compensation and are not at the centre of the investigation of the offence or the decision whether or not to prosecute. The main purpose of criminal proceedings is to establish the guilt of an accused person for conduct which is socially unacceptable. If he or she is found guilty, a penalty may be imposed, such as imprisonment or a fine or a community order. We must remember that the courts in which civil claims are heard and those in which criminal trials take place are usually different: the terminology is different, together with the process and purposes. In civil claims, the claimant need only prove his case on the balance of probabilities and increasingly, where the criminal law fails the victim of crime, he may attempt to seek compensation through the civil courts where a recognised tort has been committed.

Alternatively, the victim of crime may attempt to bring a private prosecution, although no State legal aid will be available and the Attorney General may exercise his power to stay the prosecution. The Stephen Lawrence case illustrates graphically the position of a victim of crime or that of his family where the victim has died. On failure of the police to investigate this racially motivated attack which resulted in the death of the victim, his parents initiated a private prosecution which failed for lack of evidence. In so far as those defendants were concerned, their acquittal means that the double jeopardy rule will prevent any future prosecution of them on the same charge. This would not prevent the victim's family seeking redress in the civil courts, either against the perpetrators of the attack or the police in the tort of negligence for their failure to investigate.

Thus, in some instances, conduct can be both a civil wrong and a criminal offence. In a case some time ago, a man was accused of rape, but was acquitted – the jury, having listened to the evidence, did not consider that the prosecution had proved its case beyond all reasonable doubt. Later, the victim of the alleged rape sued the defendant in the county court and recovered £50,000 in compensation, the court being satisfied that, on the balance of probabilities, battery had been committed. It was not necessary for the claimant (or, as she was called then, the plaintiff) to prove the elements of the offence of rape, but instead that the defendant had injured her.

In 1994, Sharon Allen made legal history when she issued a writ (what would now be referred to as a Statement of Claim, following the Woolf reforms of civil procedure), against George Heron, after he had been acquitted of the murder of her daughter, Nikki, alleging that he had killed her. The double jeopardy rule does not apply as between criminal offences and civil claims, and so the mother could seek compensation against Heron for the loss of her daughter.

It is also important to stress here that we are concerned only with legal responsibility, not moral responsibility. A person may, according to their own moral code, consider they have done wrong or a moral or religious code may state that certain conduct is reprehensible. Only where the rules of morality and religion converge with legal rules will a legal liability be imposed. Viscount Simonds in *R v Charles* (1976) said:

> Again it is right, we think, to shun the temptation which sometimes presses on
> the mind of the judiciary to suppose that because a particular course of conduct,

as was this course of conduct, was anti-social and undesirable, it can necessarily be fitted into some convenient criminal pigeon hole.

This statement also illustrates that the judiciary should be cautious in extending the boundaries of the criminal law, for to do so brings about a retrospective change in the law (on the date on which the offending conduct was done, it was lawful and only becomes unlawful when the court pronounces) and it can be argued that it should be for Parliament to decide whether conduct should be criminal or not.

Certainly, criminal law, of all areas of the law, demonstrates the overlap between morality and law, for example, killing of another person, stealing or robbing, the rape of another person, defrauding a person of money and so on. However, not all acts or omissions which might be considered wrong will be classed as criminal. This will be even less true of the civil law, which has developed by way of precedent in a piecemeal way rather than according to any 'grand scheme'. As we have seen in Chapter 6, the judge, in developing the law, may be willing to take into account prevailing attitudes so as to develop the law. The case of *R v R (A Husband)* (1992) is instructive. The House of Lords held that, despite several centuries where the law stated that a husband could not rape his wife, it was time for the law to reflect the changing values of society where marriage was seen as a partnership between a man and a woman rather than an arrangement in which the man treated the woman as his chattel. Rape was such a serious action that it was necessary for the criminal law to impose a sanction on those who perpetrated such an offence. It was not only the wife who was transgressed against: society should be able to show its distaste of such actions by criminalising them.

In other situations, the judge will decide not to develop the law to comply with current morality. He may state that it is the function of Parliament to act as the temperature gauge and, where change is desired, legislation should be passed. It will be risky for the judge to go on a crusade to ensure that the criminal law reflects morality. Two cases can be referred to to illustrate this. In *R v Gibson* (1991), a model's head displayed in a public gallery had earrings attached to it made from freeze-dried human foetuses and this was held to have amounted to the offence of outraging public decency. In the case of *Shaw v DPP* (1961) (the *Ladies' Directory* case), the court held that the offence of conspiring to corrupt public morals had been committed by the publishers of magazine advertisements for prostitutes.

In *R v Brown* (1993) the decision of the House of Lords by a 3:2 majority that consent is no defence to sado-masochistic acts conducted by adults in private was upheld by the European Court of Human Rights (ECHR). The judgments of the two dissenting judges, Lords Mustill and Slynn, suggest that paternalistic attitudes by the judges as to what is right and wrong are out of place. The courts have also drawn a firm line under attempts to extend the circumstances in which euthanasia does not amount to murder. The case of

Airedale NHS Trust v Bland (1993) recognised the conflict between the sanctity of life and the quality of life of a patient on a life support machine and the dilemma in keeping such a person alive, but decided that where there was no medical hope of recovery, treatment could cease, subject to the control of the court. Taking steps to end life was unacceptable and would amount to murder.

In other situations, the court recognises that a change in attitudes has taken place in society and that should be given effect to, as in *Fitzpatrick v Sterling Housing Association* (1999), where the court held that the homosexual partner of a deceased tenant could claim a statutory tenancy as a member of the deceased tenant's family.

The courts may recognise the existence of a moral rule or principle but find that the law does not offer a means of enforcing it. In *Taylor v Dickens and Another* (1997), T sued the executors of Mrs P's will, claiming to be entitled to the residuary estate not having been paid for work done between 1988 and 1995. In 1988, Mrs P told Mr T, who was her gardener, that she intended to leave him her house in her will and on being told this T stated that he would forgo any payment for doing her gardening or providing other help. Mrs P made several wills between 1991 and 1995, leaving her residuary estate to T. In 1995, Mrs P changed her will and left the residue to X. She did not tell T of her change of mind, confiding to friends that she was going to take the coward's way out, but he continued to do work for her ignorant of the changes made. The Chancery Division of the High Court held that, where a party made a promise which he or she later broke in circumstances which could be regarded as unconscionable, unfair or morally objectionable, the court could not offer any general remedy based on an equitable jurisdiction so as to interfere and enforce the promise that Mrs P had made to T.

This demonstrates that the law does not always reflect what morality would suggest ought to be done. Mrs P knew that she was going back on her promise to T and that he relied on that promise, but she chose not to confront him with her change of mind.

Until recently, those who were not parties to a contract could derive no benefits under a contract (and in turn could not incur burdens). By the Contracts (Rights of Third Parties) Act 1999, the common law privity of contract rule is reformed to permit a third party to enforce a term in a contract either where the contract expressly says so, or where it expressly identifies the party as having a benefit conferred on him and the contracting parties intend him to have such benefit.

The privity of contract rule was much criticised in failing to recognise the realities of modern life. One situation covered by this Act is where A buys a gift for D from V and it is defective. Under this Act it will be possible for D to return the item to the store, providing the terms of the Act are complied with, rather than under the common law rule, A having to seek a remedy as a contracting party.

A debate that is occurring now concerns the recovery of property confiscated by the Nazi regime in the Second World War by the rightful owners from those into whose hands the property has come. Morally, it can be argued that the true owner, or his successors, should be able to recover his property even from those who have subsequently innocently acquired it. The law may, however, recognise this as a general rule subject to exceptions. Furthermore, in this particular case, a very long time has elapsed.

In *Gotha City v Sotheby's and Another* (1998), it was held that the law favoured the true owner of property which had been stolen, no matter how long a time had elapsed since the theft. The case involved a painting which had been stolen and eventually found its way to Sotheby's, where it was to be sold. The true owners asserted their claim over it, some 50 years later, and the court held that the Limitation Act 1980 would not apply in favour of the thief or transferees who acquired the painting other than as a purchaser in good faith. Public policy demanded that the rights of the original owner should have priority.

It has been suggested on many occasions that all dishonest conduct should be criminalised, but the Law Commission has rejected this, asserting that such a course would go too far. It would have the effect of criminalising failures to pay a debt or going to a car boot sale, recognising that an item is valuable but not letting the seller know and buying it for only the small sum requested. The Law Commission prefers the idea of having specific criminal offences involving dishonest conduct which reflect the business arrangements that people enter into. This would then ensure that people can plan their future actions without fear that at a later stage a jury in a criminal trial might consider their actions to have been dishonest.

The drawback of this approach is that, given that everyone is presumed to know the law and that ignorance of the law is no defence to a criminal prosecution, where the law does not reflect morality and applies by way of specific offences, the person may be left in the difficult position of not being able to estimate from his own moral code the types of behaviour which are likely to be illegal. Clearly, it is an impossible task for everyone to know every single criminal offence in fine detail.

Personality, status and capacity

Only legal persons (whether human or artificial) can, on the one hand, incur legal liability by being in breach of duties owed to others and, on the other hand, impose liability on others. The equation that this gives rise to is the relationship that exists between A and B where A owes a duty to B; for example, A agrees to wash B's car for £5. He will be under an obligation to B to wash his car to a reasonable standard or to a higher standard, if agreed. In turn, B is under an obligation to pay A the £5 on completion, or at another time, as agreed. A has a right to expect that B washes his car to a reasonable or higher standard and B has a right to expect payment by A. Providing the conditions are present making this a binding contract in law, A can be made liable in the civil law of contract to B and vice versa. Liability as between persons can arise not only in contract, but also, the law of tort and in criminal law. Family relationships, the ownership and disposition of property, trusts and other areas of substantive law can result in liability.

We will consider personality, status and capacity in turn. The law defines personality to include humans and corporations. However, even here there are grey areas, such as when does human life begin and end? Some argue that life starts at conception and that abortion is the killing of a human person which should amount in law to murder. However, not everyone agrees with this, and the Abortion Act 1967 recognises circumstances where abortion is permitted by law. Euthanasia amounts to murder, although one is permitted to commit suicide. Aiding and abetting someone else to commit suicide remains illegal.

It might be thought that between these two extremes the legal position would be straightforward. However, instead of having simply a distinction between those who are minors with limited capacity and those of full age with full capacity, it is more complex that that. There are different ages at which one can do certain things, for example, buy alcohol (18), cigarettes (16), go into a public house but not buy alcohol (14), watch a PG film (5) at the cinema (or 15 or 18 for other films), marry with parental or judicial consent (16), without parental consent (18), be sent to prison (21) or be detained in a secure training unit (12), or in a young offenders' institution (15) or be put on probation, made subject to a curfew order or community service order (16). It is notable that s 34 of the Crime and Disorder Act 1998 imposes full criminal liability at 10 years of age and the age of consent to sexual intercourse is 16 (for homosexual intercourse it is 18 and likely to be reduced to 16 if proposals now before Parliament become law).

We have already noted that the concept of personality is important and that this starts at birth. The case of C v S (1987) is authority for the proposition that a child must be born alive if he is to acquire any rights under s 1 of the Congenital Disabilities (Civil Liability) Act 1976. An aborted foetus could have no such rights. However, in AG's Reference (No 3 of 1994) (1997), it was held that a person can be charged with the manslaughter of a child who, though born alive, dies some four months later, where the defendant had deliberately and unlawfully injured either the child whilst a foetus or the mother.

Even where personality exists, we have already seen that capacity may be limited for some purposes. A difficult area with which the courts have had to grapple is the child or young person who either refuses medical treatment or who wishes to undertake a course of action which is risky or unusual. The question will then be whether the subject has capacity to decide for himself. In one recent case, a 13 year old girl refused to have a heart operation and the

Family Division of the High Court ordered the operation to go ahead. Similarly, where a young person, or for that matter an adult, has impaired mental faculties, the court may order medical treatment to be undertaken. In another recent case, the Court of Appeal ruled that the sterilisation of a mentally handicapped 29 year old woman, whose mother feared that she might become pregnant, was not permitted. In the case of a subject wishing to undertake unusual treatment, the courts tend to err on the side of caution and refuse permission. The case of *Gillick v West Norfolk and Wisbech AHA* (1986) illustrates what has become the '*Gillick* competent' test, that is, on approaching 16, young people are to be treated as fully competent in deciding on matters affecting their future such as contraception, where they live, go to school, and so on. In this case, it was held that a local authority could prescribe contraceptive advice to girls aged under 16 without their parents' consent or knowledge.

As with legal personality, status is accorded by the law to persons. It is nothing to do, in this context, with a person's social standing or financial worth. Rather, it denotes the labels or categories into which a person fits and the types of things that a person is entitled to do in law. It does not mean that a person must do all these things, simply that he or she is permitted to do them. So, a human person may have the status of being a husband, a father, a son, an uncle, a victim support volunteer, a teacher, a first-aider at his workplace, a voter and may belong to the Samaritans. A corporation may have the status of being a plc, an employer and an owner of land. Alternatively, the corporation may be a private limited company, for example, a family run business which is not run as a partnership or a corporation sole, as with the official status of the Queen, a mayor or a borough council.

Status, then, decides the capacity that a person has in law, that is, the person's ability to do or not to do things. It may depend on age, sanity or, in the case of a natural person, whether he/she is intoxicated with alcohol or drugs. Artificial persons, such as Bromley Borough Council or Marks & Spencer plc, derive their capacity to do or not to do things, such as to employ people, own land, make contracts, sue or be sued, from the documents which establish them. A plc has two main documents, the Articles and the Memorandum of Association. The former sets out the relationship of the company with outsiders, such as lenders or contracting parties. The latter concerns the internal management of the company, including what it is permitted to do in law. The objects clause will contain the things the company is empowered to do, and if it acts in excess or abuse of those powers it can be found to have acted *ultra vires* (beyond its powers) and such actions will be void and of no legal effect. The objects clause is crucial in permitting a company to act, whether it is the ownership or disposition of land, its ability to make contracts, to buy and sell products and services, to borrow money or employ workers. Corporations, being artificial entities, will also have to be brought to an end in an official way. A legal process will be applied so as to terminate its existence. In the case of a trading company, it can be liquidated where, for example, it has become insolvent and is unable to meet its debts as and when they fall due.

Having mentioned personality, status and capacity, it is important to remember that these concepts not only demonstrate what one person is permitted to do or not to do. His or her relationship with others is important also. For example, a person cannot have the status and capacity of a mother without having given birth or adopted a child. A debate that is continuing at present concerning the relationship of parent and child is the extent to which a parent has a right to chastise his or her child. The Government has recently announced in response to a decision of the ECHR that smacking, as opposed to hitting around the head or with a slipper or other object, is acceptable.

Other relationships which emphasise the relationship between persons are teacher student, doctor patient, solicitor client, employer employee, and so on. In each relationship there is an element of reciprocity and dependence. Each gives rise to rights and duties which the law may enforce. In the context of employer employee and teacher student relationships, it has recently been acknowledged that it is no longer legally acceptable for employers or schools to insist that women or girls do not wear trousers. The Equal Opportunities Commission has supported claims by a woman employee and a girl pupil to be allowed free choice in what they wear, providing that both conform to reasonable standards of smartness. So wearing jeans is not considered of a sufficiently smart appearance.

In discussing legal liability it is important to remember that relying on the law should be a person's last resort. Not only is it costly and time consuming, and State assistance may be little or non-existent, but people often do not wish to go to the lengths of what the law will permit, they may be willing to compromise for the sake of ensuring that their relationships continue and that they remain amicable with others. If reliance is placed on the law, not only will a claimant have to show that the substantive law, such as the law of contract or tort or the criminal law, supports his claim, but also that he complies with rules of procedure and rules of evidence. Thus, he will have to use the right documents in the correct court within time limits prescribed in the Limitation Act 1980 and prove his case by eliciting admissible evidence in the form of documents or witnesses, for example. Recently, the Association of Mortgage Lenders have announced that they will in future not attempt to enforce the personal loans of mortgagees whose properties have been sold and which have not realised the full loan after six years. In law, they are entitled to do so for up to 12 years, but many former house owners have concluded that, once their properties have been repossessed and sold by their lender, that is the end of the matter. Morally, this might be so, but not in strict law, and so this announcement is an attempt to foster goodwill. It could presumably be withdrawn in the future unless a change in the law is made so that the Limitation Act 1980 would provide a six year limit for recovery of such debts, bringing it in line with unsecured debts.

Liability of children

So far as the criminal liability of children is concerned, s 34 of the Crime and Disorder Act 1998 provides that 'the rebuttable presumption of criminal law that a child aged 10 or over is incapable of committing an offence is hereby abolished'. The way in which this has been interpreted has been that a child of 10 or over (but under the age of 14 years) will not be able to plead that he or she should be acquitted because he or she did not know that what he or she did was seriously wrong.

However, in an article in the *New Law Journal* of 15 January 1999 (p 64), Nigel Walker asked whether this is correct. It could be argued that all that was abolished was the presumption, not the defence. It was for the prosecution to prove that the child knew the difference between right and wrong and that on the facts he or she knew that what he or she did was wrong. If this is the correct approach, a child aged 10 but under 14 years can still assert in their defence that he or she did not in fact know that what he or she did was seriously wrong. The burden of proving this will then fall on the defence.

In the article, reference is made to the Solicitor General being reported as saying this during the second reading of the Bill in December 1997. However, a circular distributed by the Home Office suggests otherwise, so that such children are to be treated in the same way as those aged 14 or over. The Solicitor General referred to a child with genuine learning difficulties 'and who is genuinely at sea on the question of right and wrong'. Surely such a child should be treated differently from one aged 14 or more, on the basis that not only do children develop at different rates, but a vast gap can exist between a child of 11 and one aged 15. Furthermore, given the censure from the ECHR on the trial process for those aged over 10 but under 18, this change in the law brings into serious doubt the policy aims to be achieved.

Nigel Walker suggests that it might be that the Solicitor General was mistaken in thinking that the defence and the presumption were separate. He refers to the 13th century jurist Bracton, the 1338 Year Book, Lambard writing in 1581, Hale in the 17th century, the Ingleby Committee in 1960, the Queen's Bench Divisional Court decision in *C (A Minor) v DPP* (1995) and the House of Lords, which overruled this in *C (A Minor) v DPP* (1995). None of the Law Lords saw the need to raise the question whether abolition of the presumption also abolished the defence. Walker comes to the conclusion, however, that the earlier authorities suggest that, in logic, it is sensible to have a presumption operating with a defence and so it seems that, although the presumption has been abolished, the defence would still be available, where appropriate.

At this point it is worthy of mention that, having reduced the age of criminal responsibility to 10, in the light of the ECHR ruling in *R v Secretary of State for the Home Department ex p Venables and Thompson* (1999) to the effect that children should not be tried in a formal open court, and when the Human

Rights Act 1998 comes into effect in late 2000, serious thought will have to be given as to the mode of trial for such defendants.

Minors have no special status so far as the law of tort is concerned, except that a very young child will be unable to formulate the necessary state of mind to be found to have committed a tort. In *Williams v Humphrey* (1975), a 15 year old pushed a person into a swimming pool and was held liable in both negligence and trespass to the person.

However, the courts have been reluctant to impose liability on what is described as 'the rough and tumble of life', so that in *Wilson v Pringle* (1987), intentionally rough handling by one 13 year old schoolboy of another's schoolbag being carried on his shoulder was held not to give rise to liability in the tort of battery. Minors cannot be made liable in tort if this would permit a contract on which the minor could not be held liable to be indirectly enforced. Authority for this is to be found in the case of *Leslie v Shiell* (1914).

Another issue concerns the liability of parents for the torts committed by their children. Generally, there is no rule imposing liability on a parent. Where, however, the parent would be accountable under some other rule, the claimant can look to the parent for a remedy. There are three instances where this will apply: first, under the doctrine of vicarious liability, the parent employs his or her child to carry out a job and it is done negligently; secondly, where the parent controls the child's actions; and finally, where the parent is personally negligent in failing to supervise the child properly. In *Donaldson v McNiven* (1952), the defendant allowed his 13 year old son to have an air rifle on condition that he did not use it outside the cellar of the house. Unknown to the defendant, the son fired it at some children outside and injured the five year old plaintiff. The defendant was held not liable, as he had taken reasonable precautions, and the son was usually obedient and so his disobedience could not be foreseen. This case can be contrasted with *Bebee v Sales* (1916), where a 15 year old boy injured another by firing at him with a shotgun. The father had allowed him to keep the gun despite knowing that his son had caused damage with it. The father was held liable for the injury to the other boy, as he had failed to exercise proper precautions. These cases were decided before the Firearms Act 1968 made the possession of guns by those under 14 a criminal offence and imposed criminal liability on parents for breach of statutory duty.

It is important also to remember that it is not only parents who may exercise care and control over a child. Schools must also act as a reasonable parent. This is graphically illustrated in the case of *Carmarthenshire CC v Lewis* (1955), where a four year old boy was left on his own by the teacher who was called away for 10 minutes to attend to another pupil. The boy ran out of the school premises, through an unlocked gate, down a lane and into a busy road. A lorry driver swerved to avoid him and was killed. His widow sued in negligence. It was held that the teacher had not been negligent, so vicarious liability did not apply, but the local authority had itself been negligent in failing to ensure that the child could not leave the school unattended.

A similar result was reached in *Barnes v Hampshire CC* (1969), where the local education authority was held liable when a road accident was caused when children were let out of school early before their parents or carers had arrived to collect them. In *Butt v Cambridgeshire CC* (1969), the plaintiff was a pupil, one of a class of 37 10 year olds, who lost an eye when a fellow pupil waved a pair of pointed scissors used to cut out shapes. The teacher was attending to another pupil at the time. It was held that neither the teacher nor the local authority had been negligent, as use of such scissors was an accepted practice and the teacher would not expect classroom activity to stop whilst she gave individual attention.

A child of any age can, in theory, sue or be sued, but it is usual for a parent or other responsible adult to instigate or defend a claim on behalf of a minor. Since the Woolf reforms, the guardian *ad litem* and next friend are described as litigation friends.

Section 1 of the Congenital Disabilities (Civil Liability) Act 1976 imposes liability where a child is born alive but disabled as the result of an intentional or negligent act or one arising out of the breach of statutory duty before the child's birth. The case of *C v S* (1987) is authority for the proposition that an aborted foetus derives no protection from this Act. The mother can only be made liable in negligence where she has been negligent in driving a motor vehicle when she knew or ought reasonably to have known she was pregnant. The father's liability is not limited and, in any event, in connection with driving the claim will be brought against the parent's insurer. The common law defences of *volenti* and contributory negligence (see below, pp 311–12) are available where the mother has consented or contributed to the injury. The common law rule in *Roe v Minister of Health* (1954), that health professionals cannot be made liable for treatment or advice given according to prevailing standards of care, applies to this section.

Increasingly, children may wish to initiate claims against their parents or carers. In *Surtees v Kingston-upon-Thames LBC* (1991), a child was scalded when her foster mother left her for a few moments and she turned on the hot tap to the washbasin. It was held that no negligence was proved: this was merely an instance of the hurly burly of life. In *Porter v Barking and Dagenham LBC* (1990), a 14 year old schoolboy was injured when he and a friend were left unsupervised to practise shotput. The claim in negligence against the school failed, it being said that the standard of care imposed on schools should not stifle initiative.

Corporate liability

Another grey area is the extent to which a corporation can be made criminally liable for murder. It is possible that a corporation can commit manslaughter, but there is currently a debate whether the criminal law should extend so far as to impose liability on a corporation for the intentional taking of another's life. This debate has emerged following disasters such as the sinking of *The Herald of Free Enterprise* off Zeebrugge, the King's Cross fire, the Southall and Paddington train crashes, the sinking of *The Marchioness* pleasure boat on the Thames and the Dorset canoe tragedy. It was established at the coroner's inquest into the Zeebrugge disaster (*R v P & O European Ferries (Dover) Ltd* (1991)) that a corporation could be made liable for manslaughter, and this was confirmed in *R v OLL Ltd*, which was the first conviction for manslaughter in December 1994 (the Dorset canoe case). The latter involved a small company owned and controlled by one man, and so it was far easier to find 'the controlling mind'. P & O is a large company, and the negligence was more the result of many failures within the organisation rather than something attributable to a person in charge.

In *AG's Reference (No 2 of 1999)* (2000), the Court of Appeal held on a reference under s 36 of the Criminal Justice Act 1972 that on a charge of manslaughter by gross negligence, a non-human defendant, such as a corporation, could not be convicted in the absence of evidence establishing the guilt of an identified human individual for the same crime.

In strict liability offences, liability can be imposed on a corporation on the basis of vicarious liability; those doing an act will be employed by the company. Statutory provisions may impose liability specifically on a corporation, otherwise mens rea will have to be established by way of 'the brains of the company' or 'the company's controlling mind' concepts. Those who act as the brains in the name of the company will be deemed to be the company. *Tesco Supermarkets v Nattrass* (1972) demonstrates that the workers in a company, such as those who work on the checkout in a supermarket, are in no way the controlling mind; rather, this applies to the directors or possibly only the managing director.

In civil law, liability is imposed by way of an award of punitive damages, so as to make an example of a company defendant.

The Law Commission, in its *Report on the Offence of Corporate Manslaughter*, No 237, recommended that corporate killing should result in criminal liability where a management failure (this would be a question for the jury) causes (or is one of the causes of) the victim's death and that failure constitutes conduct falling far below what can reasonably be expected of the corporation in the circumstances. Some commentators have suggested that this is too vague and will, in any event, only result in a fine which a trading company would either pass on to its customers in higher prices or to employees in longer working hours or pay reductions. In May 2000, the Home Secretary announced his intention to put before Parliament a Bill to change the law, permitting unlimited fines and remedial orders to be imposed on corporations found guilty of a new offence of corporate killing.

Vicarious liability

This concept can apply in both criminal law and the law of tort, but more usually in the latter. A distinction is drawn between an employee who works for an employer under a contract of service and an independent contractor who is employed under a contract for services. An example of the latter would be where A employs B to paint A's house and it is left to B's skill and judgment as to how he tackles the job. B will also usually supply the tools and materials and may well have employees or subcontractors working for him to complete the job.

Where a contract of service exists, the employer can be made liable for the actions of the employee done in the course of the employment. No vicarious liability attaches to the actions of an independent contractor, although in some cases the employer may owe a personal duty to the claimant or a duty to ensure that care is taken. This was the case in *Rylands v Fletcher* (1868), where an independent contractor was employed to carry out work and through negligence flooded the mines of the adjoining landowner. The defendant employer was held strictly liable for the escape of this water.

Superficially, the distinction between a contract of service and one for services is straightforward, but in practice this has detained the courts in complex discussion over many years. Several tests have been devised by the courts in an attempt to categorise a worker as an employee or as an independent contractor. Denning LJ, in *Stevenson, Jordan and Harrison v MacDonald Evans* (1952), preferred an integration test over the previously used control test. In applying a control test, the courts attempted to assess the degree of control an employer exerted over the worker, whereas with the integration test all the circumstances were to be taken into account. In recent years, the courts have adopted economic tests, again looking at all the circumstances, but taking into account the economic realities of the contractual relationship. It will be important for the parties to know the category into which a worker fits for the purposes of taxation and payment of national insurance contributions. The Inland Revenue has recently attempted to ensure that construction workers register as employees so as to prevent loss of revenue by making employers responsible for deducting income tax and national insurance contributions at source.

Where a contract of service exists, the employer will be responsible for the actions of the employee done in the course of employment. This includes the negligent, and even the fraudulent, performance of his duties. Where an act is not within the course of employment, for example, where a delivery man goes 50 miles outside his route to meet a friend, this is referred to as being 'on a frolic of his own'. A slight deviation of route or acting in an emergency will not amount to a frolic.

Other entities

Other problems exist as to whether other entities should have rights and thereby expect protection in law so that where injury, loss or damage is caused, liability should be imposed. An interesting suggestion has been made that man's nearest relative in the animal kingdom, the chimpanzee, should have rights accorded to it. If this results, then legal liability would be owed to chimps so as not to break those rights.

Similarly, the environment as an entity in its own right and distinct from the rights of persons who own parts of the environment, should have rights and in turn be owed duties enforceable in law. In these cases, a person would have to be appointed as guardians or custodians to ensure that such rights were enforced. This in itself should not present an insuperable problem, given that the law often recognises the appointment of a person as guardian, for example, the Court of Protection, trustees and executors, trustees in bankruptcy, litigation friends and so on.

Liability in criminal law

Criminal offences usually have two elements, the *actus reus* (the guilty act) and the *mens rea* (the guilty mind). For a person to be liable for a criminal offence it is necessary not only that he does an act (or in some cases, fails to act) but that he has acted deliberately, recklessly or, in some cases, negligently. We will mention later that there are a small number of offences where no *mens rea* need be proved by the prosecution. These are called strict liability offences which have been created by statute and where liability results from an act in the absence of a mental element.

In our discussion of criminal liability, we will confine our attention to the situation where one person is alleged to have committed a crime. It is worth noting in passing, however, that this may not always be the case. Two or more people may agree to commit a crime (to conspire to commit a crime) or to have others commit a crime. A person may encourage another to commit a crime (incite him to commit a crime), or a crime in its preliminary stages (as we will see in *R v White* (1910)) may not be completed, either because it is interrupted or the police or others act to prevent it, which gives rise to the separate offence of attempting to commit the main offence. Some examples include attempting to commit murder, incitement to blackmail and conspiracy to steal. These are called inchoate offences, and provide a useful additional means of penalising those who enter into criminal activities.

In considering the elements of a crime it is not only traditional but also logical to consider the *actus reus* first, so as to establish whether or not an act has been done. Having established that, the question of whether the defendant's mental state coincides with the *actus reus* can be decided. If it does, he will then be liable for his action, unless he can show a good defence, such as insanity or intoxication.

Actus reus

This usually refers to an act, or in some cases it refers to an omission or failure to act. For example, a duty to act may be imposed by statute or by contract. In other cases, a person may voluntarily assume a duty, or in others a special relationship may exist, such as between a parent and child. At common law there is no general liability for omissions. The case of *R v Miller* (1983) demonstrates that liability may attach to a person who creates a dangerous situation and then fails to act to avert damage. A squatter lit a cigarette and fell asleep. The house caught fire and damage was caused. The defendant was found guilty of arson on the basis that the *actus reus* was his original act of dropping the cigarette. It may not always be easy to distinguish an act and an omission. Difficulties may arise with silence and also in cases of medical treatment, as was shown in *Airedale NHS Trust v Bland* (1993), where to turn off a life support machine could be said to be an act, whereas failing to replace a drip would amount to an omission.

The act must be voluntary and conscious. The defendant must be shown to have his mental faculties in control of his bodily functions if he is to be said to have done an act voluntarily. The defences of insanity and automatism will be considered later, but for now it is useful to note that the former concerns factors internal to the defendant and which in law are treated as a disease of the mind, whereas the latter concerns external factors, such as a tree falling on the defendant's head which knocks him out and prevents him from being aware of his actions or conduct. The case of *Broome v Perkins* (1987) is authority for the proposition that a defendant who is able to control his bodily movements cannot be said to be acting involuntarily or as a result of automatism. So far as the defendant is concerned, these defences work better for him in negativing liability than if they are applied to the *mens rea*. This is so because a defendant who has been reckless in putting himself in the dangerous or risky position could be held liable for his act.

The term *actus reus* is shorthand for several concepts, including an act (or omission), a course of conduct, a consequence or a set of circumstances. Thus, in some offences, it is not only the act which may be in question and with which the *mens rea* must coincide, but also the circumstances surrounding the act and/or the consequences of the act. Take, for example, the offence of murder – this is the intentional killing of a human being – and this consequence must be shown to have been caused by the defendant intending to kill the victim or the intention of causing him really serious harm. If that result does not follow, for example, if the victim recovers from being shot or stabbed, an offence under the Offences Against the Person Act 1861 may have been committed instead. We shall consider some of these later.

In the offence of rape, no consequence need follow the illegal act, but the circumstances surrounding the offence are important. It will be sufficient if a man has sexual intercourse with a person who at the time does not consent and at that time he knows that the victim does not consent or is reckless as to whether he or she consents to it. An act of sexual intercourse which is consented to cannot amount to rape.

In the offence of possessing illegal drugs in s 5 of the Misuse of Drugs Act 1971, the *actus reus* is the proscribed set of circumstances of possession. No act or consequences of an act are required.

Thus, it is traditional to classify crimes into those involving actions: for example, wounding, crimes involving consequences, such as murder, and situational crimes such as possession of illegal drugs. There are few situational crimes, as the defendant will not be able easily to avoid liability. An example is to be found in *R v Larsonneur* (1933), where the defendant was deported from Ireland and brought into the UK by the police contrary to the Aliens Act 1920. In *Winzar v Kent Chief Constable* (1983), the defendant was convicted for 'being found drunk on the highway' after he was ejected from a hospital for being drunk.

We mentioned above the need to establish causation. A useful illustration is *R v White* (1910), where a son put cyanide in his mother's tea with the intention of killing her. Before she was able to drink the tea, she died from a heart attack. This broke the chain of causation between the defendant's act and his mother's death and so the defendant could not be found guilty of murder. This is called the 'but for' test. Only if the victim would not have died but for the defendant's act will the defendant be guilty. It is useful to note here that the son was found guilty of attempted murder, as he had formed an intention to kill his mother and had gone some way to accomplishing his aim.

Mens rea

Except in strict liability offences, the prosecution must prove that the defendant acted intentionally, recklessly or was negligent. We will consider each of these in turn, noting that to make a person criminally liable it is usually necessary to show that he has acted deliberately or at least took an unjustifiable risk.

Intention

This must not be confused with a person's motive for doing an act. It does not affect the imposition of criminal liability, although it may be relevant in reducing the sentence. A person who steals food to feed his family or the daughter who tampers with the life support machine on which her terminally ill mother exists so as to allow the mother to die may act from the highest moral standards, but nevertheless the first intends to commit theft and the second, murder, or at the very least manslaughter. Motives concern the reasons for doing an action, and the defence of duress may allow a defendant who has acted under threat to life or limb to escape liability, as was shown in *R v Steane* (1947), where the defendant broadcast propaganda in wartime to save his wife and children who were still in enemy hands.

It is what the defendant intended when he committed the alleged offence that the trial court is concerned to establish. If the defendant desires or wants the consequences of his act, regardless of how likely or unlikely they are, he is said to have a direct intention. Where A shoots at B, wishing or hoping to kill him, this is direct intention. However, in some situations, a defendant does not desire a particular result, but if the court finds that that result is a virtual certainty, and the defendant realises this but continues to act, he can still be said to act intentionally. In this case, it is an oblique intention. Where A shoots at B wishing to kill him and is aware that B is standing near a valuable painting, A may have no desire to damage the painting, but he realises that the chances of so doing are high; he will have an oblique intent to damage the painting and a direct intent in respect of B. This concept has seen much judicial discussion in the offence of murder. For example, D hits his child very hard when the child fails to stop crying. D does not wish to hurt his child, but the court has to apply a standard to decide whether D should be liable for the consequences of his action.

From 1960 to 1998, both the Court of Appeal and the House of Lords have attempted to ensure that trial judges do not misdirect juries in having to decide on guilt or innocence of defendants charged with murder, but who plead that they had no desire to cause the consequences of their acts. To a large extent, the law appears to have been settled by the House of Lords in the case of *R v Woollin* (1998), where Lord Steyn gave the leading judgment and the other Law Lords, Lord Nolan, Lord Browne-Wilkinson, Lord Hoffman and Lord Hope of Craighead agreed. The Court of Appeal certified a point of law of general public importance under s 1(2) of the Administration of Justice Act 1960 and the House of Lords allowed the appeal, quashing the conviction for murder and substituting a conviction for manslaughter. The case was remitted to the Court of Appeal to pass sentence.

D lost his temper and threw his three month old son on to a hard surface; the boy suffered a fractured skull and died. D was charged with murder but he denied any intention to cause his son serious injury. It was not alleged by the Crown that D desired to kill his son or to cause him serious injury. The issue of oblique intention was in question. The trial judge had applied the case of *R v Nedrick* (1986), where the test was one of virtual certainty. The trial judge then added his own words and talked of a substantial risk of serious harm. The defendant appealed against conviction on the basis that the trial judge had enlarged the mental element for murder. The House of Lords held that the reference to substantial risk was wrong, as it blurred the distinction between intention and recklessness. As a result, the conviction for murder was unsafe and, as already noted, this was quashed and a verdict of manslaughter was substituted.

Lord Steyn outlined the how the debate over oblique intention had been dealt with by the courts from 1960 to 1998.

In *DPP v Smith* (1960), the defendant killed a police officer by driving off with him clinging to the car in order to avoid arrest. The House of Lords held that the defendant was guilty of murder because (a) death or serious injury was foreseen by the defendant as a 'likely' result of his act; and (b) he was deemed to have foreseen the risk that a reasonable person in his position would have foreseen. This was reversed by s 8 of the Criminal Justice Act 1967, as (b) was grossly unfair, although the case should be considered in its historical context and that it involved a police officer acting in the execution of his duty. However, the court should only concern itself with the subjective question of what was going on in the defendant's mind at the time of the alleged offence, not what is imputed to him.

In *Hyam v DPP* (1974), the House of Lords again considered oblique intent where the defendant burnt down V's house, killing the children inside. Three different standards were given in the 3:2 majority decision: (a) the consequences of the defendant's act had to be highly probable; (b) it was sufficient if the consequence was probable; and (c) it was sufficient if the defendant had realised there was a serious risk. Needless to say, at this stage the law was seen to be in chaos.

R v Moloney was heard in 1985, and this attempted to narrow the broad approach used in *Hyam*. Lord Bridge stated in his judgment that, in order to establish the necessary intent, the probability of the consequences taken to have been foreseen 'must be little short of overwhelming'. He referred to this as a moral certainty. The House of Lords adopted a narrower test, similar to 'virtual certainty' in *R v Nedrick* (1996) This was formulated in two parts: (a) was death or serious injury a natural consequence of the defendant's voluntary act; and (b) did the defendant foresee that consequence as being a natural consequence of his act? If the answer to both questions was in the affirmative, the jury could infer an intention by the defendant to cause that consequence.

This equated with a high probability, but difficulties were still experienced with how best to direct a jury trying a case of oblique intention in murder, as the *Moloney* guidelines made no reference to probability. The House of Lords found them to be defective in *R v Hancock and Shankland* (1986). This involved two striking miners who pushed a concrete block from a bridge onto the highway, hitting a taxi in which a miner was being taken to work. The taxi driver was killed and the defendants were charged with his murder and convicted. Lord Scarman said that the greater the probability of a consequence, the more likely it is that consequence was foreseen and if foreseen the greater the probability is that that consequence was also intended. The decision is for the jury considering all the evidence. Guidelines should only be used sparingly. He did not disagree with the 'little short of overwhelming' test, nor with the model directions by Lord Lane LCJ in the Court of Appeal, where he referred to 'highly likely' consequences. It was recognised that jurors could ask probing questions of the judge, and it was crucial for answers on the degree of risk or probability of death or serious injury to assist the jury in its task.

The uncertainties continued and, in 1986, *R v Nedrick* was heard. This involved similar facts to *Hyam*, where the defendant poured paraffin through the letter box of a house and set it alight. A child inside was killed. Lord Lane CJ's observations in this case were quoted by Lord Steyn in *R v Woollin* (1998) and he said their effect was that a result foreseen as virtually certain is an intended result. He rejected claims by the prosecution that this conflicted with s 8 of the Criminal Justice Act 1967 and with statements in *Hancock and Shankland* (1986), and pointed to academic writers who suggested that it was correct.

Lord Steyn indicated that a model direction should be given in cases of oblique intent in murder and the jury should be directed 'that they are not entitled to find the necessary intention unless they feel sure that death or substantial harm was a virtual certainty (barring some unforeseen intervention) as a result of the defendant's actions and that the defendant appreciated that such was the case'.

Before leaving the question of intention and moving on to recklessness, it is worth mentioning two other forms of intent.

Specific intent

Specific intent is where an offence requires a particular intention; for example, in murder, an intention to kill or cause serious harm, or in theft, an intention to permanently deprive the owner of his property. Other examples include causing grievous bodily harm with intent in s 18 of the Offences Against the Person Act 1861 and burglary with intent to steal. The defence of intoxication may prevent the specific intent from operating, whereas an offence of general intent would not be negatived. Lord Simon, in *DPP v Majewski* (1977) concerning s 47 of the 1861 Act, is authority for this. Other basic intent crimes include involuntary manslaughter, rape, wounding or inflicting grievous bodily harm under s 20 of the 1861 Act, criminal damage and common assault. There is, however, no clear cut way of distinguishing specific and basic intent crimes, other than looking at the *mens rea* for each and every one.

Ulterior intent

Ulterior intent some offences require an additional intent. Most of these are found in the Offences Against the Person Act 1861, for example, s 18 – causing grievous bodily harm with intent. Section 9 of the Theft Act 1968 provides another example, burglary with intent to steal, cause grievous bodily harm, rape or cause damage.

Recklessness

This concept needs particular care, as its legal definition is not the same as its everyday meaning of taking unjustified risks. It is important to note that in criminal law a distinction is drawn between (a) a subjective test involving what the defendant thought at the time of the alleged offence, or perhaps more correctly, the view of the magistrates or jury as to what they believe he was thinking; and (b) an objective test involving what the reasonable man in the defendant's position would have thought (or the magistrates' or jury's view of what the reasonable man in the defendant's shoes would have thought). The first is harder to prove, and we shall see later that the second test is more often used in offences involving property.

Two cases apply these tests to recklessness. To subjective recklessness, in *R v Cunningham* (1957), the defendant broke a gas meter to steal money, the gas seeped into the neighbouring house where a person was sleeping and she became very ill. The defendant was charged under s 23 of the Offences Against the Person Act 1861 with 'maliciously administering a noxious thing so as to endanger life'. It was held that 'maliciously' equated with intentionally or recklessly, and the latter was to be assessed by means of a subjective test. A defendant would have to foresee that the kind of harm might occur but he would continue with his act. This depends on the foresight of the defendant. To objective recklessness, in *MPC v Caldwell* (1982) C, a former hotel worker, held a grudge against the owner and started a fire in the hotel. He was charged with arson under the Criminal Damage Act 1971. The *mens rea* required was intention or recklessness. Lord Diplock stated that the *Cunningham* subjective test was too narrow for this Act and said that there were two limbs, the first based on *Cunningham* and the second a wider objective test.

Paraphrasing Lord Diplock's words, the tests are these: a person is reckless as to whether any property would be destroyed or damaged (this will vary according to the offence in question) if: he does an act which in fact creates an obvious risk that property would be destroyed or damaged and when he does the act he either (a) has recognised some risk and goes ahead; or (b) has not given any thought to the possibility of there being any such risk but goes ahead. The first part is similar to the *Cunningham* subjective test and the second is based on the reasonable man who would have seen this obvious risk.

Several matters need to be considered. In *R v Reid* (1990), the court cautioned against referring to Lord Diplock's tests as objective recklessness, given that the first limb is subjective and the second is objective in part. The court will have to assess what the defendant's state of mind is, as he must be shown not to have thought about the risk he was taking. In *R v Lawrence* (1982), the test was reformulated as an 'obvious and serious' risk and the court cautioned that it has to be adapted for each offence to which it is applied. In *Elliot v C (A Minor)* (1983), the court stated that proof of an obvious risk applied only to the second limb, and use of the reasonable man standard was a very harsh one.

Caldwell creates a lacuna or loophole, that is, it fails to cover the particular situation where the defendant believes that no risk exists. This is illustrated in the case of *Chief Constable of Avon and Somerset Constabulary v Shimmen* (1986), where the defendant broke a shop window when showing off how close he could get to it without breaking it. He asserted that he was an expert in martial arts and was convinced he would avoid breaking the window. He was not believed and was taken to have known of some risk within the first limb. This lacuna was recognised in *R v Reid* (1990), where the court stressed that it could only apply to genuine and honest mistakes which are not considered to be reckless.

Given that the tests may have to be adapted for particular offences, it might be expected that the courts were clear as to which offences were covered by *Cunningham* and which by *Caldwell*. However, no such certainty exists. Generally, *Cunningham* applies in non-fatal offences against the person where the word 'maliciously' appears, and in the offences of rape and indecent assault. *Cunningham* applies in property offences such as criminal damage.

Lord Mackay, who gave the leading judgment in the House of Lords in *R v Adomako* (1994), stated that *Caldwell* recklessness did not apply in manslaughter. This has since been endorsed in the cases of *R v Watts* (1998) and *R v Khan and Khan* (1998). The result of this is that a defendant can be made liable for gross negligence manslaughter and this could, as we shall see when we consider the offence of manslaughter, make a loophole defendant liable in manslaughter, but not for offences requiring 'maliciousness' or 'recklessness'. Most commentators prefer a subjective test, and *Caldwell* blurs the line between recklessness and negligence. In the criminal law, it may be undesirable to hold a defendant liable on the basis that the reasonable man would have acted differently, as this is an arbitrary standard. Clause 118 of the Draft Criminal Code supports this.

We will now move on to consider negligence as a type of *mens rea*. This concept is most often found in the civil law of torts, either in relation to the tort of negligence, which we will see later involves the breach of a duty of care owed by the defendant to the claimant who, as a result of the breach, suffers loss, damage or injury. Other situations in the civil law involving negligence will be where a person performs a contractual service carelessly or a tort, such as nuisance, is committed as the result of the defendant's carelessness. This concept depends on an objective standard below which the defendant falls, the standard being that of the reasonable man. In civil law, the reasonable man finds himself in the shoes of the defendant, so there is a subjective element, but in the criminal law this does not apply. The case of *McCrone v Riding* (1938) illustrates how harsh this can be where a learner driver was expected to reach the standard of the reasonably experienced driver. Naturally, those who support the safety of others on the road suggest that imposing such a standard is justified. Alternatively, the law may impose strict liability on the defendant, and he may be permitted to use in his defence an 'all due diligence' defence in recognition that here, liability is strict but not absolute.

Given the basic tenet of criminal liability of imposing responsibility on those who are culpable, this is unfair in the extreme, and not much used in the common law. However, some statutes impose criminal liability for negligence, for example, s 3 of the Road Traffic Act 1988 imposes liability for driving without due care and attention. As we have already mentioned, the House of Lords in *R v Adomako* (1994) recognised the offence of gross negligence manslaughter, of which we will say more later. For the moment, it is worth mentioning that, even here, some subjective factors will be taken into account in what must amount to a very high degree of carelessness.

Having considered the need for the presence of an *actus reus* and *mens rea*, it is useful to remind ourselves that an offence may comprise more than one *actus reus* and this will be specified in the statutory provision. For each part, a different *mens rea* may be required, but in respect of the *mens rea* for a particular *actus reus* each must coincide. Two cases illustrate the difficulties that can arise and the ingenuity of the judiciary in overcoming the difficulties. In *Fagan v MPC* (1969), the defendant drove over a police officer's foot and at that time had no *mens rea*. He was told to get off the officer's foot, but the defendant told the police officer to wait. At that time, he had *mens rea* but was omitting to do an act (that is, move the car), not acting, and so no criminal offence occurred. However, the court held that driving onto the officer's foot and then not moving was one single continuous act and it was sufficient if the defendant had *mens rea* at some time during the continuous act.

In *Thabo Meli v R* (1954), the defendants attempted to kill V and, thinking they had succeeded, dumped his body over a cliff. In fact, V only died later from the fall and exposure to the elements, and the question for the Privy Council was whether the *mens rea* and *actus reus* coincided. It was held that here there was 'one transaction' and as the defendants had *mens rea* at the start this was sufficient to found liability.

Strict liability offences

The common law recognises very few offences of strict liability, for example, public nuisance and criminal libel. The case of *Lemon and Whitehouse v Gay News* (1979) established that the offence of blasphemy was a strict liability offence, so that the editor and publisher of *Gay News* were guilty of the offence when they published a poem suggesting that Jesus Christ was a homosexual. It was not necessary to prove a *mens rea*, merely the act of publication. Several hundred statutory strict liability offences exist, mainly in areas regulating public safety, consumer protection, pollution, the possession of drugs, the licensing of liquor and minor road traffic offences.

It is not always clear from the words of a statute whether Parliament intends an offence to be one of strict liability. The courts, in interpreting a provision, start with the presumption that in the absence of clear words *mens rea* is required, for it is not the function of the law to punish those who are not blameworthy. Authority for this is to be found in *Sweet v Parsley* (1970), where the landlord of a house was convicted of 'being concerned in the management of premises used for the purpose of smoking cannabis resin' contrary to s 5 of the Dangerous Drugs Act 1965 when the police found cannabis at the house, which had been let to students. The conviction was quashed on the basis that the words of the statute were not clear as to the requirement for *mens rea*. Conviction for such an offence as this would carry a stigma, and should require a *mens rea*.

However, where the words are clear and there is a need for strict standards, the courts will impose strict liability. This can be seen in the case of *Alphacell v Woodward* (1972), where the company defendant was charged with causing polluting matter to enter a river. This is a strict liability offence, and the company was liable when a defect in one of its pumps, of which the company was unaware, led to an overflow of water into the river. Thus, the company was under a strict duty to ensure that its operation functioned properly and if it did not, even where the defendant has not been negligent, the company was liable.

Another example is *Harrow LBC v Shah and Another* (1999), where it was held that selling a National Lottery ticket to a person under 16 was contrary to s 13 of the National Lottery Act 1993. The prosecution only needed to prove that the ticket was sold to a person who was under 16 at the time. The defendant did not need to be aware of the buyer's age.

Strict liability offences must not be confused with absolute offences. In the latter, no defences will be available to absolve the defendant of liability. In the former, both at common law and by statute, defences are available, for example, as acts of a third party such as a trespasser, Act of God, such as extreme flooding or other natural disaster beyond the ordinary bounds of nature, or where the defendant has not done any positive act.

It is useful to consider some of the arguments for and against imposing strict liability offences. This usually applies to 'administrative offences' involving safety or business operations, possession of drugs and the use of machinery. There may be a social policy or utility in not having to prove a mental element. Such offences are more easily proved and enforced and there may be a deterrent value. However, the arguments include: that it is unfair to impose criminal liability on those who are not at fault; the question of fault is delayed until the sentencing stage; it raises business costs, particularly those of small businesses; and there is little evidence that it raises standards.

On the whole, the argument seems to go against imposing strict liability and, as was said in *Thomas* (1976), the normal process of law should be used in all criminal offences to determine at the outset the nature of the fault or blameworthy conduct which is to be prohibited. This is in the interests of fairness, to enable a person an opportunity to take care in his actions.

Homicide

It is beyond the scope of our discussion to cover each criminal offence, but having explained the elements required in proving that an offence has been committed it is useful to explore more fully the homicide offences, in particular murder and manslaughter. Homicide does not simply refer to killing a person; rather, it refers to killing which cannot be justified or excused, for example, capital punishment where permitted by the law, or killing another in self-defence, or committing suicide. It must be noted that, although, as a result of the Suicide Act 1961, it is no longer an offence to take one's own life, it is not permitted to aid or abet another in his suicide. Murder and manslaughter are the two types of unjustifiable killing, but there are others, including infanticide by the mother, child destruction and the procuring of a miscarriage. Murder is a common law offence, defined originally by Coke CJ.

The *actus reus* of both murder and manslaughter is the killing of a human being. The victim must have been born and must be alive at the time of the offence. A person on a life support machine whose brain stem is dead is, for the purposes of the law, dead, so that intervention by others will not give rise to liability. The defendant must be of 'sound memory', not able to plead incapacity due to insanity, diminished responsibility or being under the age of criminal responsibility. There must be proved to be a causal link between the act of the defendant and the death of the victim. The 'but for' test applies, the prosecution must show that but for the defendant's act, death would not have resulted as and when it did. Where the law imposes a duty to act, a failure to do so which causes the death of another can result in liability. Interventions by third parties, natural events or the victim himself may break the chain of causation, but this will be a question of fact for the jury.

It used to be that the victim had to die within a year and a day, but this rule was abolished by the Law Reform (Year and a Day Rule) Act 1996, which provides that the consent of the Attorney General is required to bring a prosecution in fatal offences where the alleged injury which caused death was sustained more than three years before the death resulted, or the defendant has previously been convicted of a lesser offence involving the same circumstances. This was an essential rule before improvements in medical science and the use of life support machines, as it ensured that a defendant was not made liable for a death caused in some other way apart from his act or omission. However, with improvements in medicine, a defendant could escape liability if his victim died outside the 366 day limit, having undergone treatment which failed to save him. It is important that some safeguards are provided, and the consent of the Attorney General ensures that prosecutions long after the event will only proceed where justified.

The *mens rea* of murder is the intentional killing of a person or the intention to inflict grievous (very serious) bodily harm. This is often referred to as malice aforethought. Intention can either be a desire to kill or cause serious injury, or an oblique intention giving rise to a virtual certainty of such result.

The *mens rea* of manslaughter varies according to whether it is voluntary or involuntary manslaughter. In the former, the voluntary and intended killing would otherwise amount to murder, but is excused either on the grounds of diminished responsibility or provocation and the defendant is convicted of the lesser offence of manslaughter. In the latter, a lesser *mens rea* than intention is present, either constructive manslaughter, where the defendant kills by way of an unlawful and obviously dangerous act, such as an assault or criminal damage, or gross criminal negligence manslaughter. In *R v Adomako* (1994) it was said that this type of manslaughter occurred where the defendant was in breach of a duty and this caused death, providing the jury considered that a criminal conviction was justified. As already noted, this may cover the *Caldwell* loophole in cases where the defendant makes a mistake as to the risk of injury.

Much controversy has been expressed in recent years over the defences of diminished responsibility under s 2 of the Homicide Act 1957 and provocation under s 3 of the same Act, in particular regarding the availability of provocation to battered wives. In s 2, the jury are asked to decide two questions: did the defendant have an abnormality of mind? and did it substantially impair his mental responsibility? Diminished responsibility may be relied on in place of insanity (given the artificial definition of this defence and the fact that, if it is successful, the defendant will find himself placed in a mental hospital), in mercy killings by relatives (the judges and others have, for many years, criticised the mandatory life sentence for murder which applies to the whole spectrum of murder from the mercy killer to the armed robber), those who have been thwarted in marriage or family relationships where passions run high, and those with severe mental conditions giving rise to anxiety or failure to be able to control will power. In *R v Ahluwalia* (1993), a battered wife relied on the defence of provocation, but this was refused as she had planned the death of her husband following many years of abuse. She was, however, able to rely on the defence of diminished responsibility.

Provocation in s 3 is not only a specific defence in murder, but may be used in mitigation of a sentence in any offence. *R v Duffy* (1949) is authority for the rule that this is available only where there 'is a sudden and temporary loss of self-control'. If an attack has been planned with the aim of achieving revenge, the defence of provocation will not be available. Important factors in finding provocation will be the elapse of time between the words or actions which provoked the defendant, his particular sensitivities and the nature of the provocation and the circumstances surrounding it. Where a wife suddenly snaps after a severe beating, where the husband had applied domestic violence over many years causing the wife to stab him, the defence is available as in *R v Thornton* (1996). The reactions of the defendant are judged on an objective standard, that of the reasonable man standing in the shoes of the defendant. The very harsh common law standard in *Bedder v DPP* (1954) has been disapproved of in *Camplin* (1978) and *R v Morhall* (1995). In *Bedder*, the defendant, an impotent 18 year old, was taunted by a prostitute with whom he had unsuccessfully tried to have sexual intercourse. He stabbed her and she died. His defence of provocation was rejected, the jury having been directed by the judge, that the standard they were to apply was that of the reasonable man, not taking into account any of the particular characteristics of the defendant. In *Camplin*, the age and sex of the defendant were relevant, as were other characteristics of the defendant which would affect the gravity of the provocation to him. In *Morhall*, addiction to glue sniffing was relevant. It is a question for the jury as to whether the reasonable man would have reacted and, if he would, whether he would have done so in the way the defendant did. In *R v Smith* (1998), the Court of Appeal applied the objective test, relying on *Camplin* and *Ahluwalia*, with the result that the defendant's severe depression could be taken into account.

General defences

The defences of duress, necessity, consent, mistake and self-defence may allow the defendant to escape liability. Some offences are worded in such a way as to provide that, in the absence of a factor, such as consent, no offence is committed. An example is rape, where the defendant can only be proved liable if his victim was not consenting.

Other offences are worded with no such proviso as part of the *actus reus*, but where a general defence may be pleaded regardless of the wording of an offence, it has become traditional to consider whether an offence has been committed and then ask whether any defences are available.

Duress

This is merely an excuse, unlike the defence of necessity, which is a justification. The prosecution must prove that the defendant was not acting under duress, that is, an immediate threat of death or bodily injury to himself or members of his family. An objective test is applied as in *R v Bowen* (1996): was the threat of such gravity that it might well have caused a reasonable man in the same position as the defendant to act as he did? and would a sober person of reasonable firmness, sharing the defendant's characteristics, have responded to the threats as he had done? A defendant who voluntarily puts himself in this position will not be able to make use of the defence, and it is not available in murder (*Howe* (1987) and *Gotts* (1992)). There has been some debate as to whether it should be available in murder and the Law Commission in 1977 recommended that it should. No legislative change has resulted.

Necessity

This mainly operates at common law, although statutes may recognise this as a defence. The famous case of *Dudley v Stephens* (1884) suggests that such a defence might be available other than to murder. The case of *Dr Bourne* in 1939 is more encouraging; see also the cases of *Gillick v West Norfolk and Wisbech AHA* (1986) and *F v West Berkshire HA* (1990), where a 36 year old mentally handicapped woman was ordered to be sterilised for her own safety.

Consent

The absence of consent is an element of the crime in rape and so the defendant does not have to prove that the victim consented. Section 1(2) of the Sexual Offences Act 1976 provides that an unreasonable belief in the victim's consent, if genuinely held, will result in the acquittal of the defendant. This will be a question for the jury, and very often juries conclude that the defendant was not genuine in holding an unreasonable belief and convict.

Other examples where consent may be a defence include, theft, assault and criminal damage. In the cases of *Jones* (1986) and *Aitken* (1992), involving s 20 of the Offences Against the Person Act 1861, a genuine belief, whether or not reasonably held, that consent had been given where there was no intention to commit injury was a defence. Jones involved rough play, but *Aitken* involved RAF officers who poured white spirit over a colleague whilst he was asleep and drunk dressed in a flying suit. He sustained 35% burns when they set him alight. They mistakenly believed he had consented, and this was a question for the jury.

In *R v Brown* (1993), the majority of the House of Lords held that, for offences under ss 20 and 47 of the 1861 Act, consent was not available where sado-masochistic practices were entered into in private between adults. Those in the minority, Lords Slynn and Mustill, considered that consent should have been available. This decision was upheld by the ECHR. In *R v Wilson* (1996), a husband branded his initials on his wife's buttocks with a hot knife at her request. His conviction under s 47 was quashed by the Court of Appeal, who held that in marital relationships it was for the parties to decide on what was acceptable behaviour.

Mistake

The defendant may be mistaken as to a fact or one of the surrounding circumstances where this is an ingredient of the offence. The case of *DPP v Morgan* (1976) is a good illustration. Here, a husband encouraged his RAF colleagues to have sex with his wife, telling them that she might protest but to take no notice as this heightened her experience. She did not consent, but the colleagues were able to rely on their honest belief that she had consented. Their belief in her consent did not need to be reasonable.

Self-defence at common law or prevention of crime under s 3 of the Criminal Law Act 1967

The common law recognised this defence, but note the case of *Dadson* (1850), where D shot and wounded V, a poacher. The court held that the degree of force used was permissible if D had known that V was a poacher. In fact D did not know this. D's conviction was upheld on the basis that, where D seeks to rely on an excuse or a justification, he must have known or believed in those circumstances.

Two recent instances demonstrate the limitations that apply to this defence. In the case of Tony Martin, the Norfolk farmer convicted of the murder of a 16 year old burglar, the amount of force used was held to be excessive. The 'all or nothing' effect of this defence results in either acquittal or a finding of guilty to murder. It is suggested that reform is timely, permitting a finding of guilty to manslaughter. In the other case heard at Peterborough Crown Court in May 2000, a home owner and his lodger were held to have used reasonable force in striking a burglar with a metal baseball bat, causing him to sustain broken bones and a cracked skull. In sentencing the burglar, the judge made no allowance for the injuries suffered.

Incapacity

We have already considered the criminal liability of corporations and children. Here, we will consider insanity, automatism and intoxication by alcohol or drugs.

Insanity

Somewhat surprisingly, this is a legal, not a medical concept. It was defined in *R v M'Naghten* (1843) and has become known as the M'Naghten Rules, that is, 'a defect of reason arising from a disease of the mind, as not to know the nature and quality of the act he was doing; or if he did know it, that he did not know he was doing what was wrong'.

In classifying insanity, this is an internal lack of autonomy, whereas automatism and intoxication are due to external factors. Strictly, insanity is not a defence, as it is the status of being insane which prevents guilt arising. Policy suggests that such a person, as with young children, is in need of protection from themselves or others who may exploit their weakness. It does not mean that the consequences of their actions go without penalty: the insane person found not guilty of murder by reason of insanity will be confined indefinitely to a mental hospital. This is provided for in the Criminal Procedure (Insanity and Unfitness to Plead) Act 1991. This Act also gives the court a variety of detention powers in cases other than murder where the defendant has been found to be insane.

A defendant can only be insane where he does not know that what he did was legally wrong. This raises some serious questions. For example, surely this ought to apply where he knows that his act is morally wrong, and what about the defendant who thinks that his act is morally wrong but does not know it is legally wrong? In *R v Windle* (1952), the defendant was convicted of murdering his suicidal wife whom he thought it was right to kill. Killing is objectively wrong according to law, and so the subjective view of W had no bearing on guilt.

Where a defendant pleads insanity, he must on a civil burden prove he is insane. In murder, he can use insanity as a defence and, when the death penalty was in place, this served as a means of sparing the life of the insane defendant. However, now that the death penalty has been removed (and since the Crime and Disorder Act 1998), for all offences reliance on insanity is to be avoided in favour of, say, diminished responsibility.

The question of what a disease of the mind is is a legal question and, in *R v Sullivan* (1984), the House of Lords held that a minor epileptic fit which caused a temporary suspension of the mental faculties of reason, memory and understanding, during which time an offence was committed, permitted a special verdict of not guilty by way of insanity. In *Burgess* (1991), sleepwalking was included and, in *Kemp* (1957), hardening of the arteries. Curiously, this has a physical origin, but is an internal factor to the defendant. External diseases are not included, and the questions posed over diabetes have caused difficulties.

Where there is shown to be hyperglycaemia (high blood sugar), for example, where the defendant fails to take insulin to treat his condition, this is treated as a disease of the mind and the defence of insanity is available (*Hennessy* (1989)), but not the defence of automatism. Where there is low blood sugar (hypoglycaemia), for example, because insulin has been taken but without food, this is not a disease of the mind (*Quick* (1973)), but the defence of automatism will be available. We will see later that the courts have been reluctant to accept automatism as a defence except in exceptional circumstances.

In *Clarke* (1972), the defendant suffered from mild depression and was absent minded. He was accused of shoplifting when he placed items from the basket straight into his bag before leaving the shop. He pleaded guilty rather than rely on the defence of insanity and the Court of Appeal quashed his conviction, as this was not a case of insanity and he should not have been forced to choose between this and a guilty plea. The Butler Committee Report in 1975 and the Draft Criminal Code, cll 35 and 36, state that this defence should be based on medical factors.

Automatism

This is not available as a defence if caused by insanity or intoxication. It must be caused by a factor external to the defendant. Examples given in *Hill v Baxter* (1958) included stroke, epileptic fits, a blow from a stone and attack by a swarm of bees. These are cases of *novus actus interveniens* (a new intervening act). In *AG's Reference (No 2 of 1992)* (1993), monotonous motorway driving leading to 'driving without awareness' did not amount to automatism.

It is often asked whether this defence negates the *actus reus* or the *mens rea* of an offence. It is better for the defendant to have it negate the *actus* (*Broome v Perkins* (1987)), as the *actus* must be voluntary if it is to give rise to liability. If it affects *mens rea*, then should a diabetic driver be able to use this defence?

Legal history has been made in *R v Padmore* (1999). Padmore is the first accused killer believed to have been cleared of murder whilst suffering from a severe attack of diabetes. This was reported in the national press on 17 December 1999 and it is the first time that such a case has been known to the legal or medical professions. Padmore flew into an uncontrollable rage and stabbed to death his landlord and housemate with a kitchen knife after entering a hypoglycaemic state of automatism. The case foundered when the prosecution offered no evidence at the Old Bailey, having accepted that Padmore's condition, of which he was unaware and unable to control at the time, took over. In other words, his mind was not in control of his bodily movements. This lack of mental control might suggest that the court considered Padmore to be unable to form *mens rea*. However, the preferred conclusion is that automatism affects the *actus reus*. In the absence of an act, no crime can be committed.

Intoxication

This can be as the result of taking alcohol or drugs. In specific intent crimes, for example, murder, intoxication acts as a defence, but where the crime is committed with a basic intent, for example manslaughter, this will not provide a defence, unless it is involuntary and the defendant lacks *mens rea*. The leading authority is *DPP v Majewski* (1977), and this gives rise to some surprising results. Thus, intoxication is a defence to a charge of murder and will have the effect of reducing the charge to one of manslaughter. However, where a specific intent crime has no lesser offence, a successful defence of intoxication will result in the defendant being acquitted. this also applies to attempted offences. Intoxication is not a defence to a charge of rape, but it is for attempted rape. The proverbial saying of 'taking Dutch courage' removes the defence and authority for this is found in *AG for Northern Ireland v Gallagher* (1963). *MPC v Caldwell* (1982) raised interesting questions about recklessness and gross negligence in getting drunk where the basic intent crime of arson was in question.

Where the defendant can show that he was intoxicated as the result of taking prescribed drugs, he will have a defence, as this is an instance of involuntary intoxication. The case of *R v Hardie* (1984) provides an illustration. Here, the defendant took some valium which had been prescribed for his partner, as he was upset when she told him she wished to end their relationship. He set fire to a bedroom and was prosecuted for damaging property under s 1 of the Criminal Damage Act 1971. The Court of Appeal allowed his appeal, finding that he had not been reckless in taking this drug, which usually only has a soporific effect.

A common occurrence is lacing another's drink. Under s 5 of the Road Traffic Act 1988, strict liability is imposed and the person whose drink has been laced is not excused. Authority for this is to be found in *AG's Reference (No 1 of 1975)* (1975). This also applies to crimes requiring recklessness or intent.

So far as mistakes are concerned, where the subjective rule for mistake clashes with the objective rules for intoxication, the latter take priority. In *Woods* (1982), self-induced intoxication was no defence to allegations of recklessness concerning the victim's consent in rape. In *O'Grady* (1987), the defendant was not entitled to rely on a mistake of fact created as the result of self-induced intoxication. Two friends slept in a large bed, both were drunk, the defendant woke when the victim hit him, he hit back and on waking in the morning found the victim dead. The defendant was convicted of manslaughter.

Section 5(2)(a) of the Criminal Damage Act 1971 requires only an honest belief. In *Jaggard v Dickinson* (1981), the defendant, who was drunk, planned to stay with X, but by mistake went to V's house and, finding it locked, broke a window to get in. The defence was available (cf s 6(5) of the Public Order Act 1986 regarding the offences in ss 1–5).

The Law Commission's Draft Criminal Code would abolish the present law and replace it with liability based on recklessness. In its 1993 Consultation Paper No 127, the Law Commission preferred to abolish the rule in *DPP v Majewski (1977)* and/or introduce a new offence of criminal intoxication. However, in 1995, in its Final Report, the Law Commission suggested leaving *Majewski* in place.

Crimes against the person not causing death

In this section, we will consider five offences where the victim is injured in some way by the defendant, without death resulting. This is a complex area involving the Offences Against the Person Act 1861, which has been the subject of much criticism and many proposals for reform. The statute was drafted in an age where phenomena such as stalking and telephone harassment were unknown and when domestic violence was not, as it is today, so socially unacceptable, but unfortunately prevalent and yet unreported to the authorities. The Protection from Harassment Act 1997 has gone some way towards alleviating this problem with its power for a restraining order to be imposed on stalkers.

The offences we will consider are (starting with the least serious):

- assault – s 39 of the Criminal Justice Act 1988 replacing s 42 of the 1861 Act, a summary offence with a maximum sentence of six months' imprisonment or a fine;

- battery – s 39, replacing s 42 of the 1861 Act, a summary offence with a maximum sentence of six months' imprisonment or a fine;

- assault occasioning actual bodily harm – s 47 of the 1861 Act, a triable either way offence with a maximum sentence of five years' imprisonment;

- inflicting grievous bodily harm or wounding – s 20 of the 1861 Act: 'whosoever shall unlawfully and maliciously wound or inflict any grievous bodily harm upon any other person either with or without any weapon or instrument ...'; this is a triable either way offence with a maximum sentence of five years' imprisonment;

- causing grievous bodily harm with intent or wounding – s 18 of the 1861 Act: '.... whosoever shall unlawfully and maliciously by any means whatsoever wound or cause any grievous bodily harm to any person, with intent to so some grievous bodily harm to any person, or with intent to resist or prevent the lawful apprehension or detainer of any person ...' This offence is triable only on indictment with a maximum sentence of life imprisonment.

The reader will quickly see that the language is archaic and it can be difficult to decide which offence should be prosecuted for. The CPS may decide as a tactical move to pursue a lesser offence so as to ensure success; the reader's job will be to assess any facts given in a problem question and apply the law to reach a conclusion. A methodical approach looking at the facts in the light of each offence will ease this task. Given that the assault and the battery offences in s 39 are separate (if both are present, each must be charged separately, *DPP v Taylor* (1992)), but may anticipate s 47, it is easier to start with s 39 and work through each section in turn. It is worth noting that s 20 is more serious than s 47, and yet both have a maximum of five years' imprisonment. Furthermore, the difference in penalties between ss 20 and 18 seems disproportionate, given that the amount of harm in s 18 may not be that much greater than in s 20, but remember that s 18 involves a *mens rea* for murder, and simply because the act does not result in death, the defendant will escape a charge of murder with a fixed penalty of life imprisonment.

Taking assault, the *actus reus* can be words or actions which put the victim in fear of unlawful force. The common law developed the definition of both assault and battery and usually they go together – the assault is the being put in fear by threats, and the battery is the execution of the threats. Words on their own can amount to assault, as is shown in *R v Constanza* (1997). This case involved stalking, which is now covered by the Protection from Harassment Act 1997. A threat to kill amounts to an assault, but strictly, a threat to kill someone in the future is not, although the courts have taken a liberal approach to this at times.

Words can also negate the threat, so in *Tuberville v Savage* (1669) a man who put his hand on his sword to threaten force, saying that, if it were not assize time, he would use the sword against V, was not committing an assault.

The *mens rea* is an intention to cause the victim to fear the infliction of immediate and unlawful force or recklessness (*Cunningham* subjective recklessness) of the risk of creating such fear. In *R v Ireland and Burstow* (1996), silent telephone calls amounted to assault. In *Smith v Chief Superintendent of Woking Police Station* (1983), the victim was at home at night in her ground floor bedsit when she was terrified to see the defendant through the window watching her. He was found guilty of assault. Although V was locked in, the court found that there was a sufficient immediacy of fear of the infliction of harm and V anticipated some immediate violence.

Battery can be the direct or indirect application of force. An example of the latter is *Fagan v MPC* (1969), and force can be punching, touching, spitting and possibly it needs to be hostile, although Lord Goff in *F v West Berkshire HA* (1990) said this was not required. The *mens rea* is an intention to apply unlawful force or recklessness as to whether such force will be applied. This, again, is on a subjective standard.

When considering s 47, although the section only refers to an assault, the courts have interpreted this to refer also to battery, so, having established an assault or battery, the prosecution may decide to use s 47 instead of s 39, providing the assault or battery causes hurt or injury which is aimed at interfering with the health or comfort of the victim. This was explained in *R v Miller* (1954), and includes nervous conditions. The *mens rea* is either an intention to cause an assault or battery or subjective recklessness as to whether either of these results. In *R v Roberts* (1978) and *Savage and Parmenter* (1991), it was held to be sufficient that the intention or recklessness related to the assault or battery – no additional *mens rea* was required regarding the actual bodily harm caused.

Wounding is covered by s 20 or s 18 and refers to a break in the skin, even if only with a pin. *C v Eisenhower* (1984), which involved a ruptured blood vessel behind the victim's eye, was not enough. The *mens rea* in the former is an intention that the act causes some physical harm or recklessness as to whether that act causes some harm. In the latter, despite the use of the word 'maliciously', only an intention to wound will be sufficient.

Both ss 20 and 18 refer to really serious harm, although s 20 talks of 'inflicting' and s 18 talks of 'causing'. In *R v Ireland and Burstow* (1997), these were said not to be synonymous, but in practice both refer to the need for causation. This case seems to get over the difficulty highlighted in *R v Clarence*

(1888) as to whether 'inflict' refers only to direct actions as opposed to indirect ones. The defendant made repeated silent telephone calls at night to his female victims and this amounted to inflicting grievous bodily harm under s 20. The court held that 'inflicting' covered not only physical harm, but also psychiatric harm, and either could be done directly or indirectly.

In *R v Clarence* (1888), it was held that a husband could not inflict grievous bodily harm on his wife by knowingly exposing her to the risk of contracting venereal disease through intercourse. She had not feared the infliction of harm at the time, as she had consented to sexual intercourse. Compare this with the case of *R v Martin* (1881), where the defendant turned off theatre lights during a performance and in the ensuing panic members of the audience were injured. The court had no doubt that he had inflicted really serious harm on his victims. Causing may be wider than inflicting, for example, a defendant who puts another in danger and fails to warn the victim might be said to cause harm, but he does not inflict it on the victim.

Really serious harm is grievous bodily harm, and this includes a broken nose, bruising, lacerations, concussion and broken bones, as noted in *R v Brown and Stratton* (1998). This also includes really serious psychiatric injury. In s 20, the *mens rea* of serious harm is intent or recklessness whereas in s 18, only intention will do. So far as avoiding arrest is concerned, it is necessary for the prosecution to show not only an intent or subjective recklessness to avoid arrest, but also an intent or recklessness to cause harm or as to whether harm is caused.

Lord Mustill, in *R v Mandair* (1994), was also very critical of the 1861 Act, suggesting that its replacement was long overdue with legislation 'soundly based in logic and expressed in language which everyone can understand'.

Given the complexities of these provisions, the Law Commission, in its *Report on Offences Against the Person*, 1993, No 218, suggested reform so as to ensure clarity and brevity; offences based on the harm intended or contemplated by the defendant, not the harm that in fact resulted, and with clear distinctions between serious and less serious cases expressed in modern and comprehensible language.

The Law Commission would create three new offences:

- the intentional causing of serious injury bearing a maximum life sentence;

- the reckless causing of serious injury bearing a maximum penalty of five years' imprisonment;

- the intentional or reckless causing of injury bearing a maximum of 3 years' imprisonment.

In 1998, the Home Office prepared a draft Offences Against the Person Bill, attempting to bring into effect many of the recommendations of the Law

Commission. Notably, it would be an offence under this Bill intentionally to infect someone with AIDS, but it would not be an offence to do so recklessly.

Liability in the law of tort – introduction

In this section, we will be looking at the tort of negligence and how it protects a person against harm, personal injury or damage to their property caused by another who breaks a duty of care owed to the claimant and as a result causes damage. Today, this is perhaps the most used tort, but there are others which protect particular interests and which have been in existence much longer. These include nuisance, trespass, defamation and the strict liability tort regulating escapes of potentially dangerous things from the land owned or occupied by the defendant on to land occupied by the claimant. This was recognised in the case of *Rylands v Fletcher* (1868), where the plaintiff's mine was flooded by water accumulated on the defendant's land, and in recent years has not been further developed by the courts. In *Cambridge Water Co v Eastern Counties Leather plc* (1994), the House of Lords was not willing to extend the scope of this tort, saying that legislation had been passed to cover polluting incidents and there was no room for extending the common law in this specialised area, where solvents used in the tanning process had seeped into a watercourse nearby.

It is important to realise that only where a recognised tort exists will the claimant be able to seek a remedy for harm suffered. In the case of *Bradford Corp v Pickles* (1895), the defendant maliciously stopped up a stream and prevented water getting to a neighbour lower down. At that time this was a lawful action, and simply because it was done from poor motive did not entitle the claimant to a remedy.

The other torts mentioned protect various types of interest. Defamation protects a claimant against verbal or written untruths which affect his reputation in the 'minds of right thinking members of society'. Libel is an untruth in a permanent form, such as a newspaper or television broadcast, whereas a slander is a temporary form, such as a face to face conversation.

Trespass can take three forms: to the person, in the form of assault or battery; to land, where a person walks across another's garden without permission; and trespass to goods, where one person takes or touches another's personal property without permission. Here, an intention is required, but trespass is a tort actionable *per se*, without the need to prove that any damage has been caused to the person or property of the claimant.

Nuisance recognises that the owner or occupier of land has an interest in its use or enjoyment free from ongoing interference from noise, smoke, fumes or noxious substances. Unlike trespass, which is a direct interference, this is an indirect interference over a period of time. Damages may be awarded where the defendant is shown to have committed a nuisance, but the more usual remedy will be an injunction ordering discontinuance of the offending activity.

It is useful to note that we talk about the law of tort, and then promptly explain that a number of torts exist, and for a claimant to be successful he will have to ensure he brings his claim in the tort recognised in law as protecting the interest that has been injured. There is no one connecting principle between these torts, but they are types of civil wrong where the rights or interests of the claimant have been adversely affected and, usually, where no contractual liability exists to assist the claimant. The rule that where a contract existed, negligent performance only gave rise to an action in breach of contract, no longer applies. The injured party may choose which course of action to take.

An interesting development that is likely to take place will be as a result of the Human Rights Act 1998, due to come into effect in England in October 2000. Article 6 of the European Convention on Human Rights gives the citizen a right to a fair trial; it refers to access to justice, and this is taken to mean that the courts will have to ensure that new torts are created where the common law fails at present to recognise 'Convention rights' as torts, otherwise, the courts, as public authorities under s 6 of the Act, will be acting incompatibly with the Convention. By ss 7 and 8 of the Act, an individual can enforce Convention rights against public authorities by suing in damages. A notable interest that the common law has not protected by way of tort is a right of privacy. It is likely that this will receive early attention when the Act comes into force, although a delicate balance will be needed to give effect to this and at the same time preserve the possibly conflicting interest in freedom of expression. Another area that may be changed in the light of these provisions is the public policy limitations placed on extending the scope of the duty of care in the tort of negligence. Such limitations may be found to restrict unfairly an injured party in recovering damages. The case of *Osman v Ferguson* (1993), heard in the ECHR (*Osman v UK* (1999)), provides an interesting insight into how English law may have to change. A teacher at a school attended by P2 developed an obsession for him and, following a petrol bombing of the family home, investigated by the police, the teacher shot and wounded P2 and shot and killed his father. The plaintiffs, P2 and his mother, P1, sued the police in negligence in failing to protect them. The Court of Appeal held that no claim could be brought on policy grounds: following *Hill v Chief Constable of West Yorkshire Police* (1989), no duty of care in law was owed. We shall see later in this chapter that a public service immunity applies to prevent claims being brought against the police in exercising their powers. The ECHR found in favour of the plaintiffs under Art 6, which provides a right to a fair and public trial in which the full facts of a case should be heard. We will consider this and other cases in Chapter 10.

The tort of negligence

The modern law of the tort of negligence is founded on Lord Atkin's neighbour principle in *Donoghue v Stephenson* (1932). This is not to say that before that time no successful claims had been brought in negligence, but those that had succeeded tended to be only in defined categories, such as between landlord and tenant. No general principle linked the decisions which would permit the law to extend to new categories through application of principle. In *Donoghue*, Mrs Donoghue went to a café with a friend. The friend bought Mrs Donoghue a drink of ginger beer which was poured into a glass from an opaque bottle with a stopper. The friend made a contract for the supply of the drink with the café proprietor, who had made a contract with a supplier, who in turn had made a contract with the manufacturer. Mrs Donoghue consumed part of the drink, but, on pouring out the remainder, out slipped the decomposed remains of a snail and Mrs Donoghue became very ill with gastroenteritis. As she had made a contract with no one, and her friend, who had, had suffered no injury, Mrs Donoghue sought to make the manufacturer directly liable in negligence (the bottle was opaque and firmly stoppered, so could not have been tampered with after leaving the factory). This was a novel claim. It was held purely on the question of law as to whether a manufacturer could be made liable to the ultimate consumer with whom neither he, nor those in the chain of supply, had made a contract, that a claim could lie.

Lord Atkin attempted to find a general principle. He said this:

> The rule that you are to love your neighbour becomes in law: 'You must not injure your neighbour', and the lawyer's question: 'Who is my neighbour?' receives a restricted reply. You must take reasonable care to avoid acts or omissions which you can reasonably foresee would be likely to injure your neighbour. Who then, in law, is my neighbour? The answer seems to be persons who are so closely and directly affected by my act that I ought reasonably to have them in contemplation as being so affected when I am directing my mind to the acts or omissions which are called in question.

Thus, negligence was founded on a duty of care and this arose where there was reasonable foreseeability of harm. In the intervening years, it has been for later courts to fashion the development of this tort and, of all the torts, it is the one that has been applied to a vast range of situations, from supply of goods and services, to professional advice, to medical and educational services and the use of property. A relationship will have to be recognised in law as giving rise to a duty of care, some examples are doctor patient, occupier of land visitor, solicitor client and teacher pupil. In a recent High Court case, the widow of a driver was able to establish that a duty of care was owed to her husband by his driving 'buddy' while they were driving together. However, the defendant was shown to have discharged his duty of care, and so was not in breach.

The courts at different times have attempted to narrow its scope, talking of 'floodgates', and at other times have extended its scope, in the interests of justice, so as to find a remedy for an injured claimant. We will talk of liability for accidents in its everyday meaning of situations where there is some fault, whereas in law it refers to a situation where there is no fault (a pure accident).

In addition to the need to establish in law a duty of care, the claimant will also have to prove a breach of this duty by the defendant. This is also a question of law, and the standard applied is an artificial one, that of the reasonable man or, more correctly today, reasonable person, in the position of that defendant. Another component of the tort also has to be proved, and that is damage, loss or injury flowing from the breach of duty. This is the question of remoteness and falls into two parts: the question of causation – the claimant must show that the defendant caused the injury; and reasonable foreseeability of harm – not every occurrence arising out of the defendant's act or omission will automatically be recoverable for. We will now consider each of these in turn.

Duty of care

The case of *Caparo Industries v Dickman* (1990) marked a turning point in the attitude of the courts in deciding whether a duty of care should be found to exist in law in new situations. Before that time, it had generally depended on reasonable foreseeability of harm, subject to the proviso that the courts should work on an incremental approach, developing new categories of duty by way of analogy with existing ones.

In *Caparo*, three concepts were needed to found a duty of care:

* foreseeability of harm;

* proximity or neighbourhood – the parties should have a close relationship; and

* that it be just and reasonable for the claimant to be owed a duty of care by the defendant.

Before considering the facts and the decision in *Caparo*, and its effect on the development of the law by the Court of Appeal and the House of Lords, we will consider the concept of foreseeability.

The case of *Bourhill v Young* (1942), the 'pregnant fishwife' case, illustrates that a general duty type situation may exist, but no actual duty in the circumstances. The fishwife was on a tram when a motorcyclist was killed nearby, but out of her line of sight. She suffered a miscarriage from the shock of hearing the accident. This could potentially have given rise to a duty of care in the road users, but in the circumstances the motorcyclist would not have had the plaintiff (as then described) in contemplation. Her injury was not foreseeable and she was not sufficiently proximate.

The courts have in some cases been faced with the question as to what type of harm should be foreseeable and which type of claimant should be successful.

In *Haley v LEB* (1964), the London Electricity Board was held liable to a blind man who fell into a hole in the road dug by the Board which a sighted person would have been able to avoid. Defendants are presumed to be aware that people with disabilities or, as it is sometimes described, 'eggshell skulls', may be harmed by a defendant's actions. Where serious situations arise, it is also to be expected that people will do acts of bravery, such as attempt to rescue those who are trapped or injured. *Chadwick v BRB* (1967) is a good example of a rescuer at a train crash being held to be in the contemplation of the railway company so as to be owed a duty of care. *Haynes v Harwood* (1935), where a milkman ran in the path of a runaway horse in a busy road to divert him from children, is another example. Rescuers, like others, may suffer serious psychiatric injury, either with or without physical injury. The courts have had to decide the boundaries within which those who have suffered injury, loss or damage will be able to recover compensation.

Two areas above all have caused the courts particular problems in marking out the scope of the duty of care: one is where negligent misstatements have been made; the other is claims for nervous shock. We will consider each in turn.

Mention was made earlier of *Caparo Industries v Dickman* (1990), and this illustrates an area where the courts have been reluctant to extend the scope of the duty of care. Financial loss is less recognisable than physical injury, and the courts have demanded that a claimant proves that the defendant was under a duty to safeguard him against that type of loss. A special relationship will have to be proved in which the defendant assumes responsibility for the claimant's financial welfare. *Caparo* recognised three areas where such a relationship might exist, namely, where there was the performance of services, the making of statements and in the giving of advice. Historically, the principles were established in the case of *Hedley Byrne v Heller* (1963), where the plaintiffs asked their bankers to inquire into the financial stability of a company with which they had business dealings. The bankers inquired of the company's bankers, who reported favourably. Unfortunately, these references had been carelessly prepared and when the plaintiffs relied on them they incurred financial losses. The plaintiffs sued the company bankers for the loss arising out of these careless statements and would have succeeded but for the presence of a disclaimer clause. The court stated *obiter* that foreseeability of loss was insufficient. The possible class of recipients of a statement was indeterminate and so a duty of care would only arise where a special relationship was shown to exist.

In *Caparo*, auditors acted for F plc and prepared annual accounts on which the plaintiff relied. He bought shares in F plc and mounted a successful takeover bid. The accounts proved to be inaccurate and misleading as to the worth of F plc. The plaintiff claimed that, had he known the truth, he would not have bid for F plc. The House of Lords held that the auditors only owed a duty of care to shareholders collectively so as to allow them to exercise control. Thus, no duty was owed to the plaintiff, either as a member of the public or as an individual shareholder.

The court stated four conditions which must be present if a defendant is to be made liable for financial loss arising from a negligent misstatement:

- the defendant must be fully aware of the nature of the transaction which the plaintiff had in contemplation following receipt of the information;

- the defendant must either have communicated that information to the plaintiff directly or know it will be communicated to him or a restricted class of persons of which the plaintiff is an identifiable member;

- the defendant must specifically anticipate that the plaintiff will properly and reasonably rely on the information when deciding whether or not to go ahead with the transaction;

- the purpose for which the plaintiff relies on the information must be one connected with the interests which it is reasonable to demand that the defendant protects.

Many cases followed *Caparo* covering a vast range of situations, in many of which no duty of care was found to exist. Two notable cases where a duty of care was found are *Henderson v Merrett Syndicates Ltd* (1995) and *Smith v Bush* (1990). In *Henderson*, the managing agents of Lloyd's insurers placed monies in underwriting contracts on behalf of their members (who are known as Names). Huge losses resulted from insurance claims that were made against Lloyd's and these had to be met by the Names. They sued the managing agents in negligence and it was held that a duty of care was owed to them. In *Smith*, surveyors who acted for lenders gave favourable surveys on properties to be bought by the plaintiff borrowers. Express disclaimers denied any liability was owed to borrowers, but on the facts it was the borrowers who paid for the surveys, their identities were known to the surveyors who knew that borrowers would rely on the reports and suffer loss if they had been negligently prepared. The court held that the surveyors owed a duty of care to the borrowers and the disclaimers were unlawful under the Unfair Contract Terms Act 1977.

Another case which illustrates that this is a developing area of law is *Spring v Guardian Assurance plc* (1995), where the defendant employer provided a reference for an employee to a third party, with whom he was seeking a new job, which suggested that the employee was dishonest. This was a careless, not a malicious, statement and when the employee was not appointed he sued the defendant in breach of contract and negligence and succeeded.

The courts have also faced difficult questions when deciding on the scope of the duty of care in nervous shock cases. It is more usual these days to describe this as severe psychiatric illness arising out of a person's experiences in a traumatic event. It is not simply being depressed, grief stricken or upset. This condition has been recognised from the 1900s most easily where it accompanied physical injury. The case of *Dulieu v White* (1901), however, allowed a barmaid to recover for nervous shock alone when a horse van crashed into the bar in which she was serving. The courts allowed gradual extensions, so in *Hinz v Berry* (1970) the plaintiff was able to recover compensation when a car ploughed into and injured her family while they were parked in a layby. In *Attia v British Gas* (1987), the plaintiff suffered a nervous breakdown whilst watching her home burn down following a gas explosion. In *Hambrook v Stokes* (1925) a mother whose children were injured by a driverless lorry out of her sight around a corner was able to recover damages. Rescuers who attend the scene of an accident are able to recover, as is shown in *Chadwick v BRB* (1967). However, the important case of *McLoughlin v O'Brian* (1983) establishes the modern approach to this question. In that case, questions of public policy were raised – this is often described as the 'floodgates' principle – so as to limit the scope of the duty of care, the persons to whom it is owed or the damage which can be recovered for. Here a driver and his children were involved in a road accident caused by the defendant's fault. They were taken to hospital, one child was dead, the others were seriously injured. The wife and mother attended the hospital and from what she had seen suffered severe psychiatric illness. It was held that this harm was foreseeable and she was sufficiently proximate. This is described as an 'aftermath' case and the court stated that three conditions must be met to found liability:

- the plaintiff must be within the protected class of close family – spouses, parents, children and siblings;

- the plaintiff must show proximity to the accident in both time and space;

- the plaintiff must either be within the sight or hearing of the accident or it must be an aftermath case.

Further refinements have been made in the cases arising out of the Hillsborough disaster. In *Alcock v Chief Constable of South Yorkshire Police* (1991), claims were made by relatives and one fiancée. The court asked two questions:

- could relatives other than parents or spouses bring claims in nervous shock?; and

- could those not at the ground but who saw the tragedy unfold on TV recover?

The answer to (a) was that parents, spouses and children were generally the only people within the class who could recover. Siblings and remoter issue were excluded, although an exception was recognised in the case of the fiancée and a possible exception might be where a grandmother had brought up a grandchild as her own child. The answer to (b) was in the negative, regardless of how close the relationship was. An *obiter* statement suggested that, in a really horrific accident, mere bystanders might be able to recover for nervous shock, but this has been firmly rejected in the case of *McFarlane v EE*

Caledonia Ltd (1994), where the plaintiff was on a support vessel at the Piper Alpha disaster. He was out of the range of danger and was not a rescuer, but could only watch as those on board the rig burned to death.

In *White v Chief Constable of West Yorkshire Police* (1999), five policemen who assisted the injured and one who was in the mortuary, but who were not themselves in danger, were denied compensation. Their position must be compared with those police officers who had risked their own safety by dragging out victims and whose claims were settled in *Frost v Chief Constable of South Yorkshire Police* (1997). In *White*, the police officers were not primary victims of the defendants' negligence as they were not rescuers, and neither were they secondary victims, that is, relatives who witness injury to others. They had, of course, witnessed the events, but not as relatives with close ties of love and affection, and so denying the claims of siblings in *Alcock* prevented these claims. It is to be noted that subsequently, an off-duty nurse who attempted to render assistance at Hillsborough and who suffered nervous shock as a result of being unable to assist victims has been able to recover damages.

Some relationships have an automatic immunity from suit; this is clearly seen in the advocate client relationship. The cases of *Rondel v Worsley* (1969) and *Saif Ali v Mitchell* (1978) demonstrate that barristers or solicitors, when acting as advocates, act as officers of the court and cannot be sued in negligence. Where a solicitor or other legal professional offers advice or drafts a document, other than involving or immediately leading up to litigation, a duty of care is owed, not only to the client, but also to others such as the intended beneficiary under a will, and even an intended beneficiary where an amendment to a will is, through negligence, never made (*Ross v Caunters* (1980) and *White v Jones* (1995)).

Public policy may be invoked in other situations so as to prevent a duty of care from arising. Attempts to sue the police for failures to conduct investigations properly is another example of this. The 'Yorkshire Ripper' case illustrated that a false trail followed by the police in the capture of Peter Sutcliffe, whereby more murders were committed, did not permit the mother of one of these later victims to sue the police (*Hill v Chief Constable of West Yorkshire Police* (1988)). In the case of *Mulcahy v MoD* (1996), it was held that soldiers owe no duty of care to comrades. Other examples include *Aston v Turner* (1981), where the plaintiff burglar was injured by the negligence of the drunken driver of the getaway vehicle. The harm was foreseeable, but on the grounds of public policy the plaintiff was denied a claim. A claim by a child for 'wrongful life', failing an abortion being carried out when it was discovered that the mother-to-be had rubella, was also denied on the grounds of public policy.

Another area where boundaries have been drawn is in the recovery of financial loss. *Spartan Steel Alloys Ltd v Martin and Co Ltd* (1972) illustrates that where physical damage results or is accompanied by economic loss, such as loss of profit on a wasted batch of steel, these can be recovered. However, pure financial loss, in the form of loss of an expected profit for goods which cannot be produced whilst a machine is being mended or whilst the power is being restored cannot be recovered. This was confirmed in *The Aliakmon* (1986) and *Murphy v Brentwood DC* (1990). In the former, the plaintiff had contracted to buy a cargo of steel to be shipped from Korea. The cargo was damaged at sea and as the risk, but not ownership, had passed to the plaintiff he had to pay for the damaged goods. He sought to recover this loss, but it was held that as it was a pure economic loss it could not be recovered. In the latter, a subsequent purchaser of a defective house was not able to recover (either against the builder or local authority who had authorised the building plans) for this loss, despite the fact that if the house fell down it would be worthless.

Weller and Co v Foot and Mouth Disease Research Institute (1966) is also authority that no duty of care is owed for pure economic loss. Here, a firm of auctioneers were unable to recover their loss of profits following the imposition of quarantine restrictions on cattle due to an outbreak of foot and mouth disease. As no physical damage had been suffered, their claim failed.

Breach of the duty of care

This is also a question of law and the standard applied is that of the reasonable man. It is an objective standard (similar to that applied in criminal negligence). It is arbitrary, in that it is not necessary that the defendant can achieve it, as is illustrated in the learner driver case of *Nettleship v Weston* (1971), where a learner driver is expected to achieve the standard of a reasonably competent driver. *Wilsher v Essex AHA* (1986) imposed a similar standard on a junior doctor, that of the reasonably competent trained doctor. However, in part it is a subjective test, in that the reasonable man stands in the shoes of the defendant, so if he professes to be an expert, the reasonable man takes on that characteristic. In *Phillips v Whitely* (1938), the jeweller who offers an ear-piercing service is not expected to reach the standard of a surgeon, but is expected to achieve the standard of a reasonably competent jeweller who holds himself out as being able to offer this service.

Several important factors must be considered in deciding whether the defendant has reached the required standard. This is a weighing up exercise that the court must do. The seriousness of the harm, the social importance of the activity in which the defendant is engaged, the likelihood or probability of the harm and whether adequate precautions are needed and have been taken must all be considered. Thus, in *Paris v Stepney BC* (1951), a one-eyed worker who should have been supplied with goggles by his employer and who as a result of dangerous work practices lost his only eye was able to prove breach of the duty of care owed him. The classic case illustrating the function of the court here is *Bolton v Stone* (1951), where a cricket ball left the pitch and caused injury to the defendant. The court took into account the social utility of this activity, the frequency of balls escaping and the degree of precautions taken to prevent this occurrence. It was found that the precautions taken were more than adequate weighed against the likelihood of injury and its seriousness. In the result, the duty had been complied with. Given the infrequency of balls being hit out, a claim in nuisance was inappropriate.

The case of *Latimer v AEC Ltd* (1952) is also instructive, for here the plaintiff fell on a slippery factory floor, part of which had been treated with sawdust. Unfortunately, not enough of this material was available, and it would have necessitated closing the whole area. It was held that that would have outweighed the risk of injury, and so the claim failed.

A recent example of how the court approaches this question arose following the rape and murder of a schoolgirl on a trip to France. The mother of the schoolgirl Caroline Dickinson sued Cornwall County Council for failure to ensure that the outer door of the hostel where she had stayed had been locked to prevent the entry of an intruder. The question for the court was whether those who organised the trip or the teachers in charge of it had been in breach of their duty of care to the victim in failing to ensure that hostel staff locked the outer door at night. It was held that the rape and murder were not foreseeable consequences of any carelessness in leaving the doors unlocked. It had to be established as probable that the rape and murder would not have occurred but for the failure to lock the doors. The risk of such a serious assault in the event of the outside doors being left unlocked at night, even if school staff were at fault, was only at the very lowest order of probability. It was not likely, even if it had been a possibility.

Resulting damage – causation and remoteness of damage

Where the claimant can establish a duty of care, and that it has been broken, he must then prove that he has suffered reasonably foreseeable harm as a result of the defendant's breach. There are two distinct questions here. The first relates to causation, that is, there must be proved to be a causal link between the breach of duty and the damage suffered by the claimant. Any damage suffered which has not been caused by the defendant is said to be too remote. Thus, the person who is injured by the negligence of D and who, on his way to hospital, suffers further injury when the ambulance in which he is being carried overturns, cannot look to D for compensation for any further injuries suffered. This is called a *novus actus interveniens* (a new intervening act). The other question – which is usually referred to as remoteness of damage – concerns the reasonable foreseeability of damage. Here, it is the type of the damage suffered by the claimant which is found not to have been foreseeable and in that sense is said to be too remote. In reality, it may be difficult to avoid overlap between these two questions, particularly where consecutive and concurrent causes are involved.

Taking causation first, a chain of causation must be shown to exist – all the links in this chain must be present, and any damage suffered after a break in the chain cannot be recovered for against the defendant. The 'but for' test is used: if the claimant can show that but for the defendant's breach, no damage would have been caused to him, then he has proved that the defendant caused the damage suffered. *Barnett v Chelsea and Kensington HMC* (1968) is a good example. Here, a factory nightwatchman became ill with stomach pains after drinking some tea. On going to the hospital, the doctor refused to see him and told him to see his own doctor in the morning. By that time he had died from arsenic poisoning, this having been placed in his drink by an unknown person. It was held that, even if the hospital doctor had seen him, he would not have been able to prevent his death, and so no claim could be made by his widow.

A distinction is drawn between concurrent and consecutive causes. Regarding the former, the case of *Wilsher v Essex AHA* (1987) demonstrates concurrent causes. A premature baby went blind and there were six possible causes, one of which was the breach of duty of care by the junior doctor. It was proved that premature baby ailments contributed to the child going blind and that for liability to attach to the doctor it had to be shown that he caused or materially contributed to the blindness. It was insufficient to show a high risk of injury.

So far as consecutive causes are concerned, the cases of *Baker v Willoughby* (1970) and *Jobling v Associated Dairies Ltd* (1982) are a useful contrast. In *Baker v Willoughby*, the defendant negligently injured the plaintiff in the leg. Before trial, the plaintiff was shot in the leg by burglars and he had to have his leg amputated. The defendant remained liable for loss of amenity arising from the injury caused by the defendant. In *Jobling*, however, the plaintiff was partially incapacitated at work and before the trial became fully incapacitated due to an illness. The House of Lords distinguished *Baker v Willoughby* (1970) and held the defendant liable only for the plaintiff's loss of earnings up to the time he fell ill. Becoming ill was a risk everyone ran and it was not proper to expect a defendant to be made liable for such everyday risks. Additionally, it was thought improper to allow the plaintiff to profit at the expense of the defendant.

We now come to look at reasonable forseeability, which we have noted is usually referred to as remoteness of damage. This involves the determination by the court of the extent to which the claimant can recover for damage suffered by him and caused by the defendant.

The Wagon Mound (No 1) (1961) provides for the reasonable foreseeability test so that as long as the precise type of damage suffered was reasonably foreseeable, the full extent of damage suffered can be recovered for. This was an Australian case heard on appeal in the Judicial Committee of the Privy Council and, strictly, was not binding in English courts. The Court of Appeal decision in *Re Polemis* (1921) was binding, but the reasonable foreseeability test in *The Wagon Mound (No 1)* (1961) has been followed. In *Re Polemis*, stevedores negligently caused a plank of wood to fall into a ship's hold containing petrol drums and where petrol vapour had built up. The wood caused a spark which ignited the vapour and the ship was damaged. The test applied in this case was whether the fire was a direct consequence of the negligent act, regardless of whether it was foreseeable.

In *The Wagon Mound (No 1)* (1961), following an oil spill in Sydney harbour, the oil floated towards some ships moored at a wharf. Welding was being done at the wharf and this stopped pending inquiries as to the risk of a spark igniting the floating oil. On resuming welding, following assurances that ignition would not occur, the inevitable happened and the ships and the wharf were damaged. It was held that so far as the damage to the wharf was concerned, this was not a reasonably foreseeable consequence of an oil spill. In *The Wagon Mound (No 2)* (1966), the owners of damaged ships recovered in negligence as the courts hearing this case took a different view on the evidence as to what was reasonably foreseeable. Unlike the wharf owners, who had been welding and creating sparks, the shipowners did not risk the defence of contributory negligence being raised by the defendant.

Thus the harm suffered must be of a kind, type or class foreseeable as a result of the defendant's negligence – the extent need not be foreseen. This is demonstrated in *Hughes v Lord Advocate* (1963), where a hole in the road was marked by oil lamps which gave rise to a risk that a child who tampered with a lamp could be burnt. However, the plaintiff dropped a lamp into the hole, it exploded and he was burnt. The court held that as long as injury by burning was foreseeable, it did not matter whether this was direct or indirect.

In *Ogwu v Taylor* (1987), it was held that it is foreseeable for a fireman to be burned by fire, but the plaintiff was able to recover for burns caused as a result of hosed water turning to steam. In *Crossley v Rawlinson* (1981), however, an AA patrolman who ran towards a burning truck and tripped injuring his back was not able to recover damages. It was not foreseeable that he would suffer injury as a result of tripping. If he had been burned, or the cargo had fallen on him, he would have been able to recover. *Bradford v Robinson Rentals* (1967) offers another example. Here, the plaintiff suffered frostbite when driving his employer's unheated van in winter. It was foreseeable that he would suffer a severe cold, pneumonia or chilblains and frostbite was of the same kind. He recovered damages for this harm.

Causation and reasonable foreseeability must both be present if a claim is to be successful. This will depend on the circumstances, but as can be seen from *Performance Cars v Abraham* (1962), if injury has been caused by another to the claimant, and then the defendant breaches a duty to the claimant, no claim will lie against the defendant.

We referred earlier to the 'eggshell skull' person. *Smith v Leech Brain Ltd* (1961) and *Robinson v Post Office* (1974) illustrate that where a bruise would be reasonably foreseeable, but the particular sensitivity of the defendant results in concussion, the defendant can be made liable for the full extent of the injury. In the former, Smith suffered an injury to his lip from a burn. This developed later into cancer and he died. His employer was held liable. In *Robinson*, the plaintiff's leg was injured whilst he was at work. He was allergic to the tetanus injection administered and this caused encephalitis. Again, the court held the employer liable, stating that a defendant takes a plaintiff as he finds him.

Novus actus interveniens

This brings us to the *novus actus interveniens* (new intervening act) rule. If the chain of causation is broken by a new intervening act, then any damage resulting thereafter will be too remote. The chain of causation may be broken either before any damage is caused to the claimant or after some damage has been caused.

A *novus actus interveniens* is usually a new act by a third party, but it may be an act by the claimant, as in *Wieland v Cyril Lord Carpets* (1969) and *McKew v Holland & Hannan & Cubitts* (1969). In *Wieland*, the plaintiff was injured by the defendant's negligence, and soon after the accident she visited her son and needed to enter and leave his premises via stairs. She was fitted with glasses and a neck collar following her injury and was in a nervous state. When accompanied by her son on leaving, she fell down the stairs and suffered more injuries. The court held that she acted reasonably and this did not amount to a *novus actus interveniens*. In *McKew*, the facts were very different. The defendant's negligence caused injury to the plaintiff who, as a result, had occasional loss of control in his left leg. He went down some stairs ahead of his family without a stick and accompanied by young children. He was unable to recover for further injuries sustained when he fell, as his action was a *novus actus interveniens*.

Lord Reid, in *Home Office v Dorset Yacht* (1970), the case involving the escape of the borstal boys who damaged property of those living in the neighbourhood, said that the third party's act 'must at least have been something likely to happen'. In *Smith v Littlewoods* (1987), Lord Mackay LJ preferred 'probable'; here, the House of Lords rejected a claim for damages where vandals had caused a fire in a disused cinema owned by the defendants and which spread to the plaintiff's premises.

What if the claimant goes away on holiday and his next door neighbour is burgled and the burglars get into C's house because of some deficiency in security the burgled house? Compare this with the situation where the neighbour takes control of C's house, for example, he has a key on the understanding that he will keep an eye on C's house? Also note the following situation recently reported in the press. A lorry driver notices he has a puncture, so he pulls over onto the hard shoulder of the motorway. His vehicle is struck by a passing truck and as a result of the impact, the gas containers carried on his lorry explode and fly into the air. A fireball envelopes the oncoming cars and a multiple pile-up follows. One of the car drivers is killed at the wheel of his car. The cases of *Rouse v Squires* (1973) and *Wright v Lodge* (1993) might help. It was held in the first that negligent driving is not a break in the chain of causation, whereas in the second case, reckless driving can break the chain of causation.

What will the position be here, so far as the liability of the first truck driver is concerned? If the second truck driver is merely negligent, the first remains liable, but if the second is reckless, this can break the chain of causation and liability would fall on the second or his employer. In such cases, the insurers of the party found to be at fault then have to pay the damages awarded.

Res ipsa loquitur

Having considered each of the three elements that the claimant must prove to be successful in the tort of negligence, it is worth mentioning a rule of evidence which may assist a claimant.

This is the *res ipsa loquitur* rule ('let the facts speak for themselves'). This rule shifts the burden of proof from the claimant to the defendant where it is unclear from the facts whether the defendant was in breach of his duty of care. In the absence of an explanation by the defendant, the claimant wins his claim. However, if the defendant asserts that he had used reasonable care in discharging his duty, then he will have to rebut an inference of fault. There are three aspects to this rule of evidence:

- the claimant cannot establish the exact cause of the injury;

- the defendant was in the exclusive control of the situation in which the claimant was caused injury;

- this is something which does not normally happen where those in control act with reasonable care.

An example might be useful. A transport company is delivering a pink dye used in paint, when the cargo spills at a roundabout, spraying several vehicles with the dye. The owners of the vehicles discover that the dye damages their paintwork. The *res ipsa loquitur* rule may offer assistance in the proof of their claims, as is illustrated in the following cases.

In *Scott v London and St Katherine's Dock* (1865), bags of sugar fell from a warehouse onto the plaintiff below, and in *Ward v Tesco* (1976), yoghurt left on a supermarket floor allowed the presumption to apply as it did in *Mahon v Osborne* (1939), where swabs were left inside a patient undergoing an operation. Other situations where this rule may apply are cars mounting a pavement and aircraft crashing on take-off. In *Ng Chun Pui v Lee Cheun Tat* (1988), a coach veered off the road into the path of an oncoming vehicle. The plaintiff called no evidence and the Privy Council held that the facts raised an inference of fault. The defendant's case was that a car cut up the coach and this caused the coach driver to brake sharply and the coach skidded. It was held that the defendant had rebutted the inference of fault as the cause of the accident. The driver's response in this emergency, which was beyond his control, was reasonable and he had not been careless in braking.

Defences

We now move on to consider the defences available to a claim in negligence. There are two main defences and these may apply in other torts. it is usual to consider each in turn but the first, *volenti non fit injuria*, is a complete defence whereas the second, contributory negligence, is only a partial defence, in that it allows a reduction in the damages awarded to the claimant in proportion to his contribution to his injury.

Volenti non fit injuria

The courts have been cautious in allowing this defence, because its result is a complete denial of liability by the defendant to the claimant. However, a distinction is drawn between cases where the claimant consents to an intentional interference which is planned, such as an operation, and consent to run a legal risk. In *Smith v Baker* (1891), a quarry worker who knew that rocks were being carried over his head had not consented to run the risk of injury from those rocks. An assumption of risk does not apply to rescuers, as in *Chadwick v BRB* (1967), but it will to those who volunteer to undertake unjustified risks, as in *Cutler v United Dairies* (1933) where a runaway horse was stopped in an empty field.

Consent is not simply to knowledge, it must be voluntary, and it can either be express or implied, but only where the consent is to run a particular, identifiable and obvious risk. In *ICI v Shatwell* (1964), two brothers were experienced quarrymen who lit a fuse negligently, which caused an explosion which injured them. It was held that they had consented to run this risk. In *Morris v Murray* (1990), a ride in a light aircraft with a pilot who was visibly very drunk was *volenti*, whereas in *Dann v Hamilton* (1939), it was held that a passenger in a car did not consent to the driver being drunk. In *Slater v Clay Cross Co Ltd* (1956), the claimant was hit by a train in a tunnel whilst lawfully on the track. The court distinguished between ordinary risks to which the claimant was taken to have consented and those which were outside the scope of consent, such as the train driver's negligence.

The defendant may in writing or orally exclude his liability, but statute restricts his ability to do so in business dealings under s 2(1) and (2) of the Unfair Contract Terms Act 1977. In private matters, the defendant may be able to exclude his liability, but statutes, such as the Road Traffic Act 1988, prevent this in respect of road accidents.

Contributory negligence

This is governed by the Law Reform (Contributory Negligence) Act 1945 and has the effect of reducing the amount of damages which the claimant will be awarded. The defendant need only prove that the claimant has contributed to the injury suffered, although in practice he may be shown to have contributed to the 'accident' itself. The claimant must be at fault and the defendant will have to show causation and reasonable foreseeability on the part of the claimant.

In *Froom v Butcher* (1975), a 20% reduction in the award of damages was made for failure to wear seatbelts at a time when this was not a legal requirement in criminal law. In *Jones v Livox Quarries Ltd* (1952), the plaintiff ignored orders from his employer and rode on a slow moving vehicle. This was shunted from behind when its driver had to brake hard and the claimant was injured. His damages were reduced by 20%.

The case of *Sayers v Harlow UDC* (1958) illustrates that where a person is trapped and attempts to escape, the law will not penalise their attempt providing they act reasonably. With hindsight, it might be shown that they did not take the best course of action. Mrs Sayers was locked in a public toilet and tried to escape through the window. However, finding that she could not escape, she attempted to return to the floor via a revolving toilet roll holder and as a consequence injured herself. Her damages were reduced by 25%.

Rescuers also should not be penalised except where their methods of rescue are negligent, as in *Harrison v BRB* (1981), when a train guard was injured trying to pull a passenger on board and they both fell out. He had contributed to his injury when he brought the train to an immediate stop, rather than giving a signal for it to slow down. Employees also may be given the benefit of the doubt, particularly where they work in noisy or difficult conditions.

Defective premises under the Occupiers' Liability Acts 1957 and 1984

The 1957 Act covers lawful visitors and the 1984 Act provides for trespassers entering private property, including private rights of way. It has recently been announced by the government that its intention of extending rights of access to the countryside will necessitate changes in these statutory provisions so as not to cast the burden of injury on to land owners.

Section 2(1) of the Occupiers' Liability Act 1957 imposes a common duty of care and this is explained in s 2(2) to take such care as, in all the circumstances of the case, is reasonable to see that a visitor will be reasonably safe in using the premises for the purposes for which he is invited or permitted by the occupier to be there. 'Occupier' is widely interpreted, and it is not the premises that need to be reasonably safe, but the visitor. All those, whether they be the postman or woman, the police officer or the telephone engineer are protected. Scutton LJ in *The Carlgarth* (1927) expressed the sentiment well: 'When you invite a person into your house to use the staircase, you do not invite him to slide down the banisters.'

The occupier will have to take extra care of vulnerable visitors, such as children or the blind or deaf. Children may be allured onto premises and in *Glasgow Corp v Taylor* (1922) berries in a park might allure a child, and instead of being a trespasser the child will be treated as having an implied licence to enter. Naturally, if it is a place where children are expected not to enter, such as a scrap yard, the 1984 Act will apply to give more limited protection to the trespasser.

Skilled entrants are covered in s 2(3)(b), and s 2(5) provides for the defences of *volenti* and contributory negligence. Such people as gas fitters, mechanics and roof repairers are expected to be able to take reasonable care for their safety. Section 2(4)(b) allows an occupier to escape liability where he employs an independent contractor to do work and it is reasonable to entrust work to such a person providing he uses reasonable care in selecting the contractor. In *Haseldine v Daw and Sons* (1941), mending a lift required the specialist skills of a contractor, but in *Woodward v Mayor of Hastings* (1944) sweeping snow off a school step did not.

Before the Occupiers' Liability Act 1984 was passed, there was little protection for trespassers, other than child trespassers who, in *BRB v Herrington* (1972), were owed a duty of common humanity. This case overruled *Addie v Dumbreck* (1929), in which the occupier only had to refrain from deliberate or reckless acts causing injury to any trespasser. In 1984, it was felt that occupiers should ensure to a minimum standard the safety of all those who enter without permission. In some situations, entry to another's property is not malicious, and may be as the result of a mistake.

By s 1(3), the occupier is aware of a danger or has reasonable grounds to believe a danger exists in the state or condition of his property. The risk is one against which he may reasonably be expected to offer the trespasser some protection, knowing that he is in the vicinity or may come on to the premises. Reasonable belief in the trespasser's presence or likely presence is sufficient.

The occupier, by s 1(4), must take such care as is reasonable in all the circumstances of the case to see that the trespasser does not suffer injury on the premises by reason of the danger concerned. Unlike the 1957 Act, this Act only protects against personal injury, not damage to the trespasser's property.

The occupier cannot attempt to encourage trespassers not to enter by using dangerous 'man traps' under the 1984 Act and at common law he must not undertake dangerous activities, even in an attempt to see off trespassers. The case of *Revill v Newbery* (1996) illustrates this. An 82 year old man had been the subject of several burglaries and wished to prevent his garden shed from being broken into. He guarded it, and when the offender banged and shouted outside the shed, the man fired and shot the burglar. He was held liable in damages, but the court reduced the damages awarded by two-thirds. The defences of volenti and contributory negligence are available, but it is unlikely that the law will permit notices to exclude an occupier's liability to trespassers.

Employees are covered by the 1957 Act and in addition may have a claim in the tort of negligence for breach of statutory duty; for example, where the employer fails to comply with the Health and Safety at Work Act 1974, or where a fellow employee is negligent, the injured employee may either sue that employee or the employer under the doctrine of vicarious liability. Where an employee is acting in the course of his employment, albeit negligently, the injured employee can claim against the employer who is bound to have public liability insurance to meet such claims.

The defence of *volenti* will not be available against an employee and, although contributory negligence will be, the effects of the Health and Safety at Work Act 1974 are such that this dilutes the effect of this defence. Workers engaged in dangerous or difficult jobs should not be held to standards of contributory negligence; the burden should fall on the employer.

Sanctions and remedies

Introduction

In this section, we will consider the main purposes of criminal sanctions and the types of sentences imposed on adult and young offenders. We will also consider the main types of damages available in an action in tort and the purposes served by them.

Criminal sanctions

Lawton LJ in *R v Sargeant* (1974) said of sentencing:

... those classical principles are summed up in four words: retribution, deterrence, prevention and rehabilitation. Any judge who comes to sentence ought always to have these four principles in mind and apply them to the facts of the case to see which of them has the greatest importance in the case with which he is dealing.

We shall take these in turn.

Retribution

When we consider the harm involved in a criminal offence, it is useful to consider our starting point: is it the harm actually caused, or is it the harm threatened or the harm intended? Thus, a distinction can be drawn between the moral blameworthiness of an act or omission and the amount of harm that results. Serious actions do not always result in serious consequences, and trivial acts sometimes have very serious results. Sentencing policy should take these factors into account if it is to be fair to the individual offender and as between several offenders. In the words of Gilbert and Sullivan's operetta, *The Mikado*, 'the punishment should fit the crime' – there must be proportion and recognition of gravity – so where, for example, force is used, the offender will normally receive a higher sentence than one who used no force. Discretion has an important part to play in achieving proportion or justice when deciding whether to prosecute and also at the sentencing stage.

It is to be noted that during the passage of the Crime (Sentences) Act 1997 the judges, *inter alia*, were opposed to the clauses bringing in minimum sentences, as this would eliminate the element of judicial discretion in deciding on the sentence appropriate for the individual offender. Lord Bingham LCJ said in late 1996 that a judge should be free to give effect to his sense of justice in each case and should not be obliged to impose a mandatory sentence where he considered it unjust to do so. In the event, the Home Secretary, Jack Straw, agreed to a compromise in order for the rest of the provisions of the Bill to become law and judicial discretion in sentencing has been retained to a large extent.

Retribution does not aim to reduce crime and assumes that the offender is responsible for his actions, as a result of free choice. Thus, he deserves to be punished for his wrongdoing. However, studies constantly show that offenders are disproportionately deprived, both economically and emotionally, and compulsory pre-sentence reports confirm that the overwhelming majority of offenders are on State benefits, and some have no income at all. This raises the question as to effectiveness of retribution, both for the individual offender and society as a whole. Society may be said to have a vested interest in seeing the reduction in crime, and if retribution does not work, this should be through other means, such as deterrence, prevention or rehabilitation.

Deterrence

This applies not only to the offender, but members of society who might otherwise be tempted to commit crimes. Protection of the public is also an important aim of sentencing. Sending an offender to prison may 'put him out of circulation' and by default protect the public and prevent him from committing crimes. All too often, prison is seen as 'a school for criminals' and fails to discourage either the prisoner or others from committing crime. Sentences will need to be in proportion to seriousness of the act or the harm caused or threatened. For example, burglary carries a maximum sentence of 14 years, whereas robbery has a maximum life sentence. It might be argued that the only real deterrent is a high risk of being caught, rather than the penalty likely to be imposed. The resources made available for policing are themselves a very controversial issue, but unless investigation and detection of crime are effective, deterrence through stiff penalties will be wanting.

Prevention (incapacitation)

The offender is taken out of society so that he cannot re-offend. At one time, this meant transporting offenders overseas or hanging them, but the Victorians decided that prison was a more effective means of prevention. It is interesting to note that the social reformers of the Victorian age considered that prison was an effective means of rehabilitating offenders rather than a means of punishment. All too easily in recent times has prison been seen as only a means of containment without offering the prisoner means of preparing to live in society having served a sentence. This is shortsighted and no doubt contributes to re-offending.

There are several possible meanings of prevention: it could mean treatment or training for the offender; alternatively, it may involve measures taken to prevent offending or as proof that offending has taken place, such as the use of closed circuit television or better street lighting. Increasingly, such measures are improving the detection and investigation of crime and may deter or prevent offending, at least in those areas where such measures are in use. The risk is, of course, that crime will be committed in areas where such measures are not available.

Since Lawton LJ's statement in *R v Sargeant* (1974), prevention is generally used to refer to the means by which an offender is incapacitated following conviction. It is perhaps useful to note here the use of electronic tagging, which has been piloted in recent years and which allows an offender a degree of freedom, but at the same time attempts to ensure that a curfew, as to time or place, is maintained.

Rehabilitation

It has been the perennial hope of social reformers, such as Lord Longford and Barbara Wooton, that the criminal justice system be based on this ideal, leading to the reform of the offender. Probation and community service orders have replaced prison as the means of achieving this. Suspended sentences, parole, absolute and conditional discharges and binding over all attempt to have the offender treated in the community rather than being sent to prison. Treatment and/or education and training are seen as the means of encouraging a person to reform and conform to the values of society. The Rehabilitation of Offenders Act 1974, which permits some convictions to become spent, also has this aim and recent initiatives for victim support and reparation by offenders suggest a more positive and libertarian approach to the treatment of offenders.

Despite these initiatives, the Government, when invoking law and order policy, has on many occasions taken the opposite view, seeking a quick solution to high crime rates and re-offending. This has involved various hard line approaches, from the 'short, sharp shock', to 'boot camps', to 'prison works', to 'three strikes and you're out' schemes, all, it must be noted, with very little degree of success.

The case of *R v Secretary of State for the Home Department ex p Venables and Thompson* (1997) demonstrates that these four aims of sentencing are incompatible and compete with one another, so in that sense they are inconsistent. Research suggests that judges use a consistent approach in sentencing so that one aim may well take precedence.

Having considered the main aims of sentencing, we will move on to consider the main types of sentences for adults and those who come before the youth court.

Adult sentencing

Most offences carry maximum sentences and these are imposed by the statutes creating each offence. There are few offences which carry a fixed penalty, but the notable one is, of course, murder, with a penalty fixed by law of life imprisonment, which replaced the death penalty (Murder (Abolition of Death Penalty) Act 1965). By s 36 of the Crime and Disorder Act 1998, the death penalty for treason and piracy is abolished and a fixed penalty of life imprisonment is substituted. Where a mandatory life sentence is imposed, it can take one of three forms: life imprisonment for those aged 21 or over on conviction; custody for life for those aged 18–21; and detention during Her Majesty's Pleasure for those convicted of murder who are under the age of 18 at the time of commission of the offence. Even here, the courts and the Home Secretary have discretion to impose a sentence which in its effect operates for less than the natural life of an offender. Sentencing rules are found in statutes – usually Criminal Justice Acts – but three recent statutes are the Crime (Sentences) Act 1997, the Crime and Disorder Act 1998 and the Youth Justice and Criminal Evidence Act 1999. The Court of Appeal also sets guidelines on sentencing policy which are found in decided cases, involving appeals against sentence reported in the law reports. Lawton LJ said in *R v Pither* (1979) that 'life sentences, for offences other than homicide, should not be imposed, unless there are exceptional circumstances in the case'. In *R v Hodgson* (1968), it was stated that the court should consider the gravity of the offence, the offender's history and potential danger to the public, when considering whether to impose a life sentence.

The Crime (Sentences) Act 1997 creates a variation on the mandatory life sentence. By s 2, an automatic mandatory life sentence comes into force where a person aged 18 or over, who already has a conviction for a serious offence in the UK, is convicted of another offence, unless exceptional circumstances exist. Serious offences include murder, manslaughter, rape, sexual offences, use of real or imitation firearms and inchoate offences, such as attempted murder.

The Criminal Justice Act 1991 set up a new sentencing regime, but, following much criticism from magistrates and others, the Home Secretary bowed to pressure and was forced to promote changes to the 1991 Act in Parliament. It was subsequently amended by the Criminal Justice Act 1993. The main provisions of these Acts are outlined below.

By s 1(2) of the 1991 Act, as substituted by s 66 of the 1993 Act, a custodial sentence shall not be passed unless the court is of the opinion that the offence or combination of offences, and one or more offences associated with it, is so serious that only a custodial sentence is justified, or, with a violent or sexual offence, custody is the only adequate means of protecting the public from serious harm. If an offender refuses consent to a community sentence, where his consent is required, the court may then pass a custodial sentence. The court should only look at the offence and any associated offences, not the defendant's previous criminal record, in deciding whether or not to impose a custodial sentence.

A custodial sentence must be the only suitable option. In *R v Cox* (1992), it was said that a non-custodial sentence is not justified for:

> ... the kind of offence ... which would make all right thinking members of the public, knowing all the facts, feel that justice had not been done by the passing of any sentence other than a custodial one.

Section 1 refers to 'so serious', and the court may consider the offence together with one or more associated offences. These are defined in s 31(2), and are offences for which the offender is to be sentenced if he is convicted of them in the same proceedings, or sentenced for them at the same time, or offences which he asks to be taken into consideration.

The seriousness of the offence and associated offences must be considered, regardless of how many offences are involved. If they are trivial, 'a custody threshold' applies, so that custody is only warranted where the offence(s) is/are serious in itself/themselves. Section 1(4) of the Act provides that the judge must explain in open court, to the defendant's understanding, its use of s 1(2).

Section 2 of the 1991 Act prescribes that the length of sentence must be 'commensurate with the seriousness of the offence', or combination of offences, and one or more associated offences, or, in the case of violent or sexual offences, for such longer term (not exceeding the maximum) as the court considers necessary to protect the public from serious harm.

By s 3(1), the court must 'obtain and consider a pre-sentence report' in all cases where it intends to pass a custodial sentence, except indictable offences where the court has a discretion to do so. Pre-sentence reports are also necessary when the court makes orders for probation, where more than the standard conditions are imposed, community orders and combination orders. The offender must consent to probation orders, community service orders, combination orders and curfew orders.

By s 3(3)(a), the court must also 'take into account all such information about the circumstances of the offence (including any aggravating or mitigating factors) as is available to it'. Sections 28 and 29 of the Act are important here, and the court must apply these sections in its decision making. Section 28 provides that nothing in the Act shall prevent a court from mitigating a sentence by taking into account any such matters as, in its opinion, are relevant in mitigating a sentence. Section 29, as substituted by s 66 of the 1993 Act, provides that a court, in considering the seriousness of an offence, may take into account any previous convictions or any failure to respond to previous sentences. If an offence is committed whilst on bail, this is to be treated as an aggravating factor. Taking into account an offender's previous record in deciding on the seriousness of an offence must not be confused with the question under s 1 as to whether to impose a custodial sentence.

Section 29, as redrafted, gives the court a wide power to consider the whole of an offender's past record, but custodial sentences are to be the last resort and the court must consider 'community sentences' first. Thus, probation orders and combination and curfew orders have to be considered as alternatives to a custodial sentence.

Section 6 of the 1991 Act imposes obligations on the court when considering whether to impose a community sentence. The court must not pass a community sentence unless three conditions are met:

- the offence (or combination of the offence and one or more associated offences) is serious enough to warrant it;

- the court has considered which order(s) are most suitable to the offender; and

- the restrictions on liberty are commensurate with the seriousness of the offence(s).

Children and young offenders

Youth courts try children and young persons. A child is a person aged up to 14. Young persons are those from 14 to 18 years of age. The Criminal Justice Act 1991, in ss 58 and 60, extended the jurisdiction of the youth court to those aged up to 18 years of age. Those aged over 18 are adult and are tried in the magistrates' court or the Crown Court, as appropriate. By s 1(1) of the Criminal Justice Act 1982, imprisonment is not available for those aged under 21.

Section 44 of the Criminal Justice and Public Order Act 1994 provides that children and young persons appearing before magistrates on an indictable offence must normally be tried summarily, except where:

- the charge is homicide; or

- in the case of a young person, the offence is one for which an adult could be sentenced to 14 years' imprisonment or more; or

- where a child or young person is charged jointly with an adult and the magistrates consider it necessary in the interests of justice that they be transferred for trial to the Crown Court.

Section 34 of the Crime and Disorder Act 1998 abolished the *doli incapax* rule for those aged from 10 to 14 years.

No criminal liability attaches to those aged under 10. Section 50 of the Children and Young Persons Act 1933, as amended by the 1963 Act of the same title, provides that those under 10 years who have done an act which would be a crime if they were aged over 10, will be subject to the family proceedings court by way of care proceedings in which a care order or a supervision order involving a local authority may be made.

The sentences that the youth court can impose are wide and include, under ss 24 and 36 of the Magistrates' Courts Act 1980, fines of up to £250 for a child and up to £1,000 for a young person. Also, various orders can be imposed including supervision orders, compensation orders, attendance centre orders or secure training orders, if aged not less than 12. For those aged 16 years, supervision, compensation orders and community service orders can be imposed. Attendance centre orders and sentences of detention to Youth Offender Institutions can be imposed on those aged 15 or above, and secure training orders for those aged 14. The Criminal Justice and Public Order Act 1994 made provision for secure training orders, for the detention of offenders aged from 15 to 17 years and the long term detention of children and young persons.

Provisions under the Crime and Disorder Act 1998 which have yet to be brought into effect include s 97, amending the Children and Young Persons Act 1969, permitting children as young as 12 to be detained on remand to local authority secure accommodation; s 98 also amends that section, so that 15 and

16 year old boys who meet the requirements to be remanded to a remand centre or a prison and those who are physically or mentally immature or who are likely to harm themselves may be remanded to local authority secure accommodation.

In the light of the 1998 and 1999 Acts on youth sentencing, and the ruling of the ECHR in the *Venables and Thompson* appeal, it is interesting to note that ss 4 and 5 of the 1969 Children and Young Persons Act was repealed by the Criminal Justice Act 1991, having never been brought into effect. This was aimed at replacing criminal proceedings with care proceedings for young offenders. There have been, since the *Venables and Thompson* trial, some notable trials of young offenders for serious crimes, such as rape and murder, and the question of how such an offender should be tried, if at all, and how they should be treated, whether sentenced to detention or made subject to care proceedings – in which the primary aim will be their long term welfare and rehabilitation – will have to be settled very soon, given the coming into effect of the Human Rights Act 1998 in late 2000.

Section 34 lowers the age of criminal responsibility to 10, and the Act aims to have young offenders appear in court quickly and make them face up to their crimes. Section 35 extends s 35 of the Criminal Justice and Public Order Act 1994 to children aged from 10–13, with the effect that the court or jury may draw such inferences as appear proper from the defendant's silence at trial.

Sections 37–42 and Sched 2 to the Crime and Disorder Act 1998 make major changes to the way in which the police and courts will deal with young offenders. The Youth Justice Board has been operating pilot schemes and £13 million has been provided to ensure proper supervision of those on bail by probation officers and social workers. It is planned later in 2000 that offenders under 18 will be kept in custody separate from those who are older, and greater emphasis will be placed on education and rehabilitation. A range of new sentences that can be imposed have been created.

Sections 1 and 2 of the 1998 Act provide for anti-social behaviour and sex offender orders respectively. In a recent press report concerning two brothers, one aged 12 and the other 15, in Weston Super Mare, an anti-social behaviour order under s 1 was imposed on each boy. No details of the boys' activities were admitted in open court, but after a hearing lasting three hours the result of the order was to ban them from the centre of the town for two years and from causing harassment, alarm and distress to any person in a prescribed area. Many complaints had been made by local residents about the boys' behaviour, including assaults, shoplifting and breaking windows.

By s 11, a child safety order for children under 10 who are at risk of offending or who are behaving in an anti-social way can be imposed and s 14 allows for a local child curfew order.

By s 8, parenting orders will ensure that an offender's family attend meetings organised by Youth Offending Team (YOTs). Sections 67, 68 and

Sched 5 provide for reparation orders which will bring offenders into direct contact with victims and which will enable them to make amends. By s 69, action plan orders will ensure that those who in the past were given conditional discharges are now required to attend courses in which their problems are addressed, ranging from anger, drugs, home and school problems, finding a job or training to counselling. These have been the subject of pilot schemes and initial findings suggest that this approach could divert young offenders away from crime and in particular the prospect of prison in later years. Section 71 amends the 1969 Act in making supervision orders.

Sections 47–50 of the Crime and Disorder Act 1998 amend the powers of the youth court and magistrates' court in the following ways: the youth court may remit a defendant to the magistrates' court who reaches 18 either before the start of the trial or after a finding of guilt, but before sentencing; where a defendant under 18 is committed to the Crown Court for trial of a grave crime, he may also be committed to the Crown Court in connection with any other related indictable offence. It is no longer necessary for there to be a one hour interval between sittings of adult magistrates' courts and youth courts and stipendiary magistrates may sit alone in youth courts and the powers of justices and clerks are extended.

Part I of the Youth Justice and Criminal Evidence Act 1999 creates a new sentence for young offenders called a referral order, following the main proposals for reform in the 1997 Government White Paper, *No More Excuses*, which were enacted in s 39 of the Crime and Disorder Act 1998. The principal aim of the 1998 Act is to prevent re-offending.

The 1999 Act is being piloted in some areas during 2000, and this will last until mid-2001 and is likely to come into full effect in 2002. YOTs will implement the new sentence, a referral order under the 1999 Act, which is intended for first time offenders under the age of 18 referred by the magistrates to Youth Offending Panels (YOPs) (via YOTs), and it will enter into a Youth Offending Contract (YOC) with the offender, the duration of which will be set by the court. By s 9 it must not exceed 12 months, nor be less than three months, taking into account the seriousness of the offence.

Part I and Sched 1 deal with the referral order administered by YOPs to be set up by YOTs. Section 39(1) and (3) imposes a duty on local authorities to establish, in co-operation with police chiefs, probation committees or health authorities at least one YOT in their area.

By s 39(5), a YOT must include at least one police officer, probation officer, local authority social worker, a nominee of the health authority and a nominee of the chief education officer, and may include such other persons as the local authority thinks fit, after consultation with police, probation and health authorities.

Section 14 of the 1999 Act states that a YOT must provide administrative staff, accommodation and facilities for the YOP to allow it enter into a YOC with the offender. Whilst a YOC is in force, the YOT must monitor his or her compliance with its conditions. The panel member selected from the YOT must keep records of compliance and the YOT must comply with any guidance issued in future by the Secretary of State.

By s 4, a referral order is a self-contained penalty and cannot be imposed alongside any other penalty, such as binding over the parents or guardians, binding over the young offender to keep the peace or to be of good behaviour, parenting orders, fines or reparation orders, conditional discharges, community sentences such as probation orders, community service orders, combination orders, curfews, supervision orders, attendance centre orders, drug treatment and testing orders and action plan orders.

By s 3(1), a YOC is a programme of behaviour agreed between a YOP and the offender and can be revoked, if broken, or the offender re-offends. It is a flexible approach to sentencing youth offenders, especially those who offend for the first time, except for very serious offences. The Secretary of State may by regulation alter the scope of the referral order so as to expand the categories of offenders subject to them. Where the young offender breaks the YOC or re-offends when subject to a referral order, the court may revoke the referral order and re-sentence in any way it chooses, within its powers, regardless of s 1.

Section 1(1) empowers the youth court and an adult magistrates' court at first instance to impose a referral order on offenders aged under 18. The Crown Court can impose a referral order on appeal, and in other cases, may remit a young offender to the magistrates' court for sentence, where a referral order is considered appropriate. A referral order is not appropriate where a sentence is fixed by law, a custodial sentence is appropriate, or where a hospital order or absolute discharge is appropriate.

Section 1(2) and (3) provides that the court must impose a referral order where a young offender pleads guilty to an offence and any associated offences, has no previous convictions, has not been bound over to keep the peace or to be of good behaviour. He is then referred to the relevant YOP. If he pleads guilty to at least one and not guilty to at least one offence or associated offences and the other conditions are met, the court may impose a referral order.

By s 2(5), a conditional discharge is deemed to be a conviction and so a referral order will not be appropriate. Also, courts will only be able to impose a referral order where the Secretary of State has made an order that they apply in that area.

By s 5, the court has discretion to require parents and guardians or others to attend a YOP for young offenders aged 16 and over; for those aged under 16 it is mandatory for at least one parent/guardian to attend or the representative of the local authority in whose care the child is, unless, in the case of parents or guardians, it is unreasonable to attend, for example, owing to serious illness. Those unable to attend must be sent copies of the referral order. Failure to attend without good reason amounts to contempt of court.

Section 7 provides for attendance at a YOP and for non-attendance. A young offender may be accompanied by a person of at least 18 subject to YOP agreement. No express provisions permit legal representation at YOP meetings. The Government suggested during the passage of the Bill that this would be a barrier to the young offender taking responsibility for the offence. A YOP may allow any person, who appears to it to be a victim, to attend, including members of the community. Such persons can be accompanied by a person of their choice, subject to agreement of the YOP.

Section 8 provides for the first meeting between a young offender and a YOP when an agreement on the YOC can be made. The YOC will cover financial or other reparation, attendance at mediation sessions with the victim, unpaid work or service to the community, curfews, attendance at educational establishment or workplace, attendance at other times/places, staying away from specified places/persons, supervision and recording of progress and participation in prescribed activities. Electronic tagging is not permitted. A plain English written agreement must then be prepared and signed by the young offender and counter-signed by the YOP.

Section 10 covers the situation where no YOC results from the first or later meetings of YOP. The YOP may refer the young offender back to court for sentence, if all else fails. Sections 11 and 12 provide respectively for progress meetings and a final meeting.

Part I of Sched 1 to the 1999 Act covers the situation where the YOP refers the young offender back to the court and Pt II of Sched 1 deals with an offender under a referral order who is convicted of one or more offences either before or after he has been referred to the YOP.

The success of this new sentence will have to await the conduct of the pilot schemes and, in any event, must be seen in the wider context of young offender sentencing including probation and supervision orders, action plan orders and the powers under ss 65 and 66 of the Crime and Disorder Act 1998 for the issuing by the police of reprimands and warnings. The Secretary of State has power to extend the categories of young offender who can be made subject to the scheme.

Part II of the 1999 Act, ss 16–63 and Scheds 2 and 3 were made in response to the Home Office Report in 1998, *Speaking up for Justice*, and deal with the giving of evidence in criminal proceedings. Children, rape victims, and other vulnerable or intimidated witnesses giving evidence in criminal trials will, under Chapter 1, ss 16–33, have the benefit of special measures to assist them and physical measures such as informal dress, screens, closed circuit television, and pre-recorded interviews. Chapter 2, ss 34–40, provides for the examination by the defendant who chooses to represent himself of witnesses, including the victim, in serious cases. This is in response to the case of *R v Edwards* (1996), and will ensure that the court makes legal representation available to such a defendant. Chapter 4 imposes reporting restrictions and Chapter 6 imposes restrictions on the use of evidence.

Civil law remedies in tort

The main remedy in the law of tort, in particular in negligence, is an award of damages. This aims to put the claimant back into the position he would have been in if the tort had not been committed. However, other remedies may be available. Cherie and Tony Blair have recently sought an injunction of the court to prevent publication of a diary by their former nanny which they assert is in breach of a confidentiality clause in the employment contract. Such an order can be issued in the interim, pending the outcome of the claim. Some are mandatory, requiring the taking of action, and others are prohibitory, requiring that certain action cease or not be taken. Usually, the granting of an injunction in tort will only be appropriate where there is a continuing activity such as the commission of a nuisance. It is not unknown for the law to permit a defendant to take self-help, but much care is required with this if he is not to commit a tort. The dangers were noted in *Revill v Newbery* (1996).

Damages

The most usual award is of compensatory damages so as to compensate the claimant against the loss, damage or injury suffered as a result of the tort committed by the defendant. A recent illustration which was reported in the national press was an award of £275,000, made to a saleswoman who was sent by her employer on a corporate bonding exercise. She was told to put on a 55 lb sumo wrestling suit. This caused her to over-balance and injure her head. There are two types: general or unliquidated damages, and special or quantifiable damages. The judge decides on the amount of general damages, taking into account estimates arrived at in previous cases. Sums may be awarded for nervous shock, physical injury or for damage to property. Special or liquidated damages cover those losses which can be quantified by the claimant, such as his loss of earnings arising from the date of the injury or for expenses which he has incurred on medical treatment. It could be that he has had his car or other property repaired following an accident, and these costs are quantifiable.

The court is not limited to these two headings of damages, but in the particular circumstances of the case decide to make additional or alternative awards. An award of nominal damages can be made where, although the claim is good in law, the court finds that the claimant has an ulterior motive in pursuing it. If he is vexatious or is trying to make a profit, the court will award a nominal sum, such as £1. This is not uncommon in defamation claims where the claimant pursues the claim in the hope that a civil jury will make a huge award. The normal costs rule, 'costs follow the event', applies here.

Contemptuous (or derisory) damages are awarded where a tort is actionable *per se*, that is, without the need to prove damage. Thus in trespass it is the act of touching or frightening the person or treading on his land or interfering with his goods that is protected, and no damage need be done to his property. The claimant may wish to 'have his day in court' to prove a point or principle and the award of damages reflects this. No order for costs will usually be made.

In some instances, the civil courts will award punitive damages, that is, more than the sum of the injury, so as to punish the defendant. Strictly, a distinction is made between exemplary and punitive damages. The former is made to make an example of the defendant, whereas the latter is to punish him. In some cases, an award of aggravated damages is made where the defendant has been particularly nasty towards the claimant or has put up unnecessary obstacles to the claim or has delayed in the hope that the claimant would give up.

When considering remedies, it is important to remember that a claimant may have a good claim in law, but in order to pursue it he must comply with not only rules of procedure, but also rules of evidence. One trap for the unwary litigant is the Limitation Act 1980, which can be specially pleaded by a defendant so as to prevent what would otherwise be a good claim from continuing. A claim will become statute-barred usually after six years, although three years apply to personal injury claims and one year to defamation claims. Time begins to run from the accrual of the claim, that is, in torts actionable *per se*, such as trespass, from the date of the wrongful act. In other torts, time runs from the time when damage first results or when the claimant becomes aware of the injury.

In personal injury claims, s 11 provides for three years from first becoming aware of the fact of injury and even where the claimant has become aware, s 33 permits an application out of time at the discretion of the court.

It may be particularly difficult to assess either the date on which a personal injury claim accrues or the amount of damages that should be awarded. There are three heads of damages: pecuniary losses, such as loss of earnings or earnings capacity; the cost of future medical or hospital treatment; and non-pecuniary losses, such as pain and suffering and loss of amenity. Assessing damages in personal injury claims is notoriously complex and it is often said that a claimant may be drastically overcompensated or undercompensated applying the conventional rules which are supervised by the Court of Appeal. However, two alternatives may be available. In cases where there is a risk that the claimant may develop a disease or that his condition will deteriorate, a provisional award may be made. The courts are cautious as to its use and, in *Wilson v Ministry of Defence* (1991), where the claimant suffered an ankle injury and continued to experience pain with the likelihood that arthritis would at some future time set in, the court held that this was not an appropriate case for a provisional award. A lump sum payment should have been made to cover the possibility of progressive deterioration. The effect of a provisional award when made is that the court assesses damages on the basis that the deterioration or disease will not happen. If it does, the claimant applies to the court for the award of further damages.

Another alternative is a structured settlement under the Damages Act 1996. These are extremely complex in their detail, but the principles are straightforward. The defendant's liability insurers make an immediate payment to the claimant to cover losses to date and then use the balance of the sum awarded to purchase life assurance annuities so as to provide income for the remainder of the claimant's life. The 1996 Act will only apply where the parties consent and in making an award the court will have to forecast future loss.

The Court of Appeal, in a reserved judgment in *Heil v Rankin and Another* (2000), held that, for awards above £10,000, the level of damages for pain, suffering and loss of amenity in personal injury claims should be increased up to a maximum of one-third for the most serious injuries. This would ensure fair, just and reasonable compensation.

A difficulty in recent years has been in respect of claims for damage to property where this has been latent, that is, not apparent. The Latent Damage Act 1986 provides that the accrual date will be the later of the date of damage or the claimant's awareness of it, but with an absolute limit of 15 years starting from the date of breach of the duty of care.

Another question arises where the victim dies as a result of injuries. The Law Reform (Miscellaneous Provisions) Act 1934 permits the personal representatives of the deceased (his executors, if he died testate, or administrators where he made no will), to bring any claim which he would have been able to bring. The Fatal Accidents Act 1976 permits his dependants to claim via his personal representatives for any losses which accrue to them as a result of his death.

LEGAL LIABILITY

Legal and moral responsibility

- Judges may develop the law to reflect morality.

- *R v Gibson* (1992); *Shaw v DPP* (1961); *R v Brown* (1993); *Airedale NHS Trust v Bland* (1993); *Fitzpatrick v Sterling Housing Association* (1999); *Gotha City v Sotheby's and Another* (1998); *Taylor v Dickens and Another* (1997).

- Personality, status and capacity: legal persons; age of consent; age of full legal liability; human personality.

- Liability of children: *R v Secretary of State for the Home Department ex p Venables and Thompson* (1999); Human Rights Act 1998; very young children; claims brought by children against carers.

Corporate liability

- Few prosecutions have been brought: *R v P & O European Ferries (Dover) Ltd* (1991); *R v OLL Ltd* (1994); *AG's Reference (No 2 of 1999)* (2000).

- *Tesco Supermarkets v Nattrass* (1972).

- Law Commission's *Report on the Offence of Corporate Manslaughter,* No 237.

Vicarious liability

- Control test; integration test (Denning LJ in *Stevenson Jordan and Harrison v MacDonald Evans* (1952)); economic tests.

Liability in criminal law

- *Actus reus*: *R v Miller* (1983); *Airedale NHS Trust v Bland* (1993); voluntariness and consciousness; defences of insanity and automatism – *Broome v Perkins* (1987).

- *Mens rea*: *R v Steane* (1947); *R v Woollin* (1998); *R v Cunningham* (1957); *MPC v Caldwell* (1982); *R v Reid* (1990); *Chief Constable of Avon and Somerset Constabulary v Shimmen* (1986); *R v Adomako* (1994); *R v Watts* (1998); *R v Khan and Khan* (1998)) or negligence (*R v Adomako* (1994); *Fagan v MPC* (1969); *Thabo Meli v R* (1954)).

Strict liability offences

- *Sweet v Parsley* (1970).

Homicide

- Murder and manslaughter: *actus reus* and *mens rea*.
- Defences: diminished responsibility (s 2 of the Homicide Act 1957) and provocation (s 3): *R v Ahluwalia* (1993); *R v Duffy* (1949); *R v Thornton* (1996); *Bedder v DPP* (1954); *Camplin* (1978); *R v Morhall* (1995); *R v Smith* (1998).

Crimes against the person not causing death

- Assault – s 39 of the Criminal Justice Act 1988. *R v Constanza* (1997), *Tuberville v Savage* (1669); *R v Ireland and Burstow* (1996); *Smith v Chief Superintendant of Woking Police Station* (1983); *Fagan v MPC* (1969); *F v West Berkshire HA* (1990).
- Battery – s 39 of the 1988 Act.
- Assault occasioning actual bodily harm: *R v Miller* (1954); *R v Roberts* (1978); *Savage and Parmenter* (1991).
- Inflicting grievous bodily harm or wounding: *C v Eisenhower* (1984); *Ireland and Burstow* (1997); *R v Clarence* (1888); *R v Martin* (1881).
- Causing grievous bodily harm with intent or wounding: *R v Brown and Stratton* (1998); *R v Mandair* (1994).

Liability in the law of tort

- Trespass, nuisance, defamation and negligence. Extension of the scope of tortious liability: Human Rights Act 1998 (*Osman v Ferguson* (1993); *Osman v UK* (1999)).

Negligence

- *Donoghue v Stephenson* (1932).
- Duty of care.
- Resulting damage – causation and remoteness of damage.
- *Novus actus interveniens.*
- *Res ipsa loquitur.*
- Defences – *volenti non fit injuria*; contributory negligence.

CHAPTER 10

EUROPEAN LAW

Introduction

In this chapter, we will consider the historical developments in post-Second World War Europe which led to the establishment of the two main European groupings of States, namely, the European Community (EC) and its movement towards 'ever-increasing union' through the formation of the European Union on the one hand, and on the other the European Convention for the Protection of Human Rights and Fundamental Freedoms entered into by the original Contracting States of the Council of Europe at a conference held in London in May 1949. Since that time, membership has grown from 21 to over 40 Member States.

We will also consider the impact on domestic law of membership of the European Community. This, for some purposes, from September 1993, became the European Union, following ratification of the Treaty on European Union 1992 (the Maastricht Treaty). This was given domestic effect in the UK by the European Communities (Amendment) Act 1993, and further changes have been brought about by the Amsterdam Treaty 1997.

We will then consider the main provisions of the European Convention for the Protection of Human Rights and Fundamental Freedoms, as well as the implications for the UK of enacting the Human Rights Act 1998 and how this is likely to affect domestic law making and judicial decision making.

At the outset, it is important to appreciate the separate origins of these two groupings of States and their distinct purposes: the EC is primarily concerned with economic matters, such as the free movement of persons, goods and services; and the Convention is concerned with fundamental human rights and freedoms, such as the right to life, freedom from torture and the right to a fair trial. However, it is important to note that, in recent years, there has been a movement towards recognition that their purposes may well converge; in particular that, as the EC develops towards ever-increasing political union, it will wish to adopt fundamental human rights which apply generally, and not only in a business or employment context. We will consider this question in the last part of this chapter.

Historical background

Looking at an atlas reveals that a European geographical entity is not easily defined and the boundaries between Europe and Asia are problematic. However, as a continent, it is, apart from Australia, the smallest. The divide between Europe and Asia runs from the Ural Mountains in the East to the Caspian Sea in the South, including the Caucasus to the Black Sea and the Sea of Marmara and the Dardanelles. The idea of Europe as an entity is not a new one: the Greeks and the Romans considered such an entity. The Holy Roman Empire and philosophers such as Erasmus and St Thomas Aquinas considered there to be sufficient common heritage for a united entity to exist. The Romans recognised the idea of citizenship extending throughout its empire and conquest was the principal means of acquiring power. Modern leaders, too, from Napoleon to Hitler, saw the worth of political, social and economic unity.

Following the Second World War, the USA and Russia dominated the world stage, and more recently China and India are emerging as new superpowers. Emphasising the common cultural and civilisation of Europe is not enough, as the differences have led to conflict. In an attempt to prevent this, the development of economic and political groupings has been a necessity. In 1946, Sir Winston Churchill, speaking in Zurich, referred to a United States of Europe or the formation of a European Union. In May 1948, the European Movement was founded, but the formation of a federation along the lines of the United States may be far too ambitious. Britain, having had its past bound up with the Empire, and then the Commonwealth, and being an island State, has not been a willing partner in forming, or being part of, a fully unified Europe, despite statesmen such as Churchill.

In 1949, at the London conference, the Council of Europe was established by the founding 21 States. This was a consultative body based in Strasbourg. It had no legal powers, but comprised an assembly of members and a committee of ministers concerned with legal affairs, social policy, science, culture and education. Its main achievement has been the European Convention for the Protection of Human Rights and Fundamental Freedoms, signed in 1953. Britain played a large part in its creation, but it was felt that this Convention did not need to be given effect to in the UK as the rights and freedoms protected by it were already to be found in the common law and sufficiently protected. Notably, apart from Turkey, the UK has the worst record for abuses of the Convention and it was only in 1966 that UK nationals could take a case direct to the European Court of Human Rights (ECHR). As we shall see later, it is only since October 2000 (other than in Scotland) that individuals are able to rely on the Convention in domestic courts.

Following the mass destruction of European infrastructure during the Second World War, the Organisation for European Economic Co-operation (OEEC) was set up in 1948 to ensure economic co-operation and administration of the Marshall Plan – aid from the USA to allow reconstruction. This organisation was re-named in 1960, after the USA and Canada became members, as the Organisation for Economic Co-operation and Development (OECD). This is an intergovernmental organisation which does not require any member to relinquish its sovereignty, but which provides a detailed financial and statistical analysis of economic development in Europe.

In 1950, Jean Monnet and Robert Schuman devised the Schuman Plan concerning political, military and economic integration. Only the latter found support, but even this had a strong political base as a supranational authority (the High Authority) was to become responsible for the production of coal and steel. These commodities were the means by which future conflict could result, so their regulation would prevent future war or conflict. Britain was not in favour of this, given its special relationship with the USA, its Empire and Commonwealth links and the loss of political sovereignty which would result from membership. However, following the Suez Crisis in 1956 and the loss of world status, Britain's attitude began to change, but it was to be a number of years before Britain's application to the European Economic Community (as it was then called) would be successful.

In April 1951, the Treaty of Paris set up the European Coal and Steel Community (ECSC) with six founding States – the Benelux countries of Luxembourg, The Netherlands and Belgium, and also Italy, Germany and France. This took effect in July 1952.

In 1949, the North Atlantic Treaty Organisation (NATO) was established and the six founding States of the ECSC then set about forming the European Defence Community, but this came to nothing. In 1955, the Brussels Treaty set up the Western European Union, and these six States were joined by the UK, Spain, Portugal and Greece, with the aim of having a common defence and security policy.

Moves then followed to establish greater economic integration and the Spaak Report led to the Messina Conference in 1956, and as a result the European Economic Community (EEC) and the European Atomic Energy Authority (Euratom) were formed under the Treaty of Rome in 1957. A Commission, a Council of Ministers, a Court of Justice and an Assembly were established, but moves towards federalism did not find favour with the then President of France, Charles de Gaulle, who was not a proponent of federalism, and, in order to reduce conflict, the Luxembourg Compromise 1966 was agreed.

At this time, States who were unable or unwilling to join these communities formed the European Free Trade Association (EFTA). In 1960, Austria, Denmark, Norway, Sweden, Portugal, the UK and Switzerland set up this organisation and were later joined by Finland, Iceland and Liechtenstein.

In 1965, the Merger Treaty, which took effect in July 1967, merged the High Authority and the Commissions of the EEC and Euratom and the Council of Ministers. Other moves towards greater integration included the rationalisation of EC finances in 1971 whereby Member States made direct contributions to the EEC from VAT, agricultural levies and customs duties.

The UK, together with Ireland and Denmark, joined the EEC in 1972 and from that time other States have joined and the movement towards the creation of economic and political union has developed. We will mention these extensions later, noting here that as a result of the Maastricht Treaty, which took effect in 1994, it was recognised that the ethos of the original communities was moving 'towards ever-increasing union'. It is likely that the union will continue to develop, particularly as more States seek membership, although a federation along the lines of the USA is very futuristic.

Development of the EC/EU

We will now consider in more detail the main landmarks in the development of the European Union (EU). In April 1951, France, West Germany, Italy, Belgium, The Netherlands and Luxembourg signed the Treaty of Paris establishing the ECSC. As already noted, coal and steel production was to be placed under international control so as to prevent its use in any future conflicts. In May 1957, these six founding members signed two Treaties of Rome, setting up the EEC and Euratom.

By the Merger Treaty in 1965, all three communities were to share common institutions, namely the Commission, Council of Ministers, Assembly and Court. By far the most important community was the EEC, which had as its main aim the creation of a common market and the harmonisation of the economic policies of Member States. It established freedom of movement of persons, capital and services within the EEC and devised common agricultural and transport policies. Free competition, without restrictions or distortions, was also provided for.

In January 1972, the Treaty of Accession was signed at Brussels by the UK, Eire and Denmark with effect from January 1973. Norway had shown interest in joining the EEC, but did not ratify the treaty following a negative vote in its national referendum. In 1981, Greece acceded to the EEC, by which time there were 10 members. In January 1986, Spain and Portugal joined. It was not until 1995 that membership was enlarged to the present 15, when Austria, Sweden and Finland joined.

An auspicious development took place in 1985 when the Single European Act was approved by the European Council. This was signed in February 1986 and the UK gave effect to its provisions in the European Communities (Amendment) Act 1986. The rather confusing title of the Single European Act, which is a Treaty, should not be confused with domestic legislation emanating from the UK. It came into force throughout the EC in July 1987.

We will move on to consider its main provisions. The Member States agreed to establish a single internal market by the last day of December 1992, namely 'an area without internal frontiers in which the free movement of goods, persons, services and capital is ensured'. They entered into a declaration of the willingness 'to transform relations as a whole among their States into a European Union'. This was followed by an acknowledgment that their main objective was the progressive realisation of economic and monetary union.

Further, agreement was made to develop new policies in economic and monetary convergence, social policy and the environment. It is notable that, when the EC was formed, little if any provision had been made for the protection of the environment. Clearly, this was a necessity which the Single European Act sought to address. Another important provision was the acceptance that the European Parliament's law making powers needed to be strengthened and this was to be achieved by means of a new 'co-operation procedure'. It is to be noted that the Assembly, which had, since 1958, unofficially been referred to as the Parliament, adopted this as its official title. Direct elections to the Parliament were provided for in 1979. The Council of Ministers' decision making powers by means of majority voting, as opposed to unanimous voting, was to be extended to a greater range of matters.

In December 1991, the TEU, usually referred to as the Maastricht Treaty, was agreed with the aim of moving towards greater European integration – an 'ever-closer union'. Before considering its main provisions it is worth asking two questions. What is the EC/EU? Has the EU superseded the EC?

The EU is made up of the EC, ECSC and Euratom and the new areas of intergovernmental co-operation on foreign and security policy (CFSP) and justice and home affairs (JHA). Thus, the EC, the ECSC and Euratom amount to one pillar of the EU. The other two pillars are CFSP and JHA.

Action on the CFSP and JHA pillars is to be taken by way of intergovernmental co-operation. EC law does not apply, and the ECJ has no jurisdiction in these areas, although the Treaty of Amsterdam extends the European Court's powers in the regulation of asylum, immigration and in co-operation concerning policing and judicial matters. It is to be noted that, although reference to the EC or EU will depend on context, under the TEU, the Council of Ministers designates itself as the Council of the European Union for all purposes, including when it enacts EC legislation.

We will now consider the main provisions of the TEU:

- the establishment of a European Union 'founded on the European Communities supplemented by the policies and forms of co-operation' created by the TEU;

- adoption of fundamental principles, including respect for national identities, fundamental rights as a principle of Community law, development of the principle of subsidiarity and the idea of European citizenship;

- a new agreement on Economic and Monetary Union (EMU), with a strict timetable for its achievement;

- intergovernmental co-operation on a CFSP, and also in the areas of JHA, including asylum, immigration, police co-operation against terrorism and drug trafficking;

- expansion of Community powers in, *inter alia*, health protection and overseas development co-operation;

- changes in the balance of power between EC institutions, especially strengthening the law making powers of the European Parliament and the creation of the Court of Auditors.

All but the UK signed the Social Chapter Protocol, which incorporated the social policy objectives of the EC. The UK gave effect to the TEU by the European Communities (Amendment) Act 1993.

In June 1997, the Amsterdam Treaty was prepared, and it was signed in October of that year. This aimed to prepare the way for future enlargement of the Union from the Eastern Bloc and took effect following ratification by all Member States in 1999. Applications to join have been received from Turkey, Hungary, Poland, the Czech Republic, Estonia, Slovenia and Cyprus. It is proposed that future membership will extend to some 20 members.

The main provisions concern four areas:

- freedom, security and justice – common policies are to be developed on asylum, the issue of visas and immigration and border controls. The UK is exempted from applying new measures on visas, asylum and immigration. Increased co-operation between police and customs authorities is to be fostered and co-operation between enforcement authorities in each Member State in the prevention, detection and investigation of crime is made a priority. An aspect of these provisions which have angered critics of political union is the *corpus juris* or common criminal law code. Of the 15 Member States, only two, the UK and Ireland, have adversarial systems. Other Member States follow the Roman law tradition and have inquisitorial systems. The San Sebastian seminar held in April 1997, from which the *corpus juris* emerged, suggested that its main aim was to harmonise criminal prosecutions for fraud against EC funds. However, it is clear that it has a much broader effect, namely, to create a Europe-wide criminal law code. The implications of this go much further and include the removal of lay magistrates and juries in criminal trials, removal of the ancient right of habeas corpus (the right to have a prisoner or other captive brought before the court and for the captor to answer to the court for the reasons justifying continued detention), the appointment of a European Director of Public Prosecutions with powers to detain, and to issue arrest warrants throughout the EU;

- policies to benefit citizens – these will include the promotion of employment and co-ordination of policy, incorporation of a strengthened social chapter for all Member States, the achievement of sustainable development as an objective of the EC, better human health and consumer protection, and the principles of subsidiarity and proportionality to be included in a new treaty protocol;

- a common foreign and security policy;

- changes in the institutions and legislative procedures – this will include extending the scope of co-decision procedures; limiting the membership of the European Parliament to 700; extending the areas where qualified majority voting may be used in adopting the acts of the Council; reforming the Commission by increasing the powers of the President to select Commissioners; extending the powers of the ECJ by ensuring the protection of fundamental rights and providing for the consolidation of the Treaties.

What next?

The Treaty of Nice, containing the Charter of Fundamental Rights, is due to be signed in December 2000. This may adopt the European Convention of Human Rights and may permit the EU to regulate the internal politics of Member States. An interesting question arose recently when Austrians voted for a Fascist minister who in the past had made public statements in support of Hitler's Nazi regime in the Second World War. Commentators suggested that, should such a thing happen after ratification of the Treaty of Nice, the EU should be able to apply pressure to either prevent such an occurrence or apply sanctions should such things occur. Another interesting question arises in connection with Art 280 of the Treaty of Amsterdam, giving effect to *corpus juris*, and how this will take effect in relation to the right to a fair trial under Art 6 of the European Convention.

UK membership of the EC

The UK joined the EEC, the ECSC and Euratom in 1973 by way of the Accession Treaty of 1972, undertaking to establish a common market with the existing members to approximate economic policies by abolishing customs duties and trade barriers and ensuring free movement of persons, services and capital within and between Member States.

The Treaty of Accession was signed in 1972 and was brought into effect by the European Communities Act 1972. Similarly, the Single European Act 1986 was given domestic effect in the UK by the European Communities (Amendment) Act 1986, and 1993 saw the ratification of the TEU (the Maastricht Treaty) which was implemented by the European Communities (Amendment) Act 1993 following some 19 months' discussion in Parliament.

This treaty had the effect of recognising Europe as a social and political as well as an economic community. The UK, however, did not ratify the Social Chapter in the Maastricht Treaty, but in 1997 the Treaty of Amsterdam incorporated the Social Charter, as it had become, and the UK became a signatory. The Amsterdam Treaty, which came into effect on 1 May 1999, has re-numbered previous article numbers, so, for example, Art 177 of the Treaty of Rome, providing for a preliminary ruling by the European Court of Justice (ECJ), now becomes Art 234.

United Kingdom constitutional theory demands that an international treaty entered into by the Crown has no effect in domestic law unless and until it is given effect by legislation. Authority for this is to be found in the case of *Mortensen v Peters* (1906). This is an aspect of the doctrine of parliamentary sovereignty and, in legal theory, these Acts may be repealed by a later Parliament, with the result that the UK can be in breach of international law. The political reality is quite different, and any attempt to repeal this legislation would not only result in political crisis, but also call in question the position of the courts and whether the judges would comply strictly with the doctrine of parliamentary sovereignty or attempt to comply with the law of the European Community. At the present time, with the doctrine still in place, in so far as it gives effect to EC law, developments have shown the courts of the UK willing to give European law priority where there is a conflict with domestic law.

The institutions of the EU

There are four main institutions of the EU.

The Council of the European Union

The Council, formerly the Council of Ministers, is made up of one representative from each of the 15 Member States, usually the foreign minister, or the appropriate minister for the business to be discussed. For example, when agriculture is being dealt with, the UK would be represented by the Minister for Agriculture, Fisheries and Food. The Council is the principal decision making body and can conclude agreements on behalf of the Union. The presidency is rotated between each Member State on a six month basis. Decisions are reached in one of three ways: by simple majority, qualified majority or unanimously. Larger States have proportionately more votes. France, Germany, Italy and the UK each have 10 votes; Spain has eight; Belgium, Greece, The Netherlands and Portugal each have five votes; Sweden and Austria have four; Denmark, Finland and Ireland each have three and Luxembourg has two. The qualified majority on a vote is 62 out of a total of 87.

This is the supreme law maker for the EC but it can only normally legislate on receipt of proposals by the Commission. By the Luxembourg Accords, the Council has adopted the practice of unanimity for decisions involving vital national interests.

The Council of the European Union must not be confused with the European Council, which was established in 1974 and given formal recognition under the Single European Act 1986. This consists of heads of government and foreign ministers who meet in 'summit' at least twice a year as provided for under Art 2 of the Single European Act. This is not one of the institutions of the Union and it does not have general decision making power. Another body not to be confused with the Council of the European Union or the European Council is the Committee of Permanent Representatives of Member States (COREPER), which prepares the work of the representatives on the Council and is composed of ambassadors of the Member States.

This terminology can at times be very confusing and it is perhaps useful to note here that the institutions already mentioned must not be confused with the Council of Europe, which established the European Convention for the Protection of Human Rights and Fundamental Freedoms in 1953.

The European Commission

The Commission, which is located in Brussels, is the executive body, likened to a 'civil service'. There are at present 20 members drawn from Member States.

France, Germany, Italy, the UK and Spain appoint two Commissioners each and the other States appoint one. The Intergovernmental Conference has agreed that, when the EU is next enlarged, all States will only appoint one Commissioner. Commissioners swear an oath of allegiance to the Union and each takes responsibility for a subject. One is appointed President, and two become Vice-Presidents. Commissioners are appointed for five years by mutual agreement. Each is assisted by a cabinet of six or more officials appointed by and responsible to the Commissioner. They formulate proposals for the Commission's approval. *Chefs de Cabinet* meet regularly to co-ordinate and prepare for Commission meetings. The Commission is divided into departments or Directorates General, headed by a Director General responsible to a Commissioner. Each Directorate General is divided into directorates and these are further subdivided into divisions. Some specialist services, such as a legal service, are provided.

Its main function is the preparation of proposals for new legislation which are laid before the Council and the formulation of policy. It also has limited legislative powers of its own in areas such as competition policy and control of government subsidies. It also implements EC legislation and ensures that treaty obligations are observed by Member States.

The European Parliament

The Parliament, formerly called the European Assembly, has 626 members (MEPs) directly elected by Member States for a five year term. Members sit in party groupings, not according to State. Membership is as follows:

Germany:	99
France, Italy and UK:	87 each
Spain:	64
Netherlands:	31
Portugal, Belgium and Greece:	25 each
Sweden:	22
Austria:	21
Denmark and Finland:	16 each
Ireland:	15
Luxembourg:	6

The Parliament operates in two locations – it holds plenary sessions in Strasbourg and committee meetings in Brussels.

The involvement of the Parliament in law making was increased under the provisions of the Single European Act. This is known as the 'co-operation procedure'. It can accept, reject or amend proposed legislative changes and it has a power of veto over the Commission's budget proposals. It can also dismiss the Commission on a two-thirds vote, but this power has not yet been used, although events in 1998 and 1999 brought Parliament very close to doing so. In December 1998, Parliament voted not to accept the Commission's accounts for 1996 given serious allegations of fraud and mishandling of finances. This was followed in January 1999 by a report from the Court of Auditors holding the Commission responsible for maladministration and fraud. Some £3 billion had been overlooked or wasted and proper accounting principles were absent. This report resulted in a vote of no confidence in the Commission and a committee was set up to investigate and report on its work. When the committee reported, this at least demonstrated that the control mechanisms were effective, as the report clearly showed the extent to which money had been mishandled. It was merely a question of time before Parliament would exercise its power to dismiss the Commission. However, all the Commission members resigned, and Romano Prodi took over as caretaker President pending approval of a new Commission. Another development has been the appointment of Neil Kinnock as Vice President of the Commission charged with the duty of reforming its workings.

Under the TEU it can set up Committees of Inquiry to investigate contraventions of, or maladministration in, the implementation of EC law. It may also appoint an ombudsman to investigate complaints of maladministration. Under the TEU, it has powers of veto in proposals concerning the single market.

The ECJ

The ECJ interprets EC law and its application to Member States and other bodies. The Court follows the Roman law tradition in that no reliance is placed on precedent (although decisions of the Court bind the courts of Member States). An inquisitorial approach is followed and no dissenting opinions are given. Counsel make written submissions and the Court reaches a preliminary decision through Advocates General. In *Grant v South West Trains Ltd* (1998), the claimant sought equal treatment for her same-sex partner as an employee with a spouse or heterosexual partner. The Advocate General recommended to the ECJ that Art 6 of the Equal Treatment Directive could extend to same-sex couples, but the Court rejected this view.

A president is appointed by fellow judges and each Member State sends one judge to the Court. The 15 judges are assisted by nine Advocates General.

Reference may be made (and, in the case of Member States' final appeal courts, reference must be made) under Art 234 of the EC Treaty for a preliminary ruling as to the meaning or effect of EC law. The case of *Bulmer v Bollinger* (1974), in which Lord Denning MR laid down four guidelines as to whether a reference was necessary and six guidelines for the exercise of the discretion by those courts which are not final appeal courts, remains instructive as to the use of Art 234 although refined by later cases.

In 1989, the Court of First Instance (CFI) was inaugurated, with the aim of easing the burden of the ECJ and to speed up the hearing of cases. Members are appointed for six year terms by mutual agreement between Member States. It sits in divisions of three or five judges. Members may be asked to act as Advocates General, and when so acting must not participate in the deliberations of the Court, before the decision is made. The CFI decides disputes between the EC and its employees; appeals against the implementation of EC competition rules and actions brought by undertakings against the Commission under the ECSC Treaty. Appeals on points of law only against decisions of the CFI lie to the ECJ.

Use of Art 234 necessitates adjournment of a case in the domestic court pending the interpretation of EC law by the European Court. The delay may be several years and this of course increases costs for litigants.

In addition to preliminary rulings, the ECJ decides proceedings against Member States brought by either the Commission or by another Member State for alleged violations of the treaties or EC legislation. The Court can order an offending State to take the necessary measures to comply. The TEU gives the ECJ the power to impose financial sanctions. Previously, the Court could only rely on political pressure. A recent illustration is the action taken by the Commission against France and Germany to seek compliance with EC law over the lifting of the ban on UK beef.

Other disputes handled by the ECJ include actions against Community institutions brought by other institutions, Member States or possibly corporate bodies and individuals. The Court may annul acts of the Council or Commission; issue a declaration that the Council or Commission has failed to act as required by the treaties; order compensation for damage caused by EC institutions; and review the penalties imposed by the Commission.

Other organisations of the EC

The Court of Auditors

This sits in Luxembourg and scrutinises the EC's financial management. It reports to Parliament and oversees the implementation of the budget. It has 15 members, appointed every six years by the Council in consultation with the European Parliament. As a result of the TEU, the Court of Auditors is now an institution of the EC.

The Economic and Social Committee (ESC)

Representatives from Member States, drawn from employers, employees, professional bodies, consumers, farmers and those representing interests such as the environment, sit on this Committee and its opinion on proposed legislation is sought by the Council and Commission.

The Committee of the Regions

Set up by the TEU as an advisory committee, this consists of representatives from each Member State, drawn from regional and local bodies. It is consulted on proposed legislation involving education, culture and public health.

The European Investment Bank

This is also based in Luxembourg, with the function of lending money for the finance of capital investment projects.

EC Ombudsman

The TEU created this post. The Ombudsman is appointed by the European Parliament for a five year term. He deals with complaints from citizens involving maladministration by EC institutions other than the ECJ. No time limits or filter mechanism apply, as in UK domestic law. MEPs may refer complaints to him, or he may conduct investigations on his own account. He cannot impose sanctions, but depends on publicity and political pressure. He must submit an annual report to the Parliament and in each case where he finds maladministration.

Law making powers of the EC institutions

Consultation procedure

Before the Single European Act, this was the only procedure, and the Commission formulated proposals which were submitted to the Council for consideration. The European Parliament was to be consulted and could give an opinion. The Council took the final decision. This procedure is still used in respect of the European Monetary Union.

Under the Treaty of Amsterdam 1997, the Council and Parliament are placed on a more equal footing. The scope of Parliament's powers is extended and a reduction is made in the number of legislative processes. In future, emphasis is placed on reaching decisions by way of the consultation, co-decision and assent procedures.

Co-operation procedure

This was introduced by the Single European Act and involves the European Parliament more fully in the decision making process. Parliament gives its opinion and proposes amendments on two occasions:

- when the Commission proposal is submitted to the Council; and

- after the Council has considered Parliament's opinion and reached a 'common position'.

Parliament has no right of veto, merely a power to influence the decision making process. Under the TEU, this procedure was to be used in areas formerly subject to the consultation procedure, such as common transport policy decisions.

Co-decision procedure

This was introduced by the TEU and applies to most single market proposals, consumer protection, culture and public health. It follows the co-operation procedure up to the point where Parliament considers the 'common position' adopted by the Council. If Parliament approves the proposal, the Council adopts the measure. If it indicates an intention to reject the common position, a Conciliation Committee, consisting of 12 representatives of the Council and 12 MEPs, is convened to reach an agreement.

If no agreement is reached or one which is not acceptable to the Parliament, the proposal lapses. If Parliament proposes changes to the 'common position', then, following further consideration by Commission and Council, the latter may adopt the measure, provided it approves all amendments. If it does not, the Conciliation Committee is convened and both sides may agree a joint text. The measure must then be adopted within six weeks by the Council and

Parliament. If no agreement can be reached, the proposal will either lapse or be adopted unilaterally by the Council. Parliament has a power of veto and can reject the proposal by an absolute majority.

Assent procedure

This was introduced by the Single European Act and applies to applications to join the EC and agreements between the EC and other States or organisations. If the Council is to adopt a Commission proposal under this procedure, it must first obtain the formal approval of Parliament.

Sources of EC law

When considering the sources of EC law a distinction is made between treaties and secondary law. Treaties are the primary source of law, for example, the Treaties of Paris, Rome, TEU and the Amsterdam Treaty. Some are so specific in their terms that they take direct effect and provide enforceable Community rights for individuals.

Defrenne v Sabena (No 2) (1978) is authority for the proposition that the principle of equal pay for equal work (now Art 141) is directly effective, so that individuals who are discriminated against may rely on this provision and bring an action against the employer under the doctrine of horizontal direct effect. Where rights are created against the Member State, this is called 'vertical direct effect'. Many treaty provisions are too general and rely on Member States implementing them via national law.

The Council and Commission are empowered by the treaties to make three types of secondary law: regulations, directives and decisions. Recommendations and opinions are advisory only and do not have any binding effect. We shall see later the effect of each of these types of law.

The application of EC law

So far as application of European law within Member States is concerned, the view of the ECJ and the views of domestic courts have not always been identical.

The attitude of the ECJ to EC law

The European Court has, on many occasions, stated that European law takes precedence over domestic law. Authority for this is to be found in *Costa v ENEL* (1964), *Internationale Handelsgesellschaft* (Case 11/70) and *Van Gend en Loos* (1963). On 19 June 1990, the ECJ again ruled that European law was to take precedence over domestic law in what has become known as the Spanish fishermen case, which involved the provisions of the Merchant Shipping Act 1988. In *R v Secretary of State for Transport ex p Factortame Ltd and Others (No 2)* (1990), the House of Lords granted interim relief to the applicants suspending the provisions of the 1988 Act.

A distinction has been drawn between directly applicable and directly effective provisions, although this distinction is not always made clear in the judgments of the European Court. Regulations are directly applicable and bestow rights on individuals under Art 249 of the EC Treaty. No further measures need be taken by Member States to bring regulations into effect.

On the other hand, directives are binding only as to the result to be achieved and Member States are free to choose the form of implementation, subject only to a specified timetable. To be directly effective, a directive must meet three conditions:

(a) the provision must be clear and precise in its scope and application;

(b) it must not be conditional;

(c) there must be no room for a Member State to exercise its discretion in implementing the directive.

If a directive meets these conditions, but otherwise is inadequately implemented by a Member State, an individual can still rely on its terms in the domestic courts. This is known as 'vertical direct effect', in that an individual can look to his or her government for a remedy.

Authority is to be found in *Marshall v Southampton and SW Hants AHA* (1984), which concerned the compulsory retirement age of 65 for men and 60 for women. It was held that the Equal Treatment Directive had been broken and that this could be relied on as the employer was an organ of the State.

An issue then arose as to whether direct effect could apply for the benefit of individuals who wished to bring claims not against the State, but another individual or private body. This became known as 'horizontal direct effect'. The cases of *Von Colson* (1983) and *Marleasing SA v La Commercial Internacional* (1989) show that the European Court called in aid Art 5 of the Treaty of Rome (now Art 10) to get round the difficulty, with the result that States (including domestic courts) must take 'all appropriate measures' to fulfil European obligations. *Macarthys v Smith* (1979) is authority for the direct applicability of treaty articles and their horizontal direct effect. Article 119 (now Art 141) conferred rights on S which were enforceable against her private sector employer in the UK courts.

A further breakthrough was made in *Francovich v Italy* (1992) when the European Court held that Francovich should be awarded damages against the Italian Government despite the directive in question having been found to be insufficiently precise to be directly effective.

Further developments have now been seen concerning State liability to pay damages to individuals. In the cases of *R v Secretary of State for Transport ex p Factortame (No 4); Brasserie du Pêcheur SA v Federal Republic of Germany* (1996), it was held that Member States can be made liable in damages to an individual for legislation that is incompatible with European law. In both cases, treaty provisions were in question. The ECJ ruled that a right to damages lies where three conditions are met. There must be a serious breach of the law; the intention of the EC law in dispute must be to confer rights on individuals, and a direct causal link between the breach of obligation by the State and the damage suffered by the individual must be proved. These conditions were later applied in the case of *Dillenkofer and Others v Federal Republic of Germany* (1996), concerning the Package Holidays Directive which was due to be implemented by 31 December 1992. Germany only implemented the measure with effect from July 1994. In the meantime, two package tour operators became insolvent and, as a result, the plaintiffs either lost their holiday or had to return home at their own expense. It was held that the three conditions having been met entitled the plaintiffs to reparation by the German Government.

In *Van Gend en Loos* (1963), Art 12 of the Treaty of Rome (now Art 25) was held to have vertical direct effect and this ruling was soon applied to other treaty provisions which satisfied the conditions above. Horizontal direct effect of treaty provisions was recognised in *Defrenne v Sabena* (1975). In *R v Secretary of State for Transport ex p Factortame Ltd and Others (No 5)* (1997), it was held that there was no right to claim punitive damages in respect of the breaches of EC law by the UK Government passing the Merchant Shipping Act 1988, which precluded Spanish trawler owners from registering to fish in UK waters.

So far as decisions, recommendations and opinions are concerned, only decisions are binding and may have direct effect.

The attitude of the English courts to EC law

The UK courts are bound by the doctrine of sovereignty of Parliament and, whilst the UK is a member of the Union, European law is given effect under the European Communities Act 1972 and subsequent legislation.

When considering the attitude of the English courts to the application of European law, two points are worthy of note. The first point concerns the use of Art 234 of the EC Treaty for the making of a preliminary reference for the interpretation of a European provision. As we have already noted, the landmark case was that of *Bulmer v Bollinger* (1974), in which Lord Denning MR laid down guidelines to assist the court in deciding whether or not to make a reference. In his judgment, the House of Lords, as the final appeal court, was under a duty to make a reference where one or both parties wished, providing it was necessary to do so on the basis of four guidelines. All other courts had a discretion, and Lord Denning MR laid down six guidelines to assist a court with this question. Later cases have refined Lord Denning's statements and it may be that a court other than the House of Lords may be the final appeal court, in which case it will be under a duty to make an Art 234 reference.

The second point concerns the sovereignty of Parliament and how the English courts would deal with a clash between European law and domestic law. As we have already mentioned, European law is given effect by way of s 2(1)–(4) of the European Communities Act 1972 as subsequently amended. In strict legal theory this legislation could be repealed and a conflict created with European law. Even whilst remaining members of the EU, a clash between European and domestic law might arise. *R v Secretary of State for Transport ex p Factortame and Others (No 2)* (1990) involved the suspension of s 14 of the Merchant Shipping Act 1988 pending the final determination of the issues. This case, together with *R v Secretary of State for Employment ex p Equal Opportunities Commission* (1994), involving the rights of part time workers under the Equal Pay Directive, illustrates the closest the UK has come to such a clash.

The question has often been posed as to how UK judges should react, and four possibilities have been put forward: they could follow the traditional doctrine of implied repeal and give effect to the later legislation; they could ignore such later legislation unless it expressly repudiated European law; the judges could apply a rule of construction and interpret UK law consistently with European law; they could take a radical approach and apply European law.

In the light of the *Factortame* case and the ratification of the TEU in 1993 and the Amsterdam Treaty in 1997, there is every likelihood that any clash between European and domestic law will be slight and, should it arise, will be remedied, not by the courts, but by amending legislation. Should legislation be passed in the future which repeals the European Communities Act 1972, as amended, this raises much more fundamental issues and the reaction of the judges would depend on their view, not only of their role within the constitution, but of the constitution itself.

The European Convention on Human Rights

The European Convention for the Protection of Human Rights and Fundamental Freedoms was signed on 4 November 1949 and took effect on 3 September 1953. The aim was to 'reconstruct durable civilisation on the mainland of Europe'. Originally, 21 States signed the treaty, and this has now extended to over 40 States. The UK ratified the treaty in 1951, but only incorporated it in domestic law by way of the Human Rights Act 1998, although the UK granted its citizens the right to petition the ECHR in 1966. The dualist constitutional doctrine ensured that, without domestic legislation giving effect to the Convention, it could not apply directly in domestic law. It is worth noting, however, that Convention rights have been given limited credence by domestic courts. This was so where the court needed to establish the scope of the common law, as was shown in *Derbyshire CC v Times Newspapers* (1992), which was concerned with whether libel could be committed against a local authority; also where a court, in interpreting a statute, found ambiguity and called on the Convention as an aid to construction.

When founded, the Convention established three bodies: the European Commission of Human Rights (abolished by Protocol 11 with effect from November 1998); the European Court of Human Rights (ECHR); and the Committee of Ministers. All three were located in Strasbourg, and the role of the Commission was to advise the Court and offer an opinion in each case.

As we shall see later, the different traditions in drafting and interpreting legislation and the reliance on the sovereignty of Parliament doctrine in the UK will result in major changes in both substantive and procedural rules when the Human Rights Act 1998 comes into force in October 2000. Emphasis on the rule of law as found in the Convention rights and on a purposive approach to statutory interpretation will demand of the judiciary a reappraisal of its role in protecting the rights of the citizen against abuse or excess of power by the State or emanations of the State.

An applicant to the ECHR will have to identify the Convention right on which he or she relies. Some are absolute – for example, the right not to be tortured – whereas others are subject to limitations or qualifications. The Court will have to balance individual and public interests (proportionality) and also balance the interests of the majority and those of minorities. Any interference with a Convention right will have to be proportionate, prescribed by law and intended to achieve a legitimate objective. The doctrine of proportionality is far wider than the English test of *Wednesbury* unreasonableness, established in the case of *Associated Picture Houses v Wednesbury Corporation* (1948), or as Lord Diplock in the *GCHQ* case referred to it, irrationality, and so when domestic courts start to apply the Convention a new approach will be required.

It was reported in *The Times* (24 March 2000) that the *Practice Direction (Crown Office List: Preparation for Hearings)* has been issued to ensure that the backlog of cases already in process must be cleared before the Human Rights Act 1998 comes into force.

Three concepts are worth mentioning here, as they have played an important part in the development of the law by the ECHR and its influence in the domestic legal systems of its members. First, the ECHR developed a principle called the margin of appreciation to allow for the cultural and social differences between Member States. The case of *Wingrove v UK* (1996) illustrates how this works. The UK decided to ban the film *Visions of Ecstasy* under its blasphemy laws contained in the Offensive Publications Act 1956. The film director asserted that his freedom of speech under Art 10 was infringed, but the Court held that such fundamental issues as blasphemy should be decided at the local level and declined to find against the UK ban. Once the Convention is given effect to in UK law, it would seem that UK courts will not be able to invoke a margin of appreciation, but instead will be able to apply the principle of proportionality in reaching decisions. Secondly, decisions of the Court have persuasive authority and this includes both decisions of the Commission and Court, where the former were made whilst the Commission was in existence. However, this principle has to take account of the third principle. This states that the Convention is a 'living instrument' and flexibility is needed in its interpretation, as well as the recognition that, as membership increases and attitudes change, such changes should be reflected in how the Convention is applied.

We will now consider each of the main articles in turn.

Article 1 imposes a duty on signatories to 'secure to everyone within their jurisdiction the rights and freedoms' protected by the Convention. Article 2 protects the right to life. Lawful execution, use of self defence, lawful arrest, use of force to quell a riot or prevent a prisoner's escape are permitted. No derogation under Art 15 is allowed and Protocol 6 requires States to abolish the death penalty.

This article provides some notable case law, including against the UK. In *McCann v UK* (1995), the three IRA gunmen shot and killed on Gibraltar by the SAS resulted in a 10:9 majority finding of a violation of Art 2, but the costs and expenses of the applicants only were recoverable. A further challenge is at present before the Court, brought by relatives of those killed by the Security Forces in Northern Ireland. The Government's 'shoot to kill' policy is in question. In *Paton v UK* (1980), abortion was permitted, as the 10 week old foetus was not a separate life from its mother, and the father, who was separated from the mother, had no claim.

The case of *Osman v UK* (1999) has been referred to in Chapter 9. No violation of Art 2 was found, but Art 6 had been violated. However, important *dicta* are to be found in the case concerning the State's duty to protect life. The Court suggested that a breach of this duty may result merely from a failure to do all that would reasonably be expected so as to avoid a real or immediate risk to life which is known or ought to be known. This case concerned the duty of the police to prevent the commission of a crime where they had been informed that a high risk of danger to the victim was apparent. A recent instance where a young woman starved herself to death over a period of five weeks in a National Trust car park in Cornwall and where various members of the public attempted to alert the police comes to mind. Could it be that the police have a duty to protect life in such a situation? If so, what steps should be taken to comply with the duty?

Article 3 ensures freedom from torture or inhuman or degrading treatment. This is an absolute duty and cannot be derogated from under Art 15. On a scale of nastiness, torture is at the top, followed by inhuman treatment, and at the bottom is degrading treatment. *Ireland v UK* (1978) involved the latter, when the UK Government permitted the hooding of IRA suspects, the playing of loud continuous noise, deprivation of food, drink and sleep and forcing suspects to stand against a wall in an uncomfortable stance. The court identified that treatment can give rise to different results. Thus, torture amounts to very serious or cruel suffering; inhuman treatment is intense physical or mental suffering; and degrading treatment gives rise to fear, anguish, humiliation, inferiority or the breaking of a person's physical or moral resolve.

Soering v UK (1989) involved the extradition of S to the USA to face a murder trial, with the prospect that he would be held for a long period on death row. This was held to violate Art 3. The question of corporal punishment has often been raised under this article. A recent ruling finds that smacking only is acceptable. In *A v UK* (1998), a stepfather hit a boy with a stick and was acquitted under s 47 of the Offences Against the Person Act 1861, but the ECHR ruled that Art 3 had been violated.

Clearly, torture involves very serious physical or mental suffering, whereas inhuman and degrading treatment is less serious. However, treatment of asylum seekers and those facing deportation will have to be subject to control, as will the treatment of those subject to immigration rules. A recent press report concerned a man who was a US national whose mother was British and who had been brought up in the UK. He faced deportation from the UK, but left voluntarily in the hope that he would be able to return to marry. Entry was refused, and he committed suicide on what would have been his wedding day. The methods of interviewing and investigating the applications of such people will in future be subject to close scrutiny under the Human Rights Act 1998.

Prisoners and victims of crime, such as in *R v Edwards* (1996), where the victim of an alleged rape was subjected to examination at trial by the accused acting in person, will also come within this provision. Other interesting questions might arise out of the use of police batons, CS spray, the detention of paedophiles and the activities of vigilantes. Other questions will involve the use of euthanasia and the position of the 'Moors murderer', Ian Brady, comes to mind. Will the use of force-feeding to keep a prisoner alive be lawful or does a prisoner, or other person, have a right to die?

Article 4 provides for freedom from slavery and forced labour. No claims have been upheld under this article, which cannot be derogated from, although exceptions permit acting in an emergency, the carrying out of civic obligations and being made subject to prison and military service.

Article 5 protects the right to liberty and security of the person, subject to exceptions prescribed by law and Art 15 derogation in an emergency. Compensation is payable where this Article is not complied with. Questions may arise concerning the detention of mandatory life prisoners, detention of paedophiles, the use of electronic tagging and the detention of asylum seekers and patients with mental illness. The ECHR has ruled in the case of *Caballero v UK* (2000) that s 56 of the Crime and Disorder Act 1998 (amending s 25 of the Criminal Justice and Public Order Act 1994), permitting an automatic denial of bail, breached Art 5(3) and (5).

Article 6 ensures the right to a fair trial. Needless to say, this is an extremely important provision and one which no doubt will give rise to many claims, having already given rise to more applications than any other. There are three parts to this provision and they are worth mentioning in full:

- in civil and criminal proceedings, 'everyone is entitled to a fair and public hearing within a reasonable time by an independent and impartial tribunal established by law ...'. The press and public can be excluded 'in the interests of morals, public order or national security ... where the interests of juveniles or the protection of the private life of the parties so require, or to the extent strictly necessary in the opinion of the court in special circumstances where publicity would prejudice the interests of justice';

- the presumption of innocence applies to everyone charged with a criminal offence;

- five minimum rights are provided for those charged with a criminal offence: to be informed promptly of the nature and cause of the accusation in a language he understands and in detail; to have adequate time and facilities for preparation of his defence; to defend himself in person or through legal assistance of his own choosing or to have free assistance when the interests of justice so require and he has insufficient means; to examine or have examined witnesses against him and to obtain the attendance and examination of witnesses on his behalf under equal conditions; to have free assistance of an interpreter if he cannot understand or speak the language used in court.

Different jurisdictions define differently what amounts to civil or criminal proceedings: where a domestic criminal offence is in question, the ECHR has stated that this is to be accepted, but where domestically, an act is classed as non-criminal, it is for the Court to decide the question.

Article 6 is concerned with due process and this was explained in *Neumeister v Austria* (1968) and *Dombo Beheer BV v Netherlands* (1993) as a guarantee of 'equality of arms'. One side in a trial should not have an unfair advantage, so, for example, where one party is legally represented it may be essential to provide representation for the other side.

Other notable cases include *Golder v UK* (1975), where it was held that a prisoner should have access to a lawyer to allow him to defend proceedings involving a warder. In *Murray v UK* (1996), ss 34–37 of the Criminal Justice and Public Order Act 1994, concerning the right to silence, were subject to scrutiny.

M had refused to say anything on solicitor's advice after 48 hours in detention. He was questioned for 22 hours and 39 minutes over two days, and also refused to give evidence at trial. The Court held that Art 6 had not been violated, but stated that the right to remain silent was of fundamental importance, although not guaranteed. The refusal of access to a lawyer was, however, a violation.

In *Condron and Another v UK* (2000), the applicants had been advised by their solicitor not to answer police questions and the judge at trial had directed the jury that s 34 of the 1994 Act permitted the drawing of adverse inferences. The ECHR unanimously held that Art 6(1) had been breached.

In *Saunders v UK* (1996), Ernest Saunders, a defendant in the Guinness fraud trial in 1990, proved a violation arising out of interviews by Department of Trade inspectors, when he was required to answer questions without the right to silence. He alleged that such questioning and the use of evidence, obtained in this way, at trial infringed Art 6. Both the Commission and Court found in his favour but did not award him damages. The UK Government accepted that such inspectors should not have had these powers and that the law is to be amended for the future. This, of course, failed to assist Saunders, who was left without a remedy.

Some issues which may come into question under this provision are the rules for disclosure of prosecution evidence under the Criminal Procedure and Investigations Act 1996, decisions made by the Crown Prosecution Service not to prosecute, the admissibility of evidence obtained in contravention of the Convention and the trial and sentencing of juveniles. A recent case (*R v CPS ex p Simon Jones* (2000)) found that the Crown Prosecution Service was subject to judicial review in connection with its decision not to prosecute for corporate manslaughter. Simon Jones had taken vacation work in a dock and was killed on his first day whilst loading a ship with rocks. At the end of 1999, the ECHR ruled against the British Government in connection with the trial and sentencing of the killers of Jamie Bulger, Thompson and Venables. It is to be noted that the Home Secretary, Jack Straw, has, as a result of this judgment, instructed the Lord Chief Justice to review the tariff period for both defendants.

Another question arises in connection with the position of judges and judicial officers. The Commission has held that the Bailiff of Guernsey, in carrying out judicial, legislative and administrative functions, detracted from the need to ensure judicial impartiality. In a recent Scottish case tried under the Human Rights Act 1998 (which has been given effect in Scotland following devolution), the position of sheriffs has been challenged. They also carry out a mix of function, and it was found that this can affect the appearance of independence and impartiality in the conduct of their judicial functions. This will no doubt bring to mind the position of the Lord Chancellor, particularly in the light of the recent cases of *R v Bow Street Magistrates ex p Pinochet Ugarte (No 2)* (1999) and *Locabail (UK) Ltd v Bayfield Properties and Another* (1999) in which judicial independence and impartiality were questioned. The ECHR in *Sander v UK* (2000) held by a 4:3 majority that a judge's decision to deal with an allegation of racial bias in the jury trying an Asian defendant by redirection, rather than a discharge of the jury, breached Art 6(1). In the circumstances, a reasonable impression and fear of a lack of impartiality was created.

Article 7 provides for protection from the retrospective effect of the criminal law. In *Welch v UK* (1995), W was arrested on drugs charges in November 1986 and a forfeiture order came into effect in the following January. The court held that this was retrospective and amounted to a violation of Art 7, but in *SW v UK* (1995), a husband could be guilty of the rape of his wife when the common law (as decided in *R v R* (1990) was changed after the act with which he was accused had been done. Again, the detention of paedophiles, so as to protect children, when no sentence of imprisonment is in force will no doubt be questioned under this provision.

Article 8 provides a right to respect for family and private life, home and correspondence, subject to exceptions in the interests of national security, public safety or economic well being of the State, prevention of disorder or crime, protection of health or morals or the rights and freedoms of others. Some notable cases have been decided under this provision. One of the most important is *Malone v UK* (1984), which involved telephone tapping by the police of a suspect, where a violation was proved. This resulted in the passing of the Interception of Communications Act 1985 and demonstrates that where a government is found to violate the rights of its citizens, a change in the law must be made, even where no such right was previously recognised in domestic law.

In *Dudgeon v UK* (1981), which concerned serious sexual offences in Northern Ireland, domestic controls were found to be intrusive and outweighed the need to protect vulnerable persons. In *Sutherland v UK* (1998), concerning the question of homosexual consent, it was held that this should be the same as for heterosexual consent. Change in the law is awaited. Similarly, a ruling permitting homosexuals to be employed in the military services has resulted in changes in UK law. However, in *Laskey, Jaggard and Brown v UK* (1997), sado-masochistic offences under ss 20 and 47 of the Offences Against the Person Act 1861 were held not to violate Art 8. Prisoners' rights to correspondence were protected by this article in *Golder v UK* (1975) and *Silver v UK* (1983).

Some examples of future issues involving this Article include the existence of a right of privacy, which has been denied at common law; conflict between this article and Art 10 (freedom of expression); the use of listening devices and closed circuit television. Another issue likely to arise is the use of medical records and the refusal in UK law to permit changes in birth certificates following adoption and the carrying out of sex change operations. An interesting case has been reported in the press recently where a man had a sex change operation and became a woman, but who for the purposes of the law remains registered as a man. This enabled him to go through a ceremony of marriage with his female partner. It is likely that when the Human Rights Act 1998 comes into effect, a person faced with such a situation may apply to the court for his birth certificate and other records to be amended.

Article 9 provides for freedom of thought, conscience and religion. To hold beliefs is an absolute right, but limitations are placed on how they are expressed. In a recent press report, Jehovah's Witnesses were accused of attempting to convert Jews, Muslims and other people to their faith. It is beyond question that such beliefs can be held, but the methods by which they are conveyed can be subject to limitation. In *Stedman v UK* (1997), the applicant refused to work certain hours and asserted that the reason for so doing was her religious beliefs. On the facts, the Court held that her objection was not founded on her religious beliefs, but simply on her dislike of working certain hours.

Article 10 provides for freedom of expression, and this may often conflict with a right to privacy and the right to a fair trial, for example. In a democracy, a balance will have to be struck in recognition of the rights of individuals, journalists, the publication of information in the public interest and so on. In *Camelot Group plc v Centaur Communications Ltd* (1998), it was held that the Contempt of Court Act 1981 protects the rights recognised in this Article.

In *Handyside v UK* (1976), the 'little red schoolbook' case, the question for the Court was whether there was a violation of Art 10 in preventing the issue of this book, which contained a chapter on sex, to schoolchildren. The UK sought to ban the book on the basis that it offended public morality. The Court held that it was its function to supervise what took place domestically, but it should allow for a margin of appreciation in such delicate areas as were involved here. It will be interesting to see how s 28 of the Local Government Act 1988, if it remains law, will fare in relation to this Article.

Article 11 provides for freedom of assembly and association. This includes a right to join a trade union, a right to strike, to join political parties and other associations. However, such rights are not without limitation, so there is no automatic right to join a trade or professional body, such as The Law Society or the Bar, and the *Council of Civil Service Unions v Minister for the Civil Service* (1985) (the *GCHQ* case) clearly shows that a ban, imposed by the Government on civil servants at the Cheltenham communications centre, from joining a trade union, was justified in the interests of national security and so was not in breach of this Article.

Article 12 provides for the right to marry and found a family. In *Rees v UK* (1986) it was held that a right to found a family only applies in marriage, so homosexuals and transsexuals are excluded from this provision.

Article 13 provides a right to an effective remedy, but this has not been incorporated by the Human Rights Act 1998. In the case of *Govell v UK* (1998), the Police Complaints Authority was held not to provide an effective remedy to those adversely affected by the actions of the police.

Article 14 provides non-discrimination in relation to Convention rights on the grounds of sex, race, colour, language, religion, political or other opinion, national or social origin, association with a national minority, property, birth or other status. It is very wide, but not a free-standing provision. It only applies to discrimination in relation to Convention rights, for example, sex, marital status, sexual orientation, birth, military or trade union status, conscientious objection, imprisonment, property, etc. The categories are open.

Article 15 permits derogation from Convention rights in 'war or other public emergency threatening the life of the nation', provided such derogation is proportional and necessary to deal with the emergency. This was a much used provision by the UK in connection with terrorist activities in Northern Ireland.

Article 16 imposes a restriction on political activity of aliens. This is not only an outdated provision, but conflicts with Art 10, which is likely to take precedence.

Articles 17 and 18 safeguard the Convention provisions.

The First Protocol provides three additional rights: to peaceful enjoyment of one's possessions; the right to education; and the right to free elections.

The Sixth Protocol provides for the abolition of the death penalty, but this has not been ratified by the UK.

Having considered the main Convention rights, we shall move on to consider the process by which a claim can be brought to the ECHR. Since Protocol 11 was ratified, with effect from 1 November 1998, abolishing the European Commission of Human Rights, all applicants have direct access to the Court. When the Human Rights Act 1998 comes into force in England in October 2000, applicants who have exhausted all domestic remedies, where a breach of Convention rights has not been identified by domestic courts, will be able to bring their case before the Court.

Article 20 provides for the nomination of one person from each Member State to sit in the Court. They must not represent the government, but act in an individual capacity, and by Art 27(1), most cases are decided by chambers of seven judges.

Article 33 provides for complaints to be made by Member States and Art 34 for complaints by individuals. By far the most complaints are made by individuals alleging breach of their rights. This is a very slow process, although in cases of emergency the court may act quickly. The majority of cases do not surmount the obstacle of admissibility. This depends on written evidence detailing the facts relied on, domestic law and the Convention right or rights alleged to have been broken. A case which relies on past Court decisions stands a better chance of success. Litigants are not legally aided by the UK, although this should change as a result of the Human Rights Act 1998.

Complaints are registered with the secretary of the Court and full details must be provided. Committees of three judges act as a filter and decide whether a claim is admissible for hearing. The rapporteur investigates each claim and reports to the chamber of judges or refers the case to a committee. At each stage a case may be declared inadmissible. No appeal lies against such a finding. Less than 0.5% of cases reach the stage at which the committee communicates, that is, gives notice of the claim to the respondent State.

A government is likely then to make observations on the claim and these will be sent to the applicant, who can make a reply. Time limits apply, and although a case may be admitted at this stage, it may later be found to be inadmissible. The chamber of judges may hold a hearing to determine admissibility and can decide on the merits.

Article 35 provides guidelines as to admissibility. For example, anonymous claims, failure to meet the six month time limit and matters already dealt with by the Court or international process (the UK does not permit UK citizens to make direct application to the International Court of Justice in The Hague) will be inadmissible. Also, claims where domestic remedies have not been exhausted, those outside the terms of the Convention or where an abuse of process is shown, and those which are ill founded in failing to demonstrate a *prima facie* violation of Convention rights will also fail. By Art 25, it is essential for the applicant to be a victim; this includes a person who has suffered a violation of Convention rights and one who runs the risk of being directly affected in the future.

Claims which are admitted are heard on their merits unless under Art 38 'friendly settlement' is successful. An order for compensation may be made, or a decision made, or a change in the law agreed. A respondent State must demonstrate that not only the individual claimant's position is settled, but also the general position in respect of other citizens.

If a settlement fails to materialise, then oral and written submissions of evidence are made and the applicant is entitled to legal representation. The Court may seek the assistance of third parties, such as Liberty or Amnesty International, under Art 36. Short oral hearing follows, and written speeches must be submitted in advance so as to allow for translation. In some cases, such as the *Thompson and Venables* case, a Grand Chamber of 17 judges hears a case, subject to the parties' consent under Art 30.

By Art 27(2), the respondent State's judge sits *ex officio* in the chamber of judges or the Grand Chamber.

By Art 40, where a violation is proved, the Court may award 'just satisfaction', that is, damages and costs. The decision binds the Government, which must take legislative steps to implement it. The Committee of Ministers can ensure compliance with orders of the Court.

By Protocol 11, a right of appeal lies from the chamber to the Grand Chamber, subject to a three month time limit. A panel of five judges will grant a referral where a case 'raises a serious question affecting the interpretation or application of the Convention or the protocols or a serious issue of general importance'. Cases which have been held to be inadmissible are not covered by this provision.

The Human Rights Act 1998

The long title of the Act states that it is an Act 'to give further effect to the rights and freedoms guaranteed under the Convention'. The UK's tradition of parliamentary sovereignty, rather than a reliance on the rule of law as expressed in a Bill of Rights or written constitution, creates a delicate balance between giving effect in domestic law to Convention rights and retaining the doctrine of sovereignty.

Several sections of the Act deserve special mention. By s 2, domestic courts will be required to take the Strasbourg case law (since 1998, decisions of the ECHR, whereas decisions made before that time include those made by the Commission) into account, where appropriate, in reaching decisions.

Section 3 provides that all legislation, past and future, must be read and given effect so as to be compatible with Convention rights. It is important to note that compatibility does not equate with legality – the doctrine of sovereignty is maintained here, as it is in regard to the Human Rights Act 1998 as a statute, namely, in constitutional theory, it may be repealed at any time in the future. This will ensure that the judicial role adopts the purposive approach to statutory interpretation, that is, looking to the purpose for which an Act is passed, rather than attempting to find the meaning Parliament intended from the words used.

Section 6 states that public authorities, which includes the courts, must comply with the Convention, unless statute expressly prevents them from doing so.

By s 7, a victim of any action by a public authority (or other body which has power to exercise public functions) which is incompatible with Convention rights will be able to challenge the authority providing a claim is made within one year, or such shorter period as appropriate. For example, a three month limit usually applies in applications for judicial review.

Two very important issues arise here: first, as to the definition of victim; and secondly, as to the definition of public authority. The Act provides individuals denied their Convention rights with an important means of making both public bodies and private individuals accountable. The Act has a direct effect in relation to the former, whereas it has an indirect effect in relation to public bodies acting in a private capacity, such as employing workers and private individuals. The court hearing a claim involving private claims will itself be a public authority under s 6 and will be obliged to interpret statutes in conformity with the Convention, wherever possible, and in addition, as we mentioned in Chapter 9, exercise judicial discretion in applying rules of common law and equity compatibly with the convention.

Victims

Where a victim challenges a public authority, s 7 provides a new ground of illegality in judicial review where it is shown that the authority has failed to comply with Convention rights. A defence of complying with a statutory obligation is, however, provided. In addition, a victim may sue for breach of statutory duty or decide to await prosecution or civil action by the authority and then rely on the new defence of acting in accordance with Convention rights.

Who is a victim? By s 7, this is a person who is, or would be, a victim of the violation of Convention rights, namely one who is directly affected by the actions of a public authority. Article 34 and Protocol 11 place a limitation on who is protected, so public interest groups, such as Greenpeace, which have been able to seek judicial review in UK law, may be denied use of this Act. Such a group will only be able to refer to Convention rights as an interpretative tool under pre-1998 law. By s 11, the right of a litigant, who is not a victim, to rely on Convention arguments under pre-1998 law is preserved.

Public authorities

This refers to such bodies as government departments, the next step agencies, such as the Child Support Agency, and public corporations. Other bodies exercising public functions, such as the public utilities, may be included. The exercise of public functions or representing the public interest is crucial if a body is to be subject to the Act.

By s 3(2)(b) and (c), the doctrine of sovereignty of Parliament is preserved, in that express primary legislation cannot be overridden by a court but the higher courts, including the High Court, the Court of Appeal and House of Lords, can issue declarations of incompatibility under s 4. A fast track procedure is provided in s 10 and Sched 2, so that government can present legislation to Parliament to remedy any incompatibility under s 4.

So far as new legislation is concerned, ministers, when promoting Bills in Parliament, will include a statement at second reading of either compatibility or incompatibility. This will be of assistance to the court when interpreting such legislation and reference to *Hansard* will be permitted under the rule in *Pepper v Hart* (1992).

Finally, where a violation is proved, the victim will be entitled to 'such relief [against a public authority] or remedy or ... such order ... as the court considers just and appropriate'.

The relationship between the EC and the Convention in the protection of fundamental human rights

As we have noted when considering the application of the European Convention on Human Rights, the Human Rights Act 1998 will allow individuals who are victims of public authorities to seek direct redress in the UK courts. Action may also be taken in respect of violations of the Convention by individuals, where the common law fails to protect Convention rights.

Before the coming into force of the Human Rights Act, it could be argued that, in areas governed by EC law, it would be better for an individual to seek redress in EC law, rather than through the Convention. Certainly, areas of overlap exist and the EU recognises wider definitions of victim and public authority than those developed under the Convention. This is demonstrated in *Foster v British Gas* (1990). Remedies may also be more freely available as demonstrated in the *Francovich* case, where damages were awarded against the Italian Government for failure to implement EC law. Crucially, the direct applicability and direct effect doctrines of EC law allow domestic law to be overridden where the latter does not comply: see *Marshall v Southampton and SW Hants AHA (No 2)* (1993). In order to preserve the doctrine of sovereignty of Parliament, the most that can be achieved under the Convention is a declaration of incompatibility.

The EU is developing a doctrine of fundamental rights within its areas of competence. In 1977, the European Parliament, the Council and Commission issued a joint declaration which stressed the importance of protecting the fundamental rights found in the European Convention for the Protection of Human Rights and Fundamental Freedoms. Advocate General Jacobs recognised such a doctrine, in connection with EC nationals' rights of free movement in all Member States, in the case of *Konstantinides v Stadt A-S* (1993). Similar sentiments were expressed by Advocate General Tesauro in *P v S and Cornwall CC* (1996). However, in *Grant v SW Trains Ltd* (1998), the ECJ refused to follow this approach so as to extend Art 119 (now Art 141) on equal pay for equal work where sexual discrimination was found not to exist. The argument that EC law should be extended to cover discrimination on the grounds of sexual orientation was rejected.

Article 6 (formerly Art F(2)) contains the statement that the EC shall respect fundamental rights as guaranteed by the Convention as they result from the constitutional traditions common to Member States and as general principles of EC law.

The ECJ ruled in 1996 that this Article was not subject to judicial application and that accession by the EC to the Convention was not within its competence. However, in *Rutili v M of Interior* (1975), the ECJ said that fundamental human rights are enshrined in the general principles of EC law as inspired by the Convention and the constitutional traditions common to Member States.

It is not clear from the case law whether European fundamental rights equal Convention rights and whether or not the Convention is merely a set of guidelines. It would seem that, as this is a developing doctrine, there is still doubt as to the fundamental rights which should be recognised. In addition, the Convention is itself rather dated and, it can be argued, fails to provide the full range of rights required in today's world. The EC was set up as an economic free market, and so is better able to provide for economic rights, such as prohibitions on discrimination in the workplace, than the Convention.

The Treaty of Nice, incorporating the Charter of Fundamental Rights, is due to be signed in December 2000, possibly leading to formal incorporation of the Convention by the EU.

EUROPEAN LAW

Development of the EC/EU

- Historical background 1951–2000.

UK membership of the EC

- Dualist doctrine.

Institutions of the EU

- Four main institutions: Council of the European Union; European Commission; European Parliament; European Court of Justice (ECJ) (and Court of First Instance).

- Another institution is the Court of Auditors. Other bodies founded by treaty include the Economic and Social Committee (ESC); Committee of the Regions; European Investment Bank; EC Ombudsman.

- Law making powers: Treaty of Amsterdam 1997 – consultation, co-decision and assent procedures. Abolition of co-operation procedure.

Sources of EC law

- Primary sources – treaties – direct effect: *Defrenne v Sabena (No 2)* (1978).

- Secondary law: regulations; directives and decisions. Recommendations and opinions are advisory only and do not have binding effect.

The application of EC law

- European law takes precedence over domestic law: *Costa v ENEL* (1964); *Internationale Handelsgesellschaft* (Case 11/70) (1970); *Van Gend en Loos* (1963); *R v Secretary of State for Transport ex p Factortame Ltd and Others (No 2)* (1990).

- Regulations are directly applicable and bestow rights on individuals under Art 249 of the EC Treaty; directives are binding only as to the result to be achieved;

- Direct effect of directives:
  - vertical – *Marshall v Southampton and SW Hants AHA* (1984);
  - horizontal – *Von Colson* (1984); *Marleasing SA v La Commercial Internacional* (1989); *Macarthys v Smith* (1979).

- Enforcement of EC law against Member State governments: *Francovich v Italian Republic* (1992); *R v Secretary of State for Transport ex p Factortame Ltd and Others (No 4)* (1996); *Brasserie du Pêcheur SA v Federal Republic of Germany* (1996); *Dillenkofer and Others v Federal Republic of Germany* (1996).

- Preliminary rulings under Art 234 of the EC Treaty.

- The European Convention on Human Rights.

- The Human Rights Act 1998.

- Development of a doctrine of fundamental rights – *Konstantinides v Stadt A-S* (1993); *P v S and Cornwall CC* (1996); *Rutili v Minister of the Interior* (1975); *dicta* of the ECJ.

FURTHER READING

When using law texts, it is essential to acquire the most up to date editions. The dates of publication listed below are the latest editions as at April 2000. In addition to the suggested texts, students are advised to make full use of journals, particularly the *New Law Journal*, which is published weekly by Butterworths, and it should be remembered that the internet is an increasingly important source of information. Other useful commentaries on legal topics are the *Hamlyn Lectures*, published annually by Sweet & Maxwell.

The most up to date and comprehensive guide to the English legal system, and one which is relevant to every chapter of this book, is Slapper and Kelly's *English Law*, published 2000 by Cavendish Publishing.

Chapter 1   The Nature of Law

Bailey, SH, and Gunn, MJ, *Smith and Bailey on the Modern English Legal System*, 3rd edn, 1996, London: Sweet & Maxwell

Barnett, H, *Constitutional and Administrative Law*, 2nd edn, 1998, London: Cavendish Publishing

Bradney, A *et al*, *How to Study Law*, 3rd edn, 1995, London: Sweet & Maxwell

Clinch, P, *Using a Law Library*, 1992, London: Blackstone

Darbyshire, P, *Eddey on the English Legal System*, 1996, London: Sweet & Maxwell

Elliott, C and Quinn, F, *English Legal System*, 2nd edn, 1998, Harlow: Longman

Gifford, D and Salter, J, *Understanding the English Legal System*, 1997, London: Cavendish Publishing

Hart, HLA, *The Concept of Law*, 2nd edn, 1997, Oxford: OUP

Holland, JA and Webb, JS, *Learning Legal Rules*, 4th edn, 1999, London: Blackstone

Ingman, T, *The English Legal Process*, 6th edn, 1996, London: Blackstone

Jackson, P, *Constitutional and Administrative Law*, 8th edn, 1998, London: Sweet & Maxwell

Keenan, D, *Smith and Keenan's English Law*, 11th edn, 1995, London: Pitman

Mansell, W and Meteyard, BA, *A Critical Introduction to Law*, 2nd edn, 1995, London: Cavendish Publishing

Twining, W and Miers, D, *How to Do Things with Rules*, 4th edn, 1999, London: Butterworths

Chapter 2   The Sources of Law

Bell, JS and Engle, G (Sir), *Cross on Statutory Interpretation*, 1995, London: Butterworths

Bennion, F, *Statutory Interpretation*, 1997, London: Butterworths

Cross, R, *Cross, Harris and Hart: Precedent in English Law*, 1976, Oxford: OUP

Denning (Lord), *Due Process of Law and The Discipline of Law*, 1980, London: Butterworths

Manchester, C *et al*, *Exploring the Law – The Dynamics of Precedent and Statutory Interpretation*, 1996, London: Sweet & Maxwell

Chapter 3   The Courts and their Personnel

Griffith, JAG, *The Politics of the Judiciary*, 4th edn, 1991, London: Fontana

Lee, S, *Judging Judges*, 1988, London: Faber & Faber

Pannick, D, *Judges*, 1987, Oxford: OUP

Stevens, R, *The Independence of the Judiciary*, 1993, Oxford: OUP

Slapper, G and Kelly, D, *The English Legal System,* 4th edn, 1999, London: Cavendish Publishing

See, also, Runciman Commission, *Report of the Royal Commission on Criminal Justice,* Cmnd 2263, 1995, London: HMSO.

Chapter 4   The Provision of Legal Services

Abel, R, *The Legal Profession in England and Wales*, 1988, Oxford: Blackwells

Zander, M, *Legal Services for the Community*, 1978, London: Temple Smith

Also, consult texts for Chapter 1.

Chapter 5   Alternative Dispute Resolution

Baldwin, J, *The Small Claims Procedure and the Consumer*, 1995, London: Office of Fair Trading

Genn, H and Genn, Y, *The Effectiveness of Representation at Tribunals*, 1989, London: Lord Chancellor's Department

Liebmann, M, *Community and Neighbour Mediation*, 1998, London: Cavendish Publishing

Lord, R and Salzedo, S, *Guide to the Arbitration Act 1996*, 1996, London: Cavendish Publishing

MacFarlane, J (ed), *Rethinking Disputes: The Mediation Alternative*, 1997, London: Cavendish Publishing

Chapter 6   The Judicial Function

Consult texts for Chapters 1, 2 and 3.

Chapter 7   Civil Proceedings

Sime, S, *A Practical Approach to Civil Procedure*, 3rd edn, 1997, London: Blackstone

Woolf (Lord), *Access to Justice – Final Report to the Lord Chancellor on the Civil Justice System in England and Wales*, 1996, London: HMSO

Also, consult texts for Chapters 1, 2 and 3.

Chapter 8   Criminal Proceedings

Ashworth, A, *The Criminal Process: An Evaluative Study*, Oxford: OUP

Croall, H, *Crime and Society in Britain*, 1998, London: Longman

Davies, M *et al*, *Criminal Justice*, 2nd edn, 1998, Harlow: Longman

Devlin, P, *Trial by Jury (Hamlyn Lectures)*, 1966, London: Stevens

Findlay, M and Duff, P, *The Jury under Attack*, 1988, London: Butterworths

Newburn, T, *Crime and Criminal Justice Policy*, 2nd edn, 2000, London: Longman

Raine, J and James, A, *The New Politics of Criminal Justice*, 1998, London: Longman

Sprack, J, *Emmins on Criminal Procedure*, 7th edn, 1997, London: Blackstone

Wasik, M, *Emmins on Sentencing*, 3rd edn, 1998, London: Blackstone

Zander, M, *The Police and Criminal Evidence Act 1984*, 1995, London: Sweet & Maxwell

Chapter 9   Legal Liability

Allen, MJ, *Textbook on Criminal Law*, 4th edn, 1997, London: Blackstone

Ashworth, A, *Principles of Criminal Law*, 2nd edn, 1995, Oxford: OUP

Baker, CD, *Tort*, 6th edn, 1996, London: Sweet & Maxwell

Elliott, C and Quinn, F, *Criminal Law*, 2nd edn, 1998, Harlow: Longman

Elliott, C and Quinn, F, *Tort Law*, 3rd edn, 2000, London: Longman

Hocking, BA, *Liability for Negligent Words*, 1999, London: Blackstone

Jones, MA, *Textbook on Torts*, 5th edn, 1996, London: Blackstone

Reed, A and Seago, P, *Criminal Law*, 1999, London: Sweet & Maxwell

Chapter 10   European Law

Cairns, W, *Introduction to European Union Law*, 1997, London: Cavendish Publishing

Dickson, B and Connelly, A, *Human Rights and the European Convention*, 1997, London: Sweet & Maxwell

Hanlon, J, *EC Law*, 1998, London: Sweet & Maxwell

Harris, DJ *et al*, *Law of the European Convention on Human Rights*, 1994, London: Butterworths

Jacobs, FG and Whiter, RCA, *The European Convention on Human Rights*, 1996, Oxford: OUP

Kennedy, T, *Learning European Law: A Primer and* Vade-Mecum, 1998, London: Sweet & Maxwell

Lasok, D and Bridge, JW, *Law and Institutions of the EU*, 6th edn, 1994, London: Butterworths

Shaw, J, *European Community Law*, 2nd edn, 1996, London: Macmillan

Tillotson, J, *European Community Law: Text, Cases and Materials*, 2nd edn, 1996, London: Cavendish Publishing (see, now, 3rd edn, 2000)

Ward, I, *A Critical Introduction to European Law*, 1996, London: Butterworths

INDEX